The Battle of the Berezina

Other titles in the Campaign Chronicles series:

The Battle of
the Berezina
Napoleon's Great Escape

Alexander Mikaberidze

Campaign Chronicle
Series Editor

Christopher Summerville

Pen & Sword
MILITARY

In memory of Sergo Mikaberidze, Alexander Sarkisyan and Sargis Orbeliani who knew the hardships of war all too well.

First published in Great Britain in 2010 by
Pen & Sword Military
an imprint of
Pen & Sword Books Ltd
47 Church Street
Barnsley
South Yorkshire
S70 2AS

Copyright © Alexander Mikaberidze 2010

ISBN 978-1-84415-920-8

Typeset in 11/13.5pt Garamond by
Mac Style, Beverley, East Yorkshire

Printed and bound in the UK by
the MPG Books Group

Pen & Sword Books Ltd incorporates the imprints of Pen & Sword Aviation, Pen & Sword Maritime, Pen & Sword Military, Wharncliffe Local History, Pen and Sword Select, Pen and Sword Military Classics, Leo Cooper, Remember When, Seaforth Publishing and Frontline Publishing.

For a complete list of Pen & Sword titles please contact
PEN & SWORD BOOKS LIMITED
47 Church Street, Barnsley, South Yorkshire, S70 2AS, England
E-mail: enquiries@pen-and-sword.co.uk
Website: www.pen-and-sword.co.uk

Contents

The Battle of the Berezina

List of Maps and Illustrations

Maps

Illustrations

The Battle of the Berezina

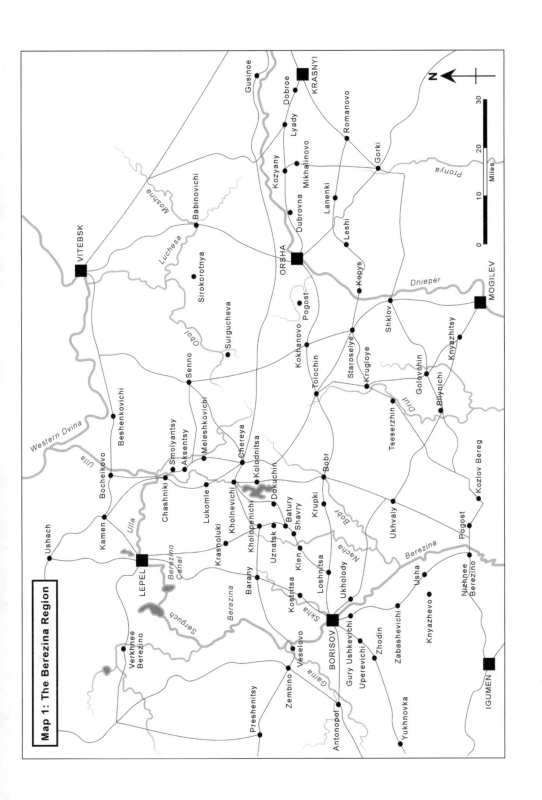

Map 1: The Berezina Region

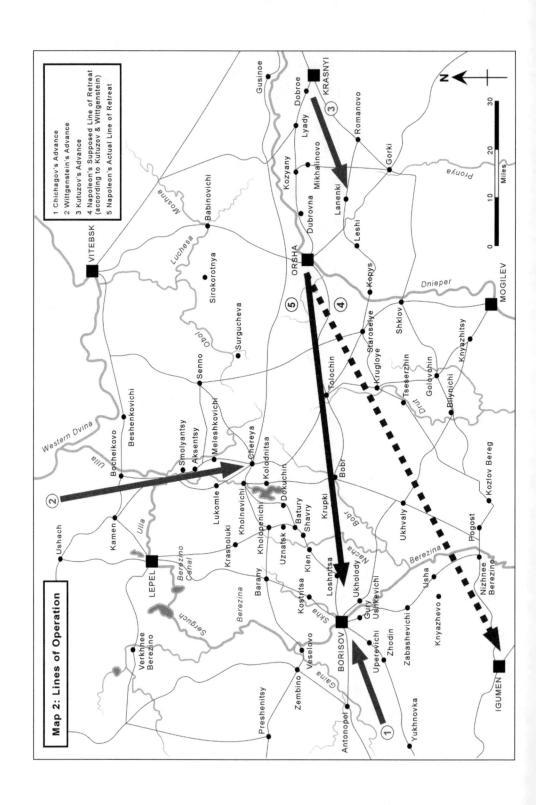

Map 2: Lines of Operation

1 Chichagov's Advance
2 Wittgenstein's Advance
3 Kutuzov's Advance
4 Napoleon's Supposed Line of Retreat
(according to Kutuzov & Wittgenstein)
5 Napoleon's Actual Line of Retreat

N

Miles
0 10 20 30

KRASNYI
Gusinoe
Dobroe
Lyady
Kozyany
Dubrovna
Mikhalinovo
Romanovo
Lanenki
Gorki
Pronya
Leshi
ORSHA
Kopys
MOGILEV
Dnieper
Staroselye
Shklov
Tolochin
Kругloye
Knyazhitsy
Tseserzhin
Golovohin
Bilyqichi
Drut
Bobr
Ukhvaly
Pogost
Kozlov Bereg
Bobr
Nacha
Berezina
Usha
Nizhnee
Berezino
Ukholody
Ushkevichi
Guty
Zhodin
Zabashevichi
Knyazhevo
IGUMEN
Uperevichi
BORISOV
Skna
Loshnitsa
Kostritsa
Klen
Krupki
Shavry
Batury
Uznatsk
Kholopenichi
Dokuchin
Koladnitsa
Chereya
Meleshkovichi
Lukomle
Kholnevichi
Krasnoluki
Barany
Gaina
Veselovo
Antonopol
Zembino
Preshenitsy
Verkhnee
Berezino
Berezina
Serguch
Berezino
Canal
LEPEL
Ulla
Kamen
Ushach
Western Dvina
Bocheikovo
Beshenkovichi
Smolyantsy
Aksentsy
Senno
Obol
Surgucheva
Sirokorotnya
Babinovichi
Mosshna
Luchesa
VITEBSK
Kozyany
Yukhnovka

Map 2: Lines of Operation

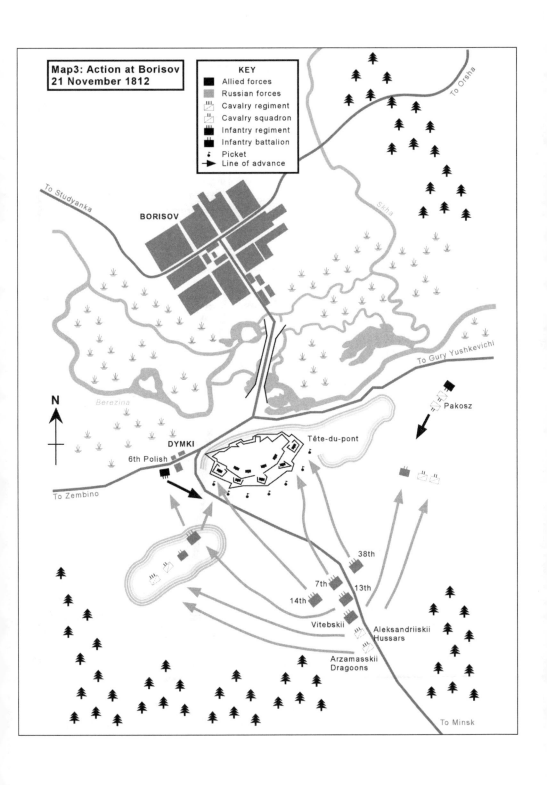

Map3: Action at Borisov
21 November 1812

KEY
Allied forces
Russian forces
Cavalry regiment
Cavalry squadron
Infantry regiment
Infantry battalion
Picket
Line of advance

To Orsha

To Studyanka

BORISOV

Skha

To Gury Yushkevichi

N

Berezina

DYMKI

Pakosz

6th Polish

Téte-du-pont

To Zembino

38th

7th   13th

14th

Vitebskii

Aleksandriiskii
Hussars

Arzamasskii
Dragoons

To Minsk

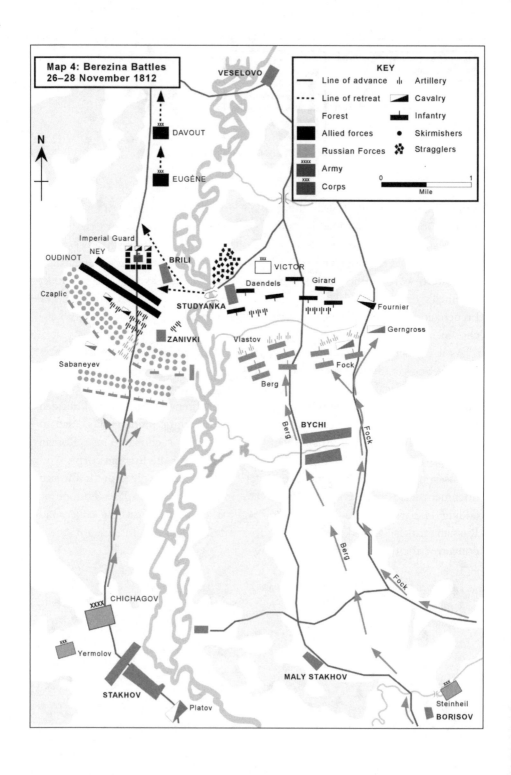

Map 4: Berezina Battles
26–28 November 1812

KEY

Line of advance	Artillery
Line of retreat	Cavalry
Forest	Infantry
Allied forces	Skirmishers
Russian Forces	Stragglers
Army	
Corps	

0   1
Mile

N

VESELOVO

DAVOUT

EUGÈNE

Imperial Guard

NEY

OUDINOT

BRILI

VICTOR

Czaplic

Daendels

Girard

Fournier

STUDYÁNKA

ZANIVKI

Vlastov

Gerngross

Fock

Sabaneyev

Berg

BYCHI

Berg

Fock

Berg

Fock

CHICHAGOV

Yermolov

MALY STAKHOV

STAKHOV

Steinheil

Platov

BORISOV

Author's Note

The name of the Polish General Jan Henryk Dąbrowski is often given as Dombrowski or Dambrowski, but I chose to adopt the original Polish spelling of his name. Similarly, Admiral Pavel (Paul) Chichagov's name has been spelled as Tchitchagoff, Tchitchakow or even Tsetshakov/Tshetshakon in Western works, although his name easily transliterates as Chichagov. Faddei Steinheil's name is often transliterated as Steingel (in the correspondence of French corps commanders, for example) but 'Steinheil' is the form I have chosen.

As it crossed the Nieman, the Grand Army included soldiers from all over Europe, and yet, despite such diversity, it is frequently referred to as 'the French Army' in historical works, although the French accounted for no more than 50 per cent of total manpower. Out of justice to non-French participants, I decided to use the term 'Allied', except when dealing with specific French units. Also, to distinguish between the Russian and Allied corps, I chose to use Roman numerals for the Grand Army and Arabic numerals for the Russian corps.

Russia used the Julian calendar until 1917 and so all dates given in the Russian documents had to be converted into the Gregorian calendar. This is done by adding 11 days to dates prior to 1800 and 12 days after. Also, the Allied and Russian armies utilized various measurements of distance and weight and I converted them into modern measurements.

1 *verst* equals 3,500 feet or 1.0668km
1 *sazhen* equals 7 feet or 2.1336m
1 *toise* equals 6.394 ft or 1.949m
1 *lieue* equals 2.5 miles or 4km

Preface

—•◦((◦))◦•—

'César a passé le Rubicon, mais il n' aurait
point passé la Bérésina.'

Henry Murger, *Scènes de la vie de bohème*

History is full of dramatic episodes and probably none more so than the Grand Army's crossing of the River Berezina in November 1812. It is hard to find another example in military history where an army in desperate circumstances suffering from cold, famine and exhaustion, surrounded by the enemies on almost all sides and pressed against a river had extricated itself more skilfully. It paid dearly for the honour it gained, but those who survived the horrors of the crossing remembered their deeds for the rest of their lives while the crossing itself became known as one of Napoleon's masterful strokes.

Almost two hundred years separate us from the passage of the Berezina, recognized by the contemporaries as one of the most tragic yet heroic events of the Napoleonic Wars. There, on the swampy shores of the previously unknown river, Napoleon should have been defeated. Yet he survived with the core of his army intact, only further augmenting the myth that surrounded him. Already on 10 February 1813, Guillaume-Joseph Roux, Baron Peyrusse, a paymaster with the Grand Army, described the crossing as 'a phenomenon' while Frédéric-François Guillaume de Vaudoncourt, the *général de brigade* who witnessed the crossing before being captured at Vilna, wrote in 1815 that 'the passage of the Berezina is an event of much importance from its political consequences and its bearings on the art of war'.[1] General Pierre Berthezène felt that 'the crossing of the Berezina, in the face of and in between enemy armies, is a remarkable military operation that will add new shades of glory to the army and its general'. Baron Henri de Jomini, the famous military theoretician, noted in his *Précis de l'Art de Guerre*,

'The celebrated passage of the Berezina by the French is one of the most remarkable operations. Never was an army in a more desperate condition, and never was one extricated more gloriously and skilfully. Pressed by famine, benumbed with cold […] assailed by the enemy in front and in rear, having a river with marshy banks in front and surrounded by vast forests, how could it hope to escape?'[2]

As years passed and participants began to write their memoirs, the passage became a symbol of endurance and perseverance of the Allied soldiers. Generations later, we cherish the memory of those *pontonniers* and sappers who, deep in freezing water, built the bridges upon which the Grand Army escaped. Over the years, the Berezina crossing inspired some prominent writers and poets to pick up their stylus – Honoré de Balzac, one of the greatest French writers, devoted one of his best novellas to the Berezina crossing, laying the foundation for a new genre of historical realism; Victor Hugo evoked the images of the retreat in his famous *Châtiments*, while Anne Bignan sang dithyrambs to the crossing in *Napoléon en Russie* and Lydia Huntley Sigourney described it in *Passage of the Beresina*.

The situation was quite different in Russia, however, where the battle was banished to the shadows of historical memory. Leo Tolstoy believed that the 'passage of the Berezina, about which so much has been written, was only one of the intermediate steps in the destruction of the French army, and not at all a decisive episode of the campaign'.[3] The Russian society largely blamed a single man for allowing Russia's arch-enemy to escape. This man – Admiral Pavel Chichagov – had seen his reputation ravaged by public gossip and outright attacks, and was compelled to spend the rest of his life as a lonely bitter exile, unsuccessfully seeking to clear his name.

Despite its fame and importance, the crossing of the Berezina has been so far generally overlooked in English-language Napoleonic studies, which, except for a few short articles in popular history magazines and brief chapters in campaign histories,[4] had seen no separate and scholarly study of this event. This gap was expected to be partially filled by François G. Hourtoulle's forthcoming book *Crossing the Berezina* but the author passed away in early 2009. Hourtoulle's study, if published, will be part of an ongoing series of titles that concentrates more on army uniforms and orders of battle rather than tactical/operational analysis. The Russian Campaign has been discussed in many English works, notably by Paul Britten Austin, Archibald F. Becke, Hilaire Belloc, Reginald Burton, Cate Curtis, Ronald Delderfield, Theodore Dodge, Edward Foord, H.B. George, Alan Palmer, George Nafziger, Nigel Nicolson, Richard Riehn, Achilles Rose, Digby Smith, Adam Zamoyski and many others. However, due to the broad nature of these books, the events of the crossing are usually described in general terms, with an emphasis on the 'French' experiences, often crediting Napoleon with a masterful stroke that deceived the Russians. Some titles concentrate on specific

The Battle of the Berezina

aspects of the war. Thus, Austin's remarkable trilogy provides a heart-wrenching account of human suffering during the crossing but provides few details on the tactical and operational aspects of the battle. In contrast, Nafziger's narrative is devoid of human experiences but contains interesting insights on tactics.

The French historiography is quite diverse and includes both general accounts of the campaign by Georges Chambray, Georges Bertin, André Castelot, Arthur Chuquet, Gabriel Joseph Fabry, Constantin de Grunwald, Jean Thiry, Jean Tranié, and titles dealing with the Berezina crossing in particular, most notably the studies by Fernand Beaucour (2006) and Alain Fillion (2005). The former provides interesting insights on the battle and includes a couple of essays written by Russian and Byelorussian scholars. The latter provides a survey of the battle, lacks tactical and operational details and looks at events from the French perspective while ignoring sources/perspectives from the German, Polish or Russian sides. A handful of German, Dutch and Polish works by Robert Bielecki, Paul Holzhausen, Curt Lindenau, Jurg Stussi-Lauterburg and others are largely unknown or unavailable to the English-speaking general public.

In Russia, historians had long ignored the story of the Berezina as well as Admiral Pavel Chichagov, the key personality in this saga, who still awaits a proper biographical treatment. For decades V. Kharkevich's *1812 g. Berezina*, published in 1893 and containing valuable primary documents, served as a standard text on the battle, although I. Vasiliev's recent work *Neskolko gromkikh udarov po khvostu tigra* (2001) provides a much needed new look. Beyond these specific Russian studies, the Berezina Crossing is dealt with, in varying levels of detail, in dozens of general campaign studies (i.e. D. Buturlin, A. Mikhailovsky-Danilevsky, M. Bogdanovich, L. Beskrovnyi, P. Zhilin, etc.) of the 'Patriotic War of 1812'. But they largely share the same weakness of glorifying Russian exploits, justifying Kutuzov's actions and blaming Chichagov.

The present book seeks to blend French, Russian, German, Swiss, Polish, Dutch and other sources to produce a more balanced account of the battle. This is a daunting task by all means and I only hope I have succeeded in it. The battle will be covered from both sides, but occasionally emphasis will be made on the Russian experiences which have been often overlooked in previous studies. To meet the requirements of the 'Campaign Chronicles' series, I had to avoid certain details but, as with my earlier book on Borodino, such information will eventually be made available at the book's companion website at the Napoleon Series (www.napoleon-series.org).

Alexander Mikaberidze
Shreveport, Louisiana (18 June 2009)

Acknowledgements

------ ◦((◦))◦ ------

I have been interested in the story of the Berezina Crossing for many years, partly because of meeting Dr. Fernand Beaucour, one of the premier French specialists of the Berezina topic, during a bicentennial Napoleonic congress in Israel in 1999. I had a long and fascinating discussion with him regarding the battle while we travelled on a bus to Mount Tabor, the site of another famous Napoleonic battle. Beaucour had tirelessly worked to commemorate the Berezina Crossing and through his efforts a special monument in honour of the Grand Army was erected on the banks of the Berezina. Sadly he passed away in 2005 but his memory will live on in his works, including his last book *La Bérézina: Une Victoire Militaire*.

In 2006 I was commissioned to write *The Battle of Borodino* for Pen & Sword and, during this partnership, we discussed the possibility of working on the 'sequel' volume dealing with the Berezina. Christopher Summerville, a Napoleonic scholar in his own right, with whom I collaborated on the Borodino book, magnanimously offered to let me write the book that he initially planned to do himself. He also kindly assisted me in editing it, so without him this book probably would not have been written and I am very grateful for his support. As always, Rupert Harding, the editor at Pen & Sword, was extremely supportive and professional throughout the process.

In the process of researching this book, I was able to utilize materials from over two dozen libraries throughout the United States and Europe. I am extremely grateful to Susie Davison and Ashley Wood of the Noel Library at Louisiana State University in Shreveport (LSUS), whose efficiency in locating materials proved to be indispensable. Special thanks go to Dr. Lucy Patrick of the Special Collections at the Strozier Library (Florida State University), one of the best Napoleonic collections in the United States. I must also extend my thanks to the staff of the King Library of Miami University, the Wilson Library of University of Minnesota, the Hornbake Library of University of Maryland, the Green Library at Stanford, the Yale University Library, the Widener Library of Harvard University and Bibliothèque Am Guisanplatz (Bern, Switzerland) who kindly copied and mailed me dozens of sources I could not obtain elsewhere. Dr. Peter Harrington sent me material from the famous Anne S.K. Brown Military Collection. I am indebted to Colonel Jack Gill for introducing me to Mark van Hattem and Mariska Poole of the Legermuseum (Netherlands) who helped me with documents on the Dutch participants. Professor Kenneth Johnson (US Military Academy at West Point) and Thanh Nguyen have kindly assisted me in research at the French archives at Château de Vincennes in Paris.

Every book is a result of collective effort. Donald D. Horward and David Markham encouraged me to write throughout the process. I am thankful to my colleagues at LSUS, especially Professors Blake Dunnavent, Gary D. Joiner, Helen Wise and Cheryl White, for welcoming me to their department and creating a jovial and collegial atmosphere that facilitated my work. I am especially grateful to Prof. Michael V. Leggiere, now at University of North Texas, a great friend and Napoleonic scholar, whose advice and encouragement I will always cherish. He was the first to read my draft manuscript, providing many insightful comments. Jack Sigler, my comrade-in-arms from the Institute on Napoleon and the French Revolution, helped me acquire a rare copy of Maurice Sautai's *Heros de la Berezina*. I have greatly benefited from the help I received from the wonderful people at the Napoleon Series forum (www.napoleon-series.org) and Napoleon On-Line (www.napoleon-online.de). Robert Goetz provided insightful commentary on parts of the manuscript. Steven H. Smith was, as always, indispensable in tracking down obscure materials. Fausto Berutti advised me on Italian sources, Thomas Hemmann, Markus Stein and Markus Gaertner shared their vast knowledge of the German memoirs while Marcin Michalski assisted me with Polish sources and Michael Hopper reviewed portions of the manuscript. Equally informative and helpful were members of the Russian Military Historical Forum (http://www.reenactor.ru), whose knowledge and ability to explain and discuss any issue, no matter how obscure, continues to amaze me. I am especially grateful to Sergei Kabrusev, archaeologist and historian from Borisov (Byelorussia) who sent me images of his home town and its environs, including the ruins of Borisov *tête-de-pont* and the crossing sites over the Berezina. On a personal level, this book could not have been written without the help and support of my family and friends. I extend my love and thanks to all of them, especially to my wife, Anna, for her unwavering support and love.

Background

---••(•)••---

As he stood on the raft moored in the middle of the Nieman, Emperor Napoleon must have felt on the top of the world. He had destroyed the Third Coalition of European powers in December 1805, routed the once-mighty Prussian Army in autumn 1806, and defeated Russia by mid-June 1807. Now, in the second week of July 1807, he and Emperor Alexander were to sign the Treaty of Tilsit, pacifying their nations and, in effect, acknowledging Napoleon's supremacy west of the Nieman.

But relations between France and Russia quickly reverted to hostility. The two nations had differing interests, which reanimated the shadows of war. For its part, Russia remained disgruntled by setbacks suffered at the hands of Napoleon and deeply concerned by his dominance over Europe. Crucially, Napoleon's economic war with Britain (the so-called Continental Blockade), which Alexander was obliged to join under the terms of Tilsit, proved disadvantageous as Russia lost lucrative trade with Britain, a major destination for wheat, timber, hemp, tallow and other resources. Without compensation for lost revenue, Russian merchants faced financial ruin. The Polish question further strained relations. The old Kingdom of Poland had been partitioned and swallowed up by Russia, Prussia and Austria between 1772–1795. Napoleon's creation of the Grand Duchy of Warsaw, 'a splinter in the body of Russia' as Alexander described it, awakened Russian fears of a full reconstitution of Polish lands and national identity. In addition, Franco-Russian interests clashed over the Germanic states and the future of the Ottoman Empire. Alexander's ambition of acquiring Constantinople through conquest appeared to be a move that Napoleon – fearing Russian interference in the Mediterranean – was determined to block. On the other hand, Napoleon's reorganization of the Confederation of the Rhine affected many German princes who were related to the Russian imperial house. Alexander's sister, Catherine, was married to the son and heir of the Duke of Oldenburg so the French annexation of that principality in 1810 looked like a deliberate insult to Alexander.

Thus, by late 1811, both sides were preparing for 'the Second Polish Campaign', as Napoleon described it, and the Emperor's Grand Army (*La*

The Battle of the Berezina

Grande Armée) of some 600,000 troops and over 1,300 artillery pieces began assembling along Russia's western frontier. Its troops were largely furnished by Napoleon's European allies, with contingents from Austria, Prussia, Saxony, Poland and Italy. By the spring of 1812, Napoleon's army was deployed in three groups – under Eugène de Beauharnais, Napoleon and Jérôme Bonaparte, King of Westphalia – along the Vistula River, stretching from Warsaw to Königsberg. Meanwhile, Marshal Jacques-Etienne Macdonald's X Corps (with a Prussian contingent) guarded the left flank of the Grand Army, close to the Baltic coastline, while 30,000 Austrians under Karl Philip Schwarzenberg covered the right flank.

Russia fielded about 650,000 men in 1812, but these were scattered throughout Moldavia, the Crimea, the Caucasus, Finland, and other regions, leaving some 250,000 men with over 900 guns (organized in three major armies and a few separate corps) in the western provinces to fend off Napoleon's invasion. The 1st Western Army of Mikhail Barclay de Tolly deployed in the vicinity of Vilna, while the 2nd Western Army under Peter Bagration assembled in the area of Volkovysk and Belostock (Białystok) in the south. Alexander Tormasov commanded the 3rd Reserve Army of Observation around Lutsk, covering the route to Ukraine. In addition to the three main armies, Lieutenant General Baron Faddei Steinheil's Finland Corps in the north and Admiral Pavel (Paul) Chichagov's Army of the Danube in the south covered the extreme flanks of the Russian Army. These forces were further supported by three reserves corps of Peter Essen, Egor Muller-Zakomelsky and Fedor Ertel.

From the Nieman to Moscow

After months of intensive preparations, Napoleon crossed the Nieman on 23–24 June, advancing to engage the armies of Barclay de Tolly and Bagration. But the Russians retreated to Smolensk, where the Grand Army followed in hope of a decisive battle. Tormasov was more successful in the south, where he pinned down Schwarzenberg in the Volhynia region. At the same time, Chichagov's Army of the Danube received orders to move from Moldavia to support Tormasov. In the north, Marshal Nicolas Charles Oudinot attacked General Peter Wittgenstein's 1st Corps (tasked with protecting the route to St Petersburg) and seized Polotsk on 26 July. But in subsequent combats the Russians prevailed, forcing Napoleon to divert Gouvion St Cyr's corps to support Oudinot. In the Baltic provinces, Macdonald became bogged down near Riga. Thus, by August 1812, Napoleon's initial plan to destroy the Russian armies in a decisive border battle had been frustrated: instead, his army suffered considerable losses from strategic consumption and desertion, as well as the usual combat casualties. There was a lack of fresh water and no forage for the horses. Meanwhile the hot weather was, according to Baron Lejeune, 'a veritable disaster to our troops'. To cap it all, the supply system had broken down, with the wagons laden with provisions bottlenecked near bridges or battling roads. These carts could not keep pace with the troops constantly pushed forward by forced marches for a battle that forever remained on the horizon.

As the armies of Barclay de Tolly and Bagration united at Smolensk, the Russians faced a crisis of command. This conflict stemmed from discord between the old Russian aristocracy and the 'foreigners' who had gained influence at court and Army headquarters. The specific reason for this tension was the difference in views regarding strategy, evident among senior officers, who represented opposing parties. Barclay de Tolly, nominal Commander-in-Chief, was surrounded by a group of officers (many of them of German extraction) who supported his defensive plans. Opposing them was the much larger 'Russian party', led by Prince Peter Bagration (ironically a Georgian), which urged an immediate counter-offensive. Anti-Barclay sentiments were so strong among the senior officers that they openly loathed the commander-in-chief and intrigued for the appointment of Bagration to supreme command. Some even encouraged Bagration to replace Barclay by force.

Bending under pressure, Barclay de Tolly agreed to an offensive from Smolensk, in an attempt to break through the French centre and destroy the remaining French corps piecemeal. But due to differences among the commanders – made worse by Barclay's vacillation – precious time was lost in futile manoeuvring, which allowed Napoleon to recognize Russian intentions and seize the initiative. He crossed the Dnieper River and rapidly advanced on Smolensk. But a resolute rearguard action at Krasnyi on 14 August enabled the Russians to prepare Smolensk for defence, while Bagration and Barclay de Tolly rushed their commands back to the city. On 15–16 August the Russians repulsed the Allied assaults on Smolensk but nonetheless were forced to abandon the city. As the Russians withdrew towards Moscow, Napoleon attempted to cut their line of retreat, but Barclay's army succeeded in clearing its way to Dorogobuzh following the indecisive Battle of Valutina Gora on 19 August.

The surrender of Smolensk further aroused general discontent in the Russian Army and society at large. Emperor Alexander replaced Barclay de Tolly with General Mikhail Kutuzov, who took command on 29 August at Tsarevo-Zaimische. Kutuzov withdrew the troops still further to the east, deploying them for battle near the village of Borodino. After receiving reinforcements under General Mikhail Miloradovich, as well as *opolchenye* (militia) forces, Kutuzov commanded some 155,000 troops, of whom 115,000 were regulars, supported by 636 guns. Napoleon fielded some 135,000 men with 587 guns.

The Battle of Borodino took place on 7 September, with Napoleon opting for frontal attacks on fortified Russian positions instead of flanking manoeuvres that might have prompted another Russian withdrawal. In a savage and bloody fight both sides displayed great bravery and steadfastness, but the French remained in possession of the battlefield and claimed victory, while the Russian Army withdrew in good order towards Moscow. At Borodino, Allied losses numbered about 35,000 men, including forty-nine generals, while Russian losses were 45,000–50,000 men, including twenty-nine generals.

During his retreat to Moscow, Kutuzov still considered engaging the enemy in front of the capital. But after a military council at Fili on 13 September, he ordered Moscow to be abandoned without a fight. The following day Napoleon's troops entered the city. Later that same day, fires started by the Russians spread throughout Moscow and continued to burn until 18 September, destroying two-thirds of the city. The fiery devastation of the Russian capital had a profound effect on the troops of the Grand Army, as they were forced to billet amid the ruins, lacking proper provisions and shelter. Discipline became lax and many troops turned to pillaging.

Meanwhile, Wittgenstein continued to hold ground on the northern flank and made preparations for an offensive that culminated in an important victory at Polotsk on 20 October, securing the northern approaches to St Petersburg. In the south, Tormasov and Chichagov guarded the south-western Russian provinces and prepared to move north to help the main Russian army. In the Baltic provinces, Russian forces continued to thwart Marshal Macdonald's attempts to seize Riga.

Throughout September and early October, Napoleon remained in Moscow while he made several peace proposals to Alexander but all were rejected. While the Grand Army remained in Moscow, Kutuzov skilfully manoeuvred from the Ryazan road (east of Moscow) to the Kaluga road (south-west of Moscow), where he established a fortified camp at Tarutino. Through this manoeuvre, the Russian commander covered the southern provinces, which were abundant with supplies and manufacturing enterprises. Kutuzov also began intensive preparations for future operations, receiving reinforcements that increased his army to 110,000–120,000 men, with additional forces to come. He encouraged guerrilla operations against the invaders and organized cavalry detachments to harass French communications and supply lines.

In mid-October, the Grand Army began probing Russian positions south-west of Moscow. On 18 October, Marshal Joachim Murat's forces suffered a sudden defeat on the River Chernishnya, north of Tarutino (the battle is often called Tarutino by the Russians). This proved to be a wake-up call for Napoleon. After General Jacques Alexandre Lauriston's peace mission to the Russian camp failed in early October, Napoleon realized he had to abandon the devastated ruins of Moscow before winter arrived and the Russians descended upon him.

Background

Departure from Moscow

After spending just over one month in Moscow, Napoleon finally departed the city on 19 October 1812. His forces had dwindled to about 115,000 men,[5] accompanied by thousands of non-combatants and an enormous baggage train laden with loot. The non-combatants included members of the French community in Moscow as well as foreigners and Russians (servants, women and petty criminals) who had thrown in their lot in with the occupiers. Pierre-Armand Barrau lamented about the state of the army: 'Anyone who did not see the French army leave Moscow can only have a very weak impression of what the armies of Greece and Rome must have looked like when they marched back from Troy and Carthage.' Count Adrien de Mailly, an officer in the Carabiniers à Cheval, thought that this 'was no longer the army of Napoleon but that of Darius returning from a far-flung expedition, more lucrative than glorious'. The number of vehicles accompanying the army was truly staggering and, depending on sources, is estimated at between 15,000 and 40,000. Traffic on this scale not only slowed the army's movements but also distracted the troops, many of whom were more concerned about securing their portion of booty than on maintaining discipline. As Colonel Griois summed up: 'This mass of men, of horse and of vehicles resembled rather the migration of a people on the move than an organized army.'[6]

But looks can be deceiving: the Grand Army was still a potent tool of war. While the cavalry was significantly reduced, thanks to herds of worn-out horses, the infantry was rested and eager to leave the hostile land. Cesare de Laugier, an

The Grand Army by mid-October 1812 (according to Georges Chambray)

Unit	Infantry	Cavalry	Artillery
Imperial Guard	17,871	4,609	112
I Corps	27,449	1,500	144
III Corps	9,597	901	71
IV Corps	23,963	1,661	92
V Corps	4,844	868	49
VIII Corps	1,916	775	34
Cavalry (from I, II, III and IV Reserve Cavalry Corps	–	5,000	67
Total	89,640	15,314	569

officer in the Italian Guard, noted in his diary that one could 'read joy on every face at the prospect of leaving [...] We were thinking only of our native land [...] of our families ...'[7]

Napoleon planned to move his forces to the western provinces of Russia, where supplies and magazines already had been prepared. 'We are going to withdraw to the frontiers of Poland,' he told his trusted aide Jean Rapp, 'I shall take good winter quarters and hope that [Emperor] Alexander will make peace.' For Napoleon, it was a strategic withdrawal, not a retreat, a point he tried to reinforce in his memoirs dictated at St Helena.[8] The route from Moscow to Smolensk, via Gzhatsk, was devastated after the Allied forces had fought their way to the Russian capital from July through September. Napoleon decided, therefore, to advance by the Kaluga route, towards the intact south-western regions, before veering north. Initially, Napoleon successfully deceived the Russians about his plan. Despite the Cossack outposts and Russian flying detachments around Moscow, the Grand Army filed from the capital in such secrecy that Kutuzov did not learn of its departure for two days. And secrecy was crucial to the success of Napoleon's plan, for, if alerted, Kutuzov could have cut the route to Kaluga with ease.

But this promising start was soon marred. The Grand Army, burdened as it was, grinded along, gridlocking when obliged to negotiate various streams and defiles. And to make matters worse, heavy rains turned the roads into rivers of mud. Meanwhile, the Russian scouts soon observed the long lines of enemy infantry and cavalry moving south-west and immediately informed Kutuzov, who dispatched General Dmitry Dokhturov's 6th Corps to intercept the enemy at Maloyaroslavets.[9]

Turning Point: The Battle of Maloyaroslavets

After an exhausting march over bad roads and in rain, Dokhturov's men arrived at Maloyaroslavets in the evening of 23 October, just in time to anticipate the arrival of the Grand Army's advance guard. In the ensuing battle, the fighting proved to be savage in the extreme, and the town changed hands up to a dozen times. The fighting ended around 11 p.m. with the Allied forces in control of the burning wreck of the town.[10] In total, Napoleon committed approximately 27,000 men to this battle, while about 32,000 Russians opposed them. The Grand Army's casualty estimates vary depending on the source: the official Bulletin listed as few as 1,500 men; most Anglo-French studies refer to 4,000–5,000 men; and recent Russian studies arguing in favour of about 7,000 French casualties. As for the Russian Army, the official report quoted 6,665 losses, but did not account for some units (especially among the *opolchenye*) so the total number probably exceeded 7,000 men. Among the casualties were eight French and Italian generals (including Delzons, Pinot, Fontana and

Background

Giflenga), while the Russians lost General Dorokhov, who was seriously wounded.

On 25 October Napoleon – who arrived too late at Maloyaroslavets to influence the outcome – conducted a reconnaissance on the southern bank of the Lusha, barely escaping capture by Cossacks near Medyn. Although the Emperor's troops had gained a tactical victory at Maloyaroslavets, his effectives had dwindled to around 70,000. Realizing he could not break through the 90,000 Russians that opposed him, Napoleon – following a council of war on the evening of the 25th – ordered a withdrawal to Smolensk by way of Borodino and Gzhatsk. Remarkably, Kutuzov – unbeknown to Napoleon – had ordered his army to retreat south, fearing a flanking manoeuvre. Thus both armies simultaneously withdrew in opposite directions! In the opinion of the British commissioner to the Russian Army Sir Robert Wilson, 'Napoleon's star no longer guided his course, for after the [Russian] rearguard had retired, had any, even the smallest reconnaissance, advanced to the brow of the hill over the ravine – had the slightest demonstration of a continued offensive movement been made – Napoleon would have obtained a free passage for his army [...] through a fertile and rich country to the Dnieper.'[11]

The Battle of Maloyaroslavets was the third largest battle of the campaign (after Smolensk and Borodino) but probably second in its importance and impact on Napoleon's campaign in Russia. The march to, and fight at, Maloyaroslavets consumed seven days – and this loss of time would prove fateful, as the ferocious Russian winter set in a couple of weeks later. Technically an Allied victory, the battle was a strategic defeat for the Grand Army, since it was prevented from reaching the rich southern provinces and was forced instead to retrace its steps along the devastated route via Smolensk. Given the battle's importance, Napoleon should have taken direct control and used more troops to flank and defeat the Russian defenders before Kutuzov's arrival. The battle signalled a change of character in the campaign. Napoleon's strategic withdrawal from Moscow now turned into a retreat, which, although commonly counted from 19 October (when the French abandoned Moscow), technically should be dated from 26 October. From this point, the Grand Army ceased offensive operations and sought to withdraw from the occupied provinces as fast as possible. The Russians, on the other hand, assumed a more aggressive stance, which many Russian/Soviet historians described as the start of the 'counter-offensive' stage of the campaign, following Joseph Stalin's famous postulation. But in truth Russian actions hardly constituted a 'counter-offensive'. Kutuzov avoided open confrontation with Napoleon at Maloyaroslavets and chose to withdraw, despite the objections of his lieutenants.[12] Nevertheless, Maloyaroslavets was the starting point for Kutuzov's 'parallel march' strategy, designed to dog Napoleon's footsteps without risking costly clashes, thereby reducing unnecessary losses. This strategy would play an important part in events leading up to the Berezina.

From Maloyaroslavets to Smolensk

After the Battle of Maloyaroslavets, Napoleon directed his army to Mozhaisk, where he returned to the Old Smolensk Road, which had been devastated in the August–September fighting. The morale of the army, already undermined by the retreat, was further lowered when the troops marched across the Borodino battlefield still covered with corpses, half-eaten by wolves or pecked at by carrion crows. To move faster, Napoleon ordered the wounded to be evacuated on wagons and carriages but the troops, who were forced to give up their places, were angered by the decision and this led to abuses. Napoleon's Master of the Horse, Armand de Caulaincourt, shuddered as he saw

> drivers deliberately drive their horses at speed over rough ground, in order to rid themselves of the unfortunates with whom they had been over-weighted; and although they knew that hoofs would mutilate them or wheels crush them, they would yet smile triumphantly when a jolt freed them of one of those wretches.[13]

And so the army marched on to Vyazma.

In the meantime, Kutuzov spent a couple of days regrouping his army before launching the pursuit. The main Russian army moved along the Kuzovo–Suleika–Bykovo route while the advance guard, led by Miloradovich, operated between Kutuzov and the Old Smolensk Road, and Ataman Platov's Cossacks pressed the enemy along the Old Smolensk Road. In addition, the flying detachments were always at hand to harass the enemy.

On 29 October the Grand Army reached Vyazma, a major town in the Smolensk province, and occupied it after a few minor skirmishes with local forces. The three-day march from Maloyaroslavets had exhausted Napoleon's troops. The weather was becoming colder and the nights of 27 and 28 October saw temperatures plunge to as low as minus 4 degrees Centigrade. Allied troops began competing for the quickly diminishing supplies, while lack of forage weakened horses. In fact, in order to transport artillery, horses were taken from private (frequently trophy-laden) wagons, which were abandoned along with the wounded men they contained. The march of tens of thousands of men and animals on earthy roads soon created a muddy morass, causing further delays and exacerbating the suffering of the troops. 'From the very first day, our retreat had the semblance of a rout,' lamented Fezensac. 'Woe betide those who allowed themselves to be knocked over,' recalled another French officer, 'they could not get up, were trodden underfoot and caused others to trip and fall on top of them. In this manner mounds of men and horses, dead and dying, gradually piled up, blocking the way. But the crowd kept coming, banking up and cluttering the approaches to the obstacle [...] People quarrelled, pushed each other away, knocked each other over, and then one could hear the cries of the unfortunates, who, knocked over, trampled, were caught and crushed beneath the wheels of carriages ...'[14]

The Battle of Vyazma

In early November, Napoleon led the Grand Army towards Smolensk. Ney's III Corps and Davout's I Corps stayed behind to act as rearguard. On 3–4 November the Russian forces under Miloradovich and Platov attacked the Allied forces and captured Vyazma. The battle, while a Russian victory, was also a missed opportunity. Kutuzov's main army, despite being in proximity, did not participate but continued its march to Bykov. Kutuzov was probably concerned that an attack on his part would oblige Napoleon to turn back, thus leading to a major battle, which Kutuzov was not willing to risk at Vyazma. In response to Miloradovich's pleas for reinforcements, Kutuzov dispatched cavalry reinforcements which however took no part in the fighting. Many Russians criticized Kutuzov's actions and Yermolov noted that 'had our [main] army, located nearby, joined the advance guard, the enemy would have been routed from its initial position, its remaining forces would have been pursued and destroyed piecemeal'. Robert Wilson, British Commissioner to the Russian Army, wrote to Lord Cathcart, British Ambassador at St Petersburg, asking him to lobby for Kutuzov's dismissal.

The battle had a disruptive impact on the Grand Army's retreat and accelerated demoralization among its troops, especially in rear units, where chaos spread in a chain reaction. 'Here at Vyazma we witnessed for the last time the actions of the enemy forces that had spread horror with their victories and earned our respect,' wrote a Russian officer. 'We could still see the skill of their generals, the obedience of their subordinates and their energy. But, there were no orderly enemy troops left; the experience and abilities of their generals were now of no use, discipline had disappeared and the soldiers seemed to have lost their last strength, each of them now a victim of hunger, exhaustion and the cruelty of [the] weather ...'

Smolensk

On 5 November, Napoleon received reports of the action at Vyazma and decided to halt to concentrate his forces. He initially considered falling on the pursuers but the idea was soon abandoned. The weather was becoming colder and the first snow already covered the ground, further increasing the misery and disorganization in the Grand Army. Friedrich Klinkhardt, a Westphalian officer, recalled, 'Snow fell heavily and severe cold immediately froze it so the horses could move on the hard crust without sinking. It did not last for long but I managed to freeze my nose, ears, hands and feet and could move around and get on a carriage only with assistance.' Claude François Meneval recounted that 'In one night the thermometer went down to twelve degrees below zero and two days later to eighteen degrees. From that time forward the cold grew worse and worse.'[15]

As snow began to fall, the countryside turned a monotonous white, contrasted by the dark procession of snivelling stragglers creeping onward, hoping to reach their native lands. Severely lacking provisions and with no proper clothing or footwear, the Allied soldiers suffered terribly. The number of stragglers – most of them unarmed – rapidly increased, morale declined, and discipline gave way to the instinct of self-preservation. Everyone looked to Smolensk and its large supply stores as towards a promised land.

Napoleon entered Smolensk on 9 November and the army poured into the city over the next four days. Cold and hungry, the soldiers – many of whom had subsisted on horseflesh for the past few days – ravaged the magazines, leaving virtually no provisions for those who arrived after them. Meanwhile, Napoleon ordered the Imperial Guard to be furnished with all necessary supplies, which only increased the antagonism felt by regular units towards the privileged guardsmen.

While at Smolensk, Napoleon received news from France, informing him that a false report of his death had led to a failed coup by General Claude François Malet in Paris. On hearing the news, Napoleon exclaimed with deep feeling, and in the presence of his generals, 'Does my power then hang on so slender a thread? Is my tenure of sovereignty so frail that a single person can place it in jeopardy?' As Mathieu Dumas informs us, news of the Malet Conspiracy

> struck Napoleon and made him sensible of the necessity of quitting the army as soon as he could so with safety, and of hastening to Paris to revive the spirits of the people by his presence and create by the ascendancy and the resources of his genius the means of repairing such unexpected reverses.[16]

As his forces concentrated at Smolensk, Napoleon weighed his options. The strategic situation had turned against him. During the fourteen days since the Grand Army left Moscow, it had suffered staggering losses, with battle-ready forces reduced to an estimated 60,000 men. And with each passing day, the number of men under arms diminished, while those of the stragglers swelled.

Remaining in Smolensk was pointless, since the city was untenable and the stores were nearly exhausted. Meneval notes that 'each night at the bivouacs we lost thousands of horses, whose flesh served to stay the hunger of the soldiers. Our cavalry found itself on foot, our artillery was without teams'. The army had already been reduced to a fragment of its original strength, with troops tired, hungry and cold. Now, with Wittgenstein closing from the north and Chichagov from the south, Napoleon believed his only change of escape was to quit Smolensk, beat the Russian converging forces to the Berezina, and seek better winter quarters further west.

The Battle of Krasnyi

On the cold morning of 14 November, Napoleon left Smolensk with his Imperial Guard and proceeded along the main road through Krasnyi, followed by the remaining corps. This movement made the army vulnerable to attack. By 13 November, the main Russian army had already approached Smolensk from the south and, having by-passed it, made a direct thrust to Krasnyi, threatening to cut the Grand Army's line of retreat. On 14–16 November, the Russian forces made repeated attacks on three Allied corps (Eugène, Davout, Ney) while they were marching from Smolensk to Krasnyi. Each corps was temporarily cut off, and Ney's corps even surrounded, but none of them were forced to lay down their arms; Ney was cut off from the main army, but conducted a heroic retreat across the Dnieper River. Still, Napoleon's main army proceeded pell-mell to Orsha on the right bank of the Dnieper. To Mathieu Dumas

> This march […] was the most afflicting scene that can strike the eyes of a French soldier. It was painful to see the Emperor on horseback, making his way with difficulty through the crowd of soldiers, the greater number of whom were disarmed and kept no order or rank. A sudden thaw increased the embarrassments of this day; the greater part of the infantry passed the Dnieper on the floating ice, which was already underwater, while the horses and carriages went over the bridge […] [At Orsha], we found some resources; the remnants of the corps of the army, whose losses both in men and *matériel* were immense, were rallied and re-organized as much as it was possible.[17]

The Battle of Krasnyi was not a battle on the scale of Borodino or Maloyaroslavets but rather a series of isolated engagements spread over three days. Yet, as at Borodino, the victor at Krasnyi seems to be in the eye of the beholder. Many Francophile historians claim it as a French success, although it is hard to accept this conclusion. Even though Napoleon escaped Russian encirclement, he lost up to 10,000 killed and over 20,000 captured, including seven generals, some 200 guns and six flags.[18] Eugène and Davout suffered heavy casualties and Ney's corps effectively ceased to exist. The Grand Army's combat-ready core of troops was now reduced to about 30,000 men with perhaps forty guns. Chambray estimated that Allied cavalry amounted to about 2,000 men: 1,600 in the Guard cavalry, 200 in Latour-Maubourg's corps and 200 men in the remaining units. Thiers estimated the total strength of the Allied infantry at some 23,000 men: 8,000 in the Guard, 8,000 in I Corps (Davout), 1,500 in III Corps (Ney), 3,000 in IV Corps (Eugène), and 2,500 in V (Poniatowski) and VIII Corps (Junot).[19] And crucially, the Grand Army lost a large portion of its artillery during the retreat, making it vulnerable to Russian artillery bombardment in future combats. While the army still nominally counted 'corps' and 'divisions', in reality these were all but skeletons, with many of the latter reduced to regimental strength. Meanwhile, the army remained heavily burdened by tens of thousands of stragglers.

The Russian army, having left the Tarutino Camp with about 100,000–110,000 men, numbered some 60,000–65,000 men at Krasnyi. This attrition is explained by the strategic consumption, which required the Russian command to divert forces, but also by losses due to combat, weather elements and lack of supplies. Thus, on 12 November, the 3rd Corps mustered 8,286 men (with ninety cannon) but over 5,700 men were in the hospitals. The 12th Division was reduced to 2,611 men after over 4,200 men fell sick. The cavalry fared no better, with the 1st Cuirassier Division reporting 1,908 men present and 300 sick, and the 2nd Cuirassier Division having 1,261 men present and 679 sick.

Until recently, Russian and Soviet historians tended to exaggerate the importance of the battle at Krasnyi, largely because Kutuzov described it as a decisive victory in his reports. Buturlin, Mikhailovsky-Danilevsky, Garnich, Beskrovny and others called it the 'decisive battle' brilliantly won by the Russians, and Zhilin went as far as to claim 'the three-day-long battle at Krasnyi ended with a complete rout of Napoleon's army ...'[20] In reality, the Russian troops attacked separate corps (Eugène, Davout, Ney) as they were marching from Smolensk to Krasnyi. Although each corps was temporarily cut off and Ney's corps even surrounded, *none* was forced to lay down arms. Thus, an opportunity to destroy the Grand Army was squandered.

Kutuzov himself facilitated such embellishment when he wrote on 18 November, 'Yesterday the enemy suffered a new and violent defeat at Krasnyi. The confusion, in which he now remains, is indescribable. Napoleon himself fled with his entourage, abandoning his army to the slaughter [perpetrated] by our warriors ...'[21] His report to Alexander was more measured but effectively claimed that the Grand Army was routed, and this assertion was supported by the presentation of Marshal Davout's captured baton. To celebrate this victory, Alexander conferred the title 'Prince of Smolensk' on Kutuzov, and generously rewarded senior Russian commanders involved in the battle. But Alexander also understood that more could have been accomplished. He had already complained

Background

about Kutuzov's 'inexplicable inactivity' after Tarutino, Maloyaroslavets and Vyazma: 'It is with extreme sadness that I realize that the hope of wiping away the dishonour of the loss of Moscow by cutting the enemy's line of retreat has vanished completely,' he told the field marshal, warning him that 'all misfortunes stemming from your actions would be your personal responsibility'.[22] Reading Kutuzov's report on Krasnyi, Alexander would certainly have expected more than captured baggage and a mislaid baton.

Contemporaries, likewise, were dissatisfied with the results of Krasnyi. General Nikolai Rayevsky criticized Kutuzov for representing this battle as 'decisive'.[23] Colonel Eyler, who commanded the Russian reserve artillery, hoped for much better results, considering that 'the French were driven back like a herd and they were resisting only when their route was blocked, abandoning wagons, carriages and even artillery without any defence'.[24] Yermolov notes that, in his reports, Kutuzov

> portrayed the indecisive and sluggish actions of our army at Krasnyi as being major battles fought over several days, whereas the battles against [Napoleon's] corps were fought separately, without [...] any general plan [of action]. Yet, our timid actions had to be presented in a beneficial light and what could have been better than describing them as battles? But, in reality, they were carried out arbitrarily.

Denis Davydov echoes Yermolov's criticism:

> The action at Krasnyi, that some our military scholars pompously named as a three-day battle, should instead be described as a three-day search for hungry, half-naked Frenchmen; only insignificant detachments such as mine, not our main army, might be proud of these trophies.[25]

Robert Wilson was probably the most vocal in the Russian army, as he complained about 'all the dilatory and discursive marches' that, in his opinion, were 'consistent sequences of [Kutuzov's] predetermination to make the victor weep, to see the vanquished fly!' At Krasnyi, Kutuzov 'might have concluded the war', Wilson claimed. And in a letter to Alexander, Wilson openly criticized the Russian commander and sought

> to bring to Your Majesty's attention a few comments on the remarkable sluggishness of our movement to Krasnyi [...] and [Kutuzov's] difficulties in executing any kind of plan of attack against the enemy.[26]

Meanwhile, Armand de Caulaincourt agreed that while Napoleon 'defied adversity at Krasnyi, the Russians profited little from their advantages'.[27]

Kutuzov's actions at Krasnyi, although hard to explain, are important in order to understand the subsequent course of events. A more vigorous attack might have produced decisive results and potentially changed the course of history. His motives for restraining the army are inscrutable because of his very personality – intelligent, shrewd and manipulative. Scholarly opinion is divided on this topic. Some suggest that Kutuzov's age and poor health had some effect on his judgment, and that he did not want to jeopardize his place in posterity by risking open combat with Napoleon. Kutuzov's documents certainly reveal his concern regarding Napoleon's whereabouts, and he repeatedly requested his commanders to 'use all means necessary to locate the exact position of the [Imperial] Guard', noting that without such information, 'the field marshal does not intend to attack'.[28] But the notion of Kutuzov 'fearing' to fight Napoleon – which is quite popular in Western historiography – seems the least plausible, considering Kutuzov's prior actions. If Kutuzov had no qualms of fighting Napoleon (with his relatively intact Grand Army) at Borodino and Maloyaroslavets, why would he dread facing the weakened enemy at Krasnyi? More credible is the argument that Kutuzov wanted to preserve his forces and let starvation, exhaustion and the elements complete the destruction of the enemy. He told the captured French Chief Commissary, General Puibusque, that

> I was convinced of your defeat [due to starvation and weather] and had no desire to sacrifice a single soldier to achieve this [...] This is how we, barbarians of the North [barbares du Nord], conserve our men.[29]

Instead of pitched battles, Kutuzov preferred using Cossacks and flying detachments to harass the retreating enemy and capture stragglers by the hundreds, if not thousands. As noted above, the Russian army lost about half of its strength between Tarutino and Krasnyi and Kutuzov certainly was concerned about such high losses. Napoleon's defeat could no longer be doubted, and winning one more battle was not as important as future political developments in Europe and Russia's role in them. According to Prince Eugène of Württemberg, Kutuzov told him that

> our young hot-heads are angry at me for I restrain their frenzy; but they do not realize that the circumstances are more effective than our weapons. We cannot reach the frontiers with empty hands [i.e. without an army].

Wilson, who continually criticized Kutuzov's actions and urged more dynamic operations, was incensed when Kutuzov bluntly told him that

Background

I do not care for your objections [...] I am by no means sure that the total destruction of the Emperor Napoleon and his army would be such a benefit to the world. His succession would not fall to Russia or any other continental power, but to that which already commands the sea [i.e. Britain], and whose domination would then be intolerable.

Arguing with Bennigsen over strategy, the Field Marshal told him, 'We will never come to an agreement; you are only thinking of the benefit for England while to me, even if that island sinks to the bottom of the sea, I would not sigh.'[30] Besides, as Kutuzov put it, '[it is] so sweet to chase the best commander in the world'.[31]

Ensnaring the Eagle: The St Petersburg Plan

In order to understand what happened on the banks of the Berezina in the last days of November, we must look back to early September, when Napoleon and Kutuzov fought at Borodino and both claimed victory there. Napoleon considered himself the victor since the Russians retreated from the battlefield and his 18th Bulletin proudly proclaimed 'the victory was never uncertain'. But the Russians had a different view, and during the night after the battle, Kutuzov prepared a report describing with much fanfare the Russian victory at Borodino. The report reached St Petersburg on the night of 10/11 September and was presented to Emperor Alexander. The following day, as the Imperial family attended a mass at the Alexander of Neva Monastery, Kutuzov's report was announced (and later published) to a joyous public. News of the victory was rapturously celebrated throughout St Petersburg, where church bells pealed forth and trumpets blared. The American envoy to Russia, John Quincy Adams, wrote in his letter that 'St Petersburg was illuminated'. Meanwhile, an English traveller, Ker Porter, described that 'with the victory being publicly declared, the *Te Deum* was chanted, every voice united in the strain which gave glory to the God who had fought, and covered her people with immortal honours'. The news spread to other towns and provinces and in the process became embellished. Thus Joseph de Maistre informed the Sardinian foreign minister that he had heard that 'by the end of the battle the French had completely run out of ammunitions and were throwing stones'.[32]

It was natural then for many to assume that with Napoleon defeated at Borodino, the Russian Army should undertake more aggressive measures to complete the enemy's destruction. On 13 September, Emperor Alexander and his advisors, still unaware of the Russian retreat and the subsequent abandonment of Moscow, came up with a new plan of operations, which was entrusted to Flügel Adjutant Alexander Chernishev (the famed Russian spymaster who penetrated the French Ministry of War in 1810–1811) to deliver

The Battle of the Berezina

to Kutuzov. Chernishev found the retreating Russian Army only after Moscow had been surrendered and Kutuzov's headquarters established at Krasnaya Pakhra on the old Kaluga Road. He presented the Russian commander-in-chief a set of orders designed to change the tide of the war. Kutuzov was permitted freedom of action according to circumstances, while Chichagov, Tormasov, Wittgenstein and Steinheil were given specific orders to follow.[33] The 'St Petersburg Plan' – as this strategy became known – is often overlooked in campaign studies, although it is crucial for a correct evaluation of subsequent events at the Berezina. Not developed overnight, the plan was the product of a long list of strategic considerations. It was based on the general assumption that, after Napoleon had pursued the main Russian army deep inside Russia, the remaining Russian forces – the 3rd Reserve Army of Observation, Army of Moldavia and Wittgenstein's Corps – should intensify their actions to force Napoleon to halt his advance and turn around. Thus, as early as mid-August, Barclay de Tolly urged Chichagov to undertake more vigorous campaigning and explained to him that 'current circumstances do not permit the 1st and 2nd Armies to operate in such a manner as to protect the heartlands of the Fatherland in case of even a minor setback in a general battle […] The outcome of the war depends on rapid and offensive movements of the Army of Moldavia and the 3rd Reserve Army of Observation. Such movements conform with the general plan of war, which envisions a part of our troops containing the main enemy forces while the second group of our troops, facing fewer enemy forces, is to overwhelm them and threaten the flank and rear of the main enemy army'.[34] A similar idea was expressed by the Swedish Crown Prince Karl Johann – formerly Marshal Jean Baptiste Bernadotte – who finally broke with Napoleon by signing the secret Treaty of Abo with Russia in late August 1812.

Following the Battle of Borodino, the Russian court, misled by initial reports that Napoleon's army was defeated, thought the situation was ripe for a coordinated attack. The St Petersburg Plan, therefore, called for a coordinated offensive by all Russian forces against the French line of communications and Napoleon's dispersed corps in the north and south, all for the single purpose of isolating (and potentially destroying) Napoleon's main army. Kutuzov – the 'hammer' – was to push Napoleon westwards, while Chichagov and Wittgenstein – the 'anvil' – were to block the French escape. Alexander argued that 'we must take advantage of the relative isolation of the main enemy forces to rally our communications and direct superior forces from Polotsk beyond the Dvina to engage the left flank of the two enemy corps of Oudinot and Macdonald'. Having isolated and defeated them, the Russians should then direct their efforts to 'the northern regions of the Minsk province', where Chichagov's army was expected.

Background

In fact, Chichagov was entrusted with a key element of the plan. Following the conclusion of the Peace of Bucharest with the Ottoman Empire in May 1812, his Army of the Danube (also known as the Army of Moldavia) spent the summer regrouping in the Volhynia region and was now ready to enter the fray against Napoleon. Alexander envisioned Chichagov leaving Volhynia via Pinsk to Nesvizh, where his army would threaten French communications through Minsk. Chichagov would then establish close contact with Tormasov (who was tasked with pinning Schwarzenberg around Slonim), merge with Fedor Ertel's reserve corps and take up positions along the Berezina, thus blocking Napoleon's escape route. The ultimate goal was to drive 'the Saxons into the Duchy of Warsaw, the Austrians into Galicia, the Prussians and Württembergers across the Nieman, while the French must be annihilated to the last'. Chichagov was instructed to defend the Berezina line by building a fortified camp near Borisov (reinforcing positions along the River Bobr, which would add depth to his defensive line) and establish direct contact with Wittgenstein, who was supposed to operate from the north. Wittgenstein was instructed to seize Polotsk and drive Marshal Gouvion St Cyr back towards the Nieman. He was then supposed to take up a defensive line along the River Ulla to block potential escape routes between the Rivers Berezina and Dvina.[35]

According to this plan, Wittgenstein and Chichagov were provided with substantial reinforcements. Tormasov's 3rd Reserve Army of Observation was supposed to protect Chichagov's rear from Schwarzenberg and Reynier and try to push them back towards the Duchy of Warsaw or Galicia. Steinheil's Finland Corps, which was transported across the Gulf of Finland to Revel, was ordered to launch an offensive against Macdonald, in order to prevent him supporting St Cyr against Wittgenstein. Steinheil would then assist Wittgenstein in pursuing St Cyr and Macdonald to the Nieman, serving as a strategic reserve to the Russian forces blocking Napoleon's escape. Overall, Alexander envisioned concentrating some 160,000 men along the Rivers Ulla and Berezina by 27 October, while Kutuzov's main army would be driving Napoleon from the east. 'With the help of the Lord, we will force the enemy to abandon not only Russian provinces but all of Byelorussia and Lithuania,' he told Michael Oginski in early October.[36]

In truth, the 'St Petersburg Plan' had both strengths and weaknesses. Napoleon's line of communication was stretched over a vast territory between the Nieman and Moscow and a setback on either flank would have dangerously exposed it. On paper, the plan assigned sufficient forces (the Army of the Danube and the 3rd Reserve Army of Observation in the south, plus Wittgenstein's and Steinheil's corps in the north) to execute the pincer operation and provide the Russians with numerical superiority. The area selected between the Rivers Dvina, Dnieper and Berezina also seemed appropriate, since Napoleon's line of operation between Smolensk and Vilna ran between the

The Battle of the Berezina

Dvina and Dnieper and followed two major routes: Smolensk–Vitebsk–Bocheikovo–Glubokoe–Vilna and Smolensk–Orsha–Borisov–Minsk–Vilna. The latter route was the most convenient and was full of magazines constructed at Napoleon's command. Both routes were also intersected by rivers and streams – the most important being the Dnieper, Ulla and Berezina – which the Russians could exploit to defeat Napoleon.

But Alexander and his advisors failed to consider certain elements. Most important was the fact that the initial plan was based on Kutuzov's misleading Borodino report. Once the true picture emerged and news of Moscow's surrender reached St Petersburg, it became clear that the plan could not be implemented under current circumstances. But Kutuzov also knew that rejecting the imperial plan outright would not be wise, so upon receiving it he summoned a council of war to consider the options. The council was attended by Kutuzov, Levin Bennigsen (a Hanoverian who understood little Russian and required the plan to be translated into French), Karl Toll and Peter Konovnitsyn, who approved the plan – although they knew well that it did not correspond to circumstances and could not be implemented.[37] As one historian rightly observed: 'Kutuzov acted in his customary manner: he made no essential objections and sent the necessary instructions to Wittgenstein and Chichagov. But in reality he did not approve the plan; he did not desire its realization, and thought it was impracticable.'[38] So, in his response to Alexander, Kutuzov obscurely referred to 'difficulties' while pretending to have accepted the plan.

The plan called for close coordination between three armies separated by vast distances. Such coordination was of a paramount importance, since failure to adhere to the timetable would allow Napoleon to engage (and perhaps defeat) each attacking army separately. The seed of this problem was present from the very start, since Kutuzov essentially ignored the plan while Chichagov sought to implement it. Meanwhile, Alexander's involvement only complicated things further, since he mistrusted Kutuzov and frequently went behind his back to issue instructions directly to Wittgenstein and Chichagov. Thus the commanders operated disjointedly and without a common goal. In addition, communications were difficult and even in late November the Russian generals were still not in direct contact with each other. In fact, Kutuzov's dispatches generally reached Wittgenstein after a delay of three to seven days.

Meanwhile, Alexander – without first-hand knowledge of the situation on the ground – began dictating movements to his commanders: he gave detailed instructions to Wittgenstein on how to capture Polotsk; ordered Chichagov to be at Pinsk on 7 October, Nesvizh on 13 October, and Minsk by 21 October; while Tormasov was given specific dates by which he had to coordinate his actions with Chichagov. Alexander assigned these dates without understanding the situation each commander faced.

Background

Russian Leadership

The success of the St Petersburg Plan largely depended on the commanders entrusted with its execution and required a high level of coordination between them. Such coordination was hard to achieve, not only due to the vast distances involved but also because of the different and conflicting personalities of those who led the Russian armies.

The Russian commander-in-chief was Mikhail Illarionovich Golenishchev-Kutuzov, a 65–year-old who had spent most of his life in the military. Born into an ancient Russian noble family, he enlisted at 14 and later distinguished himself fighting the Turks. Barely surviving two wounds to the head (that left him blind in one eye), Kutuzov later served as ambassador to the Ottoman Empire, showing his considerable diplomatic skills. Returning home, Kutuzov was appointed governor of several Russian provinces and directed the famous Engineer and Artillery Cadet Corps, which produced generations of Russian officers. In 1800–1801, Kutuzov served as military governor of St Petersburg. Following the murder of Emperor Paul, he disagreed with his successor, Alexander, and retired in 1802. Three years later, he was called back to lead the Russian army against Napoleon. After the Austrian defeat at Ulm in October 1805, Kutuzov's sound advice on avoiding battle with Napoleon was ignored by Alexander, who called for an immediate offensive. After the subsequent Allied loss at Austerlitz, Kutuzov was unfairly blamed for the defeat and spent the next four years in disgrace, governing provinces in Ukraine and Lithuania. In 1810, Kutuzov was given command of Russian forces in the Danubian principalities. Facing a familiar foe, he showed his military prowess by crushing the Ottoman army in November 1811 and negotiating a much needed peace treaty with the Turks by May 1812. These successes, together with his reputation for capable command made Kutuzov a popular figure in Russian society, leading to his selection as the new commander-in-chief in late August 1812.

Despite the popular western perception of him, Kutuzov was far from being a sluggish and simple-minded man. Although his career was largely based on victories against the decadent Ottoman Empire, Kutuzov's military talents are hard to deny and a contemporary described him as a 'good military tactician and very courageous under fire'. Yet he was also a shrewd diplomat and adroit courtier, who rarely spoke his mind openly and could skilfully manipulate people around him. Suvorov famously described him as 'Crafty, crafty! And shrewd, very shrewd! No one can deceive him.' Kutuzov was a subtle personality and Robert Wilson found him to be 'polished, courteous, shrewd as a Greek, naturally intelligent as an Asiatic and well-instructed as a European'. Describing his eloquence, one officer commented, 'Kutuzov did not speak, but rather played with his tongue like another Mozart or Rossini, who enchanted their listeners.'[39] Yet Kutuzov was also a sybarite, who valued power and honours. And he remained a womanizer into old age. One Russian general, who served under Kutuzov in the Danubian principalities, left a vivid and critical portrait of him:[40]

> Kutuzov was a very smart man but also extremely weak in character, combining agility, shrewdness and true talents with incredible immorality. Extraordinary memory, serious education, benevolent treatment, ability to maintain interesting conversation and good-heartedness (which was pretended but pleasant to trusting individuals) – these were sympathetic features of Kutuzov; at the same time his ruthlessness, rudeness when angered or dealing with people he did not have to fear, his obsequiousness, which often bordered on slavery to persons of greater stature, impenetrable laziness that consumed everything, his apathy, egoism, free-thinking and indelicate attitude to financial affairs, comprised the opposite sides of the same man [...][40]

The effects of this indulgent life were evident by 1812: the 65-year-old Kutuzov had grown stouter since the days of Austerlitz, walked heavily, was often out of breath and had difficulty riding a horse, preferring to use his carriage. Madame de Staël, an ambitious French writer who passionately hated Napoleon and lived in exile, visited Russia on the eve of war and described Kutuzov as

> an old man with the most graceful manners and animated expression [...] Looking at him, I was afraid he would not be equal to the struggle against the strong and ruthless men who were swooping down upon Russia from every corner of Europe [...] I was moved when I bid farewell to the illustrious Marshal Kutuzov and did not know whether I was embracing a conqueror or martyr but I could see that he understood all the greatness of the cause for which he was now responsible.[41]

Some contemporaries, including Kutuzov's rival Levin Bennigsen, claimed the Russian field marshal had lost the habit of mental work; Alexander Langeron, commanding a corps in the Army of the Danube, lamented that Kutuzov's

> assistants, adjutants and secretaries did whatever they wished with him and, although Kutuzov was undoubtedly much smarter and knowledgeable than them, he never bothered to check their work, not to mention to correct it. He signed everything presented to him in order to quickly free himself of daily business, to which he already dedicated only a few minutes per day, before delegating it to the duty generals.

Background

According to Sergei Mayevsky, 'for Kutuzov, to write ten words was more difficult than for some people to produce 100 pages ...' But, below that drowsy and absent-minded appearance was a very keen judgment, cunning and patience.

The commander of the 3rd Western Army, Admiral Pavel Vasilievich Chichagov, turned 45 in the summer of 1812 – a year that proved fateful in his life. The son of Admiral Vasily Chichagov, he graduated from the Naval Corps and began military service in 1779. Over the next decade, he served on various ships in the Mediterranean and Baltic and distinguished himself during the Russo-Swedish War of 1789–1790. He had the honour of delivering news of the Russian victory at Vyborg to Empress Catherine II, for which he was promoted to captain in July 1790. After the war, Chichagov resided in Britain (1792–1793) and upon returning home, commanded various ships-of-the-line. The death of Catherine II in November 1796 was a turning point in Chichagov's career, since Emperor Paul, who disliked him, had him discharged in 1797. Chichagov was later pardoned and promoted to rear admiral in 1799, only to be disgraced again and imprisoned on false charges. An investigation proved him innocent and Chichagov was released and his rank restored. Later that same year, Chichagov participated in the expedition to Holland, for which he received the gift of a golden sword with diamonds from the British sovereign.

Chichagov's prospects improved with the death of Paul in March 1801. Under Alexander, he became a vice admiral and Deputy Minister of Navy in 1802. Over the next five years, Chichagov introduced a series of reforms to modernize the Russian Navy. He was appointed the Minister of Navy with the rank of admiral in 1807 and supervised Russian naval forces for the next four years before resigning due to the death of his English wife and his own poor health. In the spring of 1812, he was called back to service when Alexander appointed him to replace Mikhail Kutuzov in the Danubian principalities. Chichagov's new position was a rather odd one – 'Commander-in-Chief of Moldavia, Wallachia and the Black Sea Fleet' – combining both land and naval commands. The appointment was initially kept secret but news quickly leaked. Joseph de Maistre claims that Kutuzov was secretly notified (by Chancellor Nikolai Rumyantsev, Chichagov's enemy) that 'unless he signed the peace treaty at once, it would be signed without delay by Admiral'.[42] Kutuzov was naturally upset by this appointment. He had spent two years fighting the Turks, routing their army near Ruse in November 1811 and pressuring them to accept Russian conditions for peace. Chichagov's appointment meant that this admiral would be able to sign a peace treaty with the Turks and reap the glory of concluding the war. So Kutuzov did his best, through promises and threats, to pressure the Turks to accept Russian conditions before Chichagov assumed the command. Kutuzov's efforts proved fruitful as the Turks signed the Treaty of Bucharest on 26 May

1812, thus depriving Chichagov of any share in the victory, but this haste also meant that Russia, after six years of fighting to secure Moldavia and Wallachia, had to surrender these provinces to the Porte. Nevertheless, Kutuzov bested Chichagov, who now faced the mundane task of managing an army on the periphery of the empire.

Chichagov and Kutuzov both felt slighted in this incident: the former was robbed of fame, while the latter scorned the upstart who almost deprived him of his laurels. Upon reaching the Army of the Danube, Chichagov further strained his relations with Kutuzov when he began filing reports about mismanagement and abuses in the army, which he blamed on his predecessor. Chichagov described abandoned villages, whose residents fled to avoid maltreatment by Russian troops, and the entire army suffering while Kutuzov occupied himself with mistresses: 'Should one be surprised to see soldiers mismanaged when General Kutuzov, solely concerned about his personal pleasures, had no qualms about kidnapping and exiling a member of the *Diwan* [Governing Council] of Wallachia, who happened to be a husband of one of his mistresses?' lamented Chichagov.[43] Such sentiments did not help improve relations between Kutuzov and Chichagov, which would play a crucial role when, only months later, these two generals were called upon to cooperate in a major operation against Napoleon.

Chichagov is an interesting personality, neglected by historians and undeservedly maligned.[44] Contemporaries were divided over this man and left contrasting portraits of him. Known for his candour and honesty, which earned him many enemies, Chichagov expressed his opinion bluntly, even when dealing with sovereigns (his remarks once angered Emperor Paul so much that he ordered Chichagov imprisoned).[45] Meanwhile, Joseph de Maistre praised Chichagov as 'one of the most remarkable men in Russia. Nowadays, there is no one here to [...] equal him in judgment, sharpness of intellect, strength of character, sense of justice, impartiality and even austerity of morals'. In one of his letters, de Maistre also noted that 'Chichagov is feared because he insists on order and is despised because he does not allow anyone to steal in his ministry.'[46] Karl Toll thought Chichagov 'a strange man', but spoke of his 'determination, firmness, conviction and independent spirit', as well as his 'arrogance' and 'pretentiousness'.[47] Countess Catherine de Bouzet, the Admiral's youngest daughter, later remembered her father as a man of extremes, who took 'frankness to carelessness, unselfishness to deception, modesty to neglect of his own reputation, hoping that posterity will give him his due ...'[48] Count Fedor Tolstoy – who served under Chichagov and knew him quite well – described him as a

> very intelligent and educated man, of upright character, remarkably uninhibited and, like no other minister, plain in his relations and

40

conversations with the Emperor and the royal family. Chichagov knew well his superiority in sciences, education, as well as honesty and firmness of character, over court sycophants, and treated them with great inattentiveness, oftentimes even carelessly for which he was, naturally, hated virtually by the entire court and all the empty-headed but haughty nobility. However, Chichagov treated his subordinates and petitioners well, accepted them without distinction of rank or title and always listened to their requests with great patience.[49]

Nevertheless, Chichagov's constant criticism of the Russian nobility and his desire to reform society were perceived as a hatred of his own motherland, earning him the derogatory tags of 'Jacobin' and 'liberal'. De Maistre, who praised Chichagov so much, had to admit that 'his excellent character traits' were eclipsed by two 'grave flaws': indifference towards religion and 'loathing, even a profound hatred, towards every principle established in this country, in which he only sees feeblemindedness, ignorance, transgression and despotism'. De Maistre did note, however, that the admiral 'despised not Russia herself but rather the evil that corrupts her; alas, such delicate intricacies are beyond the majority's understanding'.[50] The fact that Chichagov had once expressed admiration for Napoleon – even displaying his bust in the Navy Ministry's office – was certainly not lost on his numerous opponents.[51] The naysayers, like State Secretary Alexander Shishkov, wondered, 'how could a man, who expressed so much disgust for everything Russian, enjoy such closeness to the Emperor?'[52] But despite intrigues and hearsay, Alexander continued to trust Chichagov, whom he repeatedly praised and considered among his most trusted advisers. In September 1812, when he had to choose between Chichagov and Tormasov to lead the newly-created 3rd Western Army, Alexander told Kutuzov that 'among these two men I consider Chichagov the ablest because of his decisive character'.[53]

Chichagov's appointment to the Army of the Danube unleashed a variety of reactions. Many probably agreed with a Swedish general's comment, that it was 'a strange idea to entrust a land army to the admiral'.[54] Alexander's decision was criticized, as was his continued disregard of Kutuzov, one senior official writing that '[The Emperor's] prejudices against [Kutuzov] following the Austrians campaign [of 1805] [...] remain as strong as ever, even though the Fatherland stands on the edge of destruction.'[55] Shishkov – who had loathed Chichagov since youth[56] – described him as 'haughty, boastful of his imaginary merits, with audacious tongue, and hateful of his own motherland'.[57] Langeron left one of the most critical portraits of Chichagov, helping us appreciate how contemporaries perceived the Admiral:

He was not devoid of mental powers, if one can give such a name to a mixture of slang, garrulity, and a very superficial education. His brain was like a volcano: every minute it produced some new project, and this project, which was usually either absurd or impracticable, had to be executed instantly. He would allow neither argument nor delay in the execution of his whims. Not one of his ideas was sound. The stiffness of his character and his excessive *amour-propre* prevented him from listening to or taking any advice. With unyielding obstinacy he followed whatever he had conceived in the delirium of his extravagant imagination. He was a no better judge of men than of events, and could never abandon a prejudice [...] [As the Minister of Navy] he had ruined the Navy. He had no idea about land operations and his ignorance of our organization and manoeuvres soon made him the laughing-stock of his army. Chichagov's character accorded perfectly with his mind; he was hard and autocratic, ungrateful and coarse. He had every vice of the heart just as he had every extravagance of the mind. At one time a fanatical admirer of the English, at another time ridiculously enamoured of the French, he had only one constant emotion: hatred and scorn of his own nation, a scorn which he never stopped expressing [...] However. Chichagov had one precious quality: he was honest and disinterested. [Yet] he carried this virtue to excess both for himself and for others ...[58]

Reading Langeron's account, however, one must remember that this general had served under Chichagov in the Army of the Danube and was certainly unhappy (and offended) when the admiral revealed poor conditions in the army. Chichagov himself was tepid towards Langeron, noting in one of his letters to Alexander that he hoped 'to be delivered from Langeron [...] who could have been a good [general] if he were not empty-headed and absent-minded'.[59]

Toll, another of Chichagov's detractors, acknowledged that Chichagov, after taking command of the Army of the Danube, vigorously studied army regulations and manuals and soon 'surprised generals and even NCOs with his knowledge'. But the admiral failed to 'comprehend the higher levels of military art and had no clear and firm conceptions on troop deployment on the battlefield'.[60] As a result he often relied on his generals, especially Chief of Staff Sabaneyev, but, as Tyrconnell reported, he never fully trusted them.[61]

Unlike Chichagov, Lieutenant General Peter Khristianovich (Peter Ludwig Adolf) Wittgenstein (Sayn-Wittgenstein-Berleburg) was widely admired in Russian society and the military. This 43–year-old general was the son of a Prussian lieutenant general (who entered the Russian service in 1762) and a Russian princess from the powerful Dolgoruky family. Young Wittgenstein was brought up in the family of his uncle, the famous Russian Field Marshal General

Background

N.I. Saltykov and was enlisted in the Life Guard Semeyonovskii Regiment in 1781. He quickly advanced through the ranks, fighting the Polish rebels in 1794 and the Persians along the Caspian Sea in 1796 and delivering the keys of the captured fortress of Derbent to St Petersburg. A colonel in 1798, he became a major general the following year. In 1805, he participated in the campaign against Napoleon, distinguishing himself at Amstetten and Austerlitz. The following year, he briefly served against the Turks in Moldavia before fighting the French in Poland, earning a golden sword for courage. Promoted to lieutenant general in 1807, he led a corps in southern Finland between 1808 and 1811. In 1812, Wittgenstein commanded the 1st Independent Corps, covering the routes to St Petersburg, and was quite successful in containing Oudinot's forces. After winning a battle at Polotsk on 18 October, thereby protecting the route to the capital, he became widely popular in Russian society. Dubbed 'the Saviour of St Petersburg', Wittgenstein advanced to general of cavalry on 3 November 1812 with seniority dating from 18 October 1812. A contemporary, who was clearly fascinated by him, described Wittgenstein as a

> tall man, with an aquiline nose, ardent eyes […] tall forehead […] and a smile that expressed his beautiful soul which can be seen in all features of his calm and attractive face. He laid his path to distinction through personal courage, not intrigues and slavishness. Masculine appearance revealed a hero in him; his captivating manners showed a man who knew his talents and never put down others through aloof treatment or careless glance. He was perceptive and cautious but also quite brave.[62]

Indeed, Wittgenstein was known for his reckless gallantry. As one of his contemporaries commented, Wittgenstein belonged 'to those rare heroes who owe their fame not to fortune but to genuine military talent […] Fearlessness, firm decisiveness and personal courage – valiant companions of genuine heroes – were his essential merits'.[63] But the general was not without his weaknesses. Generous and open-hearted to friends, often chivalrous and inspirational, Wittgenstein also was haughty, impulsive and incapable of executing large military operations. Until 1812, he had mainly commanded at brigade level and, although he successfully led a corps against Oudinot, his shortcomings would be partly revealed at the Berezina, and fully at Lützen and Bautzen in the spring of 1813. One Russian general noted Wittgenstein's

> carelessness with respect to internal management of the army, which led to such disorder that the locations of some regiments were oftentimes completely unknown. The main headquarters was akin to a market square […] Out of kindness of heart, he never restricted access to himself to

anyone. His room was always full of idle officers, who discussed and spread news about any issues, even those confidential.[64]

These commanders were supported by a host of generals and senior officers whose names are often left out of the pages of history, although they all played relevant and often key roles in the events at the Berezina. They came from different ethnic origins but most shared a common trait – nobility. On average, they were in their early forties and had served in the military since boyhood.[65] Wittgenstein's and Chichagov's officers had honed their skills in two to four campaigns, most serving against Poland (1792–1794), Turkey (1787–1791 and 1806–1812) and France (1805 and 1806–1807), but some had also fought the Persians (1796) and Swedes (1808–1809).

The 40-year-old Karl Osipovich Lambert was a French *émigré* officer in Russian service. He was descended from a prominent French noble family, and began his service in the French Royal Guard, fleeing his homeland during the Revolution and entering Russian service in 1793. The following year, Lambert fought against the Polish rebels, distinguishing himself at Maciejowice and Praga, for which he was decorated with the Order of St George (4th class). In 1796–1797, he participated in the campaign against the Persians along the Caspian Sea and, upon returning to Russia, was promoted to colonel (1798) and given command of a cuirassier regiment (1799). In late 1799, Lambert served under General Alexander Rimsky-Korsakov in Switzerland, fighting his former compatriots at Zurich, where he distinguished himself and was later promoted to major general. When Emperor Paul I began purging the Russian army, Lambert found himself among those discharged from military service. A year later – and following Paul's assassination – Lambert was reinstated. In 1806, he again faced the French, this time on the barren fields of Poland. Fighting at Czarnowo, Eylau and Friedland, Lambert garnered several awards. By 1811, he was already in charge of a cavalry division, which he commanded in the early stages of the 1812 Campaign. He distinguished himself at Kobryn and Gorodechnya and was promoted to lieutenant general on 2 November 1812 with seniority dating from 12 August 1812. A contemporary described Lambert as

> among the best cavalry generals of Emperor Alexander's era. In peace time, he maintained his troops in excellent condition […] In war, he was one of the most efficient and valiant commanders […] Kind, very polite to everyone, he was a quiet and modest person. Unassuming in his speech and actions, he was adored by his subordinates and deeply respected in the entire army.[66]

Louis-Alexandre Andrault Langeron was another French *émigré* officer, whom some scholars compared to a 'soldier of fortune', while the Prussian officers

Background

later described him (unjustly) as a 'miserable poltroon'.[67] Born into a prominent French noble family, Langeron began service in the French Royal Army and participated in the American Revolutionary War before fleeing France during the Revolution to enter Russian service. In 1805 he commanded one of the Russian columns at Austerlitz, being unjustly blamed for the Russian defeat and sent to govern Odessa, on the Black Sea, in disgrace. He also served in the Danubian principalities and distinguished himself fighting the Turks. After the Napoleonic Wars, he made a successful career as governor of Odessa, which flourished under his rule. By 1812 – with thirty-three years of service behind him – Langeron was perceived as a competent general. But he was also known as a faultfinder, frequently expressing criticism of his Russian comrades-in-arms, including his superiors, which garnered him few friends.[68] Still, a contemporary portrayed him as a cheerful figure, 'constantly in a good mood, especially when in the midst of fighting. With canister and bullets flying, a smile often graced his lips and he often made witty remarks. Incapable of anger, he usually humorously reprimanded his subordinates'.[69] Another contemporary remembered Langeron as a 'kind, helpful and affable person […] In society, he was known for his politeness and unordinary witticism. At the same time, he was an absent-minded and ambitious man'.[70]

General Yefim (Eufemiusz) Czaplic (Chaplits), 44 years old, descended from a Polish noble family. He began service in the Polish army but entered Russian service in the fall of 1783. He distinguished himself during the Russo-Turkish War in 1788–1791 and later served against his own compatriots in Poland in 1792–1794. Two years later, Czaplic participated in the Persian Campaign and was promoted to colonel. In 1805 he served under Prince Peter Bagration, earning promotions and awards for his actions at Lambach, Amstetten, Schöngrabern (Hollabrunn) and Austerlitz. The following year, he again distinguished himself fighting the French, this time on the fields of his native Poland. After serving as a divisional commander in 1808–1810, Czaplic commanded a cavalry corps in 1811–1812. During Napoleon's Invasion of Russia, he took part in combats at Kobryn and Slonim, for which he was later promoted to lieutenant general. In the fall of 1812, Czaplic led the advance guard of Admiral Paul Chichagov's army and played an important role in the events at the Berezina. In later years, he fought at Leipzig (1813) and commanded a corps in Poland in 1814.

Ivan Vasilievich Sabaneyev played an important – albeit not always a positive – role in the events on the Berezina. 'One of the best officers in this army,' as he was described by a British officer,[71] Sabaneyev was 17 years old when he enlisted in 1787, and by the time he fought on the Berezina, he was already an experienced officer. A graduate of the University of Moscow, he served in Jäger regiments most of these years, fighting the Turks in 1790–1791, the Poles in

The Battle of the Berezina

1792 and the French in 1799. Following his exploits at Urzern (where he was wounded) and the Devil's Bridge, Suvorov recommended him for promotion to lieutenant colonel, but Sabaneyev was seriously wounded in the Muottethal Valley and left with other Russian wounded at Glarus. After spending over a year in French captivity, he was released as part of the rapprochement between Napoleon and Paul I in 1801. Imprisonment in France proved consequential for Sabaneyev, since he had opportunity to study French tactics. Mikhailovsky-Danilevsky, who knew Sabaneyev well, left the following pen portrait:

> Agile and smart, passionate in his emotions and willing to engage in a lively conversation, Sabaneyev easily befriended the French officers. Taking advantage of their affinity, he began following them to their training camps and learned French tactics. He was especially surprised to observe the French skirmisher training in open order, then little known in Europe.[72]

Returning home, Sabaneyev prepared a special memo on improving Russian skirmishing tactics and was soon considered an authority on this topic. He commanded various Jäger regiments and served in the North Caucasus before being sent to Poland to face the French again in 1807. Serving in Prince Peter Bagration's advance guard, he fought at Guttstadt, Heilsberg and Friedland, where he was wounded in the face: his gallantry earned him the Order of St Vladimir and a golden sword. In 1808–1809, Sabaneyev fought the Swedes in Finland, was wounded at Alavo, and participated in the famous crossing of the Gulf of Bothnia. Promoted to major general in December 1809, he was sent to the Danubian principalities and distinguished himself fighting Turks at Silistra, Ragrad, Shumla, Batin and Ruse, where Kutuzov destroyed the Ottoman Army in late 1811. Sabaneyev was appointed the second plenipotentiary to the Bucharest conference – which in itself indicates the high opinion Kutuzov had of him – and helped negotiate the Russo-Turkish peace in May 1812. The same month, Sabaneyev was appointed Chief of Staff of the Army of the Danube.

Contemporaries spoke of Sabaneyev's literary knowledge, his honesty, and his devotion to Russia. Philip Vigel described him as 'a small, thin, intelligent and enterprising man', while in the words of Mikhailovsky-Danilevsky, Sabaneyev was a 'man of small and frail stature, with pale yellow face, shortsighted, wearing green glasses, suspicious and quick tempered'. Vladimir Rayevsky, whom Sabaneyev had arrested for radical ideas in 1822, sniped that Sabaneyev was no taller than 5 feet 2 inches, 'with red nose, full lips, rather shortsighted eyes …' But even he acknowledged that the general had 'many honourable traits. He knew military art, read profusely, and wrote excellently, never concerning himself with decorum but always about soldiers' benefits'. Langeron, who was known for his critical assessments, thought Sabaneyev a

courageous, educated and enterprising officer. However, his military talents were curtailed by his weak vision, since he was almost blind and this is a major weakness for a general during a war. In terms of honesty, he was an ideal person, very kind and responsible, but he also had a very abrasive character and he was unable to constrain himself and his outbursts and frankness were often out of place.[73]

Campaign Chronicle

W e already have seen that Tormasov celebrated a victory at Kobryn in the early weeks of the campaign. This caused Napoleon to divert the two Polish divisions of Kosinski and Jan Henryk Dąbrowski to support the Austrians. In early August, the combined forces of Schwarzenberg and Reynier launched an offensive against Tormasov, who was defeated at Gorodechna on 12 August and forced to retreat to Lutsk. Schwarzenberg, however, did not exploit his success, allowing the Russians to bring up the Army of the Danube in mid-September. This tilted the balance of power in their favour and prevented Schwarzenberg from taking any offensive operations. On 22 September 1812, the 3rd Reserve Army of Observation and the Army of the Danube were merged into the 3rd Western Army, under the overall command of Chichagov, while Tormasov was recalled to the main army.

11 October–17 November: Minsk

Taking advantage of a large force at his disposal, Chichagov drove Schwarzenberg and Reynier back to Brest, which was occupied on 11 October. Schwarzenberg then retreated to the left bank of the Bug, allowing Chichagov to march on Minsk. It seemed that the first stage of the St Petersburg Plan could be accomplished without difficulty. But Chichagov spent the next two weeks at Brest, gathering supplies and fearing that Schwarzenberg was intentionally retreating before him. Ideally, Chichagov would have exploited his numerical superiority to defeat Schwarzenberg and turn to block Napoleon, but the crafty Austrian refused to be drawn into a major battle. Finally, after days of vacillation, Chichagov decided to divide his forces. He left General Sacken with about 27,000 men at Brest with orders to monitor Schwarzenberg, and marched north-east with the rest of the 3rd Western Army.[74] Still, Chichagov was concerned about his rear, advancing slowly, in order to better aid Sacken should Schwarzenberg attack him. His worst expectations seemed to materialize when he received word that Schwarzenberg and Reynier were marching on Volkovysk, but this was followed by more heart-warming news: Sacken fought a series of actions around Volkovysk between 14–16 November and, although unable to defeat the numerically superior enemy, prudently began retreating to Brest, thus diverting Schwarzenberg and Reynier from the 3rd Western Army, which was quickly marching on Minsk.[75]

The town of Minsk held an important place in the French line of communication and Napoleon himself described it as 'the grand depot of the army'.[76] Governed by Polish General Mikolai (Nicolas) Bronikowski since July, the city was protected by a small garrison of some 2,200 men, supported by General Ksawery Kossecki's Lithuanians (some 3,500 men). Not far away, Jan Henryk Dąbrowski's 17th Division was spread out between the Dnieper and Slutsk, where it faced the Russian troops of Ertel, Ignatyev and Zapolski.[77] There were no other significant forces in the vicinity, since Claude Victor-Perrin's corps (located at Smolensk) was sent to assist St Cyr against Wittgenstein.[78] On 28 October, Victor instructed Dąbrowski to concentrate his forces on the Berezina but later changed his orders, diverting some 3,000 men to Minsk, which Dąbrowski was able to accomplish due to Ertel's idleness.[79] But Bronikowski was in a difficult situation and failed to rise to the occasion. Aware of Chichagov's advance from Nesvizh, he chose to delay it by sending out a portion of his troops (under Kossecki) to defend the crossing over the Nieman at Novy-Sverzhen.[80]

The Russian advance guard, led by LG Lambert, routed Kossecki at Novy-Sverzhen and Kaidanov on 14–15 November, capturing the crossings intact. The Admiral proudly reported that these 'brilliant actions' produced 'two flags and two guns captured, while the entire corps [sic], except for its general [Kossecki], who ran away with a hundred of horses, was either captured or destroyed ...'[81] The Polish command seems to have regarded Kossecki in different terms, since Dąbrowski later nominated him for the Legion d'Honneur.[82] Colonel Justin Laffitte of the 18th Dragoons described the fighting retreat, where 'a numerous cavalry assailed us in open countryside and we ended up suffering considerable losses. Two battalions of the newly raised Lithuanian troops threw down their arms and refused to fire; or rather, they lay down on the ground and nothing could lift them out of this posture'.[83] On 15 November Bronikowski unhappily reported that Kossecki's forces were destroyed and that within hours, he expected to battle 8,000 Russians with only twelve guns at his disposal.[84] Dąbrowski, believing the Russian advance guard to be 12,000 strong and supported by the rest of the 3rd Western Army, concurred that Minsk could not be defended.[85] According to Vaudoncourt, Bronikowski promptly decided to abandon Minsk and withdraw to Borisov but made no preparations, which caused the garrison to retreat in disorder. Bronikowski's failure to defend the town surprised the Russians and Count Louis-Pierre de Rochechouart could not 'understand how the Governor of Minsk came to be taken by surprise. Why was he not forewarned of the march of our army? How did he not deploy scouts, if only to keep in touch with Prince Schwarzenberg?' In Rochechouart's opinion, the answer lay in Napoleon's propaganda: 'No doubt this feeling of security arose from the inaccurate reports given by the *Grande Armée*, which announced victories everywhere, and the annihilation of the Russian armies.'[86]

On 16 November, the Russian advance guard entered Minsk, while Chichagov's main forces arrived a day later. The Russians seized large quantities of supplies the Poles left intact, including hundreds of thousands of rations, over 2,500 muskets and plenty of ammunition. They also captured hundreds of Allied soldiers (Chichagov reported 2,224 men but Vaudoncourt claimed as many as 4,700 men) convalescing in local hospitals, and liberated 110 Russian prisoners of war.[87] In his letter to Alexander, Chichagov described dreadful conditions in hospitals and the town in general. The Russians found

> corpses that lay with the living soldiers for the past ten days [...] The road is lined with gallows, with a corpse hanging on one gibbet and up to twenty others awaiting theirs. Yet, despite all of this, the Poles still admire Napoleon: lightheaded, exultant or plain ignorant, they still believe that they are contributing to their cause ...[88]

Among the captured Poles was an entire Polish military orchestra, which the Russians now put to work for their amusement. As Mikhailovsky-Danilevsky informs us, the 14th Jägers 'entertained themselves for a long time by forcing the musicians to play songs that our enemies had written to celebrate Russia's defeat'.[89]

The occupation of Minsk was of great importance for the success of the Russian plan to entrap Napoleon. Chichagov's men deprived the Grand Army of key supplies and interrupted one of Napoleon's lines of operations from Smolensk to Vilna. Furthermore, the Russian control of the Berezina River would spell doom for the Grand Army, so it was of paramount importance for Napoleon to secure this site. The French emperor sent orders to Dąbrowski to concentrate his division at the crossing and take any measures necessary to protect it. He then instructed Oudinot to leave Victor and hasten to Borisov, where he was supposed to assist Dąbrowski. Napoleon hoped that even if the Russians seized Borisov, he would be able to defeat Chichagov's army before Kutuzov's arrival and thus clear his path to Minsk. But Oudinot's diversion to Borisov weakened Victor against Wittgenstein's corps. Napoleon instructed Victor to conceal Oudinot's departure and, by covering routes to Rosha, Borisov and Vilna, to deceive Wittgenstein on the true direction of the French retreat. The imperial order instructed 'to induce a belief that the Emperor is advancing on General Wittgenstein, a movement natural enough'. After the army passed Borisov, Victor's force would turn into a rearguard to protect its withdrawal.[90]

The 3rd Western Army spent several days in Minsk. The Admiral soon received news that Wittgenstein had occupied Vitebsk and Chashniki on his way towards Borisov, while Kutuzov was continuing his march parallel to the Grand Army, which was moving towards Borisov. Kutuzov advised the Admiral that 'the main [Russian] army was and will remain on the left (southern) side of the enemy: first, I thus maintain contact with our breadbasket provinces; second, it is easier to maintain communications with you, and finally, the enemy, seeing me constantly beside himself, would not dare to stop, fearing I may flank him'. Unaware of the fall of Minsk, Kutuzov commended Chichagov on moving to this town, since 'your movement would be remarkably decisive in current circumstances'. The following day, the Russian commander-in-chief repeated his sentiments in a letter to Emperor Alexander, arguing that Chichagov's march on Minsk 'promises to have most favourable consequences', particularly because this town was located only two marches from Borisov, where the Russians planned to intercept Napoleon.[91]

'After resting the troops, tired out with the incessant marching, and in supplying them plentifully with everything they needed',[92] Chichagov held a council of war, which agreed to march to Borisov at once, secure the bridgehead over the Berezina, and then occupy Vilna. The Admiral then belatedly received the imperial letter of 26 October, urging him to act more rapidly: 'Calculate time and expanses well ...' Alexander advised him, 'Think about the consequences if Napoleon manages to cross our borders and gather a new army. Trust your intelligence, enterprise and willpower.' Chichagov did not need extra reminders about the importance of his actions but, as Czaplic tells us, he felt that the responsibility for this operation was squarely placed on his shoulder, although 'the success of the [St Petersburg] plan largely depended on precise actions by *everyone* [my emphasis] involved in it'.[93] Unaware of the strength of Victor and Dąbrowski, Chichagov estimated they had some 50,000 men and believed that his army lacked sufficient force to contain Napoleon on its own, especially if the Austrians suddenly woke from their relative idleness to threaten from the west.

So, before continuing his advance, the Admiral tried to strengthen his army by gathering additional troops, notably Ertel's reserve corps, which was ordered to march through Igumen towards Minsk. This would have given the Admiral an army of some 45,000 men – which would have better prepared it for the difficult task ahead – but Ertel failed to comply with orders.

Chichagov was furious, accusing Ertel of indecision and insubordination.[94] In a letter to Alexander, the Admiral acidly noted that

> since insubordination is often left unpunished [in Russia], Ertel chose to take advantage of it. To clear my conscience, I would like to remove him from command and court martial [him] for his actions [...] If his corps were with me, I would have left a detachment at Minsk at once and marched with the remaining forces towards Napoleon or Victor; I would

have been sufficiently strong even without merging with Wittgenstein and, although I will do the same now, my forces are not as strong and yet the game, which we all are playing, requires as few risks as possible [...] Unfortunate are those armies where people like Ertel are tolerated.[95]

Chichagov soon replaced Ertel with MG Tuchkov and ordered the disgraced lieutenant general to travel to the main army, where his conduct would be reviewed.[96] Chichagov was not the only one upset with this general and Alexei Yermolov – Kutuzov's chief of staff – also complained about Ertel's indecisiveness, which caused 'precious time [to be] wasted [...] [because of] his meaningless questions'. Like many generals, Ertel was arrogant and brutish, unwilling to accept orders from an admiral. In December, Armand Domergue – stage-manager of the imperial theatre at Moscow, who fled with the Grand Army – observed him in Vilna 'standing in the midst of some twenty men whom he abused in the most cruel manner. Not satisfied with insulting them with worst cursing, the General was punching these men's faces, which were covered in blood. Their crime was following their masters, who, like us, fled with the French army'.[97]

Yet, Ertel had powerful allies at the Russian headquarters, who knew how much Kutuzov disliked Chichagov and were ready to please the Commander-in-Chief. Ertel himself was well aware of this and, according to Joseph de Maistre, by disobeying Chichagov, he hoped to gain Kutuzov's approval.[98] In late October, Ertel received orders from Kutuzov to gather supplies for the approaching main Russian army and prepare to engage the enemy. Kutuzov's orders specified that Ertel was only to do this if he had no other instructions from Chichagov. Although failing to properly execute any of these orders, Ertel used them to justify his neglect of Chichagov's requests. When Chichagov demanded Ertel's court martial, Yermolov tells us, 'Duty General Konovnitsyn, knowing about Prince Kutuzov's animosity towards the Admiral [Chichagov], found a way to preclude General Ertel from any responsibility for his insubordination and thus not exasperate the Field Marshal!'[99] Instead of court martial, Ertel was welcomed at the headquarters, nominated for the prestigious Order of St George (3rd class) for an inconsequential combat at Gorbachevichi (15 September) and later appointed general-police-master of all Russian armies. Thus he was effectively cleared of Chichagov's charges. Furthermore, when Kutuzov reported the events of the Berezina to Emperor Alexander and criticized Chichagov, he conveniently forgot to mention Ertel's failure to support the Admiral. As a result, Alexander would later grant Ertel the Order of Alexander of the Neva – one of the highest imperial awards – for his 'dedicated' service in 1812.

The whole affair reveals tense relations between Chichagov and Kutuzov, with the latter failing to provide important intelligence to a man he considered his opponent. On 18 November, George Carpenter, 3rd Earl of Tyrconnell, who served as an acting aide-de-camp to Robert Wilson and was attached to Chichagov, informed William Cathcart, British ambassador to Russia, that

> Kutuzov's communications to the Admiral are not only seldom, but extremely brief: he informs [Chichagov] about his location, but provides no details on the enemy forces, his intentions, etc. An officer who recently arrived from the main headquarters told us about lamentable discords and envy reigning there …

The following day, Tyrconnell received letters from Wilson about Russian operations and later met Chichagov, 'telling him about our operation more than he was aware of. [The Admiral] was extremely dissatisfied with the letters he received from Kutuzov, since they never contain any significant information on enemy intentions, about which we are so keen to learn at the moment'.[100]

18–22 November: Struggle for Borisov

Despite these problems, the Admiral was full of hope that Napoleon's army would be surrounded on the banks of the Berezina. In anticipation of victory, he made preparations to capture Napoleon, even issuing a manifesto with his description – 'of minor stature, heavy, with pale skin, short and fat neck, large head and black hair' – and advising the locals to 'capture and deliver to me any short man'. On 19 November Chichagov dispatched Lambert with some 4,500 men to Borisov with instructions to occupy the town and open direct communications with Wittgenstein. Chichagov himself remained in Minsk until 20 November, before advancing in several columns. Colonel Lukovkin's Cossack detachment moved to Igumen to observe Polish forces at Mogilev, while Czaplic's detachment marched to Zembin to secure routes towards Vilna. Langeron's column proceeded along the main route and Voinov's forces advanced to Antopol. A small detachment led by Colonel P. Knorring was left behind to protect Minsk, keep an eye on the Austrians, and maintain supply lines.[101]

The Russian offensive was spearheaded by Lambert's advance guard, consisting of the Aleksandriiskii Hussars, Arzamasskii Dragoons, three Cossack regiments, supported by the Vitebskii Infantry, 7th, 13th, 14th and 38th Jägers Regiments, and the 34th Battery and 11th and 12th Horse Artillery Companies (HACs).[102] After covering some 35km from Minsk, Lambert rested his troops at Zhodin on 20 November and deployed Cossack patrols along the routes leading to Borisov: the latter soon captured a couple of Polish officers, from whom Lambert learned that Borisov was defended by a small garrison of about 1,500 men, while reinforcements (prisoners mentioned both Victor and Dąbrowski) were on the march. To anticipate their arrival, Lambert decided to make a forced march of some 30km at night and, at dawn on 21 November, his exhausted infantrymen finally reached the edge of woods, from where they could see the *tête-de-pont* in front of Borisov.

In 1812, Borisov was a small town in the Minsk province located on the eastern bank of the Berezina. The French reconnaissance report described it as a town of '350 wooden houses' and even twenty-six years later, the town only counted 376 houses and about 2,300 residents.[103] In 1810, a Russian officer, sent on a mission to survey Byelorussian provinces, described the town as being located 'on a flat plain on the left bank of the Berezina River and the right bank of the Skha River, which joins the first mentioned river at this site. On one side the town is surrounded by considerable heights, which dominate the low-lying right bank'. Two decades later, an Englishman remembered it as 'an old, irregular-looking place, with a heavy wooden church in the centre of an open square'.[104] The town was located at a crossroads where a major road from Brest-Litovsk to Moscow split into several directions: Polotsk and Vitebsk to the north, and Mogilev and Bobruisk to the south. Borisov had seen much bloodshed during the Russo-Polish wars of the seventeenth century before the rising Russian state secured its possession in the late 1670s. Still, the Poles contested it until after the Third Partition of 1795. In 1810, the Russian authorities launched an ambitious plan to strengthen fortresses along the western frontier and, as part of this plan, MG Opperman conceived and Lieutenant Colonel N. Sazonov supervised the construction of the Borisov *tête-de-pont*, consisting of two redoubts and several redans, surrounded by a ditch and

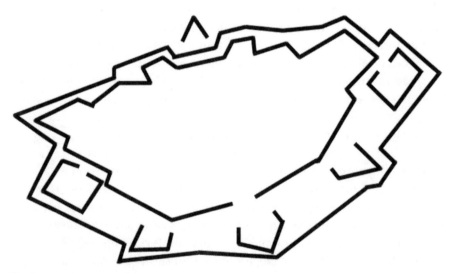

The Borisov tête-de-pont.

connected via retrenchments on the western (right) bank. The fortification was designed to protect a long and narrow bridge across the Berezina.[105] Although construction began in the summer, the fortifications were not completed by November and, according to Wilson, 'these works were in a very unfinished state [...]'[106] After the French occupied Borisov in July 1812, Napoleon instructed Marshal Davout to either destroy these fortifications or reinforce them with new ones.[107] Although Davout decided to destroy them, local commanders – as so frequently happens – occupied themselves with other concerns, so the demolition process did not begin until the fall, when Napoleon had already begun his retreat. This was a quite inopportune moment, since the half-destroyed fortifications now became strategically important in protecting the Allied line of communications and retreat.

The local garrison largely consisted of poorly trained troops, many of them raised from the local Polish and Lithuanian population. Although this bit of intelligence probably encouraged Lambert as his fatigued troops approached the town, he was quickly disappointed to learn that the Polish reinforcements – some 2,500 men and twelve guns led by Dąbrowski – had arrived the previous evening, bringing the garrison's strength to about 4,200 men. General Czeslas Pakosz's detachment of some 650 men was also en route.[108] But the Allied forces – mostly Polish, but with French and German troops – lacked cavalry and artillery and, overall, were downhearted following the recent news of defeats at Novy-Sverzhen, Kaidanov and Minsk. Captain Heinrich von Brandt, of the 2nd Vistula Regiment, recorded 'considerable anxiety as some fugitives had come into town [...] [with] news that our communications with Minsk and Vilna had been cut and that there was no way of getting over the Berezina! We were astonished ...'[109] Brandt saw

the town was filling up with refugees of all types: the cadres of regiments in the process of forming, Lithuanian and Volhynian emigrants and a clutter of scoundrels who filled the cafes and bars and did nothing but drink and play at cards. The most extreme form of anarchy ruled in this confusion and we were frequently obliged to brandish our pistols in order to preserve our host from unwelcome visits.

General Bronikowski, after arriving from Minsk with the remnants of his garrison, hardly made any arrangements to defend the town. Some participants blamed this Polish general for failing to defend Borisov, questioning his military skills: 'It has been said that Bronikowski was better at organizing dinners than fighting war.'[110] Vaudoncourt criticized Bronikowski for his indecisive actions during the few days he spent at Borisov, including the failure to 'put the inner works of the kind of retrenched camp, formed by the *tête-de-pont*, in a good state, erect batteries there, and, in short, prepare some means of defence [...] [Yet] nothing of all this entered his head'. It must be said, however, that Bronikowski lacked manpower, commanding less than 1,500 men (before Dąbrowski's arrival) in the face of the entire 3rd Western Army. As his letters reveal, he also had no news from Schwarzenberg or Victor and was certainly unaware of what transpired with the Grand Army.[111] Concerned that he might be cut off from the main Allied forces, Bronikowski kept only the 6th Battalion of the 93rd Line and a few troops from the 7th Württemberg Regiment (led by Colonel Lalance) deployed on the Borisov redoubts, while the rest of his forces were moved westwards as he planned to abandon Borisov.[112] According to Vaudoncourt, he and the Portuguese General Pamplona persuaded Bronikowski to stay in town and wait for Dąbrowski and Oudinot; Bronikowski, Vaudoncourt claimed, appeared 'ill-informed or wishing to appear so' and gave only 'fictitious' explanations for his actions.

Upon Dąbrowski's arrival, Bronikowski assured him that all approaches to the town were guarded by patrols and he should rest his fatigued troops after their long march. Dąbrowski, believing Bronikowski, kept his cavalry and artillery (eight guns) on the eastern bank and moved six battalions with four regimental guns to the *tête-de-pont*.[113] Vaudoncourt commented that since no staff officer was sent to examine the positions, the deployment of the newly-arrived troops proved to be faulty. According to Kołaczkowski, 'not knowing the terrain as needed, Dąbrowski chose to wait until morning to deploy his troops in position'. Wilson agreed with both: 'There was no officer or guide to conduct [Dąbrowski] on his arrival to any point of the entrenchments, and therefore, passing somewhat beyond, he posted his troops, in the best manner the darkness permitted.'[114] One report, based on a Russian officer's interviews of local residents, claims that, upon his arrival, Dąbrowski dispatched Captain Bronezki with a company of *voltigeurs* 'to spot [Russian] troops in the direction of Minsk' and refused to believe the latter's report that Chichagov's army was en route.[115] So the 1st Polish Infantry Regiment was placed in the centre, covering the road from Minsk, the 6th Infantry Regiment was sent to support the French and the Württembergers on the right flank, covering the road from Zembino, while the 6th Battalion of the 93rd Line and the Mecklenburg soldiers were moved to the left flank. Some fifty Württembergers, led by Captain Georgi, were deployed in a line of outposts ahead of the fortifications.[116] Looking from a house on a hill overlooking the river, Heinrich von Brandt and his comrades observed 'the hasty measures taken to defend the Borisov bridge, which, to us, seemed most ineffective'.

Later that same night, Dąbrowski decided to inspect positions more closely and, around 3 a.m., travelled to the western bank of the Berezina. Most troops were asleep or relaxing around fires, but Colonel Malachowski's 1st Infantry

Regiment remained on guard and sent its baggage train across the river. Unable to reconnoitre in darkness, Dąbrowski had a brief conversation with Malachowski and returned to Borisov, hoping for a calm night.[117]

But Dąbrowski's hopes were dashed. That morning, Lambert approached Borisov and, although aware of Dąbrowski's arrival, decided to attack at once to prevent him from fortifying his positions and receiving help from Oudinot. At dawn, Lambert reconnoitred the Allied positions, where, as Otroshenko tells us, the Russians could see 'enemy pickets in an open field, sitting around the fires, unaware that we were surrounding them'. Count Rochechouart, sent 'at the head of the skirmishers, to reconnoitre the position and the strength of the enemy', gathered 'at once, from the weak and uncertain defence, that our foes were not Frenchmen, but troops of various corps and nationalities'.[118] Lambert had a major advantage over his foes – he had information on the layout of the fortifications from a Russian engineer officer who was tasked with preparing them on the eve of war. Based on this information, Lieutenant Colonels Ikskul and Magdenko deployed artillery (34th Battery Company and 11th HAC) on the edge of the woods in front of the *tête-de-pont*. Lambert kept his cavalry, the 13th Jägers, Vitebskii Infantry, and the 12th HAC in reserve and launched an attack with the 14th Jägers, led by Krasovskii, attacking the northern redoubt, the 38th Jägers, commanded by Oldenburg, marching to the southern redoubt and the 7th Jägers, accompanied by Lambert himself, charging in between.[119]

With the sun still not above the horizon,[120] the Russian Jägers quietly approached the enemy positions, where a sleepy sentry mistook them for Poles and failed to raise the alarm in time. Veering to the left from the road, Krasovski instructed the 1st Battalion of the 14th Jägers, led by Major Goremykin, to move towards the bridge, while Major Otroshenko led the 2nd Battalion along the ditch surrounding the redoubt. On its march, the 2nd Battalion, still undetected, had to cross the main road where it encountered the Polish soldiers (probably of 6th Polish Infantry Regiment), moving just a few dozen metres away. Otroshenko initially wanted to open a point-blank volley but Krasovskii disagreed with him, hoping to take a full advantage of a sudden attack. He walked ahead of his troops and shouted in French, so that the Polish officers assumed these were French troops redeploying to a new position. As the 2nd Battalion slowly marched forward, it came across another enemy column and this time Otroshenko decided to open fire. The unexpected volley claimed the lives of the first few enemy troops while the rest fled in confusion, allowing the Russians to enter the redoubt, yelling 'hurrah' and capturing two guns. At the same time, the 1st Battalion, led by Goremykin, charged towards the enemy positions, where it engaged the 6th Battalion of the 93rd and fought its way towards the bridge but, as Vaudoncourt tells us, 'a Württemberg battalion, which was not far off, took the alarm on the first fire, hastened to the spot, drove back the [Russian] troops that had advanced, and regained a lodgement in the flèche which immediately covered the bridge'.[121]

Within the first half an hour of the attack, the Russians managed to drive back Dąbrowski's right flank but the French and Württemberger battalions continued to hold out in the centre. The situation was more serious on the left flank, where the 38th Jägers charged positions of the 1st Polish Infantry Regiment, which, as mentioned above, was placed under arms earlier that morning. The battle-ready Poles, led by Malachowski (who would be nominated for the Legion d'Honneur for his actions)[122] drove the Russians back towards the edge of the woods but suffered when the 7th Jägers attacked their right flank.[123] The Russian infantry was supported by artillery that bombarded the enemy positions, but also suffered losses, including the death of Staff Captain Andreyev, who commanded a four-gun battery of the 34th Battery Company. Yet, Ensign Zedelman, despite being wounded, skilfully directed two guns (from the same company) to repel the enemy attacks and silence enemy guns. Meantime, as Major Mikheyev reported, the 7th Jägers, despite 'heavy enemy musket fire and canister', organized itself into three battalion columns on nearby heights, where it remained for over an hour. The artillery cannonade produced losses on both sides, including, as Rochechouart recalled, 'Colonel Michaud, a distinguished Piedmontese officer and chief of the staff of the division [who] was wounded in his right arm [...] [which] was amputated on the battlefield'.[124]

After the artillery softened the Allied positions, the 7th and 38th Jägers charged once more towards the southern redoubt, enveloping it from several directions. Mikheyev divided his regiment, moving the 1st Battalion to the left while the 2nd and 3rd Battalions, supported by the 3rd Battalion of the 38th Jägers, attacked on the right.[125] Ensign Stolyarovsky (from the 7th Jägers) was first to climb the walls of the redoubt but was seriously wounded in the process. MG Engelhardt, who commanded the 7th Jägers, was killed leading his troops and was replaced by Major Mikheyev. At the same time, Ensign Karvovski was more successful, as he led some thirty skirmishers into the ditch surrounding the redoubt and directed its fire against the crews manning the enemy guns. Unable to seize the redoubt, Mikheyev asked for artillery support and deployed a horse artillery gun to the left of the redoubt. The officer in charge of this sole cannon acted with great success, disordering the enemy, which allowed the 1st Battalion of the 7th Jägers to break into the redoubt. It was quickly supported by the 38th Jägers led by Lieutenant Colonel Zhitkov, who, as a senior officer, took charge of securing the fortification, seizing two guns and some 500 prisoners. Mikheyev, wounded in the right shoulder, was replaced in charge of the 7th Jägers by Major Levitskii of the 3rd Battalion.[126] On the opposite side, Dąbrowski praised Malachowski for 'repelling with intrepidity three enemy charges to his front'.[127]

Campaign Chronicle

Following the loss of the forward redoubts, Dąbrowski's men retreated towards the entrenchment located behind them. Vaudoncourt described Dąbrowski establishing his forces in front of the bridge, placing his artillery park and train behind Borisov and keeping six cannon, which he posted at the entrance of the town, towards the river, in order to flank the bridge.[128] On the Russian side, Levitskii, after deploying the 7th Jägers into a column, pursued the enemy, supported by the 38th Jägers and two guns of the 11th HAC that Lieutenant Colonel Apushkin deployed inside the captured redoubts. A portion of the Polish troops, the 6th Regiment led by Julien Sierawski, whose actions that day earned Dąbrowski's praise,[129] became cut off on the western bank at the village of Dymki, and tried to charge in the rear of the 14th Jägers, which occupied the right redoubt. However, Lambert dispatched the 13th Jägers who pushed the Poles back to Dymki. Simultaneously, Rochechouart, leading a handful of skirmishers, noticed a weakness in the extreme right side of the enemy position and moved 'near the river, the banks of which are very steep'. Realizing he lacked sufficient force, he placed his men behind a small hill while he 'set off at a gallop' to Lambert. The Russian general, unwilling to commit his remaining infantry reserves, turned to 'the fine regiment of [Aleksandriiskii] hussars', of which he was the chef. He ordered some 300 hussars dismount, telling them *'Mes enfants*, I am giving you a grand opportunity to distinguish yourselves; you are going to take those entrenchments in company with the grenadiers, who are not strong enough. Forward! *A la Carabine*!' He also allowed Rochechouart to take four companies of the 7th Jägers, which had just captured the southern redoubt, and 'promised to delay the attack of the centre and right wing to give [Rochechouart] time to carry out the operation on the left'.[130]

Lambert first ordered an artillery bombardment of the remaining Polish guns on the opposite banks of the Berezina and then attacked with his centre and left wing, which diverted Dąbrowski's attention. This allowed Rochechouart's detachment to 'penetrate the almost undefended line' and his appearance so near the bridge forced the Polish and French troops to rush 'down the long wooden bridge' to Borisov. Dąbrowski tried to counter-attack but the Russian artillery prevented him. Yet, with Rochechouart's troops entering the bridge, Lambert was compelled to silence his guns to avoid hitting his own troops. The Polish general quickly utilized this to his advantage as he dispatched Major Winnicki with a half of the 3rd Battalion of the 14th Polish Regiment to drive the Russians back, which the Poles achieved and then barricaded the bridge. Dąbrowski later extolled Winnicki for 'regaining twice position at the bridge and inflicting heavy casualties on the enemy'.[131]

It was late morning by now. The Russians were in control of both redoubts but faced the Polish-occupied retrenchment that prevented them from crossing the river into Borisov. As the artillery cannonade slowly died down, the Poles received much needed reinforcements when Pakosz (with one infantry battalion and two squadrons) appeared on the Russian right flank, moving from the village of Gury-Ushkevichi (Ushkovich). On the Russian left flank, Sierawski also rallied his remaining troops and made another attempt to break through to the bridge.[132] Facing attacks on both his flanks, Lambert quickly responded by diverting a battalion of the Vitebskii Infantry Regiment and the Arzamasskii Dragoon Regiment to support two companies of the 14th Jägers that halted Sierawski's attack, and then moved another battalion of the Vitebskii Regiment and four squadrons of the Aleksandriiskii Hussar Regiment, with the 12th HAC, to face Pakosz.[133]

Both Polish attacks were defeated. Sierawski was again driven back to Dymki, where his troops occupied houses to better resist Russian attacks. On the opposite flank, Pakosz was still deploying his troops, when the Russians attacked. He hastily dispatched his lancers to charge the enemy infantry but they were met by canister directed by Lieutenant Riman III's two guns. The Russian hussars then charged the 3rd Battalion of the 6th Polish Infantry Regiment, capturing some thirty men. Further Polish attacks were repelled, forcing Pakosz to retreat to Gury-Ushkevichi, where he was pursued by the Russian cavalry and lost several dozen more men. Nevertheless, the Polish commander was able to ford the river and join Dąbrowski later the same day.

By noon, Lambert began preparing for a decisive assault to carry the town. Across the river, Dąbrowski, observing the enemy preparations, told Bronikowski that they must do their best to defend their positions for a few more hours until Oudinot's arrival – the French Marshal was already at Bobr, not far away. The Polish General could have easily destroyed the bridge to prevent the Russians from crossing the Berezina, but he knew how important this bridge was and chose to keep it intact. Instead, taking advantage of a lull in the fighting, Dąbrowski began sending ammunition and supplies to Malachowski's troops, dug in near the approaches to the bridges on the western bank. But the Russian Jägers were so close to the bridge that they were able to fire on the enemy caissons, killing a few horses as they moved across the bridge. Lambert also redeployed the 12th HAC closer to the river, which allowed the company to open fire directly into the town, setting a few buildings on fire and threatening the bridge, which Dąbrowski had to protect at any cost. To deal with this threat, Vaudoncourt set up a counter-battery on the opposite side of the river and, in his memoirs, described the heroic exploit of the young officer Pardaillan, who experienced his baptism by fire that day. After a cannonball hit the ground under his horse and bruised Pardaillan, Vaudoncourt jokingly asked him if he liked the 'common compliments of war', to which the young officer responded, 'Is that what it was? From now on I would never miss another battle!' The young lad would barely survive the campaign, losing six fingers on both hands to cold.[134]

The French counterfire failed to suppress the Russian cannonade. As Ivan Sukhetsky, a local teacher of mathematics, tells us, '[Russian] cannonballs began to land in the centre of the town and a few even beyond it so that a Jewish woman [living outside town], who climbed on the roof of her house to observe the battle, was killed by a cannonball'.[135]

After almost two hours of bombardment, Lambert launched the attack, sending the 13th and 38th Jägers, which were, however, repelled with serious losses; Lambert, who rushed forward to rally troops, was wounded in the knee while Colonel Velisarov, commander of the 13th Jägers, was seriously injured. As his adjutants rushed to help him, Lambert supposedly refused to leave the battlefield and shouted to his troops: 'I am staying here with you. I will either die or wait till you take me into Borisov.'[136] The Russians, led by MG Vyazemskii, regrouped and decided to resume artillery bombardment of the Polish positions; the *Journal of the Advance Guard of the 3rd Western Army* recorded that the battery of the 12th HAC 'maintained canister fire at a close distance and spread terror among the position still occupied by the enemy', while the *Journal of the Military Operations of the 3rd Western Army* specified that the battery was deployed 'almost at pistol's range'. After an hour or so (around 3 p.m.), the Russians launched another attack, with Krasovski leading the charge of the 7th and 38th Jägers, supported by the 14th Jägers, which threatened the Polish right flank. This attack proved more successful and the Poles, fearing to be cut off, abandoned two spiked guns and withdrew across the bridge, leaving some 500 wounded in the entrenchment. As the Russian Jägers rushed in pursuit, Dąbrowski ordered up the guns of Major Gugenmus (protected by Polish infantry) to open canister fire, which stopped the leading 1st Battalion of the 14th Jägers in the middle of the bridge.[137] As his men vacillated, the Russian battalion commander, Otroshenko, charged forward, leading his men across the bridge and engaging the Polish troops protecting the cannon. In the ensuing combat, the Poles lost several senior officers, including Generals Dziewanowski (wounded in the waist), Dąbrowski (bruised in the leg), Pakosz (bruised in the chest), Bronikowski (bruised in the chest), and Dąbrowski's chief of staff, Colonel Cedrowski. Dąbrowski's three and Bronikowski's and Pakocz's two adjutants were seriously wounded as well.[138] As the 14th Jägers struggled to secure the bridgehead, the remaining Russian troops poured into the town. Major Boltnev led three squadrons of the Arzamasskii Dragoons, followed by the Aleksandriiskii Hussars, galloping through the streets of Borisov, capturing one eagle and pursuing the Allied troops, who were now quickly abandoning the town. By 5 p.m. Lambert was in control of Borisov.[139]

Both sides suffered relatively heavy losses in this battle. Dąbrowski estimated the Russian loss at some 900 men, but in reality they lost up to 2,000 men, of which some 600 were killed. The officer corps was particularly hard hit: 3 officers and 17 NCOs killed and 39 officers and 41 NCOs wounded; among the casualties were Generals Lambert, Engelhardt and Vyazemsky.[140] On the Allied side, Vaudoncourt estimated some 500 killed, 1,000 prisoners and four guns captured, Wilson referred to 1,500 dead and 2,500 prisoners (with two standards and eight guns) and Chambray thought that only 1,500 men (with fifteen guns) escaped out of some 5,000 Dąbrowski had available at Borisov. Dąbrowski himself reported the loss of six guns, and some 1,800 killed and wounded.[141] Russian sources provide different statistics. The *Journal of the Advance Guard* claimed up to 2,000 killed, 43 officers and over 2,500 men captured, together with eight guns and two eagles. In his letter to Wittgenstein, Langeron referred to 3,000 prisoners, six guns and two eagles, while Kutuzov and Chichagov noted over 2,300 captured with one flag and seven guns and the *Journal of Military Operations* recorded that the Allied forces lost 53 officers and over 2,284 rank-and-file captured (together with seven cannon and one colour) in and around Borisov.[142] The Polish historian Robert Bielecki provides the most detailed estimates, which show that some Polish regiments lost almost 90 per cent of their men. Thus, the 1st Infantry Regiment counted some 70 men out of 670 that entered the battle. Sierawski's 6th Infantry Regiment suffered even heavier losses as some 980 men were killed and wounded out of 1,000. The 6th Battalion of the 93rd Line fared slightly better, losing about 200 men, while the Mecklenburgers lost some 50 men and Lithuanian losses accounted for 80 men. In total, Bielecki estimated that Dąbrowski lost close to 2,500 men, while Kukiel estimated over 1,800 men. Colonel Lalance reported that his 7th Württemberg Regiment lost 314 men out of 484.[143]

The capture of Minsk and Borisov were important victories for the Russians. Chichagov now controlled a strategic position on the western bank of the Berezina and effectively stood in Napoleon's way out of Russia, controlling the routes to both Vilna in the north-west and Minsk in the south-west. According to Caulaincourt, Napoleon received the news in a convent at Tolochin on 22 November and was

> momentarily dismayed; to him this news meant the loss of supplies – of all the resources he had counted on, since leaving Smolensk, to rally and reorganize the army. Moreover, and worse than that loss, he now had to face the disturbing certainty that [Chichagov] was not moving to join forces with Kutuzov [...] as he had hoped all along, but was massing instead to cut off our retreat.[144]

As Lambert rested his men after the battle, Langeron's column reached Borisov in the evening, while Chichagov was expected to arrive the following day. The stay in Borisov is noteworthy for a crucial (and faulty) decision to move the troops and supply train across the river and take up position inside the town. It seems the lessons of Friedland had been forgotten and the Russians again chose to take a position with a river (and imperfect crossing) behind them. The decision to cross the river was, and still is, largely blamed on Chichagov, but the Admiral himself blamed Langeron. Chichagov writes that, upon arriving at the head of Voinov's column on 22 November, he was quite upset to discover that Langeron

> found it more convenient to spend the night in town and, without my orders, moved his troops, with a great number of baggage train, across the river. I immediately ordered the train to return but my order was executed very slowly, since many people found it convenient to have their carriages with them.[145]

The Admiral soon had no choice but to cancel his order and, as one Russian officer described, 'the army bivouacked on the right side of the river, while the Admiral with his entire headquarters, as well as the staffs of the corps commanders, crossed the bridge and occupied quarters in the town on the left riverbank'.[146]

Yet, the Russian generals should have acted more carefully in light of important intelligence they discovered in Borisov. Langeron seems to have believed that Napoleon 'must be at Bobr, three marches away, and Victor should arrive here today'.[147] However, after the battle, Count Rochechouart accompanied Lambert to 'a beautiful house, the residence of the ex-commandant of Minsk'. Here, the Count noticed a fireplace – 'a rare luxury in those parts' – where a large fire had nearly burnt up some papers. Realizing these should be important documents, Rochechouart tried to save a few remaining scraps and, in doing so, made a crucial discovery. Among the burnt, but still legible, documents was a letter to Bronikowski advising him of Napoleon's arrival at Borisov by 23 November and requiring specific arrangements to be made. 'It is easy to imagine our surprise on learning that the next day we should have the whole of the Grande Armée upon us,' recalled Rochechouart; Lambert recalled finding two letters, written by Napoleon's aide-de-camp Sulkowski, regarding the arrangements to be made at Borisov for Napoleon's arrival. The content of these letters was immediately communicated to Chichagov, who found it difficult to believe Napoleon could be so close to Borisov, since he still had no intelligence from Kutuzov about the Grand Army's location and direction. Indeed, communications between the two Russian armies were virtually non-existent; the *Official Journal of Incoming Correspondence*, maintained at Kutuzov's headquarters, contains no records of Chichagov's letters for this period, which indicates there was no direct communication between the two armies throughout the first two and a half weeks of November, although the *Journal* does show reports from

Seslavin, Platov and Wittgenstein regarding Chichagov's progress starting on 21 November.[148] Rochechouart wrote that

> we did not know where Napoleon, or his army, might be; we did not know what army corps we might be called upon to fight, or its numerical strength. We did not know the deplorable condition of the French army. Our constant marches had deprived us of all regular communications. We went on at a venture, but very cautiously.[149]

Under the St Petersburg Plan, Chichagov was supposed to build a fortified camp around Borisov, protect the routes from Bobr to Borisov, and select a series of defensive positions between these two towns. These positions would have been useful in discovering Napoleon's intention and strength and, if attacked, Chichagov could gradually move from position to position, allowing Kutuzov to catch up with Napoleon and attack from behind. Although it looked good on paper, the plan could not be implemented as conceived because Chichagov lacked sufficient manpower. By the time he reached Borisov, his 3rd Western Army counted slightly over 32,800 men with 180 guns.[150] The Admiral could not afford to do everything stipulated in the plan with such a meagre force. He earlier hoped for a union with Ertel's entire corps but this did not happen. Besides manpower, a fortified camp also could not be constructed due to terrain. As Chichagov noted: 'A camp built at the front, on the riverbank from which Napoleon was expected to arrive, would have been disadvantageous with the Berezina behind it.' The Admiral was concerned that 'the nearby heights dominated terrain' and the enemy could deploy artillery to bombard him. Overall, he 'had very little time left for works, and yet the soil was frozen and there was only one engineer officer [Colonel Michaud] who could direct such [construction] works, but he was wounded during the attack on Borisov'.[151]

By 23 November, the 3rd Western Army was largely concentrated at Borisov. Czaplic had occupied Zembino and Stakhov by the 22nd, before being recalled to Borisov, while Lukovkin's Cossacks held positions at Zabashevichi in the south. Chichagov issued several orders redeploying his troops along the Berezina and destroying bridges up and downstream from Borisov.[152] He then decided 'to march along the main road to Bobr to occupy a position there and cut off the route not only to the main enemy forces but also force Victor's corps, which was at Chereya, to retreat, which would allow me to unite with Count Wittgenstein'.[153] Ideally, the plan would have worked well, with Chichagov engaging Napoleon in front, Kutuzov attacking from the rear, and Wittgenstein converging from the north. MG Czaplic observed that the Admiral decided to cross the Borisov bridge still thinking that the enemy army was beyond the Dnieper and that by moving forward, he would merge with Wittgenstein somewhere between the Dnieper and Berezina. As a result of these considerations [we] made a mistake [of crossing the river] following the capture of Borisov – a mistake that seemed so inconsequential and pardonable that the Admiral decided to take responsibility for it instead of blaming somebody.[154]

The General then criticized his comrades-in-arms for failing to rise to the occasion: 'There are no excuses for the actions of Count Langeron, General Voinov and Prince Sherbatov, while General Sabaneyev, as a person belonging to the headquarters, deserved to be court-martialled.' Langeron presented a different view on Chichagov's plan and described 'our Admiral conceived a plan of operation that only he could have imagined in the position that we were in, a plan in which danger balanced out nonsense and we all would have been victims if it had been carried out'.[155] Langeron claimed 'all generals were in despair [over this plan], but nobody dared to speak against it. I finally understood this silence and went to find Colonel Renné, a very good officer and in whom [Admiral] appeared to have a little more confidence than in others'. He sought unsuccessfully to persuade Renné to make changes to Chichagov's 'disastrous dispositions' and delay the advance.

Since Lambert was wounded in the last battle, the Admiral had to find his replacement. According to Major Yason Khrapovitskii, commander of the 2nd Ukrainian Cossack Regiment, 'for some unknown reason, none of the generals wanted to assume command over the advance guard'.[156] Chichagov personally favoured Yefim Czaplic, an experienced 44–year-old cavalry commander, whom Chichagov described as 'the most capable man to replace Lambert'. But this general was on a mission to reconnoitre Zembino and destroy the bridges there,[157] so a temporary commander had to be found. The Admiral next turned to MG Joseph O'Rourke, a 50-year-old general of Irish descent, who had distinguished himself in the wars against the Turks. However, O'Rourke and Ivan Sabaneyev (Chichagov's Chief of Staff), knowing well the subtleties of military service, politely pointed out to the Admiral that O'Rourke's appointment might cause some displeasure, since there were other, more senior, officers – particularly MG Pavel Pahlen – who, although younger (he was 37), was senior in rank. Chichagov hesitated, arguing that he 'needed a man tested for a mission of such importance'. Upon being assured of Pahlen's qualities, Chichagov agreed – though he would soon regret his decision.[158] In the meantime, some 3,000 cavalrymen, including Cossacks, were sent out in different directions to gather forage, but no preliminary reconnaissance was undertaken. As Khrapovitskii noted, the selection of advance guard commander took more than a day and 'during this time, the advance guard, lacking an actual commander, suspended all its actions, and so no patrolling or reconnaissance was undertaken; in short no one knew for certain where the enemy was and what he was doing'. Years later O'Rourke also lamented, 'Our mistake was that, with Lambert wounded, we did not quickly appoint an advance guard commander, who probably would have dispatched the Cossacks ahead on the road to Orsha to reveal enemy movements. Instead, the time was wasted ...'[159]

23 November: Combat at Loshnitsa

Early in the morning of 23 November, the 3rd Western Army began preparing for a march towards Bobr. According to Staff Captain Silvestr Malinovskii, the army by now counted 59 battalions, 88 squadrons and 13 Cossack regiments, making a total of 32,800 men with 180 guns.[160] Chichagov ordered Pahlen to lead his advance guard towards Bobr around 6 a.m. (the army would follow at 10 a.m.), reconnoitre the area and as many defiles as possible, in order to block the enemy movement and facilitate direct contact with Wittgenstein. The advance guard included the Vitebskii IR, 7th, 13th, 14th and 38th Jägers, 4 squadrons of the Aleksandriiskii Hussars and Arzamasskii Dragoons, 11th and 12th HAC, making a total of 2,800 men. Pahlen had barely covered 12km when he was suddenly attacked by the French advance guard from Oudinot's corps. But before getting into details let's change sides for a moment, to look at what had happened on the Allied side over the preceding few days ...

By mid-November, Oudinot (II Corps) and Victor (IX Corps) were facing Wittgenstein near Chereya. Napoleon had earlier ordered Oudinot to push Wittgenstein back to Polotsk and protect the escape route for the retreating Grand Army, but Oudinot and Victor proved unable to accomplish this. The two marshals disagreed on strategy, with Victor arguing in favour of a flanking attack, while Oudinot preferred to remain in front of Wittgenstein to protect the Grand Army's lines of communication, and to prevent Wittgenstein from uniting with Chichagov. On 16 November, Victor finally suggested remaining in position for another day but, next morning, Oudinot withdrew south so Victor had to follow. With the news of Wittgenstein's capture of Vitebsk and Chichagov's entry into Minsk, the French marshals realized the situation was becoming critical. On 18 November, Victor even issued a special circular, instructing his troops to take various precautions against potential Russian raids, including barricading occupied villages and strengthening patrols.[161]

On 19 November, Napoleon ordered Oudinot to hurry to Borisov and, after uniting with Dąbrowski's Poles, recapture Minsk. Victor was supposed to stay put, in order to cover Oudinot's movement from Wittgenstein and make the Russian general think the Grand Army would attack him.[162] After receiving the order on 20 November, Oudinot led his corps to Bobr, where he arrived on 21

November and, at 4 p.m., wrote to Dąbrowski (who was already fighting Lambert), advising that II Corps would arrive at Borisov on the morrow.[163] But later that day he received the first reports of the combat at Borisov,[164] and in the middle of the night, as Ségur writes, 'Bronikowski arrived to announce […] his own defeat, as well as that of General Dąbrowski [and] that Borisov was taken and that the Russians were following close at his heels'.[165] Marbot tells us that 'the Marshal received [Bronikowski] with displeasure, and ordered him to return with us to Borisov' but, according to Josef Szymanowski, Bronikowski blamed the defeat on Dąbrowski, causing Oudinot to remark that Dąbrowski 'deserved to be executed'.[166] Vaudoncourt, Dąbrowski's friend, was particularly critical of both Bronikowski and Oudinot, arguing that if they had acted more energetically, the Grand Army would have avoided the Berezina fiasco altogether. Despite his attempts, Vaudoncourt, who reached Bobr at midnight, could not meet Oudinot until 9 a.m. on the 22nd when he was told that the Marshal was finally ready to meet him. 'It was about time,' Vaudoncourt wrote, 'I could not contain my indignation and told the messenger and his chef to go to hell.' He also found it difficult to believe that the advance elements of II Corps – only 'three *lieues*' [~12km] away from Borisov – could not hear the cannonade and alert Oudinot. The Marshal himself could have acted more vigorously and dispatched Merle's division, which could have reached Borisov by late afternoon to turn the tide of the battle.[167]

On 22 November, Oudinot, still at Bobr, wrote to Berthier and broke the news of the loss of the Borisov bridge.[168] Still hoping to surprise the Russians, he then advanced via Nacha to Loshnitsa, where he was joined by the remnants of Dąbrowski's 17th Division (about 700–800 men) and the 6th Light Cavalry Brigade of General Jean Baptiste Corbineau.[169] Corbineau had left the Bavarian troops of General Karl Wrede (12,000 men with forty guns) at Glubokoe five days before and skilfully avoided Wittgenstein's troops as he marched to rejoin Oudinot. He initially planned to cross the Berezina at Borisov, but, after finding it in the enemy hands, Corbineau searched for another way across. Although the French (and most English) sources simply refer to Corbineau locating the ford, the credit for the discovery belongs to his Polish troops, who proved helpful in dealing with the local population. Major Dominik Radziwiłł, of the 1st Guard Chevauléger, owned a large estate near Borisov and knew the area quite well. He advised the French commander of an advantageous position near Studyanka. Colonel Thomasz Lubienski, commander of the 8th Chevauléger Regiment, was tasked with finding the crossing site and he sent out a few parties, including one with Jean Chlopicki, a native of the Lithuanian provinces. As Ségur tells us: 'Not knowing at what point to cross the river [the Poles] accidentally saw a Lithuanian peasant, whose horse seemed to be quite wet, as if he had just come out of it. [They] laid hold of this man, and made him a guide.' Thus a ford at the small village of Studyanka was discovered. According to Captain Drujon de Beaulieu, of the 8th Lancers, Oudinot was so surprised to see Corbineau that he greeted him with a question: 'How did you get through, my dear General? Have you grown wings to fly over the enemy blocking your path?'[170]

On 22 November, Napoleon, after receiving Oudinot's report, issued a new set of instructions. Oudinot was to proceed as fast as he could to Borisov and drive the Russians out of town by 23 November. If the enemy managed to destroy the bridge, he was to find crossing sites upstream or downstream and begin constructing two bridges protected by earthworks. Napoleon also informed Oudinot that General Colbert had previously discovered a ford near Zembino.[171]

In the morning of 23 November, Oudinot continued his march to Borisov, sending a letter to Berthier that shows that the French Marshal had no illusions about securing the bridge at Borisov:

> I must draw Your Excellency's attention to the fact that, even if I should manage to drive [the Russians] out of the town, its probable they will burn the bridge, whose re-establishment would be absolutely impracticable. This can be confirmed to you by anyone who knows the Berezina's swampy banks and Borisov's formidable position.

While he awaited new instructions from Berthier, Oudinot was informed of a Russian detachment (Pahlen's advance guard) moving in his direction. The Allied advance guard, led by General Bertrand Pierre Castex, consisted of 7th, 20th, 23rd and 24th Chasseurs à Cheval, 8th Chevaulégers, 2nd and 7th Polish Lancers, 4th Cuirassier Regiments, two battalions of the 26th Léger, the 6th Polish Line and General of Brigade Corvin Kossakowski's Lithuanian *chasseurs à pied*, making a total of some 3,600 men with twelve guns.[172]

Pahlen, leading the Russian advance guard, made the mistake of not deploying strong patrols ahead of his column, choosing instead to rest his men for the night near a windmill close to Loshnitsa. His scouts soon captured a couple of enemy soldiers, who told the surprised Russians that Oudinot was marching to Borisov, followed by Napoleon himself. Pahlen immediately sent a staff officer (Malinovskii) with a message to Chichagov, requesting reinforcements. Remarkably, Chichagov ignored the warning, reasoning that Pahlen was facing only a small enemy detachment – 'probably some partisans [!?]' as the *Journal of Military Operations of the 3rd Western Army* recorded. He ordered Pahlen to continue his advance while allowing the rest of the army to enjoy lunch before the scheduled march on Bobr.[173] The Admiral did, however, decide to strengthen positions on the right bank and make preparations to destroy the bridge in case the enemy appeared. According to Tyrconnell, in preparations for the march all carriages, wagons and [the] larger portion of [the] artillery were moved across the bridge, entering and even passing the town. This hasty intention of leading the entire army through the town and fighting the enemy on the opposite riverbank was, however, cancelled because of strong insistence of [Chichagov's] officers and, around 11:00 a.m., orders were issued to fortify [the] heights on the [right] bank and make arrangements for the burning of the bridge.[174]

Still, Chichagov assumed the threat was remote and Pahlen would certainly inform him if there was a major enemy offensive.

Despite possessing intelligence regarding the enemy's presence, Pahlen advanced without deploying outposts and was surprised by Castex's troops, who inflicted heavy losses on the Russians. Drujon de Beaulieu described the 'brilliant charges' of the Polish lancers and the 4th Cuirassiers, and so did Oudinot himself, who reported 'the light cavalry, supported by a cuirassier regiment, had made an extremely brilliant charge'.[175] During the combat, as Marbot describes with bravado, the French

cuirassiers, who, having had very little fighting in the course of this campaign, had begged for the honour of being placed in the first line. At the sight of these magnificent regiments, which were still strong and well mounted, and with the sunshine sparkling on their cuirasses, the Russian cavalry stopped short. Recovering their courage, however, they advanced again. Then our cuirassiers with a furious charge overthrew them ...[176]

The Aleksandriiskii Hussars tried to counter-charge but were overwhelmed, losing some fifty men. The Russian Jägers, facing the enemy lancers and cuirassiers, organized a square and began a fighting retreat back to Borisov. Polish lancers, thirsting for revenge, now had an opportunity to exact punishment on their adversaries, repeatedly charging the Jägers' formation; several officers from the 2nd and 7th Lancers would be later nominated for the Legion d'Honneur for their actions in this combat.[177] As Otroshenko described:

The cavalry moved in a thick column and we met it with a devastating fire, spreading death all around. Yet, despite the danger, the cavalry charged along the road in uninterrupted columns. We were firing at cavalrymen at a very close range, but they ignored our fire and charged, one may say, as a solid wall ...

The Russian Jägers soon ran out of ammunition and had to beat a hasty retreat through the woods.

The Battle of the Berezina

23 November: The Second Battle of Borisov

Shortly after midday, Chichagov received the alarming news that his advance guard had been ambushed and was retiring on Borisov, pursued by the enemy. Pahlen described a 'narrow road, which made cavalry impossible to use, while infantry was not in sufficient numbers'. The Admiral was incensed by Pahlen's failure to properly conduct reconnaissance and, in his letter to Emperor Alexander, he acidly commented that Pahlen

> acted in such a manner that one could say of him that which was said of Epaminondas, but in reverse: the troops who fought like lions the day before, ran like sheep with him today. This advance guard, which was supposed to contain the enemy's advance [and] was strong enough to achieve this, instead accelerated the enemy's arrival …[178]

His sentiments were shared by the Earl of Tyrconnell, who noted (with embellishment) that

> the very same troops who had been courageously assaulting fortifications defended by a twice [!] superior enemy a day before, now fled in disorder before the enemy, due to the lack of trust in Count Pahlen […] This would not have happened if Count Lambert still commanded.[179]

Langeron also concurred, noting that

> these were the same experienced and excellent soldiers who had fought in fifty battles in Turkey, Illyrie, etc. and now fled almost without fighting. This failure would not have taken place if Lambert had remained at the head of this detachment. Pahlen was, no doubt, brave but he did not have Lambert's military skills. The troops did not know him and he was not familiar with them either.[180]

In later years, a slightly different emphasis was added to this story. The official *Journal of Military Operations* recorded that 'Count Pahlen, observing the enemy's superiority, abandoned the town [Loshnitsa] and took up positions on the right bank', without mentioning anything about the Russian commander being surprised and forced to retreat. Similarly, when Dmitri Buturlin, one of the earliest historians of the Russian Campaign, published his French-language account of the war, he covered this battle relatively briefly, which compelled the Russian translator of this work to add a long note highlighting Pahlen's actions but blaming the Admiral for the defeat. In this version, Pahlen conducted a heroic fighting retreat, constantly sending requests for reinforcements to Chichagov who refused to budge and thus sacrificed the advance guard.[181]

Following Pahlen's defeat, Chichagov faced two decisions: either to cross to the left bank of the Berezina and fight the approaching enemy (whose strength he did not know) or retreat to the right bank and defend the crossing. He chose the latter and ordered the deployment of 'a few guns on the heights to halt the enemy and allow the advance guard to retreat in good order, as well as to gain time for the carriages that were moving through the town'.[182] The hundreds of cavalrymen (some 3,000 men according to the *Journal of the Military Operations of the 3rd Western Army*) dispatched to gather forage were immediately recalled but it was some time before they actually returned. MG O'Rourke was sent to meet Pahlen but was surprised to find the advance guard in disorder. Pahlen himself, one of the officers recalled, 'was in a state of despair impossible to describe'. Meanwhile, O'Rourke recalled: 'I encountered our horse artillery company rapidly moving back and ordered it to slow down in order not to panic our troops.' He then came across the cavalry units deployed on a meadow in the woods. He asked for Colonel Yefimovich of the Aleksandriiskii Hussars and ordered him to cover the retreat, assuring him that the Jägers would support him; in response, Yefimovich stunned O'Rourke by blurting out that 'the Jägers are gone, captured by the enemy'. Not believing him, O'Rourke rode ahead, observing first hand that the Russian infantry was already scattered through the woods, while the French skirmishers, noticing a senior officer, opened fire on him and wounded his horse. Returning to the meadow, the Irishman was upset to find the cavalry in disorder, with the troopers telling him that they could not find their commander. O'Rourke then personally took charge of the troops and gathered a few dozen Zhitomirskii Dragoons, led by Colonel Ivan Argamakov II and sixty Aleksandriiskii Hussars, under Lieutenant Colonel Madatov, to delay the enemy advance. As he approached Borisov, O'Rourke dispatched Major Yason Khrapovitskii with a request for reinforcements, which MG Aleksey Sherbatov honoured by dispatching troops from the Apsheronskii Infantry Regiment. Yet, with the enemy already on the outskirts of the town, the regiment vacillated and 'without reaching the middle of the bridge, it turned back [*sharakhnulsya nazad*]'.[183] Khrapovitskii rallied the troops and tried to make them cross the bridge, but they returned to the safety of the right bank instead. On the Allied side, according to Marbot

after executing a charge, the big horses of the heavy cavalry, especially the cuirassiers, could not go on galloping. It was, therefore, the 23rd and 24th Chasseurs who were ordered to pursue the enemy while the cuirassiers came on at a slackened pace in the second line.

The Battle of the Berezina

Jean Calosso, of the 24th Chasseurs, remembered that on the approaches to Borisov, his regiment

> fell furiously on the enemy. Having sabred some squadrons of [Zhitomirskii?] dragoons with the aid of a light battery, which was following our rapid movements, the regiment fell on Finnish infantry, defending the town's approaches, rolled it up, and, without serious losses to ourselves, took them all prisoner.

Calosso's account is interesting for its reference to 'Finnish infantry', which Russian sources do not confirm. Yet, another participant – Belgian officer Scheltens, sergeant of the 2nd Grenadiers à Pied – also described the 24th Chasseurs attacking 'Finns' defending the earthworks, which were surrounded and captured.[184]

Back in Borisov, Chichagov ordered MG Sherbatov, commander of the 18th Division, to organize the defence of the town. Sherbatov was not particularly pleased with the assignment since, as he recalled later, 'the town, full of various heavy wagons of the populous headquarters as well as numerous transports with provisions and military supplies, was already in great disorder'. Sherbatov rushed towards the nearby heights, protected by the marshy banks of the Skha, to start deploying the available artillery and infantry, but had barely begun when 'a disordered mass – a mix of infantry, cavalry and artillery' appeared from the woods. These were Pahlen's men running in disarray from the enemy. Many of these troops rushed to the fords near Borisov, showing its location to the French, who could flank Sherbatov's position. To avoid this, Sherbatov ordered his troops to retreat across the bridge, abandoning three Jäger regiments (7th, 14th and 38th) and hundreds of cavalrymen who were still foraging in the woods.[185]

One can only imagine the 'utter disorder' – in the words of Captain Ivan Arnoldi – that spread through the 3rd Western Army upon the appearance of the enemy. It was afternoon and many were enjoying lunch when the French attacked. Rochechouart writes:

> I was dining with [...] the wife of the Chief of Commissary of Stores of our army. In the middle of dinner we saw some Russian hussars who had formed part of the advance guard, galloping up. They were shouting 'Frantzouzi, Frantzouzi [French, French]', and making for the bridge [...] A prey to terror, and drunk with fear, if I may use the expression, they shouted 'Frantzouzi, Frantzouzi', incapable of saying anything else.[186]

The news spread like a wildfire and the Earl of Tyrconnell 'had never seen such a disorder before'. Lieutenant Martos recalled

We were about to have a lunch when the French cavalry, on the heels of our hussars, rushed into the streets of Borisov. We were compelled to flee at once, leaving numerous wagons [...] I cannot describe the mayhem that reigned at that moment, it is simply beyond any description.[187]

According to Langeron

no one expected the enemy and [we] were calmly having lunch, with our horses unharnessed, when cannonballs began to whistle in the streets. Our people – cavalry, infantry, gunners with their cannon – rushed pell-mell towards the bridge, pursued by the French, who were charging with terrifying yells. One cannot describe the confusion and disorder that reigned at headquarters, which was so imprudently placed close to the outposts. Everyone was running around, abandoning their carriages and dainty lunches [...] [Meanwhile, Pahlen's retreating horse artillery] galloped through the town, knocking down, or crushing everything in its way.[188]

Lieutenant Falenberg saw Chichagov, after abandoning his own lunch, rushing towards the bridge with the other generals and staff officers, who began clearing the bridge for the commander-in-chief to pass:

The wagons of *cantinièrs* became the first victims as they were pushed, together with horses and goods, over the bridge, and I almost shared their fate as the rear legs of my horse were already hanging over the bridge, but I grabbed hold of the rails, keeping myself and horse on the bridge until some soldiers rushed to help me [...] I soon observed a moving scene, as Countess Lambert accompanied her wounded husband, who was riding a horse, and gently held his leg so that it was not damaged amid the chaos.[189]

According to Rochechouart, Madame de Lambert stopped a few hussars, asking them, 'will you forsake your wounded general?!' The hussars 'carried their leader on their shoulders; four mounted hussars leading the horses of the comrades, went first to clear the way and protect the wounded officer'. Among the few who managed to save some belongings was Langeron, who had three carriages, 'a barouche and two small wagons'. One of them contained provisions while the other held the papers of his chancellery and a considerable sum of money from the army chest, which Langeron received to buy alcohol for the soldiers. Although he lost the former wagon, the General was glad to have preserved the latter, since 'responsibility for it would have been much greater'. Yet, this early sense of delight would later disappear as he and his adjutant would have virtually nothing to eat for more than one week.[190] The disorder in town was so great,

The Battle of the Berezina

Marbot writes, that

> Castex's two regiments often found their march hampered by the vehicles which the enemy had abandoned. This hindrance became still greater when we entered the town, the streets of which were crowded with baggage and draught horses, among which were streaming the Russian soldiers, who had thrown away their arms, and were trying to get back to the Russian regiments.

The French cavalry had orders to reach the bridge and try to cross it, but, as Marbot writes,

> in order to do this, it was necessary to know where the bridge was, and none of us was acquainted with the town. At length my troopers found a Jew, whom I questioned in German; but whether it was that the scamp did not understand that language or pretended that he did not, we could get no information from him [...] Still, we had to get out of the fix somehow; so we divided into several *pelotons* to explore the streets until at last finding the Berezina. That river was not yet sufficiently frozen for us to be able to cross it on the ice, so that it was necessary to pass over the bridge. But to take the bridge we required infantry, and ours was still three leagues away.

Marshal Oudinot, riding ahead of his main force, observed the situation around Borisov and ordered General Castex to dismount most men in his two *chasseur* regiments and attack the bridge formed into a 'small battalion' armed with carbines. Marbot and his comrades 'hastened to obey, and, leaving our horses in the neighbouring streets guarded by a few men, made for the river, under the lead of General Castex, who chose to march to this perilous undertaking at the head of his brigade'. The French hoped to exploit the existing chaos to get to the bridge and Marbot 'ordered the section who should first reach the right bank to capture houses near the bridge, so that holding both ends of it we could defend it till our infantry came up'.[191]

Chichagov, 'fearing every moment the arrival of the Grande Armée',[192] ordered the bridge to be destroyed. Under cover of artillery, a band of Russian pioneers, armed with torches, rushed to set the bridge on fire. Marbot's men attacked them, killing or throwing into the river the greater number of them. They then put out the fire, which had barely caught, but Russian grenadiers forced the French to abandon the bridge at bayonet point. The Russians then ignited the bridge, which 'became a huge furnace' and its blazing heat compelled both sides to withdraw. At the sight of this enormous bridge burning, the Allied troops knew that they 'had to renounce all hope of crossing the Berezina by that

bridge, and their retreat was cut off. This terrible calamity decided our fate ...'[193]
As one Russian report descibed it, 'The bridge has burned in two[194] places and
the *tête-de-pont* is fortified so that any crossing or attack from this position is now
impossible.' But the destruction of the bridge also stranded many troops from
Pahlen's advance guard, who were scattered through the woods and only
approached Borisov later that evening. Major Otroshenko's battalion fought its
way to the River Skha, where it tied several boards with officers' scarves and
used these improvised rafts to cross the narrow rivulet to the opposite bank. The
Jägers were joined by other groups of soldiers on their way to Studyanka, where
they all crossed the Berezina in a small boat. By 24 November, Tyrconnell
reported that some 600 Jägers and three hussar squadrons had managed to break
through the French lines and cross the river.[195]

Meantime, with Borisov in their hands, Oudinot's men turned to sharing the
spoils and provisioning their wagons and saddlebags. 'In view of our penurious
state,' writes Calosso, 'this was truly a windfall.' Sergeant Scheltens let his troops
pillage the house where one of the Russian generals was billeted and which was full
of biscuits, meat, tea, rum and other provisions. Indeed, the victory at Borisov
delivered hundreds of carriages and wagons that could not be hastily evacuated
across the long, narrow bridge over the Berezina. Napoleon's 29th Bulletin claimed
that the French captured 2,000 men, 500 carriages and six guns. Dąbrowski
estimated over 1,000 prisoners, and Oudinot reported that his troops seized 300 to
400 wagons with supplies, six cannon with plenty of abandoned caissons and some
800–900 prisoners.[196] Russian sources generally acknowledge 1,000 killed and
wounded, but the material losses were indeed enormous. According to Marbot:

> The booty was immense! A hundred times more, indeed, than the brigade,
> could carry [...] It seemed that Chichagov's officers took good care of
> themselves, for never has such a profusion of hams, pâtés, smoked fish,
> meat, and wines of all kinds, not to mention biscuit, rice, cheese, etc., been
> seen in an army's supply train. Our soldiers also benefited by the furs and
> boots which they found in the wagons [...] [After capturing dozens of
> horses], we selected the best to replace any our troops were complaining
> about ...

Besides hundreds of lost transports, the Russians also had to abandon hundreds
of wounded. Martos states that 'our wounded were left to the mercy of the
enemy and they soon died in the fire that overtook the town'. Langeron also
lamented that

> we suffered enormous and irrevocable losses; our wounded and sick were
> abandoned with all their belongings in hospital and they all [later] perished;

the army chapel, richly adorned, was lost as well; the engineer chancellery, which stored all invaluable plans of the wars against the Turks and the charts of regions drafted by our staff officers, and of which there were no other copies, was left behind and captured by the French.

Also lost was Chichagov's personal carriage, with his favourite silverware, and chancellery. More importantly, however, the Russians managed to destroy the bridge and effectively stranded Napoleon's army on the eastern side of the river. Some contemporaries criticized Oudinot for his failure to secure the bridge and Curély commented in his memoirs that:

> If our cavalry had charged vigorously into Borisov, it would have prevented the burning of the bridge, the only passage which was open to the French Army; it did not do so, and was not at fault, but, on such an occasion and when it is a question of saving an army, one must dare more ...[197]

Oudinot tried to justify his actions and, in a letter to Davout, he noted an interesting (but often overlooked) circumstance. He wrote:

> The enemy withdrew in disorder into the city, where we would have entered with him if he had not set fire to a bridge which exists in the entrance to the city. This obstacle prevented us from saving the main bridge [*grand pont*] over the Bérézina, which was set on fire in three places at once.

The bridge in question was over the Skha, and Oudinot's chief of staff, Lorencez, confirms the commotion on the 'small bridge', which forced the French 'to lose several minutes at a moment when every second was so precious'. He described the Berezina bridge being set on fire in three places – evidence of the Russians' determination 'to ensure its destruction'.[198]

The 3rd Western Army bivouacked in the open fields on the right riverbank and, as one officer described, 'earth-houses were dug out for the Admiral and the headquarters'.[199] Days earlier, Chichagov dispatched Colonel and Flügel Adjutant Alexander Chernishev, with a Cossack regiment, to open communications with Wittgenstein and, as the latter reported, the Colonel 'marched through the enemy forces, swam across four rivers and, having destroyed numerous transports and supplies gathered by the enemy, delivered the first news about the operations of Chichagov's army'.[200] By 24 November, the two commanders-in-chief were in contact (albeit tenuous at times) and could start preparing for joint operations against Napoleon. Czaplic believed that the loss of Borisov, despite being a defeat, also had positive side to it: 'This failure not only had no harm for us,' he argued, 'but, in my opinion, had some favourable consequences since we could observe the enemy operations and learn about his movements.' But, as the Russian historian V. Kharkevich observes, 'the loss of Borisov and the withdrawal to the right bank of the Berezina considerably complicated Chichagov's task, reducing it to a passive defence of the river. Besides, the defeat of 11 [23] November had a major impact on morale – it made a tremendous impact on Chichagov's confidence and influenced his subsequent actions'.[201]

24–26 November: Chichagov and Oudinot's Feint

Although the capture of Borisov was a major success, Oudinot knew well that it was far from being decisive. The strategically important bridge was destroyed and the Russians still controlled the key heights on the opposite bank. Unaware of the full Russian strength, he estimated it at some 20,000 men but anticipated the arrival of additional forces, not to mention Wittgenstein's corps, which was not far away.[202] Meantime, Napoleon, appraised of the situation at Borisov, studied this area on the map that his ambassador to St Petersburg famously pilfered from the Russians. The map showed a convenient crossing site at Veselovo and Napoleon initially instructed Oudinot to construct bridges there: 'Try to make yourself master of the ford of Veselovo as soon as possible: having passed, we can fall upon the enemy in the *tête-de-pont* of Borisov, and then march on Minsk, or proceed by Vileika, which road you found practicable; but the first great and chief object is to secure a passage across the Berezina.'[203] This was a difficult assignment and Oudinot and his officers were well aware of it. As Jacob Anthony Tellegen, the 41-year-old Dutch officer from the 128th Line commented: 'on paper, such can be executed in five minutes but the difference between cackling and laying an egg is large indeed'.[204]

In the evening of 23 November, Oudinot, accompanied by Claude Charles Aubry de la Boucharderie (chief of artillery) and Corbineau, explored the vicinity of Borisov.[205] The area was marshy, especially along the river, with the western bank overlooking the eastern bank. The marshes would have been frozen this time of the year if not for a warm spell in mid-November. As a result, near Borisov, the river flowed in the swampy valley up to 500m wide,[206] which presented a substantial challenge to the would-be bridge-builders; besides, the Russian army was overlooking the town and would have prevented any bridging there. So Oudinot had to find a better place. He knew about a ford near Veselovo from his prior stay at Borisov and Corbineau had earlier informed him of the crossing site near Studyanka (Studenka), which he reported to Berthier on 23 November.[207] He had earlier dispatched several scouts to reconnoitre the vicinity, who confirmed the existence of a couple more fords within 10–20km distance from Borisov. Oudinot could choose between Ukholody (Ukholod') (12km south of Borisov), Stakhov (10km north), Studyanka (16km north) and Veselovo (some 20km north).[208]

The Battle of the Berezina

Comparing these crossing sites, Oudinot decided that the one at Studyanka had the most potential: it had better terrain than Veselovo and was further away from Borisov than Stakhov and Ukholody, promising less resistance from the Russians. In addition, Corbineau had used this ford to cross the river just days before and reported that the water there was not deep (perhaps only 3.5 feet), which would make bridge-building easier. Thus the French Marshal decided to construct the bridge here and cross the river with his corps to secure a bridgehead for Napoleon's forces. On 23 November, as II Corps secured Borisov, Oudinot wrote a letter to Berthier informing him of his intention 'to dispatch Corbineau with an infantry regiment and a company of *pontonniers* to Stuzianca [*sic*]. I have great hope that we will secure this passage …'[209]

In selecting the site at Studyanka, Oudinot acted on his own and not on Napoleon's orders, as it is often suggested. This issue was debated by contemporaries after early campaign histories credited it to Napoleon, who referred to Veselovo, not Studyanka, in his orders. Lorencez, Oudinot's chief of staff, sought to clarify this issue in his memoirs, and in letters to Philippe-Paul de Ségur[210] (whose work was among the first to appear after the war) declared that the decision to bridge at Studyanka

> belongs to Marshal Oudinot [alone]. His correspondence with the Prince of Neuchâtel supports this. Napoleon had not prescribed anything. The Duke of Reggio acted on his own initiative and took precaution to seize the road through the marshes of Zembin [*sic*], without which the army would have had its line of retreat cut.[211]

Following his decision, Oudinot secretly moved a portion of his troops closer to Studyanka[212] and dispatched Aubry's men to conduct preliminary works for bridging.[213] The 128th Line remained at the shattered bridge in Borisov to keep the Russians believing the crossing might be forthcoming there. As Tellegen described:

> We were no farther removed from one another than a gun shot, but neither [Russians] nor we discharged a single shot. We were well pleased that they let us be. We could do them no harm yet they had the chance to destroy us at any moment …[214]

Since Russian patrols were observed on the opposite bank, the French chose to conduct limited reconnaissance of the ford and relied on local peasants for information. On 25 November, Aubry reported that the river itself was about '35–40 *toises* [68–80m] wide' and the recent warm weather had thawed the marshy riverbanks; the peasants told him that water depth was over three feet deeper than normal due to the thaw. The general also expressed concerns about the presence of Russian forces at Brili (see below), which could quickly occupy the heights and prevent the crossing.[215] At the same time, Oudinot received reports concerning Russian troops observed on the right bank, and assumed they were reinforcements dispatched by Wittgenstein to Chichagov, but in reality they were stragglers from Pahlen's detachment.[216] Oudinot now believed that his II Corps – even if it crossed the river at Studyanka – would not be able to deal with a reinforced Chichagov.

These were discouraging tidings indeed, and Oudinot had earlier confided to Berthier that he could not 'guarantee the success of this enterprise, but will do everything possible to make it succeed'.[217] It appeared necessary to divert the Russians' attention and prevent them from realizing where the Allies were preparing to cross. On 24 November, Oudinot explained to Berthier: 'I have set myself on the crossing point at [Studyanka], where I intend to carry out my crossing tonight and tomorrow morning. I increased diversions towards Oukholoda and Stadhof [*sic*] in order to divert the enemy ...'[218] Indeed, some three hundred troops and several hundred stragglers were sent towards Ukholody, with instructions to collect there, with as much noise as possible, all the necessary materials for the construction of a bridge. Oudinot even had, as Ségur writes, the 'whole division of the cuirassiers promenading on that side within view of the enemy'. Most importantly, Lorencez used locals to deceive the enemy – he gathered several residents, whom he interrogated with great minuteness relative to the Ukholody ford, and the roads leading from it to Minsk. Then, pretending to be very pleased with their answers, he released them, expecting them to rush to inform Chichagov.[219]

The French attempt to divert the Russian forces proved to be important for erroneous decisions made by the Russian leadership. Chichagov was demoralized by the events of 23 November and showed poor judgment over the next few days. As Czaplic noted

> [our immediate] concern was to learn the central point where the enemy intended to direct his operations and this was the most difficult task to resolve. We initially thought that it would be more rational for the enemy to force his way to the Minsk route [...] if we had known precisely the location of the enemy crossing, the Admiral could have committed all his forces to that spot and sacrificed them to prevent the enemy escape. But we had to maintain watch everywhere and over all points and therefore had to divide our forces into detachments. Until now, [Chichagov] had no direct communications with either Count Wittgenstein or with the main army; he could not possibly observe the enemy movements because they were concealed from him. So how was he supposed to perceive the direction [Napoleon's] army would take?

The Battle of the Berezina

This opinion was seconded by MG Sherbatov, who also complained of poor communications between the Russian armies, leading to the lack of 'precise and detailed intelligence on the French army's retreat from Moscow ...'

As a result, Chichagov initially believed that the French would try to cross the river at Borisov or in its immediate vicinity, and decided to remain with his army at the *tête-de-pont* and dispatch detachments up and downstream to watch for any French movements. MG Czaplic was told to operate north of Borisov.[220] Czaplic's main force (14th and 32nd Jägers, Pavlogradskii Hussar Regiment, three squadrons of the Tverskii Dragoons, supported by eight guns of the 13th HAC) was deployed near Brili; MG Umanetz (with the Kinburgskii Dragoons and the Bashkirs) was moved to Zembino and Pleshenitsy, while MG Kornilov (with 28th Jägers, Dyachkin's and Melnikov's Cossack Regiments and four guns of the 13th HAC) proceeded to Brili and Veselovo. At the same time, MG O'Rourke's detachment – six Replacement Battalions of the 2nd Grenadier Division, Pavlogradskii Hussars (two squadrons), Mariupolskii Hussars (two squadrons), Volhynskii Uhlans, and Lukovkin's, Isayev II's, Barabanshikov's and Grekov VIII's Cossack Regiments, a half-company of pioneers and the 12th HAC, totalling about 4,000 men – was sent to operate south of Borisov with instructions to take the village of Ushkevichi and observe enemy movements as far as Nizhneye Berezino.[221] O'Rourke deployed most of his cavalry to observe the river between Borisov and Gliven and kept his infantry concentrated at Gury-Ushkevichi, about 8km from Borisov. Overall, the Russians observed the Berezina along some 80km from Brili to Nizhneye Berezino. The northern sector, from Borisov to Zembino, was better protected and, in case of enemy attack, Chichagov could concentrate his army there within a day. The southern sector was less favourable and, if the French tried to cross the river near Nizhneye Berezino, Chichagov estimated that it would take him two or three days to concentrate his army in that direction.[222]

On 24 November, Chichagov was informed of minor enemy movements near Ukholody and Brili but no specific location for the crossing was determined.[223] At this moment, he received several letters that had significant consequences for the Berezina operation. Knorring reported from Minsk that Austrian and Saxon forces appeared near Slonim, with their patrols proceeding to Pinsk. This was worrisome news. 'I thought that Schwarzenberg would advance to keep me at bay,' Chichagov explained. 'This also indicated that Napoleon might have been marching in [a southerly] direction.'[224] Next came a letter from Wittgenstein about Victor's retreat from Chereya (discussed in the next chapter). Wittgenstein speculated that Napoleon's army had probably turned southwards to Bobruisk since Victor occupied too advantageous a position to abandon it if Napoleon were planning to proceed to Borisov or take a north-westerly direction.[225] At the same time, another letter, from Kutuzov, also advised Chichagov that Napoleon might turn from Tolochin or Bobr towards Igumen and urged the Admiral to watch his southern flank.[226] According to Rochechouart, Kutuzov ended his letter as follows: 'You have to do with Napoleon, a general of the greatest genius; he is sure to make a demonstration of crossing at one point, in order to attract your attention, while he crosses at another; therefore, prudence and vigilance.'

Virtually all participants who served under Chichagov in 1812 agree that these letters had a great influence on the Admiral. MG Sherbatov lamented: 'I wish [Kutuzov's] letter had never reached us …' and Tyrconnell also confirms that the arrival of the letters convinced Chichagov of the need to move south.[227] According to Czaplic,

> [Chichagov] hurried to carry out this order from the General Field Marshal of all armies [Kutuzov], especially since it coincided with the news received from Count Wittgenstein.[228]

Chichagov complained that neither of his fellow commanders could tell him of Napoleon's precise location and instead their letters 'misled me'.[229] After the war, Kutuzov's supporters tried to defend their idol and argued that Kutuzov's letter did not specifically 'order' Chichagov to move south but only 'advised' him to do this. Langeron explains:

> This order, which Tchitchagoff [sic] made me read, was very simple, precise and clearly written: Kutusof [sic] did not irrevocably order the Admiral to move to his right but rather advised him to do it if the enemy were to move in that direction; he wrote that he could guess Napoleon's intentions and let Tchitchagoff act on his own discretion if these conjectures proved false; they indeed were such, but Tchitchagoff was persuaded by Kutuzof's advice to make a movement much more absurd than that which he conceived on 11/23 [November].[230]

Martos' memoirs provide additional insights on Chichagov's reasoning. Scolding the 'partisans of Kutuzov' for blaming everything on Chichagov, Martos argued that, after receiving the above-mentioned letters

> it became more important for Chichagov to prevent the French crossing in the direction of Igumen, rather than in the vicinity of Zembino […] By breaking through to Igumen, Napoleon would have significantly reduced his line of retreat to Warsaw and would have gained an opportunity to join Schwarzenberg at Slonim. His army would have then increased to 100,000 men, which [Napoleon] could have calmly [put into] winter quarters on the

left bank of the Vistula or between that river and the Bug. Chichagov's failure to perceive Napoleon's intentions are more excusable since the river separated him from the enemy and prevented him from directly observing enemy movements. Count Wittgenstein, who did not face such obstacles, was equally deceived by the enemy ...[231]

Thus, Chichagov did not simply fall for a distraction set up by Napoleon or Oudinot as it is often portrayed, but was rather guided by a set of multiple considerations that pointed him in the wrong direction. He had letters (one of them from the Commander-in-Chief himself, who was supposed to be better informed regarding the strategic situation) at hand informing him that Napoleon was probably moving south, either to Bobruisk or Igumen. 'I could not simply ignore the information provided by the commander-in-chief,' Chichagov later wrote, in an attempt to justify his actions. This view is further reflected in Rochechouart's memoirs: 'Having received information, directions and advice from his Commander-in-Chief, the Admiral was bound to follow the counsel of his superior.'[232] As one officer commented in the notes to Vaudoncourt's memoirs:

> There was a deception, and a very great deception [...] but the Admiral [was] deceived not by the enemy, in opposition to whom he had taken every possible precaution, which his force would admit of, but by friends, no doubt unintentionally, against whose conduct he had not been sufficiently on his guard.[233]

Yason Khrapovitsky tells us that 'all these letters only placed [Chichagov] in the most difficult position, since the enemy crossing, no matter where it occurred, remained his personal responsibility'.[234]

The defeat of his advance guard at Loshnitsa convinced Chichagov that the Grand Army was still a force to be reckoned with. Reconnaissance reports seemed to confirm Kutuzov's and Wittgenstein's supposition. The Russian patrols noticed no preparations at Borisov or north of it, but did observe enemy troops massing downstream, which, in reality, were Oudinot's troops attempting a diversion. In addition, the French effort to mislead the Russians through misinforming the local community (as noted above) – 'this wretched ruse' as one Russian officer commented[235] – paid off after three locals rushed to the Russian camp with news of the French preparations near Ukholody.[236] The enemy correspondence, which the Russians captured earlier in Borisov, had indicated that Napoleon was expected to arrive at the Berezina by 25 November and, with no major construction works observed around Borisov and seemingly credible intelligence pointing southwards, Chichagov naturally assumed that Napoleon changed his plans and intended to cross the river downstream. This supposition was further reinforced by the newly-arrived reports from the commandant of Minsk, who reported Austrian detachments moving towards Nesvizh and Novy Sverzhen and the 2,000–strong Polish detachment at Svisloch. The Admiral was alarmed by 'the enemy detachments, grouped in a semi-circle, appearing in my rear and on my right flank …' The troops from Novy Sverzhen could reach him in three marches, while the Poles from Svisloch could threaten him in only two marches.[237] Their only goal, Chichagov assumed, was to facilitate the Grand Army's crossing in the south. In a letter to Alexander, two weeks after the crossing, Chichagov – already exasperated by rumours blaming him for Napoleon's escape – wrote:

> Three days we faced the enemy that manoeuvred to deceive us, while we had no signs of the approach of our armies, which, I believed, were closely pursuing the enemy. Based on my calculations of marches the enemy could make, he was supposed to be at Borisov earlier than happened; I had no knowledge of whether the enemy forces there included Napoleon with his entire army or just a small corps that was seeking to contain and distract us. In such a difficult situation I received a letter from Prince Kutuzov in which he warned me of Napoleon's movement along the Berezina towards Bobruisk, where he could cross the river in direction of Igumen and Minsk. I also received a letter from Wittgenstein, which informed that the enemy army was divided into several columns, with one of them moving to Borisov and the rest to Bobruisk. But where was Napoleon? No one knew it; probably where he was least expected …[238]

And so, in light of 'similarity of news from Kutuzov, Wittgenstein, and Knorring',[239] Chichagov made a fateful decision to redeploy his forces to better suit the perceived circumstances. His Chief of Staff, Sabaneyev, and other generals, voiced their opposition and urged the Admiral to wait another day before moving the troops. Chichagov, convinced he had no time to waste while Napoleon was moving south, overruled them.[240] He instructed O'Rourke to move from Gury-Ushkevichi[241] to Nizhneye Berezino, where, as Rochechouart tells, 'there was a good road and a solid bridge' and, leaving some 5,000 men (the 15th Division, eight guns of the 38th Battery Company, Zhitomirskii and Arzamasskii Dragoons) under Langeron to guard the Borisov *tête-de-pont*, he then personally led the remaining forces (up to 16,000 men) south to Zabashevichi (Shabashevichi), where he arrived during the night of 26 November.[242]

O'Rourke departed Gury-Ushkevichi at 2 p.m. and later that evening reached the village of Usha, where he rested his infantry while moving his cavalry to Nizhneye Berezino, which he occupied by 4 a.m. on 26 November, after marching 'all night, in terrible cold and along very bad roads'. The local bridge and ferry were destroyed but, according to Rochechouart, the Russians 'saw no trace of the French army'.[243] Still, a squadron of Polish lancers was soon found at a nearby village and forty-one of them, including three officers, were captured. After searching the Polish commander's correspondence, the Russians discovered an order instructing him to proceed to Borisov, where the crossing was expected. O'Rourke immediately forwarded his letter to Chichagov …[244]

As his army rested at Zabashevichi, Chichagov received a series of reports that caused him to question his earlier decisions. To start with, Knorring informed him that the Austrian outposts on the Nesvizh road had withdrawn and all intelligence indicated Schwarzenberg was in retreat.[245] Of greater importance was a new letter from Wittgenstein, who wrote of his pursuit of Victor in the direction of Kholopenichi, north of Borisov.[246] Reading the letter, Chichagov realized 'to my chagrin, that Wittgenstein, instead of hurrying with his 45,000 men to join me and jointly protect the crossing, intended to pursue the French and essentially leave me with my insufficient forces to face Napoleon alone'. The Admiral replied immediately, urging Wittgenstein to follow the original plan and hasten to Borisov. His memoirs inform us:

> I immediately dispatched the same courier back to Wittgenstein […] I did not dispatch another courier because the officer who delivered the letter begged me to let him carry out this assignment as well. Since he accomplished the first mission diligently and bravely, I agreed and he went back around 10 p.m. Yet, instead of rushing as soon as he could (as he promised), he travelled for a few miles and then stopped for the night, reaching Borisov only at 10 a.m. the following morning [!] […] Thus this young man, without fully comprehending the utmost importance of mission entrusted to him, betrayed my trust. My letter did not reach Wittgenstein, who kept pursuing his ill-timed objective.'[247]

While his messenger was en route, Chichagov began rescinding some of his orders. Czaplic, who was guarding Brili and Zembino, thus received contradictory instructions. In his Order No. 1165, Chichagov initially instructed him to move his troops to Borisov to support Langeron, leaving only minor patrols to guard the northern direction. After receiving new intelligence, Chichagov issued Order No. 1170 directing Czaplic to return to Zembino, reoccupy his positions and establish direct contact with Wittgenstein. He even advised Czaplic that the enemy might try crossing at 'Veselovo or some other nearby site' and instructed him to use all available forces to prevent such attempts.[248] Simultaneously, Langeron was advised to be 'alert' and ordered to dispatch 'an infantry regiment and the 38th Battery Company' to reinforce

Czaplic.[249] At dawn on 26 November, Chichagov, still at Zabashevichi, received additional reports about the French preparations for crossing at Ukholody, north from his bivouac, which further reinforced his suspicions.[250]

Meantime, Czaplic, as he wrote in his recollections, 'became almost certain that the enemy would direct his efforts to cross the river either at the sites that I occupied or near Brili or Veselovo'. At dawn on 24 November, the Cossack post at Brili observed the arrival of considerable enemy forces and the following day their numbers only increased. The Cossacks saw 'unusual movement among the enemy units and at times the sound of wood chopping could be clearly heard'.[251] Hiding in bushes on the riverbank, Czaplic 'personally observed as the French studied the site [at Studyanka] and, under the pretence of watering their horses, which, however, remained the same, they kept changing those people conducting observations'. He also observed 'enormous bonfires that revealed concentration of large masses of people'.

At noon on 25 November, Czaplic received an order to move to Borisov but in light of the things he had witnessed across the river, decided to disobey it. Instead, he wrote a letter describing events he witnessed and requested permission to remain at his current position. By the evening, the Russian outposts could hear the sound of trees being cut down across the river, while the bivouac fires continued to multiply. The higher eastern bank, however, prevented Czaplic's scouts from clearly observing what was happening across the river. And so, during the night of 26 November, Czaplic sent some 300 Cossacks, led by Colonel Melnikov, across the Berezina and had them capture prisoners, including the elder of a nearby village. The prisoners told Czaplic that the Allied army was already concentrating between Stary and Novy Borisov but had no information on where, precisely, the crossing (which was expected on the 26th) would take place. The village elder's information proved especially valuable, since he spoke of the enemy's orders to construct two bridges near Brili and Veselovo. Czaplic again sent messengers to Langeron and Chichagov with this important intelligence. But as one participant notes: 'almost twenty-four hours had passed while Czaplic's messenger reached the Admiral and Langeron received new orders to assist Czaplic. The enemy took full advantage of this time ...'[252]

What happened in the meantime is indeed remarkable. Langeron, unaware of Chichagov's new order (No. 1170), sent a stern reprimand threatening Czaplic with a court martial if he did not comply with the initial order (No. 1165) at once.[253] It is hard to understand what caused this experienced general to act in such a manner – in his memoirs he claimed that had he known of Chichagov's new order he would have acted differently.[254] Yet, Langeron did not require Chichagov's order or Czaplic's reports to realize that something sinister was brewing across the river. Observing increased enemy activity in the vicinity of Borisov, Langeron himself grew suspicious and, late in the evening of 25

The Battle of the Berezina

November, he sent three groups of Jägers across the river to gather intelligence, but they all failed to produce any prisoners due to vigilant enemy outposts. At dawn on 26 November, Langeron was told of another enemy attempt (in reality, another diversion) to build a bridge at Ukholody but a few minutes later a new messenger arrived, telling that the enemy had abandoned the village. By now, Langeron could observe 'large enemy columns, with artillery and transports, moving *upstream* [my emphasis] from the Orsha road through Borisov towards Veselovo or Rogatka …' He wrote to the Admiral:

> It can be assumed that larger enemy forces marched in this direction during the night, since we observed only the column's tail this morning. Judging from the number of enemy troops marching there, it can be also presumed that all enemy forces seek to cross the Berezina some 20 or 30 *verstas* [15–20 miles] upstream from Borisov …

By 9.30 a.m., Langeron sent another letter to Chichagov, informing him that the deserters from Eugène's IV Corps had told him: 'Napoleon with his entire army is here, seeking the crossing site. The enemy troops march to the left [northwards] of the town, where immense columns are visible.'[255]

Yet, despite all this intelligence, Langeron not only failed to act but, as mentioned above, insisted on Czaplic's withdrawal to Borisov. Receiving a harshly-worded order, Czaplic decided to comply, without waiting for the return of his adjutant, who was dispatched to Chichagov during the night and was on his way back with new instructions. Chichagov also ordered Langeron to keep Czaplic at his earlier position and maintain a 'strong detachment at Zembino so as to prevent enemy movement in that direction and try to open communications with Count Wittgenstein'.[256] But it was too late. In the morning of 26 November, Czaplic had recalled Umanetz from Zembino and left Kornilov with the 28th Jäger and two Cossack regiments, supported by four light guns (13th HAC), to guard Brili; the rest of Czaplic's detachment marched to Borisov.[257]

Some historians hold Czaplic responsible for failing to adequately respond to circumstances. Russian historian Bogdanovich claimed

> the specific news in his possession should have caused Czaplic to remain at Brili and the upper Berezina, but he, instead, recalled detachments from Veselovo and Zembino, and, at dawn of 14 [26] November, retreated to Stakhov […] and then even further, almost to the [Borisov] *tête-de-pont*.

American historian Curtis Cate argued that 'had Chaplits [*sic*] been more courageous, he would have risked defying Langeron's orders in order to deal with the threat that was building up before his eyes'.[258] But, with hindsight, these accusations are unfair and easy to make. Czaplic sent available intelligence and warned his superiors of the situation at Studyanka and Veselovo but was overruled by Langeron, whose failure to comprehend the situation is largely forgotten or ignored. Only one modern Russian historian accused him of 'doing a disservice [*medvezhya usluga*] to the plans of the Russian command'.[259] Indeed, Chichagov later complained that 'amidst all this turmoil, stirred up by undeniable signs of the enemy preparations for crossing, Langeron very inopportunely ordered Czaplic to leave all three posts – at Zembino, Veselovo and Brili – and join him at Borisov ...'[260]

Still, Czaplic is not without fault. He withdrew his troops rather hastily and failed to completely destroy the wooden causeways (*Zembinskie gati*) and 'three long bridges of some 300 *toises* [600m], separated by 100 *toises*-long [200m] intervals', built over 'the impassable marshes ...' as Chambray described them,[261] on the western bank of the Berezina leading to Zembino, as well as a nearby dam that could have flooded the bank. Czaplic believed that 'while holding on to Zembino, I would have enough time to destroy the bridges [across the marshes] and the dam to cut off the enemy'.[262] Historians Kharkevich and Apukhtin criticized Czaplic for his failure to destroy the log roads, arguing that it had 'crucial consequences and probably was one of the main reasons why the remnants of the French army managed to escape their perilous situation'. Chambray agreed that 'if the enemy had destroyed these bridges, it would have closed to the French army the route to Vilna'. Similarly, MG Foerster, who was sent to examine the Berezina battlefield in December 1812, reported that, in the Zembino defile, 'the narrow paths and unstable bridges, surrounded by marshes, would have contributed to the almost complete annihilation of the enemy if only the defiles were properly reconnoitred and the bridges destroyed'.[263]

Chichagov also noted that Czaplic's detachment 'failed to burn the long bridges across the marshes, some half a mile from the Berezina, leading through Zembino to the road to Vilna. In my instruction to Czaplic, I specifically suggested destroying them'. Yet, this criticism has a weak spot in itself. Czaplic explained that 'the local terrain did not present advantages to thwart enemy intentions, since the heights were on the enemy bank and the swamps, on both sides of the river, *completely froze* [my emphasis]'.[264] Chichagov initially concurred that destroying log roads would hardly make a difference, since the swamps froze with the onset of cold weather on 27 November. But in another passage, the Admiral incredulously claims that Czaplic deliberately failed to destroy the log roads so that Napoleon, having no clear route to Vilna, would have been forced to divert his forces south and destroy Chichagov. It speaks volumes of acrimony that developed between the Russian generals in the wake of the Berezina that Chichagov thought one of his officers (whom he highly praised not long ago) was trying to engineer his destruction.

The Battle of the Berezina

Thus, by the morning of 26 November, as a result of confusion and crucial mistakes, Chichagov had shifted his centre of gravity from Borisov towards Zabashevichi and weakened the northern sector of his position, just where Napoleon intended to cross the river. The Admiral later second-guessed this decision and tried to compensate by keeping Czaplic at Zembino, but Langeron's inactivity and stubbornness to follow the orders he received to the letter only confounded the problem. That morning, standing on the western bank of the Berezina near Brili, Captain Arnoldi could 'see materials – timber, brushwood and straw – being moved and collected on the opposite bank while numerous enemy troops were gathering at that site'.[265] Despite this, Czaplic's detachment, compelled by Langeron's orders, broke camp and marched to Borisov. Across the Berezina, Napoleon was preparing to launch an attack across the river to clear the opposite bank when he was told of the Russian movement. As he observed the Russian troops moving southwards and clearing their positions, Napoleon could hardly believe his eyes: 'Gentlemen,' he told his companions, 'I have fooled the Admiral!'[266]

Northern Front: Campaign Summary

As previously stated, in the opening moves of the campaign, Oudinot unsuccessfully battled Wittgenstein at Polotsk in late July, compelling Napoleon to divert Marshal St Cyr's corps to support Oudinot's operations. In the Baltic provinces, the Franco-Prussian forces of Macdonald and Yorck occupied Bausk, Mittau and Dunamund, fighting the Russians at Gross-Eckau before laying siege to Riga (defended by LG Ivan Essen I, the town's Military Governor), where they became bogged down for the next two and a half months. In late September, Wittgenstein received reinforcements, increasing his main forces to 38,085 men (not counting minor detachments) and giving him numerical superiority over Oudinot and St Cyr.[267] With his primary goal to seize Polotsk and isolate the French marshals from Napoleon, Wittgenstein decided to manoeuvre along the right bank of the Dvina, while Steinheil's newly-arrived Finland Corps operated on the left bank.[268] Steinheil's appearance from the Baltic provinces was due to the animosity that existed between him and LG Essen, which had resulted in an unsuccessful offensive against Yorck and Macdonald in the vicinity of Riga. Between 18–20 October, Wittgenstein resumed his offensive, defeated the French and occupied Polotsk, but was unable to cross the Dvina after the French destroyed the bridges.

As Marshal St Cyr retreated southward, Napoleon instructed Victor to march to his aid from Smolensk. The two marshals joined their forces between 29 and 30 October: the II and IX Corps were merged into a single formation and Victor assumed overall command, since St Cyr had been wounded at Polotsk days earlier. Victor reorganized his newly-created corps and marched to Beshenkovichi on 29

October. At the same time, Wittgenstein finally crossed the Dvina and advanced southwards to engage the French. His troops encountered the enemy in front of the village of Chashniki on 30 October, where Wittgenstein's advance guard – led by Prince Lev Yashvil (Iashvili) – drove the French outposts back to the village. Victor had deployed his forces in a strong position with the divisions of Generals Merle and Maison deployed in the first line on the left bank of the Lukomlya and the remaining forces in the second line on the heights behind the river. The French right flank was protected by a rivulet, while the left was anchored on thick woods, occupied by infantry. Early in the morning of 31 October, Yashvil led the first attack on Chashniki (while Wittgenstein's main forces were en route) but was beaten back. Around 10 a.m., Wittgenstein reached the battlefield and organized another assault, which forced the French to retreat across the Lukomlya. Unable to cross the river, Wittgenstein chose 'to preserve my troops' and opened up artillery fire on the enemy positions. As darkness descended, Victor broke away and retreated further south-west to Senno, in the province of Mogilev. After crossing the River Ulla, Wittgenstein rested his troops and diverted some to occupy Vitebsk on 7 November. He was still unaware of Chichagov's actions, although he dispatched officers towards Borisov in an attempt at direct communications with the Admiral.[269]

Combat at Smolyany

Both sides spent two weeks resting in their positions until Napoleon, concerned by Wittgenstein's proximity to his line of operations, demanded more aggressive actions from Victor and Oudinot.[270] Oudinot was wounded at the first battle of Polotsk in August and, after recovering, he now rejoined his corps on 9–10 November.[271] On 12 November, the French marshals marched towards Chashniki, where Wittgenstein's forces were located and, the following day, General Louis Partouneaux's division and François Fournier's cavalry engaged the Russian advance guard. After a combat, the advance guard was compelled to withdraw to the village of Smolyany (Smolyantsy) and informed Wittgenstein of the enemy offensive. The Russian corps commander had his Jägers at Smolyany and deployed Steinheil's troops on the right bank of the Lukomlya to cover the route to Polotsk, and MG Berg's forces on the left bank, while a strong artillery battery swept the main road leading to the Russian positions. Late in the morning of 14 November, the French forces attacked Smolyany, which changed hands several times – Wittgenstein himself reported that possession of the village was contested six times. Despite Victor's attempt to flank the enemy, Wittgenstein was able to utilize his numerical superiority to counter his manoeuvres. Unable to break through the Russian positions, Victor recalled his forces and retreated on Chereya.[272]

The Battle of the Berezina

The Watching Game

Following the combat at Smolyany, Victor and Oudinot remained at Chereya, with an advance guard pushed ahead to Lukomlya, while Wittgenstein kept his main forces at Chashniki and occupied Lepel with Vlastov's troops.[273] Both sides observed each other's positions while avoiding open conflict. The combat at Smolyany, which claimed some 2,000 Russians and up to 3,000 French, had important consequences. Despite his resolute attacks, Victor failed to accomplish his primary mission of driving Wittgenstein back and removing the threat to Napoleon's right flank. The two French marshals now disagreed on what to do next. Napoleon had given them a difficult mission of driving the Russians back to Polotsk and maintaining communications with the retreating Grand Army. To accomplish this, Victor favoured attacking Wittgenstein's right flank to prevent his union with Chichagov. Oudinot thought this would be too dangerous because it would threaten their communications with Napoleon. Instead, he proposed attacking the Russian left flank while Victor would remain in front of Wittgenstein to cover the retreating Grand Army and maintain contact with Napoleon.[274] Ultimately, Oudinot's arguments won over, causing General Auguste Ameil to grumble about the General's 'stupidity and unwillingness' to accept Victor's idea.[275] Yet, both marshals were reluctant to pursue vigorous attacks against Wittgenstein since they were well aware of the declining conditions of their corps and knew that any flanking manoeuvres, which required marching off roads in the cold and snow, would result in further reduction of their forces. Victor was told of lack of supplies and increasing insubordination in the IX Corps while Oudinot complained that the II Corps was 'fatigued, dying of hunger, and disorganized. It has no more than 5,000 combatants. Each march, each nightly bivouac greatly reduces our numbers'.[276]

On the opposite side, Wittgenstein remained near Chashniki almost a week. Although his troops occupied Vitebsk, he failed to defeat the French forces ranged before him or to open direct communications with Admiral Chichagov, whose army was quickly proceeding in a north-easterly direction. Wittgenstein apparently felt that, with Victor in front of him and Macdonald and Wrede behind him, he was in a dangerous situation, and if he were to suffer a defeat in another combat, his line of retreat might be cut. This consideration prevented him from vigorously attacking Victor and seeking to reach the Berezina to help Chichagov stop Napoleon's Grand Army. Prominent Russian historian, Kharkevich, justly noted:

> Wittgenstein limited himself to the achieved success because he believed that any decisive offensive against Victor would deprive him from already

gained advantages. By remaining at Chashniki, he had complete freedom of action and, if the French army moved against him, he could engage it on strong positions at Chashniki, Bocheikovo or Lepel. With no news on Chichagov and the remnants of the Bavarian corps at Glubokoe, further offensive seemed quite risky since, in case of defeat, Wittgenstein would not only lose the defensive line on the Ulla but also see his own line of retreat threatened.

Communications between the Russian commanders were extremely difficult: on 18 November Wittgenstein informed Emperor Alexander of the arrival of Flügel Adjutant Chernishev with the news of Chichagov's approach to Minsk, although by then Chichagov was already north-east of the city. A copy of that letter reached Kutuzov only on the 25th, when Chichagov was already in possession of Borisov. Wittgenstein, who had dispatched a messenger (escorted by a group of Cossacks) to Kutuzov on 13 November, was still unsure if the dispatch had been delivered ten days later.[277] In addition, the *Official Journal of Incoming Correspondence*, maintained in Kutuzov's headquarters, reveals that Wittgenstein's letters often arrived out of sequence and at least five days late, depending on the difficulties couriers encountered on their way.[278]

In light of these difficult conditions, it is hardly surprising that Kutuzov's new set of instructions only further complicated the situation. Kutuzov, in two consequent instructions, expressed his supposition that Napoleon, with his main army, would proceed against Wittgenstein. On 15 November, the Russian Commander-in-Chief argued that Chichagov's capture of Minsk would 'force [Napoleon] to take a new direction from Rosha to Senno, Lepel [...] and further into Lithuania, and thus attack you with his main forces'. To avoid defeat, Kutuzov suggested that Wittgenstein should take up 'a strong position or *defile* where the enemy would have to march and destroy all crossing in order to delay him'. Kutuzov and Chichagov would, in the meantime, converge and 'use all means to destroy the main enemy army'.[279] The letter halted Wittgenstein's operations and, by remaining at Chashniki, he believed he held a central location, allowing him to intercept enemy movements to the north-west. But this left Chichagov unsupported on the Berezina.

And so almost a week passed in relative inactivity, which benefited the Allied forces.[280] On 20 November, Napoleon's new orders arrived at the French marshals' headquarters at Chereya, advising Oudinot to proceed to Borisov (see previous chapter), while Victor was to continue protecting the northern flank against Wittgenstein, conceal Oudinot's departure, and protect the passing of the Grand Army; he could then retreat in a south-westerly direction to rejoin the main army near Borisov and take charge of the rearguard.[281]

The Battle of the Berezina

Following imperial orders, Victor remained at Chereya, keeping Wittgenstein's advance elements in check. His troops, however, were quickly dwindling due to cold and disease. General Baron August Ameil complained in his campaign notes of 'excessive cold [and] lack of provisions', while Victor reported that 'the IX Corps suffers greatly due to disease and the weakened soldiers are marching with difficulty. The 12th Division, which is composed of young troops, alone has lost 2,000 men in the last eight days'.[282] Honoré Beulay, of the 36th Line, described the misery he and his comrades experienced during these cold days: 'some wept, crying out plaintively to their parents; some went raving mad; some died under our eyes after a horrible agony'.[283] One of Victor's most reliable and disciplined units, the Badenese brigade, was able to retain some 2,240 men, but Lieutenant Colonel de Polentz, of the Saxon von Low Infantry Regiment, reported to the Saxon minister of war that the 'regiment is in a miserable condition, after too many long marches and bivouacs without water and wood'. The von Low Regiment had over 330 men sick and disabled, while the von Rechten Regiment barely counted 500 men. The Hessian Joseph Steinmüller recalled struggling to find firewood and seeing half-frozen men rudely pushed away from fires and refused water: 'We marched in bitter cold on slippery roads. Many, not knowing the road, got lost in the darkness and perished.'[284]

Wittgenstein was informed of the French withdrawal from Chereya and the departure of some of their troops, but did not realize it was Oudinot's entire corps. He ordered Vlastov to proceed to Kholopenichi and dispatched his advance guard to Chereya, following with the main forces in its wake.[285] Wittgenstein's main forces proceeded in two columns, with the right led by Steinheil reaching Lukoml' and left, led by Berg, arriving at Meleshkovichi.

On 22 November, Wittgenstein received important news. A messenger, dispatched by Langeron a few days earlier, finally delivered news of the 3rd Western Army's successes at Kaidanov and Minsk, and its expected arrival at Borisov. In addition, Langeron (after consulting intercepted French letters) informed Wittgenstein that Napoleon was expected to reach Bobr by 22 November and that Victor was moving towards Borisov. Consequently, Langeron urged Wittgenstein to hurry to Chichagov's aid.[286] Indeed, on 22–23 November, Victor redeployed his forces as he slowly withdrew southwards. To lighten his corps, he instructed his troops to discard any excess transports and specified how many wagons and transport horses each ranking officer should retain. The 12th Division was moved to Batury, the 28th Division at Pereselki and the 26th Division at Kholopenichi, with Fournier's cavalry at Dokuchin and Delaitre's rearguard at Strazhavichi. Victor established his headquarters at the village of Pereselki and kept his reserve artillery at Batury.[287]

From Chereya to Loshnitsa

The next couple of days (the 22nd to the 24th) proved relatively peaceful but full of movement. Wittgenstein, informed of the French departure from Chereya, had occupied it on 23 November and sent reinforcements to Vlastov's detachment, which became isolated as it marched towards Batury and threatened the French line of retreat. Indeed, that same day, the French advance guard engaged Vlastov's troops and pushed them back to Uznatsk, clearing the way for Victor's corps. The Russians, however, captured a large number of prisoners.[288] That night Victor received new instructions from Berthier, who informed the Marshal of Oudinot's arrival at Borisov and Napoleon's sojourn at Bobr. Victor was instructed to cover the right flank and proceed towards Barany. But these new instructions complicated his mission. Vlastov's detachment was already at Kholopenichi[289] and Victor was reluctant to engage them, fearing he would be pinned down, allowing Wittgenstein to strike from behind. In addition, Victor's reconnaissance reported poor roads and difficult terrain in this direction, which would have delayed his movement. Instead, the Marshal decided to continue his march towards Loshnitsa. This could have been a consequential decision, since Victor's movement left Oudinot exposed at Studyanka and if Wittgenstein were aware of the French bridge-building activity there, he could have approached unopposed. Napoleon later reprimanded Victor for his action.[290]

Yet, luckily for the French, Wittgenstein came to quite a different conclusion. He learned of the French defeats at Krasnyi and of Kutuzov's passage of the Dnieper.[291] After hearing from Langeron of Chichagov's occupation of Borisov, he became convinced that the only reason for Victor's continued retreat was Napoleon's intention to cross the Berezina south of Borisov. When Count Arakcheyev forwarded a letter to Wittgenstein, written by Sir Robert Wilson (British commissioner to the Russian Army), warning of Chichagov's dangerous position, Wittgenstein refuted it by citing Langeron's report. But this report was already outdated and Wittgenstein was unaware of the Russian defeat at Loshnitsa and Oudinot's recapture of Borisov.[292] On 23 November, he wrote to Kutuzov: 'In light of these circumstances I believe that the enemy would turn from Tolochin to Mogilev.'[293] He sent a messenger with similar observations to Chichagov, informing him: 'Although it is said that the enemy army is proceeding to Borisov, I think that he has turned to Bobruisk, since otherwise Victor would have certainly remained at Chereya to protect the march of [Napoleon's] troops.'[294] As explained in the previous chapter, Chichagov believed this flawed supposition and later made his key decisions based on it.[295]

By 24 November, Victor concentrated his corps around Batury and then proceeded to Shavry, leaving behind a small rearguard. That day Wittgenstein's advance guard – led by MG Harpe – attacked Delaitre, who took up a strong position on the edge of some woods and defended it for a few hours before slowly retreating. The Russian cavalry made several attacks on the French rearguard, which included Delaitre's cavalry and Daendels' division. On one occasion, according to Victor's report, some 900 Cossacks and Bashkirs charged near the village of Duby, but suffered greatly when the Badenese hussars counter-attacked. At the same time, there was a rearguard action between the Russians and Fournier's cavalry, the latter succeeding in containing the attackers before retreating.[296] Steinmüller described how his unit moved by platoons and observed Cossacks following it on both sides of the road. Later, as the troops relaxed around the bivouac fires, the Cossacks attacked them:

> Our troops quickly gathered on a favourable position and we barely occupied it as we saw Russian columns about to attack us [...] We fought with resolution and, when the enemy tried to occupy the woods that we had to pass, our 2nd Battalion moved by forced march to stop them. Our losses were light despite heavy enemy fire. When our large train was beyond any danger, the corps slowly retreated under cover of darkness [...] The enemy closely pursued us and, unfortunately, seized all our cattle.[297]

Meantime, that same night, Wittgenstein received Chichagov's letter informing him of Pahlen's defeat at Loshnitsa and urging him to attack Victor at once.[298]

On 25 November, Wittgenstein received several important reports. Vlastov informed him of the French departure from Shavry in the direction of Loshnitsa,[299] while the outposts in the north reported on the Bavarian forces of Wrede, which were moving from Glubokoe towards Dokshitsy, to threaten the Russian right flank.[300] Platov, who was operating with his Cossacks near Kokhanovo, also reported that he expected Napoleon to march on Vileika.[301] All these reports confused the Russian corps commander. Previously, he had been fairly convinced that Napoleon was not seeking to escape via the north but was rather attempting to cross the Berezina south of Borisov. In light of Wrede's movement and Platov's report, Wittgenstein now thought Napoleon might be diverting the main Russian forces south, while intending to break through between Chichagov and his own forces. Wittgenstein, therefore, instructed Vlastov to send his cavalry in pursuit of Victor, while he himself moved his main forces towards Barany to intercept any enemy movement in a north-westerly direction. He informed Yermolov of his decision and advised him to keep a watchful eye on the southern routes to Bobruisk, in order to reveal any French attempts to cross the Berezina downstream of Borisov.[302]

By late afternoon on 25 November, Victor's corps had arrived at Loshnitsa. The cold weather, sickness and fighting had reduced his corps to no more than 12,000 men, many of them war-fatigued and wayward. Victor complained to Berthier that my generals complain a great deal about their troops, who, generally speaking, are serving quite badly. It is difficult to control them. The generals ascribe this to the misery these troops suffer but I believe that it is more reasonable to attribute this problem to their deleterious composition. The Dutch regiments, above all, are absolutely worthless [absolument nuls]. The only infantry which holds up and always marches in good order is the Badenese brigade.[303]

That same day, Victor's troops united with Napoleon's main army, or, to be precise, what was left of it. Unaware of conditions in the Grand Army, Victor was stunned to see

a mob of tattered ghosts draped in women's cloaks, odd pieces of carpet, or greatcoats burned full of holes, their feet wrapped in all sorts of rags [...] [Victor's troops] stared in horror as those skeletons of soldiers went by, their gaunt, grey faces covered with disfiguring beards, without weapons, shameless, marching out of step, with lowered heads, eyes on the ground, in absolute silence, like a gang of convicts.[304]

'It is nearly impossible to describe the sight,' recorded Lieutenant Zimmermann. 'We were stunned to see a formerly so beautiful army in such degree of disorder. It seemed as if skeletons, fresh out of graves, staggered past us.' General Wilhelm Hochberg, future Margrave of Baden proclaimed:

I will never forget that day. I ordered my brigade to stop to observe the scene, the likes of which none of us had ever witnessed. We first saw twenty non-commissioned officers carrying flags, followed by generals, some on foot, others mounted, many of them in women's silk-lined fur coats [...] The weather was wonderful that day and the sun brightly shone on the scene, so painful for us to watch.

Steinmüller saw troops moving 'without any semblance of order or discipline [...] Only around the flags and eagles one could see armed men marching; the rest had no arms and covered themselves in furs and rags'.[305]

Hochberg's men had been greatly cheered when they had come across a convoy from Karlsruhe with food and supplies of every sort. The men exchanged worn-out uniforms for new ones and enjoyed the much-missed delicacies, which led to many amusing scenes:

Every officer had received something from home and everyone jumped on the packages destined for them. Thus it was that I saw Colonel Bruckner, standing on one of the wagons, open up a large box, which I assumed to be full of victuals, and from it he drew a wig and, quick as a flash, he removed the old one he had on his bald head and donned the new one, trying to fit it to his head with his hands.

After sending a portion of the supplies to Berg's brigade, Hochberg had all transports burned and horses assigned to the artillery.

The following day, around 8 a.m.,[306] Victor proceeded to Borisov, leaving General Fournier with four light cavalry regiments near Ratulichi and General Partouneaux's 12th Division at Loshnitsa to observe Russian movements and assure the safe passage of the Grand Army's rearguard, which was lagging behind at the village of Nasha.[307]

Central Front: From Krasnyi to Orsha

The operations in the south and north were sideshows for the main event: the Grand Army's continued withdrawal from Russia. After the Battle of Krasnyi, Napoleon's troops marched to Lyadi on the way to Orsha, while the army's rearguard covered the retreat between Dubrovna and Lyadi. On the march, Napoleon was 'on foot, with a stick in his hand, walking with difficulty and repugnance, and halting every quarter of an hour' and was often heard 'groaning and exclaiming, that the misery of his poor soldiers cut him to the heart, and yet that he could not succour them without fixing himself in some place [...] He was no longer strong enough to halt; he must reach Minsk as quickly as possible'.[308] According to Désiré Chłapowski, during the Allied march to Lyadi, 'the Cossacks kept up a constant fire on us with their artillery. At times the shots landed close to the Emperor, who was walking on foot with the Grenadiers of the Guard. Our cavalry had to see the Cossacks off with a number of charges'.[309]

The cold weather only complicated things since, as Sergeant Adrien Jean Baptiste François Bourgogne described, 'roads became so slippery that we fell down continually, and many were seriously hurt'. Captain Coignet saw 'the horses dying of hunger and cold [...] The roads were like glass. The horses fell down, and could not get up. Our worn-out soldiers no longer had strength to carry their arms. The barrels of their guns were so cold that they stuck to their hands'. Caulaincourt recalled

the frost was more severe than ever, and the road therefore more difficult. The country was covered in hills; the steep descents had become impracticable. It is impossible to form any idea of the difficulties that the artillery and transport had to surmount on this march, or of the number of horses lost by the former. We had reached our destination by a road that descended so steeply, that was so sunken, and a part of whose frozen surface had been so polished by the large number of horses and men who had slipped on it, that we were obliged like everyone else to sit down and let ourselves slide on our posteriors. The emperor had to do likewise, for the many arms that were offered to him provided no adequate support. That fact will give some idea of the plight of soldiers with their rifles and equipment – of artillerymen and transports – but especially of the horseman, who risked being crushed by the weight of his faster-rolling mount.[310]

Fortunately for the Allied troops, the weather became milder and snow turned to sleet. Dominique Larrey remembered that, after the battles at Krasnyi, the temperature increased by 'ten or twelve degrees and we were not suffering from the cold as much'.[311] Castellane's diary recorded the start of thaw on 18 November, noting that sledges quickly became useless.[312] This temporary thaw alleviated some hardships, but the melting ice and rains that began on 20 November turned roads into quagmires and frozen rivers into fast-flowing torrents. As Amédée de Pastoret, a young *intendant* of the Vitebsk province, remembered:

the ground turned into a thick mud, which was stirred up by the passage of the masses of men, making the road impassable. Numerous transports got stuck in this mud and many artillery pieces were abandoned. Those who, by prudence, had earlier placed their baggage on sledges, now lost both the baggage and transports.

Westphalian soldier Jakob Walter found it impossible

to recognize one another except by voice. Everyone was disguised in furs, rags, and pieces of cloth; they wore round hats and peasant caps on their heads, and many had priest's robes from the churches. It was like a world turned upside down […] In every bivouac soldiers who looked like spectres crept around at night. The colour of their faces, their husky breathing, and their dull muttering were horribly evident; for wherever they went they remained hopeless; and no one allowed these shades of death to drag themselves to the fire …

On 18 November, upon arriving at Lyadi, Guillaume Peyrusse recorded in his diary:

We were bewildered by the sight. People massed in large groups, without any order; soldiers were mixed up as well. The officers, not to waste their efforts, did not issue any orders at all. All the traces of discipline vanished. It was difficult to require anything of a soldier who was given nothing and for whom plunder and destruction became a necessity.[313]

Still, Lyadi offered some shelter and food to the troops. Pastoret recorded that Lyadi was

> the first village where we found some residents, albeit confused and frightened but courageous and sensible enough not to flee upon our approach and prefer mistreatment for the next five–six days to destruction of their houses. The Jews reappeared and with them appeared all the necessities of life …

In Lyadi, Caulaincourt was happy to see 'chickens and ducks [running] about in the courtyards. We had seen no such signs of plenty since crossing the Niemen; and every face cheered up, and everyone began to think that our privations were at last at an end'. But this joy proved temporary and chickens and ducks were quickly devoured. Ségur soon reported the increasing disorder among the Allied troops and saw that

> when an immense crowd [of stragglers] had been collected, these wretches called out 'The Cossacks' with a view to quicken the march of those who preceded them, and to increase the tumult. They then took advantage of it to carry off the provisions and cloaks of those whom they had thrown off their guard.[314]

By November 1812 the leadership of the Grand Army had undergone major changes during its five-month sojourn in Russia. The campaign would eventually claim nine Allied generals of division and twenty-one generals of brigade killed or mortally wounded. At Borodino alone, Napoleon lost eight generals, among them two generals of division (Caulaincourt and Montbrun) and six generals of brigade (Compère, Huard, Damas, Lanabère, Marion and Plauzonne). On 18 October, Generals Pierre-Cesar Dery and Stanislas Fiszer were killed at Winkowo (Tarutino). Alexis Delzons and Joseph Levie died at Maloyaroslavets on 24 October, Czeslas Pakosz was mortally wounded at Minsk on 14 November, while Louis François-Lanchantin fell at Krasnyi on 17 November. Besides generals, dozens of other senior officers (colonels, majors, etc.) were killed, wounded or captured in the battles preceding the Berezina. By early 1813, the Russian Campaign had taken the lives of fifty-three colonels, thirty-three of whom died on the battlefield.[315] Between 5–7 September at Shevardino and Borodino, as recent studies indicate, the Grand Army saw 1,928 officers killed

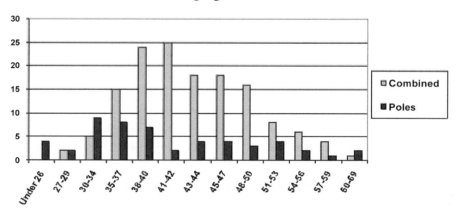

Age of the Grand Army's generals in 1812. (Combined data based on 142 persons; Polish data based on 52 individuals)

or wounded. Over 120 officers were killed and wounded at Maloyaroslavets and another 150 in the actions at Vyazma, with many more lost in the actions at Polotsk, Tarutino, Smolyany, etc.[316] After three days of fighting at Krasnyi, Kutuzov reported that 'the captured alone include six generals and 190 staff and junior officers'.[317]

With troops from almost every corner of Europe, one might have expected a nationally diverse officer corps. Yet, while officers at company level were mostly of ethnic origin, general officers were largely French. At army level, out of 166 generals studied, 130 were French (plus one Corsican). And among twenty-five generals serving in the II and IX Corps, which bore the brunt of fighting at the Berezina, twenty-one were French, the rest hailing from Holland, Portugal, Hesse-Darmstadt and Baden. They came from diverse backgrounds, but foreigners tended to belong to the nobility, while the French largely represented the 'Third Estate'. The 57–year-old Jean Claude Moreau was the oldest and, with forty-one years of service, the most experienced general; Markgraf Wilhelm von Hochberg of Baden, at just 20, was the youngest and least experienced. At the same time, among the forty-six infantry and cavalry regiments serving in these same corps, less than half (15) were French, and the rest consisted of Berg (5), Badenese (4), Swiss (4), Dutch (4), Polish (4), Hessian (3), Saxon (2), Westphalian (2), Croat (1), Piedmontese (1) and Portuguese (1) units. If one adds to these the brave Poles of the Vistula Legion, or the gallant Dutch *pontonniers* or Doumerc's Dutch cuirassiers, the ratio of non-French and French troops would further increase.

With the Grand Army suffering greatly from lack of provisions and warm clothes, the supply depots at Smolensk were quickly exhausted and one participant complained of profiteers charging three francs for a single biscuit.[318]

The Battle of the Berezina

A few fortunates, like Colonel Jean François Boulart of the Guard Artillery, still had provisions left, but the remaining 'biscuits and sugar were hard like rock and this dry food damaged our teeth and tore our gums'. The less well-off, like the Württemberg officer, Christophe-Ludwig von Yelin, suffered immensely:

> I walked, feeling completely spent, having no food except horse meat, no shoes and in tattered clothes that could not protect from cold [...] Physically and morally exhausted, I began to fall behind ...

At one of the bivouacs, the hungry Yelin patiently waited for a French soldier to nod off near the fire before snatching a pot containing precious pea soup.[319] Heinrich von Roos, a physician in the Grand Army, saw that some soldiers

> were becoming weak-sighted and, indeed, many had gone blind. One saw men dragging their comrades along by sticks, like beggars [...] The chief cause of this eye disease was the smoke of campfires, because in order to warm themselves as best they could, people used at night to put their head and hands over the flames. In addition, the snow wastes across which we struggled during the day were extremely injurious to many eyes ...[320]

Auguste Thirion de Metz, of the 2nd Cuirassiers

> discovered a new way of feeding myself. I possessed a small tin casserole [...] and when I found a horse near our halting place, I inserted a knife blade as gently as possible between the ribs, held up my little casserole to catch the blood which flowed from this wound, and then cooked it.[321]

Coignet was not shy of tasting horsemeat either, noting that

> the soldiers opened the horse's skin with their knives and took out the entrails, which they roasted on the coals, if they had time to make a fire, and, if not, they ate them raw. They devoured the horses before they died.

Many units lost their appearance as the soldiers sought to protect themselves from cold. Thirion de Metz found it difficult to

> distinguish between generals and officers. Like soldiers, they wore anything they could lay hands on. Oftentimes a general was covered in rags while a soldier wore a rich fur coat [...] All army uniforms were intermixed. The northern fur, so praised and sought, covering the silk-lined coats of various colours walked amidst common infantry *capote* and cavalry *manteau*, figures

wrapped and covered in colourful headscarves, leaving only narrow openings for eyes. The most prevalent clothing was a wool blanket with a hole in the middle to put a head through and cover the entire body. Mainly the cavalrymen wore it since, after losing their horses, they usually preserved blankets, which, however, became tattered, dirty and burnt, in short, disgusting. Besides, the people had not changed clothes or undergarments in three months and were suffering from fleabites.

Ida Saint-Elme, a Hungarian actress and self-styled adventuress who was passionately in love with Ney, recalled that 'the Emperor made an often quoted joke during the awful retreat [...] Seeing one of his officers wrapped up in a magnificent fur coat, he called to him, laughing, "Where did you steal that?" – "Your Majesty, I bought it!" – Yes, you bought it from someone who was asleep!' Senior officers suffered as much as the rank-and-file: for example, Marshal Davout 'had lost everything, [and] was actually without linen and emaciated with hunger'. Davout complained that 'none but men of iron constitutions could support such trials, that it was physically impossible to resist them; that there were limits to human strength, the utmost of which had been exceeded'. Another officer noted that

There was no longer any discipline or any human feeling for one another. Every sentiment of humanity was extinguished. No one would have reached out his hand to his father; and that can be easily understood. For he who stooped down to help his fellow would not be able to rise again [...] The men became insensible to every human feeling.[322]

One Russian general, pursuing the Grand Army, recorded that

The loss of life greatly exceeded everything else. There were thousands of dead and freezing people. There was no refuge or shelter; villages and settlements were all turned into ashes and the increasing number of prisoners, all wounded and sick and many non-combatants, were all doomed to await inevitable death. The never-ending sight of suffering humans exhausted compassion and dulled the very feeling of remorse. Each of these unfortunate men seemed to cease to be a human being in the eyes of the others. Everyone suffered and the calamity was beyond imagination! Without any means to help them, we saw them as victims doomed to die.[323]

Napoleon, concerned by increasing disorder in the army, tasked Junot, the Duke of Abrantès (who had hardly distinguished himself during the campaign) with re-establishing discipline.[324] He instructed Junot to guard the bridge at Orsha [...] and endeavour to establish the greatest order in the city, distribute rations [...] detain all unattached men and class them by their corps [...] hinder all kinds of pillage and all excesses committed by the stragglers [...] and if there are any who pillage and behave badly, have them taken before a military tribunal and shot.[325]

Yet Junot was unable to accomplish his mission and his attempts to regulate the passage of stragglers over the bridge led to massive crowds gathering on the one side of the river. Bourgogne saw 'some *gendarmes* and a few Poles' who were 'horror-struck at seeing our miserable condition, and at the enormous number of stragglers in such disorganization'. Laugier observed 'officers and *gendarmes* stopping masses of soldiers, separated from their unit, and forcing them to return to their colours'. As the army began crossing the Dnieper, Westphalian officer Friedrich Wilhelm von Lossberg saw a stampede of 'people, horses and wagons' developing on the two bridges with some units forced to use the threat of bayonets to clear their way.[326] A similar observation was made by Griois, who saw the newly-arrived *gendarmes* attempting the impossible task of regulating the traffic on the bridge.[327] As Ségur writes:

> the officers and *gendarmes* [...] had been sent for the purpose of stopping on the two bridges of the Dnieper the crowd of stragglers, and making them rejoin their columns. But those eagles, which formerly promised everything, were now looked upon as of fatal omen, and deserted accordingly.[328]

Indeed, anxious about their lives, hungry and cold, the disheartened soldiers and stragglers sought to cross the bridge and neither proclamations nor threats of execution could pacify them. Fortunately, the magazine at Orsha allowed some rations to be issued to the troops, but it was not enough to satisfy all. Walter watched as 'none of the doors [to storehouses] could be opened, since everyone pushed and shoved each other in order to get close to ...' When the doors finally opened, a mass of soldiers rushed inside but could not re-emerge due to the pressure of the crowd outside: 'Many weak soldiers lay on the floor and were trampled down, screaming frightfully.' According to General Antoine Baudouin Gisbert van Dedem van de Gelder:

> In Dubrovna and Orsha we found some food but the disorder which reigned in the army had made its distribution impossible, and the result had been the same as in Smolensk; some got more supplies than they needed, and others got nothing, eventually dying of hunger.[329]

Campaign Chronicle

On the 19th, Napoleon, knowing well of disorder spreading in his army, personally appealed to the grenadiers of the Imperial Guard, reminding them of their responsibility and urging them to set an example for the rest of the army. Some witnesses described the Emperor, dressed in fur coat and accompanied by the splendidly-dressed Murat, whose 'assurance and joyfulness were not affected by the cold and our disastrous position' and the grimmer Berthier, dressed in a common blue coat, addressing his troops:

> Grenadiers! We are retreating without being conquered by the enemy, let us not be vanquished by ourselves! Set an example to the army. Several of you have already deserted your eagles and even thrown away your arms. I have no wish to have recourse to military laws to put a stop to this disorder, but appeal entirely to yourselves! Do justice among yourselves. To your own honour I commit the support of your discipline.

Although the words had an immediate effect on the units Napoleon appealed to, as Ségur commented, 'when the march was resumed, they were quite forgotten'.[330]

During his stay at Dubrovna and Orsha, Napoleon also received distressing reports from Marshal Victor regarding Wittgenstein's offensive towards Chereya. The Emperor also received Bronikowski's news about Chichagov's march on Minsk and, as already described, he undertook measures in both directions to safeguard his passage.

Meantime, Napoleon set about reorganizing his remaining forces. The army presented but a shadow of its former self. Divisions were reduced to regimental strength and regiments often counted no more than a battalion. Colonel Griois lamented that IV Corps comprised 'several thousand unfortunate men, broken by fatigue and stupefied by misery, who only preserved enough energy for self-preservation'.[331] Davout's corps was reinforced with the Orsha garrison and reorganized into three battalions. Eugène's forces and Poniatowski's V Corps included two battalions each, while Ney's corps, after joining the army, was also converted into three battalions. Junot's VIII Corps had some 400 men left, effectively constituting a battalion. Of the hundreds of cannon Napoleon brought into Russia, only a fraction had survived by November – most having been captured or disabled and sunk in lakes and rivers. The remaining artillery, augmented by thirty-six guns found in Orsha and thirty cannon (from the Swiss regiments) detached from Victor,[332] was divided into several batteries, which were then assigned to the corps of Eugène, Davout and Ney. The number of forces at Napoleon's disposal has been subject to various claims. No exact computations were made in Smolensk or Orsha, while eyewitness testimonies vary, so must be used as estimates only. Cesare Laugier, thus, estimated that the Imperial Guard had 7,000 men, I Corps 5,000, IV Corps 4,000, V Corps, VIII

The Battle of the Berezina

Corps and the cavalry combined for 2,000 men. Ségur believed the Guard had some 6,000 men, I Corps 4,000 and IV Corps less than 2,000 men. Zajączek reported that his V Corps counted some 660 men.[333] Most sources agree that Napoleon probably had about 20,000 men still capable of fighting (excluding Victor and Oudinot's troops) and as many as 30,000–35,000 non-combatants.

At a meeting in a local monastery, imperial adjutant Eustachy Sanguszko advised the Emperor that many ammunition wagons were laden with loot and that Jean-Ambroise Baston-de-Lariboissière, the Inspector-General of the French artillery, who was still in a deep depression following the death of his son at Borodino in September, had lost his grip on the artillery and was tolerating the presence of plunder.[334] Napoleon ordered most of the baggage train destroyed. All surplus wagons and carts were burned and their horses assigned to the artillery. Pastoret informs us that marshals were allowed to retain two wagons, senior officers one, while Berthier was given six transports. At one point, Napoleon personally went to the bridge and

> with a cane in hand, performed the functions of wagonmaster-general for two hours. Transports entered the bridge one after another; he asked each of them which unit it belonged to and, thanks to his unbelievable memory, he kept their designations in mind, letting some transports pass while others he stopped and ordered to burn …

But after Napoleon's departure, the process quickly unravelled: the Emperor left Berthier in charge, but the latter – his hands full with other military business – quickly gave this assignment to one of his subordinates, who also delegated it, until a lowly staff officer was eventually left in charge. By then, darkness had descended, and the rest of the army, with thousands of wagons intact, was allowed across the river and 'the disorder continued'.[335]

Among the wagons selected for destruction were the surviving *pontonnier* wagons, a portion of which had been destroyed in Moscow and then at Vyazma. The remaining wagons, carrying heavy equipment, employed several hundred horses badly needed by the rest of the army. As Gourgaud tells us, Napoleon did not expect that 'the important post of Borisov would fall so readily into the enemy's power' and was concerned that heavy bridge equipages would be a needless burden. And so Napoleon ordered the pontoon train to be burned, despite the protests of its commander, General Jean Baptiste Eblé. Although complying with the imperial order, Eblé burned most vehicles except for two field forges, six artillery caissons full of equipment and tools and two wagons full of charcoal. And to save additional tools, he ordered his *pontonniers* to carry tools and clamps in their hands.[336] Eblé's foresight, albeit in contradiction to Napoleon's order, would play a decisive role on the Berezina only a week later.

Campaign Chronicle

From Orsha to Bobr

Napoleon departed Orsha at noon on 20 November and reached nearby Barany that same evening. As Gourgaud recounts, Napoleon was dining with Marshal Lefebvre when 'some Polish officers had arrived in the city demanding succours for Marshal Ney ...' According to Caulaincourt, 'we knew nothing definite about the III Corps [...] Not a single dispatch officer had returned'. Hearing the news, the Emperor immediately rose, and seizing Gourgaud by his arms, said to him with the greatest emotion 'Is this true? Are you certain of it?' It was indeed true – Ney was back. 'Then I have saved my eagles,' Napoleon reputedly exclaimed on hearing the news, 'I would have given three hundred millions from my treasury sooner than have lost such a man [Ney].'[337] But Ney's heroic return was marred by his bitter conflict with Davout, whom he accused of abandonment near Krasnyi. Davout argued that he could not have done anything to help Ney, as his own corps would have been isolated and destroyed by the Russians. According to Caulaincourt, it was 'impossible to describe the unbridled rage and fury that everyone showed towards [Davout]'. Ney, meantime, was widely acclaimed as the hero of the campaign: 'never has a victory in the field caused such a sensation. The joy was general; everyone was drunk with delight ...'[338]

Meantime, Napoleon weighed his options. He could select one of two major roads in the area: Orsha–Borisov–Minsk or Vitebsk–Bocheikovo–Glubokoe. The latter route seemed unfavourable for a number of reasons: Wittgenstein's offensive had already threatened it and, furthermore, taking it would require Napoleon to march north not west, losing precious time. Finally, the Vitebsk–Glubokoe route was not as well supplied as that of Orsha–Borisov–Minsk. Napoleon, therefore, chose to proceed to Bobr and cross the Berezina at Borisov. This road ran through thickly wooded territory and, beside a major bridge at Borisov, additional crossing sites were available at Veselovo and Nizhneye Berezino. Beyond the Berezina, the road led to a narrow defile near Zembino and then reached the major road connecting Minsk and Vilna. But the road had its own disadvantages, the most important being the threat from Chichagov. Napoleon had earlier received the news of Chichagov's advance on Minsk but according to Caulaincourt, 'the informant was unable to tell [Napoleon] exactly when [Chichagov] had started or how far he had progressed. All he knew was hearsay, picked up from someone else'. Discussing this threat with his trusted Master of the Horse, Napoleon told him:

> Chichagov intends, no doubt, to join Tormasov and they will send an army to the Berezina. As I have always thought, Kutuzov is leaving us alone now in order to head me off and attack me when this reinforcement has joined him. We must hurry. Time has been lost since we left Smolensk, although if my orders have been carried out I will also have my forces on the

Berezina. We must hurry to get there, for that is where great things may happen.[339]

Concerned by this new threat, Napoleon issued fresh instructions to Oudinot and Victor, as previously discussed, advising Oudinot to proceed to Borisov while Victor was to continue protecting the northern flank against Wittgenstein.

By 21 November, Napoleon moved his headquarters to Kamenitse, near Kokhanovo, while the remnants of the Grand Army left Orsha, destroying bridges over the Dnieper and marching west: Junot's VIII Corps led the way, followed by the Poles (Zajączek), the Imperial Guard, the III Corps (Ney) and IV Corps (Eugène) while Davout's I Corps served as a rearguard. Oudinot's corps was already near Bobr, while Victor was holding ground near Chereya. The same day, Napoleon received a second, more ominous report on Chichagov's progress: a Polish officer told of the fall of Minsk and the Russian march to Borisov, which, as Caulaincourt tells us, 'roused the Emperor to anxious thought'. The immense stores on which the Emperor had been counting since Smolensk were irrevocably lost. And now the Russians were marching north to Borisov, where Dąbrowski's forces were too weak to defend the town, the loss of which would endanger the entire army. The news cost Napoleon a restless evening and night as he paced up and down: 'Shall we get there in time?' he asked Caulaincourt, while Ségur overheard him remark: 'We have now nothing to do but to clear ourselves a passage with our bayonets.'[340] Doubts beset the Emperor:

> Will the Duke of Belluno [Victor] take the offensive soon enough to divert Wittgenstein? If the Berezina crossings are closed to us, something may turn up – something unforeseen, some setback – so that we will have to cut our way out with the cavalry of the Guard. How far could [we?] get with them in five or six days, with their horses in the state they are in now? How far, without letting the weakest fall by the wayside? With my Guard and the remaining brave men, it is always possible to break through. I must find out what my corps on the Dvina and Schwarzenberg's [corps] are up to.[341]

What Napoleon could not comprehend yet was that Schwarzenberg had long given up active campaigning against the Russians and, despite urgent dispatches instructing him to head for Minsk, he preferred to preserve his corps instead of making a dash to save Napoleon. Later that night Napoleon sent General Dode to Oudinot and Victor with orders for the former to proceed immediately from Chereya to Borisov, and the latter to remain opposite Wittgenstein, allowing the main army to reach the Berezina.

Finding a brief moment to rest, Napoleon laid down and asked Daru and Duroc to stay with him. The three discussed the situation at length before the

Emperor dozed off and the two officers withdrew to a nearby room. They conversed for quarter of an hour before Napoleon awoke and interrupted them. He inquired what they were discussing and Daru told him they were wishing they had a balloon. 'What for?' asked Napoleon. 'To carry Your Majesty away!' replied Daru. 'Good God!' exclaimed the Emperor. 'Things are bad enough then. You are afraid of being taken prisoners of war?' 'No, not prisoners of war, because they won't let Your Majesty off so lightly as that.' Napoleon continued: 'The situation is very grave, that is a fact. The issue is growing more complicated.' Then, in an attempt to lighten the mood, Napoleon concluded: 'Just the same, if my leaders set a good example, I am still stronger than the enemy. I can very well afford to disregard the Russians, if their troops are all that stand in my way.'[342]

On 22 November, as he arrived at Tolochin, some fifty miles from Borisov, Napoleon was surprised to hear of Dąbrowski's defeat and the loss of the Borisov *tête-de-pont*.[343] Chambray tells us that Oudinot's adjutant first delivered this news and the irate Napoleon exclaimed: 'So it is then decided that we must commit only follies.'[344] A few moments later, General Dode, returning from Oudinot and Victor, approached the Emperor, succinctly telling him, 'They are there,' meaning that Admiral Chichagov's troops were already at Borisov. 'This damned sailor brings me nothing but bad luck,' Napoleon is said to have remarked of Chichagov, while probably remembering Nelson's past victories as well.[345] Ségur commented that 'this disaster was wholly unexpected by Napoleon' and that with this news, 'the leaders themselves began then to look around them with consternation; their imagination, tormented with such a long continuance of frightful spectacles, gave them glimpses of a still more fatal futurity'.[346]

Napoleon faced a difficult situation: the Grand Army was already extended along the road leading to Borisov. Its advance elements were at Bobr, followed by the Imperial Guard and the remaining forces at Tolochin. Oudinot was approaching Loshnitsa, while Victor was protecting the right flank at Chereya. The Russians were slowly converging: Chichagov's 3rd Western Army (some 30,000 men) had already beat Napoleon to Borisov and cut the line of retreat. In the north, another 30,000 men under Wittgenstein pressured Victor, while Kutuzov's main Russian army was not far behind (see below), with its advance elements at Orsha, Kopys and Babinovichi.[347] A coordinated effort on the part of these Russian commanders would have certainly surrounded the Grand Army and inflicted heavy casualties, if not destroyed it outright.

Having crossed the Dnieper, the Allied army now operated in an area surrounded by four rivers: the Dnieper in the east, the Berezina in the west, the Western Dvina in the north and the Ulla in the north-west. The region was also intersected by a number of small rivulets (i.e. Drut', Bobr, Nacha, Skha, Obol') while several lakes, marshes and rolling hills presented difficult terrain for military operations. It must be said, however, that of the four rivers, only the

The Battle of the Berezina

Dnieper – in its width and flow – presented a major obstacle, but it was already behind the Grand Army. The Ulla was a minor river and its width averaged 25–40 metres. The natural gap between the Ulla and the Berezina was sealed by the Berezinskii canal (constructed in 1797–1805 between the small lakes Bereshta and Plavio) and the Serguch rivulet, connecting the Berezina to the Ulla, which in turn flowed into the Western Dvina and allowed for transportation of goods to both the Baltic and Black Seas. In 1797, a government survey described the area between these two rivers as 'full of woods, rocky terrain and relatively high hills'[348] – features the Russians could use to delay Napoleon's advance.

The Berezina, some 600km long, is one of the major rivers in Byelorussia. Rising in the marshes of the north-west, it flows south-east into the Dnieper, which carries its waters into the Black Sea. In 1812, the river averaged a width of 10–30 metres upstream but occasionally broadened to some 80–100 metres downstream. There were a number of fords along its flow, which probably explains why, even as late as 1838, the river had only two major bridges, one at Borisov and another at Bobruisk.[349] The riverbanks were relatively flat but marshy, prone to flooding in the spring and freezing solid in wintertime. There were rolling heights on both sides of the river, the higher being on the western bank. The marshes, as Napoleon's 29th Bulletin noted, extended for some '300 *toises* [~ 600m]' along both banks and, in combination with woodland, made cavalry operations challenging: an important advantage for Napoleon, since the Russians could not exploit their superiority in this arm. In 1848, a study by the Russian General Staff noted that the Berezina and Ulla rivers presented a 'remarkable defensive line' due to the 'nature of local terrain, largely wooded, marshy, with sparse and poor roads, which provide means to contain [an] enemy for a considerable time'.[350] The areas north of the main road were densely forested and swampy, while the fortress of Bobruisk protected the southern regions. Considering the Grand Army's direction, the best place to cross the Berezina was between Veselovo and Borisov, where the terrain was more suitable and the river flowed in relatively narrow confines. The Berezina had seen its share of military operations and just over 100 years before Napoleon, the maverick King Charles XII of Sweden campaigned in the area during the Great Northern War (1700–1721); despite Russian efforts, Charles successfully built two bridges across the river in June 1708. Now, in 1812, Napoleon – an avid student of history who read of Charles' campaigns – faced a similar task, albeit in different circumstances and, most importantly, in a different season.

As he considered his options, Napoleon invited General Dode inside his tent, where they talked over the map of Russia. Dode argued that it was impossible to cross the Berezina at Borisov or south of it. Instead, he suggested moving north to Lepel, the junction of the Berezina and Ulla, where the Berezina was relatively shallow and easily fordable; joined by Oudinot and Victor, Napoleon could defeat Wittgenstein and clear a path to Vilna via Glubokoe. Napoleon objected to this proposal on the grounds of a lengthy detour from the main road and the possibility that Chichagov and Kutuzov could corner him between two rivers. He favoured turning towards Minsk, where he hoped to procure supplies and join Schwarzenberg and Reynier. As he explained his objections, Napoleon traced with his finger the course of the Berezina and the Dnieper, reminiscing about King Charles XII's campaigns. Spotting Poltava, the site of the great Russian victory over the Swedes in 1709, Napoleon reputedly murmured, 'Poltava, Poltava!' as his generals watched in silence.[351] Berthier, Murat, Prince Eugène and Jomini soon joined the conversation. Jomini, who had previously served as a local governor, was familiar with the area and could give sound advice.[352] Jomini agreed with Dode that there were no favourable crossing sites south of Borisov, but suggested advancing on Borisov and crossing the river above the town, and then proceeding to Vilna. Jomini explained to Napoleon that he had travelled this area in August–September and knew of several roads that led to Vilna; he first suggested a road that ran through Zembino and Molodechno, but if it were blocked by the enemy, the Grand Army could cross the Vilia near Vileika and still reach Vilna. Napoleon seems to have favoured moving on Chashniki to destroy Wittgenstein, before turning back to deal with Kutuzov. Jomini advised against this, arguing that 'this might have been done in the Souabe or Lombardie but not in a deserted and devastated country some six hundred *lieues* from France'. Napoleon asked Dode for his opinion once again and the General agreed with Jomini.[353] As the subsequent course of events showed, this was sensible advice but, at the time, Napoleon still vacillated before accepting it and advancing directly to Borisov. He ordered Oudinot to spearhead the Allied movement and drive Chichagov's troops out of Borisov, clearing the path for the rest of the army. Victor was instructed to guard the northern flank, notably the Lepel road, and pin down Wittgenstein.[354]

On 23–24 November, the Grand Army, after further reducing its baggage train,[355] continued its march on, as Ségur writes, 'a wide road (skirted by a double row of large birch trees) in which the snow had melted, and through a deep and liquid mud. The weakest were drowned in it; it detained and delivered to the Cossacks such of our wounded as, under the idea of a continuance of the frost, had exchanged their wagons for sledges'. In the late afternoon of 23 November, Napoleon arrived at Bobr. He urged Oudinot to become 'the master of the crossing of the Berezina and establish bridges there'. To accelerate the march, he ordered the destruction of private wagons: the horses, freed after the destruction of so many transports, were placed under command of General Sorbier, who commanded the Guard artillery.[356] The dismounted Guard cavalrymen, only 1,800 strong and lacking weapons, were reorganized into several battalions. General Latour-Maubourg's Reserve Cavalry, which once counted tens of thousands of men, now accounted for less than 200 and was merged with the 'Sacred Squadron', whose purpose was to protect Napoleon in an emergency and in which, as Chambray tells us, 'brigade generals were employed as lieutenants and colonels as sous-lieutenants'.[357] Napoleon had already ordered the destruction of state papers while the colours and eagles of non-existent regiments were burned as well.[358] For Bourgogne:

> the days were so short – it was not light till eight o'clock, and it was dark by four in the afternoon. This was the reason why so many unfortunate men lost their way, for it was always night when we arrived at the bivouac, and all the remains of the different corps were in terrible confusion. At all hours of the night we heard the weak, worn-out voices of new arrivals calling out 'Fourth Corps!' 'First Corps!' 'Third Corps!' 'Imperial Guard!' and then the voices of others lying down with no strength left, forcing themselves to answer, 'Here, comrades!' They were not trying any longer to find their regiments, but simply the *corps d'armée* to which they had belonged, and which now included the strength of two regiments at most, where a fortnight earlier there had been thirty. No one now knew anything about himself, or could mention which regiment he belonged to.[359]

Lieutenant Heinrich August Vossler, from Württemberg, was tasked with

> assembling the stray *chasseurs* wandering along the road and re-forming them into a fighting unit. Being on foot I had some success by day in gathering and keeping together a few of them, but as soon as night fell and we had to look for sleeping quarters they discovered that I had not so much as a bite of food or anything else to offer them. So away they melted again.

Captain Johann von Borcke, from Westphalia, heard

> a dark rumour that two new enemy armies were threatening our line of retreat, after Kutuzov's army had let us out of its clutches and halted behind the Dnieper [...] On the march these rumours steadily gained substances and the names 'Chichagov, Berezina' passed from mouth to mouth. At the time of our advance four months earlier the river had looked very insignificant to everyone, but now that it seemed possible that the crossing might be fiercely contested, people remembered clearly the long wooden bridge at Borisov and the black marshy bank; and these recollections were enough to make us shudder at the prospect of having to fight our way across against a fresh Russian army [...] Gloomy, silent and

with downcast gaze, this rabble of dying men walked from Orsha to the Berezina like a funeral procession.

According to Bourgogne, Napoleon, to motivate his Guard

> placed himself amongst the Grenadiers and Chasseurs and made them an address, telling them that the Russians were waiting for us at the crossing of the Berezina, and had sworn that not one of us should pass over. Then, drawing his sword and raising his voice, he cried: 'Let us all swear to die fighting rather than not see our country again!' The oath was taken. Bearskins and caps were waved at the points of bayonets and shouts were heard of 'Vive l'Empereur!' Marshal Mortier made us a similar address, and was received with the same enthusiasm, and so on with all the regiments. It was a splendid moment, and for the time made us forget our miseries. If the Russians had only been within our reach then, we should have made short work of them, even had their numbers been six times greater than ours.[360]

The supply problems were still prevalent and, lacking food, the soldiers had to resort to eating horses, which became scarcer with every passing day. Thirion informs us that

> we cut a slice from the quarters of horses still on their feet and walking, and the wretched animals gave not the least sign of pain, proving beyond doubt the degree of numbness and insensitivity caused by the extreme cold [...] We saw some of these poor horses walking for several days with large pieces of flesh cut away from both thighs; there had been a change in the colour of the coagulated blood, which had turned white or rather yellow, and had become pus.[361]

On 24 November, Napoleon learned of Oudinot's success at Loshnitsa and Borisov, where he had driven Chichagov's army across the river. Despite the loss of the bridge, Napoleon was inspired by the news and dispatched his *officier d'ordonnance*, Mortemar, to instruct Oudinot to quickly bridge the Berezina. As Napoleon's headquarters was established at Loshnitsa in the evening of the same day, Mortemar returned with Oudinot's report that Chichagov's army proved to be more numerous than expected, and that the grave challenges relating to organizing the crossing required the Emperor's personal presence. Napoleon instructed Mortemar to inform the Marshal that he was 'mistaken in believing the enemy to be superior' and should instead hasten to bridge the river. He then ordered Generals Eblé (head of *pontonniers*), François Chasseloup-Laubat (head of engineers) and Jomini to travel to Borisov and assist Oudinot in constructing the bridges. The 400 *pontonniers* (2nd, 7th and 9th Companies of the 1st Battalion and 2nd, 3rd, 4th and 5th Companies of the 2nd Battalion) and some 450 sappers and the marines (*bataillon du Danube*) were ordered to proceed to the town by forced marches.[362] On 25 November, Napoleon received intelligence that Kutuzov was three days' march behind him. According to Caulaincourt, this news 'put the Emperor at his ease'. Although the situation was still critical, Napoleon calculated the moves open to each side and knew he had the advantage of time over Kutuzov. He became confident that 'the issue was in his hands' and that he had time to organize a crossing of the Berezina.[363]

But Where is Kutuzov?

Following the battle at Krasnyi, Kutuzov moved slowly towards the Dnieper. On 19 November, Major General Borozdin captured Lyadi and proceeded to Bolshie Koltovki, while the main army remained at Krasnyi. On 20 November Kutuzov reached Romanovo and the following day was at Lanenki. By 22 November, Platov, pursuing the Allied troops, occupied Orsha. Yermolov, having crossed the Dnieper at Dubrovna, was moving to join Platov at Orsha. Kutuzov's main force, which included the 3rd, 4th, 5th, 6th Infantry and the 4th Cavalry Corps were not far from Lanenki, still on the eastern bank of the Dnieper; a part of the 8th Infantry Corps was at Romanovo. The Russian advance guard, commanded by the dashing Miloradovich, and consisting of the 2nd and 7th Infantry and 1st and 2nd Cavalry Corps, was at the village of Goryan, on its way to Kopys on the eastern riverbank. Of the several flying detachments harassing the Allied forces, Davydov's and Seslavin's were already at Kopys, Count Ozharovsky's near Gorky and Adjutant General Golenishchev-Kutuzov's at Babinovichi. At the same time, Wittgenstein was at Chashniki and Chichagov was still watching Borisov from the western bank of the Berezina.[364]

Of the three Russian armies converging on Berezina, Kutuzov's was the largest but also the most fatigued. While the Grand Army moved along the main road (albeit a devastated one), the Russian regiments marched on remote paths and cross-country, exhausting the men and delaying the supply train. The army thus lacked proper winter clothing and adequate provisions. Although Kutuzov's headquarters did its best to organize supplies, the army still suffered due to rampant corruption in the commissariat and the shortcomings of local authorities. In his official report, Intendant General Egor Kankrin (Cancrin) acknowledged that, during the pursuit of the Grand Army, the supply trains often lagged behind, leaving the main army with 'very limited' provisions.[365] As late as 28 November, Alexander Chicherin complained in his diary: 'It is already twelve days since the Guard received bread, while the army has not seen it for the past month.'[366] On 5 November Lieutenant Uxküll recorded that

Men and horses are dying of hunger and exhaustion. Only Cossacks, always lively and cheerful, manage to keep their spirits up. The rest of us have a very hard time dragging on after the fleeing enemy, and our horses, which have no shoes, slip on the frozen ground and fall down, never to get up [...] My undergarments consist of three shirts and a few pairs of long socks. I am afraid to change them because of the freezing cold and so am eaten up with fleas and encased in filth since my sheepskin never leaves me.

Nikolai Mitarevsky acknowledged that 'it is wrong to blame only the French for burning and looting everything along the road. We did the same [...] When we went out foraging, those soldiers who in time of peace passed for scoundrels and cheats became extremely useful. Nothing escaped their eagle eye'.[367] Colonel A. Karpov described how some of his men caught cold at bivouacs and noted that 'it was said that half of the troops in the army were sick, which must be true since, in our company alone, less than a third of the men were healthy'. Another officer recorded: 'it was hard and sad to watch as, having stopped near some village, each regiment would send out a detail to fetch firewood and straw. Fences would shatter, roofs fall in and whole houses disappear in a flash'. When there were no houses to dismantle, half the men would spread their greatcoats on the snow while the other half used theirs for overblankets as they lay down, pressed together for warmth.[368] Ivan Zhirkevich remembered bitter cold, blizzards and piercing winds, observing that 'quite often we even saw the lads of the Guards frozen along the road ...'[369] Ilia Radozhitsky left a revealing account on the conditions in the Russian army:

Our soldiers were blackened and wrapped in rags, some in half-coats, others in greatcoats; some in *kengi* [special winter boots lined with fur], others in felt boots and fur caps so that once they put away their weapons, they no longer resembled soldiers. The officers were dressed no better. I myself barely survived the cold wearing a coat [*tulup*] and double felt boots, with my head wrapped in a large shawl. The cloth was so heavy it was difficult to walk for long but severe cold did not allow for sitting [...] In such instances we found delight in the precious cask of the Kizlyar vodka that was stored at the lieutenant colonel's feet, inside the sledge [in which he travelled, wrapped in a bearskin coat]. During this winter campaign I, who had never been a drunkard and had never drank a shot of vodka, had to down two glasses every day, without any snacks, so that by the end of the march, entering warm quarters, I was burning as in a fire, my head spinning and barely able to stand. Many officers and soldiers became seriously ill or had their limbs frostbitten from this strenuous life: almost everyone had some part of the body exposed to the frost and I personally had my heels frostbitten. In such a condition, we could not but wonder how the French, lacking all means of supply, managed to survive ...[370]

The main Russian army at the Tarutino camp counted some 120,000 men, including irregular forces. In the subsequent weeks of pursuit and fighting, it had suffered heavy losses, mainly due to attrition and exposure, and, by late November, was reduced to some 50,000 men. Later, Captain Pushin complained in his diary that

> no one can explain why we did not anticipate Napoleon on the Berezina or appeared there simultaneously with the French Army. We are no less exhausted and yet reap no benefit from it. We suffered heavy losses due to marching and any given regiment hardly has more than 50 men under arms in each company.

Nikolai Muravyev described how his

> legs were aching unbearably. My boots lost their soles and my clothes consisted of some blue pants and a uniform coat, whose buttons were torn off and sewn onto undergarments; with no waistcoat [*zhilet*], my clothes were covered with a soldier's overcoat [*shinel'*] with burnt edges and strapped with a wide French cuirassier's *porter l'epée* that I found on the road ...

Personal hygiene was difficult to maintain and many suffered from parasites: 'I could not change my shirt in a very long time and slept dressed,' Muravyev recalled. 'My clothes were replete with lice who constantly bothered me; sitting by the fire, I killed them by hundreds. I often took off my shirt and steamed it over the fire, taking pleasure in the cracking sound of burning lice.' Dmitri Bronevskii, a midshipman recently transferred to the infantry, also complained about wearing the same shirt for two months: 'One can imagine,' he wrote, 'what happened to my body after who knows what insects infested this shirt. The only way to get rid of them was through steaming [...] It was so pleasant to put on the shirt after this cleansing.'[371]

Kutuzov knew of the hardships his men endured and he tried to inspire them anyway he could. As one participant recalled:

> the Field Marshal came across the Life Guard Izmailovski Regiment and inquired if they had enough bread: 'None, Your Excellency,' was their response. 'And wine?' – 'None, Your Excellency' – 'How about meat?' – 'None.' With frowning face, Kutuzov told the troops: 'I will have those commissariat officials hanged. Tomorrow you will receive bread, wine,

meat, and will have time to rest.' 'Thank you Your Excellency!' the soldiers shouted. 'But …' Kutuzov added, 'while you rest, the villains [*zlodei*] will make good use of this time to make their escape!' 'We do not need these things,' yelled the troops, 'we need no wine or biscuits, just let us pursue the enemy.'

By 25 November, as Napoleon's forces approached Borisov and Chichagov erroneously began redeploying his troops southwards, Kutuzov's main forces were still far away from the future battlefield on the Berezina. Count Ozharovsky moved south and occupied Mogilev, where he captured vast supply depots. Platov's Cossacks were at the village of Nacha and Yermolov rested his men at Krupki. Miloradovich, with the 2nd and 7th Infantry and 2nd Cavalry Corps, marched from Kopys to Staroselye and reached Tolochin. The Cossack *Ataman* was the closest to the retreating army and should have been more aware of his actions, but he failed to grasp the situation correctly. On 24 November, after hearing from Wittgenstein of Victor's movement to Batury, Platov assumed that Napoleon would take a northerly direction. Then, as he learned of Chichagov's capture of Borisov on 25 November, Platov changed his opinion and became convinced that the northern route was well protected and the enemy would be forced to seek a southerly escape route towards Bobruisk. Accordingly, on 25–26 November, he was busy redeploying his troops to the south of the main road, but the movement was complicated by dense forest and marshes.[372]

Kutuzov was well aware of Napoleon's march on Borisov but still continued to believe that he would make a turn south. Despite the growing distance between his army and Napoleon's, he was in no hurry to assist Chichagov, who could not stop the Grand Army alone. As Kharkevich commented, 'Kutuzov willingly deprived himself of the chance to control these critical actions and thus remained a mere observer of subsequent events.' This can be partially explained by Kutuzov's assumption that Wittgenstein would arrive on the Berezina in time to assist the Admiral, and his (erroneous) belief that Chichagov had merged with Ertel's corps and had some 40,000 men. Furthermore, as previously discussed, Kutuzov sent several letters to Chichagov sharing his considerations, which only further misled the Admiral into believing that Napoleon would be seeking to escape southwards.

Kutuzov's sluggish actions had long been the subject of debate, and contemporaries were no less divided than future historians. As early as 12–13 November, Emperor Alexander wrote a few harshly worded letters to Kutuzov that reveal how exasperated he was by the conduct of the war. He spoke of Kutuzov's

inexplicable inaction following our victory of the 6th [18] of October at Tarutino, which wasted all the benefits we could have gained from it, as well as your unnecessary and distressing retreat following the battle at Maloyaroslavets, which destroyed all the advantages of your position, since you had an opportunity to accelerate the enemy's retreat to Vyazma and isolate there the three corps of Davout, Ney and the Viceroy [i.e. Eugène] [...] Having a superb light cavalry, you did not have [place?] enough outposts on the Smolensk road, which could have informed you of the enemy's actual movements [...] Your actions put Count Wittgenstein's Corps in jeopardy, since Napoleon can leave three corps in front of you and, having reinforced St Cyr with his Imperial Guard, attack Wittgenstein with superior forces. I advise you that all misfortunes stemming from these actions would be your personal responsibility.[373]

A week later Kutuzov responded, assuring the Tsar that Wittgenstein was facing no immediate threat and that 'the enemy army is no position to break away from me. I am constantly following on his heels'. Yet Kutuzov knew quite well that he was misleading Alexander, since in separate letters to his local commanders, he discussed exactly the same possibility of Napoleon joining his forces with St Cyr against Wittgenstein.[374] General Alexei Yermolov could see that

Napoleon retreated with incredible haste, fearing to be overtaken by our army before crossing the Berezina. But he had nothing to fear since, despite the precise intelligence on the enemy forces, the Field Marshal refused to move, believing that the prolonged retreat, worsening winter weather, raging hunger and the forthcoming combat on the Berezina would bring the French army to the verge of destruction without the involvement of the main army.[375]

Kutuzov's actions particularly incensed his old nemesis, former Chief of Staff Levin Bennigsen. Commenting on the Field Marshal's orders and his belief that Napoleon would turn south, Bennigsen wrote:

On 7 [19] November our army left the main road and, consequently, separated from the enemy, proceeding along local paths to the village of Dobroye. This village was located not far from the main road, on which the enemy was moving to Borisov. We knew of his direction, and yet, we maintained our march, further distancing ourselves from the enemy. On 8 [20] November we reached Romanovo, having covered 25 *verstas*. On the 9th [21st], the army approached Lanenki, where it remained until the 10th [22nd]. On the 11th it marched to Morozovo (18 *verstas*) and on the 12th to Kopys (18 *verstas*), where it had a break on the 13th. Looking at the map, one can observe that these settlements are not very far from the main road leading to Borisov. Is it possible to believe that Prince Kutuzov, who had 40 Cossack regiments, was unaware that the enemy was making no diversion to induce us into believing that he was intending to leave the main road? Yet, Prince Kutuzov was doing exactly this, moving away from the main road with each march: on the 14th [26] he was at Staroselye (17 *verstas*); on the 15th – at Krugloye (28 *verstas*); on the 16th – at Somre (36 *verstas*), on the 17th – at Mikheyevki (16 *verstas*) and on the 18th [30th] he finally reached Usha, where our army crossed the Berezina.'[376]

Thus, the old Field Marshal would play virtually no role in the events on the Berezina, where his troops could have destroyed the Grand Army. By the time he reached Usha on the last day of November, Napoleon had already made his escape ...

26 November: The Crossing, Day 1

After marching all night, Jomini,[377] Eblé and Chasseloup brought their troops and six wagonloads of tools, two forges and two wagons of coal to Borisov by 5 a.m. on 25 November.[378] After a meeting with Oudinot and his staff, it was agreed that two companies of *pontonniers* and one of sappers would remain in town to divert the Russians, while the remaining companies would proceed to Studyanka, where they arrived between 4 and 5 p.m.[379] By now, Aubry and Corbineau, dispatched earlier by Oudinot, had been busy gathering and preparing bridge materials for some twelve hours. The newly-arrived Eblé and Chasseloup thus found about twenty bridge trestles completed by Corbineau and Aubry, using timbers from the nearby village.[380] Caulaincourt described Corbineau doing his best to 'prepare whatever was necessary in the way of bridge construction. Without tools, without iron, with virtually no material [...] his zeal, aided by the tireless energy of Colonel Chauveu of the artillery triumphed over all difficulties'. Corbineau himself described building the first few trestles with the help of Oudinot's *pontonniers* led by Aubry on 24 November, while Oudinot was trying to feint a crossing at Ukholody. To avoid Russian attention, Corbineau had hidden his men in a ravine half a mile east of the river, out of the enemy's sight. To obtain essential materials, he had several ammunition wagons destroyed to get clamps and nails and a few houses dissembled to obtain necessary planks.[381] As Curély writes, the cavalrymen lacked supplies and dispatched a foraging party to obtain some provisions. The troopers soon came across a farm, still occupied by some Cossacks, where they captured ten Cossack horses and, most importantly, 'provisions of all kinds, more than 200 sacks of flour and alcohol for the entire brigade'.[382]

* * *

The Battle of the Berezina

Upon their arrival, Eblé and Chasseloup examined the area and, as Marbot noted, 'no enemy preparations for defence were to be seen on the further bank, so that if the Emperor had kept the pontoons which he had burnt a few days before [at Orsha], the army might have crossed the Berezina on the spot'. Wilson agrees: 'if only fifteen of the sixty [pontoons] had been preserved, a bridge might have been constructed in two or three hours'. Besides lacking equipment, Eblé also faced another major problem. A recent thaw had melted the ice and the river, which would have been frozen and passable a few days before, was now flowing and full of large blocks of ice.[383] Eblé inspected Corbineau's completed trestles and found most of them (Dutch Captain, George Diederich Benthien talks of twenty) built from thin wood and not solid enough to withstand the weight of a crossing army. He and Chasseloup decided to build three bridges: two were to be constructed by *pontonniers*, and one by sappers, assisted by the marines, many of them veterans of the Danube crossings of 1809.[384] So the night of 25/26 November was spent gathering material for new trestles and preparing planks and fascines. Napoleon, unaware of the problems his engineers faced, kept urging them to start construction at 2 a.m. but the order was simply ignored.[385] Pils recorded in his journal that

> The aspect of the countryside was gripping; the moon illuminated the ice flows of the Berezina and, beyond the river, a Cossack picket made up of only four men. In the distance beyond, one could see a few red-tinged clouds seemingly drift over the points of the first trees; they reflected the campfires of the Russian army ...[386]

As previously stated, the river was not frozen but covered in large chunks of floating ice. The precise width of the river is hard to determine, due to variations in contemporary sources, and as a Dutch officer, Tellegen of the 128th, remarked, most participants later exaggerated the width of the Berezina, which was 'within its banks [...] as all rivers are in that country in the winter season'. Marbot agreed that the

> river, which has been imaginatively described as of enormous width, is at most as wide as the Rue Royale at Paris, opposite the Ministry of Marine. As for its depth, it will be enough to say that the three cavalry regiments of Corbineau's brigade had forded it without any mishap three days before, and did so again. Their horses either never lost the bottom or had at most to swim two or three fathoms.

The riverbed itself was about 80–100 metres wide; Napoleon's 29th Bulletin claimed '40 *toises* [~80m]', Chapelle and Chapuis believed the river was '50 *toises*

[~100m]' wide, while Benthien refers to '280–300 feet [84–90m]' and 2–4 metres deep on average; but the half-frozen swampy and low banks, which Caulaincourt described as 'a good five hundred yards wide', required the construction of larger bridges that would extend for some distance at either end, since 'saddle-horses could only cross [them] with difficulty, while wagons went in up to the axletrees'.[387] A greater obstacle was the Russian control of the heights on the western bank, which allowed them to direct artillery fire against any bridging attempt.

By early morning Eblé and Chasseloup realized there was not enough material for three bridges and decided to continue work on two: one for the infantry and another for cavalry and transports. This would naturally slow down the crossing and Murat's chief of staff, Belliard, mused in his journal: 'Two bridges are insufficient for one army; a third one is necessary for a faster crossing.'[388] There seems to have been an acute professional rivalry between the sappers, engineers and *pontonniers*, since, as Marbot tells us, 'each of them claimed the sole right to build the bridges, with the result that they got in each other's way, and no progress had been made …' The *pontonniers*, many of them Dutchmen, were experts at making trestle bridges and they had the necessary equipment that Eblé had shrewdly preserved at Orsha. Chasseloup, realizing that lack of equipment prevented his men from doing anything independently, soon placed them at Eblé's disposal. The engineers gathered material while the *pontonniers* fixed the trestles.[389] Lejeune remembered 'all the wood found in the village, even that of which the houses were built, being quickly converted into trestles, beams, planks, etc.' François Pils, with his sketchbook in hand (see his drawing), recorded 'the preparatory work and construction of trestles was conducted behind a fold in the ground encasing the river and so preventing enemy scouts from seeing the workmen as they moved about'.[390]

In the meantime, Napoleon, after proceeding from Loshnitsa to Borisov, reached the latter late in the evening on 25 November and spent the night at the estate of Baron Kossak (who managed the nearby estate of Prince Dominic Radziwiłł) at Stary Borisov, before departing at dawn on the 26th.[391] During his brief stay at Borisov, the Emperor, with Murat, Berthier, Eugène, Caulaincourt and Duroc, briefly examined the local fortifications. He seems to have still considered marching on Minsk, where he hoped to join Schwarzenberg.[392] Caulaincourt tells us of Napoleon's discussion with the commissary officer regarding the availability of supplies and the nature of the country around Minsk; he also inquired about the route through Ukholody. He then spent some time observing Russian positions and Sergeant Major Calosso could see Napoleon 'standing a few paces away from us without dismounting, and train his spyglass on the enemy camp [at Borisov]', where Dumonceau could see a 'considerable state of agitation'. The bridge was still standing across the river, broken in several places but not destroyed in its entirety, except for some 40 feet of it missing on the Russian side. So Caulaincourt and Napoleon 'had gone on foot to the end of the remaining quarter of the bridge'.[393] With the Russian forces massed around the *tête-de-pont* and artillery – Legler counted 18–20 cannon on the far bank – deployed on the nearby heights, Napoleon realized the difficulty of breaking across the river at Borisov.

Only after receiving General Corbineau's update on the work at Studyanka and Victor's report on Wittgenstein's pursuit, did Napoleon make his final decision to cross the river at that location. To keep the Russians guessing, he continued diversions southwards and Calosso saw new orders being delivered to the various divisions: 'The 1st Cuirassier Brigade which had bivouacked behind us, mounted and took the road that follows the Berezina downstream. A few battalions, followed by a lot of military baggage, marched in the same direction.' Oudinot was told to move the rest of his corps to Studyanka at night but some 100 Dutchmen from the 124th Line and 150 Württembergers remained at Borisov to guard prisoners and conduct a diversion.[394] To inspire his troops, Napoleon also granted various promotions and rewarded troops for their service. The Swiss troops were among those who received the Legion of Honour: the 1st Swiss earned thirteen, the 2nd Swiss eight, while the 3rd and 4th Swiss received six awards each. Although proud to receive this highest recognition, the soldiers also realized its fleeting importance: 'It all looks very nice,' one of them commented, 'if we were at home one could just be proud of it, but we are not there yet. There will be many empty shakos before then.'[395] Looking across the river, Maurice Tascher could see the reason for this: 'the whole line of the Russian campfires …' At the same time, Dominique Larrey seemed to forget the perils of life, as he was fascinated to see 'how serene the sky was and the cold rather sharp. I could not help being struck by the appearance of a comet, moving parallel to the horizon and situated due north. It seemed to be going down toward the Arctic pole …'[396]

As Oudinot's men marched northwards, Captain Abraham Rosselet, of the 3rd Swiss, saw his comrades moving in 'the strictest order and profound silence, in closed ranks, and with no one permitted, on any pretext, of leaving them'.[397] Arriving at Studyanka, as Calosso described, Oudinot's men 'without delay, got busy demolishing the best preserved houses to obtain the materials needed to build a bridge'. The rest of the Grand Army was still en route: the survivors of the III and V Corps (led by Zajączek after Poniatowski was wounded)[398] were between Loshnitsa and Nemanitsa, Eugène's troops at Nacha, Davout between Nacha and Krupki and the IX Corps at Ratulichy.[399] Observing troops at Borisov, Pastoret reflected upon

the horror of our situation. Our men were ready to drop with exhaustion, discouraged by hunger, worn out by cold. Half of them no longer bore any weapons. The cavalry was destroyed [...] the artillery altogether lost, and gunpowder was lacking. It was in these circumstances we, after five weeks of marching, were going to have to cross a difficult swift-flowing river, carry positions, and triumph over three armies who were waiting for us ready to deliver a last blow.[400]

Later that morning Napoleon travelled to Studyanka, where the *pontonniers* and engineers were preparing materials for the bridges. He reached Oudinot's headquarters inside a lumber cottage between 7 and 8 a.m., just as Pils

opened its door, which was fixed by a tourniquet and bumped into the Emperor, who asked, 'Is Oudinot there?' Recognizing Napoleon's voice, the Marshal came hurrying out. His Majesty was wearing a fur and a green velvet cap, lined with furs, which came down over his eyes. The Prince of Neuchâtel [Berthier], who was with him, was wearing the same costume, albeit of a violet colour. [Oudinot] took them down to the Berezina's bank. After going upstream as far as Studyanka, the Emperor examined the area, visited the works and asked about the state of II Corps.

The Marshal told him that the corps had preserved all its artillery as well as 'fourteen additional pieces captured from the Russians on the banks of the Drissa'. The troops were eager to fight Chichagov's army as soon as they crossed the river, Oudinot informed Napoleon, who rubbed his hands together and cheerfully noted, 'Very well! You will be my locksmith to open the passage.'[401]

Despite the seeming success of Oudinot's diversions, Napoleon was still anxious on the score of Russian resistance to the crossing. His concerns were soon allayed. Earlier that morning, as Rapp remembered, Marshal Ney took him aside and told him:

'Our position is unheard of. If Napoleon gets away with it today, he is the Devil himself.' We were quite worried, as we unquestionably had every reason to be. [Murat] came up to us, he was no less worried: 'I have suggested to Napoleon,' he told us, 'that he save himself and cross the river a few miles away. I have got Poles who would answer for his safety and take him to Vilna. But he won't hear of this proposal. For my part, I do not believe we can escape.' All three of us had the same thought; Murat went on: 'We are all dead men because there can be no question of surrendering.'[402]

One can only imagine their utter surprise when they suddenly observed the Russians marching off downstream. The enemy campfires went out and masses of troops vanished: 'All we saw were the tails of [Russian] columns losing themselves in the woods, and 500 or 600 Cossacks spread about the fields,' recalled Rapp. Not far away, the Swiss officer Legler could not believe his eyes when 'some 1,500 enemy infantrymen filed by, taking with them two field guns and between 600 and 800 Cossacks. The Russians seemed to be nothing but passive spectators'.[403] Calosso overheard his comrades in the 24th Chasseurs, equally surprised by the enemy's movements, exclaim, 'We will just have to believe those imbeciles do not grasp the advantages of their position.'

Meantime, Rapp hurried to headquarters to inform Napoleon of this fortuitous turn of events. He found the Emperor deep in conversation with Marshal Oudinot: 'Sire, the enemy has quit his position' – 'It cannot be possible!' At that moment, Murat and Ney arrived confirming Rapp's news. Napoleon rushed outside and looked at the riverbank, where the Russians were indeed absent. 'Transported with joy,' Rapp continues, 'Napoleon threw a glance to the other side of the river. "I have fooled the Admiral (he could not pronounce Tchitschacof's [*sic*] name). He thinks I am at the spot of the feint attack. He is hurrying off to Borisov!" His eyes lit up with joy and impatience.'[404]

Despite the persisting danger, the Grand Army now faced a more favourable situation. By 26 November, Russian forces were deployed over a wide area and only a small portion were close enough to contest the crossing. With Czaplic on his way to Borisov, only Kornilov's detachment was guarding the riverbank. Langeron was at Borisov, while Chichagov and O'Rourke were two or three marches from the town. Wittgenstein's corps was in and around Barany in the north-east. Kutuzov was still further away east, with the main army at Kopys, Miloradovich at Tolochin, while Platov and Yermolov were at Slobodki (near Krupki) and Malyavka.

After Czaplic's main force withdrew, all Napoleon could see on the opposite bank were a few Cossacks on the edge of the woods. Around 8 a.m.[405] he ordered his cavalry to secure a bridgehead on the opposite bank (see below). Caulaincourt described Napoleon examining the riverbank and deploying 'strong artillery' (from the Guard Artillery and II Corps) on the heights to protect the crossing.[406] The Emperor then told Eblé to start the bridge construction and moments later, Captain Benthien led some 200 *pontonniers* from the 7th and 11th Companies of the 1st Battalion into the icy water to start installing the trestles.[407] The distance between the bridges remains unclear. The eyewitnesses, Chapelle and Chapuis, noted that the bridges were '100 *toises* [~ 200 metres]' apart, a number repeated by Vlijmen, Roguet and others. Adam Zamoyski's recent study refers to a distance of 50 metres, while German historian Heinrich Beitzke favoured '250 steps' and Russian scholar Ivan Kolodeev, who lived in Borisov and spent years researching the environment, believed the bridges were 182 metres apart; he even had two small monuments constructed at the supposed bridge entrances. Interestingly, Major General Foerster, who examined the bridges three weeks after the battle, noted that they were 'some 500 *sazhens* [~ 1,000 metres]' from each other.[408]

Captain Arnoldi, who commanded the 13th HAC and was left with Kornilov's detachment, was standing on a hill early that morning observing through a spyglass the opposite riverbank, where he saw the enemy gathering woods, hay and other materials. He, like other Russian scouts, was handicapped by the fact that the eastern bank was higher than their own, so he could not see over the crest of the embankment, where the *pontonniers* were building trestles. Still, he saw

> numerous officials at one site and then further away, some forty guns deployed on the heights to the left of the village (Studyanka) and overlooking the place where the woods and hay were gathered. Seeing this, there could be no doubt that the crossing would take place at this site and not somewhere else.

Czaplic referred to 'fifty heavy calibre guns' deployed on the heights and claimed that 'this enormous battery forced me to recall all my outposts and, not to endanger them in vain, I deployed them in the woods next to the position'.[409] A messenger was immediately dispatched to Chichagov with this crucial news. Arnoldi, in charge of four remaining guns, unlimbered on an unfavourable position on the edge of the woods and swamps, fully realizing the seriousness of his situation. His battery included only light pieces that could not reach their targets on the opposite bank. So Arnoldi 'hoped to at least inflict some damage on the bridge and target its workers when the construction reached the middle of the river'.[410]

At this dramatic and decisive hour, General Eblé rose to the occasion and his unwavering leadership, in effect, saved the Grand Army. As one scholar justly noted, 'the name of Jean Baptiste Eblé is one to be uttered with all honour and reverence as that of a man who, besides being a master of his profession, was in very truth a hero, upright, modest, self-sacrificing, and literally faithful unto death'.[411] The son of an artillery sergeant, Eblé was 54 years old in 1812, with thirty-nine years of military service behind him. After enlisting in the Auxonne Artillery Regiment in 1773, he rose to captain in 1792 and served in the Armies of the Ardennes and North during the Revolutionary Wars. His talents were quickly recognized and he was promoted to general of division in 1793 and commanded artillery units in Netherlands, southern Italy and on the Rhine in 1794–1800. Napoleon appreciated his skills and made him a member of the Artillery Council in 1801. Four years later, Eblé became chief of artillery in I Corps and participated in the War of the Third Coalition. In 1806, he saw fighting in Prussia, where he later served as a military governor of Magdeburg.

The Battle of the Berezina

In 1808–1810, he was the Minister of War in Jérôme Bonaparte's Kingdom of Westphalia, playing a prominent role in creating the Westphalian Army. In 1811, Eblé was sent to command artillery in Portugal and was present at the famous sieges of Almeida and Ciudad Rodrigo before returning to Germany, where Napoleon was assembling his Grand Army for the invasion of Russia. In 1812, he was made commander of the *pontonnier* units and constructed bridges over the Nieman, Dvina and Dnieper rivers as the invasion progressed deeper into Russia.[412]

Now, in November of 1812, Eblé stood on the bank of the Berezina supervising probably the most important mission of his career. It was said in the army that he and Larrey, the chief physician, could ask the impossible and it would be done. And Eblé did just that. As one historian aptly described, he

> declared to his troops that the fate of the army was in their hands, inspired them with his own sentiments and obtained from them promise of the most absolute devotion – a promise which bound them, although they had just marched during two days and nights, and the cold had again become most intense, to remain in the water throughout the whole of the night and the following day, in the midst of enormous masses of ice, and exposed to the bullets of the enemy, without an hour of repose, and only taking time to snatch a morsel of the roughest food.[413]

The precise number of men involved in constructing the bridges varies, but there were probably over 500 men involved in the operation. It is often assumed that the brave men who ventured into the river were French, when in reality only a small portion of them were from France proper. We had already discussed Captain Benthien, who commanded the Dutch *pontonniers* building the infantry bridge. Captain Busch led another team of Dutchmen working on a second bridge.[414] Polish involvement in bridge construction is frequently overlooked. Yet some eighty men from the 3rd Engineer Company (Captain Jean Fiedorowicz) and 5th Engineer Company (Captain Salvator Rakowiecki), assisted by Captain Jean Bujalski's twenty *pontonniers* and supervised by five officers contributed to the work.[415] When called upon, the *pontonniers* had stripped to their underpants and, struggling against the river current and ice, they, as Bourgogne describes, 'worked, standing up to their shoulders in ice-cold water, encouraged by their General'. Marbot watched as these brave men 'leapt into the cold water of the Berezina and worked there for six or seven hours, though there was not a drop of spirits to give them, and they had no bed to look forward to for the following night, but a field covered with snow'. Captain Benthien described that his men came out of the water stiff and half-dead from cold and, to find volunteers for the work, he had to offer a reward of fifty francs.[416]

One shudders to think of the desolate conditions in which these brave souls worked. Mecklenburg officer Otto Raven described the weather as 'very cold with no wind'[417] and Ségur tells us that

> the rising of the waters had made the traces of the ford entirely disappear. It required the most incredible efforts on the part of our unfortunate sappers [i.e. *pontonniers*], who worked in the water up to their mouths, struggling against the ice carried down by the current. Some of them died of the cold or were forced under by the great blocks of ice.

According to Pils, the *pontonniers* 'went into the water up to their necks with a courage of which one can find no other example in history. Some fell dead, and disappeared with the current, but the sight of such a terrible end did nothing to weaken the energy of their comrades'. Later that day, Maciej Rybinski, of the 15th Polish Line, saw a group of Polish *pontonniers* working on the bridge:

> Half immersed in the water, these men were repairing separated beams and other damage. I told the officers in Polish, 'These men are so devoted to their mission! This night they may repair the damage but tomorrow they will all succumb to cold and will die.' They replied, 'Yes, but the army will pass through.'[418]

According to Captain Rigau (from Berthier's staff) these men showed 'an heroic devotion – quite superhuman; they perished sacrificing their lives; their sole motive being honour and obedience to duty'. Laugier speaks of the 'noble sacrifice and devotion of *pontonniers*' whose 'memory will remain immortal'. Years later, Marshal Davout remembered how 'the army admired the courageous devotion of the sappers and *pontonniers*, who spent hours working in the icy water'.[419] Rybinski was right and most of the men working in the river died over the following days and, of some 200 Dutchmen Captain Benthien led into the waters, only forty remained by 29 November.[420] Eblé himself would become seriously sick and die of exhaustion at Königsberg on 31 December 1812. As Captain Heinrich von Brandt of the 2nd Regiment (Vistula Legion) justly remarked:

> From the point of view of aesthetics, the [infantry] bridge certainly lacked a great deal. But when one considers under what conditions the bridge was constructed and that it undoubtedly saved the French Army from total catastrophe, and that for each life sacrificed in its construction a thousand lives were saved, then it is obvious that this bridge was the most sublime achievement of the war, perhaps of any war.

The Battle of the Berezina

A British officer praised these men for indefatigable powers of endurance and labour, which 'entitled them to a high meed of praise: the Berezina was for them a monument of reputation'.[421] Oudinot's aide-de-camp, Le Tellier, commented:

> When the foundations of that historic bridge, the sole hope of safety offered us, had to be laid in the Berezina, at the voice of their chief those men of duty and resolution marched silently into the water, never interrupting their work save to turn aside the huge pieces of ice which threatened to cut them in two like a sword. They drove in the piles, the ground-work of the construction, and went on striking their blows until the moment came when they felt death seize them. Not one came out alive, but others stepped in to complete the work – the work of a day which should leave an immortal memory![422]

Participants left varying accounts on Napoleon's actions that morning. We know from François Pils that the Emperor, after ordering the construction, had returned to Oudinot's quarters and 'was served with a cutlet which he ate standing up'. He then returned to the bridge, where he was seen standing by many participants. Some portrayed him as dejected and gloomy and Ségur and Constant described the Emperor, in a fit of despair, ordering the burning of the eagles, which represented 'a sad spectacle, the men stepping from the ranks one by one, and throwing down [into fire] what they loved more than their life'. Yet, Gourgaud, famously, denied any of this, noting ironically that 'it was impracticable [to burn them] as these eagles were made of copper', while Castellane recorded the destruction of eagles belonging to cavalry regiments days earlier at Bobr. Jakob Walter, a private in a Württemberg regiment from the III Corps, claimed that Napoleon's 'outward appearance seemed indifferent and unconcerned over the wretchedness of his soldiers; only ambition and lost honour may have made themselves felt in his heart; and, although the French and Allies shouted into his ears many oaths and curses about his own guilty person, he was still able to listen to them unmoved'. Borcke wrote that 'Napoleon stood continually at the entrance to the bridge' inspiring the troops with his presence. Tellegen also saw Napoleon 'at the bridge with Oudinot and at least twenty other generals behind him, such as the King of Naples [Murat], Ney, etc., he was dressed in his grey coat over the Green Outfit, the outfit he cherished most'. Pils recalled the Emperor watching the *pontonniers* 'without leaving the riverbank, where he stood with [Oudinot], Prince Murat and other generals, while [Berthier] sat on the snow expediting correspondence and writing out orders for the army'. Yet, some soldiers (Bourgogne) claimed that at one moment 'the Emperor himself [was seen] handing wine to the *pontonniers*'. Dumonceau recalled Napoleon 'walking to and fro along the shore from one bridge to the other'. One moment, Calosso saw the Emperor pass close by us to mount a small hillock that dominated the river on our side. All our eyes were fixed on him. Not a sigh, not a murmur arose from our ranks. The *pontonniers* throwing the bridge were up to their necks in water. They were wholly unopposed but it was exceedingly cold. The Emperor was generous with encouragement.

Marbot recalled 'the Emperor striding about, accompanied by Murat, going from one regiment to another, and talking to men as well as officers'. Lieutenant Colonel Baudus thought that 'at this solemn moment Napoleon himself recovered all the elevation and energy that characterized him'. Overall, most participants agree that Napoleon demonstrated composure in what was a critical situation and exerted strong influence over the troops. Laugier, writing fifteen years after the battle, felt that 'the troops – no matter their origin, be it French, Italian, Polish or German, suffering from lack of food and alcohol, exhausted and tormented – were inspired by the sight of their Emperor, forgetting their hardships and misfortune'. Calosso believed that the most important factor was 'at such critical circumstances we still had faith in his genius …'[423] This sentiment is echoed in the memoirs of Jean François Boulart, who noted that the army's confidence in the Emperor was 'prodigious', and by Ségur who explained,

> The sight of its Emperor revived [the army]. It had been long accustomed not to look to him for its means of support, but solely to lead it to victory. This was its first unfortunate campaign, and it had had so many fortunate ones! It only required being able to follow him. He alone, who had elevated his soldiers so high, and now sunk them so low, was yet able to save them. He was still, therefore, cherished in the heart of his army, like hope in the heart of man![424]

The Battle of Brili
Meantime, Arnoldi, standing next to his cannon across the river, watched as the *pontonniers* were constructing the bridge and, despite the distance, decided to do something to delay them. Low-lying marshy terrain prevented him deploying his guns close to the river, so 'when the bridge construction began in earnest', Arnoldi explained,

> I decided to open fire to see if the cannonball would somehow reach the opposite bank; and if not, then to see where they would land to determine when I could inflict substantial damage on the enemy. I personally aimed the guns and gave the order to fire but we barely fired the first round when we were greeted by a forty-gun battery that showered us with cannonballs and soil from head to foot. Men and horses fell all around me and I was

convinced that I had no means of preventing the crossing, and especially with my guns, whose rounds were landing in the middle of the river, while the enemy cannon, being of larger calibre and firing from higher ground, could pick us out at will as if from a rifle. As soon as I shared my thoughts with Major General Kornilov, a Cossack officer appeared from the left side of the road to Zembino with news that the enemy cavalry, in considerable numbers, was fording the river directly in front of Zembino and that both Cossack regiments were retreating.

Since the western bank was covered with thick forest, Kornilov dispatched his infantry to delay the enemy cavalry, while Arnoldi redirected his artillery to the left, to face the new threat.[425] On the French side, Rossetti saw Arnoldi's guns rolling into position and firing before suffering from counter-fire. He noted that 'The Emperor then ordered our guns to remain silent for fear of their recalling Tchaplitz [*sic*] as the bridge had hardly been commenced'.[426] Rapp's memoirs provide an interesting detail: the French battery was commanded by 'Brechtel, a brave officer with a wooden leg. During the action, a roundshot had carried the leg away and thrown him over. "Fetch me another leg out of wagon No. 5," he told one of his gunners. He then strapped it on, and continued firing'.[427]

The Cossack retreat was caused, according to Caulaincourt, by 'a number of light cavalrymen – our fearless Poles – [who] crossed [the river] without difficulty, and drove away some Cossacks prowling on the other bank, who never fired a shot until they had been driven beyond the marshland'.[428] Colonel Jacqueminot, Oudinot's aide-de-camp, seems to have led the 7th (Boguslawski) and the 8th (Thomasz Lubienski) Polish Lancers and the survivors of the 18th Lithuanian Lancers (Count Karol Przezdziecki) in the first wave, followed by the 20th Chasseurs (led by Chef d'Escadron Sourd), each of whom had a *voltigeur* (from the 11th Light) riding pillion.[429] The Poles were leading the way and Załuski watched as 'under our eyes the Berezina ford was tried by an officer of Lubienski's 8th Regiment, aided by a few lancers'. They were followed, as Rossetti tells us, by some 'fifty *chasseurs* carrying *voltigeurs* on their cruppers. Then two frail boats which in twenty voyages carried over 400 men'.[430] Gourgaud also remembered 'three rafts' transporting the troops, which were the Polish infantry from the 1st and the 6th Regiments. The Emperor, 'impatient to secure the opposite bank',[431] also ordered Gourgaud to swim across to observe 'if the nature of the soil on the opposite bank would permit the passage of artillery, without being obliged to employ fascines'.[432]

As the cavalrymen entered the chilling waters of the river, the ice-floes bloodied their horses' chests. Marbot wrote that 'all our horses crossed the river easily', confirmed by Caulaincourt, who noted that 'there was no great depth except for a stretch of 20 or 30 feet, across which the horses had to swim to gain the other bank, which was rather steep. On our side the water came up to the horses' bellies'.[433] Dumonceau described the opposite bank as 'a low-lying marshy swamp rising farther off to slightly higher wooded ground that bounded it a thousand paces away. There were some groups of our cavalrymen who had just swum the river and were moving about in the distance to explore its limits. All eyes were fixed on them, anxiously waiting to see what they might find, for each of us appreciated the importance of the enemy not being there to dispute our crossing'.[434]

On the Russian side, Arnoldi observed

as the French *voltigeurs* and the infantry, transported by the cavalry across the river, spread inside the woods and drove back our infantry, while another enemy column proceeded along the road. At my position inside the woods, I could only deploy four guns in line and the road itself was so narrow that only two guns could be set up there with difficulty. Meantime, the enemy numbers increased and the bridge construction accelerated. There were no means to defend the crossing even before the French fording at Zembino, and, after the enemy cavalry forded and transported the infantry, it would have been senseless for MG Kornilov to remain at this position, exposing his troops to a flanking fire of the enemy's forty-gun battery without any opportunity to respond in kind. And so in this difficult situation this courageous general decided to make a fighting retreat, delaying the enemy at every step of the way.[435]

Jacqueminot, meanwhile, led several charges and, although the Russian infantrymen retreated in good order, one of them was captured. Young artillery officer François Lassus-Marcilly saw Jacqueminot as he had reached the far bank and seized a Russian infantryman (some sources refer to an NCO), whom he placed on his horse and brought back to the Emperor's bivouac: 'I will live for centuries before I forget that brief apparition,' Lassus-Marcilly wrote,

Dressed in a brilliant uniform, Jacqueminot halted his horse and threw the prisoner down just like a horseman might throw a truss of hay to the ground, and then went off, doubtless to change his clothes. Stupefied, the wretched soldier had difficulty in getting up, and blinded by the brightness of the fire put his hands in front of his eyes. 'How many men in your battalion?' the Emperor asked, a question translated by Prince Poniatowski or General Krasinski. Someone [it was Vincent Krasinski] replied, 'He does not know.' Same answer when the Emperor asked: 'How many men in your company?' and finally, 'In your squad?'[436]

The Battle of the Berezina

The prisoner was not able to tell him much but Napoleon did learn a crucial bit of information: Chichagov with the bulk of his forces was below Borisov and only a minor detachment stood in front of Studyanka.[437]

Back on the eastern riverbank, the *pontonniers* worked emphatically to finish the crossings. Rosselet could see Napoleon with

> his back resting against some trestles, his arms crossed inside his overcoat. Silent, having an air of not paying attention to what was going on, only fixing his glances from time to time on the *pontonniers* a few paces away, sometimes up to their necks amidst the ice-floes, busy placing the trestles, which they seemed to have the greatest difficulty in fixing deeply, while others, as soon as they were in place were laying the planks on them.

Napoleon seemed impatient to see the bridge complete and Roguet saw him 'personally encouraging the troops and putting his foot on each plank as it was laid'.[438] As he grew dissatisfied with the speed of construction, Napoleon occasionally had outbursts of ill temper. Captain Louis Bégos (of the 2nd Swiss) witnessed one of them:

> Napoleon was no longer the great Emperor I had seen at the Tuileries; he looked tired and worried [...] My friend Captain Rey of the 1st Regiment was in a good position to study him at his leisure and, like myself, he was struck by [Napoleon's] worried expression. Having dismounted, he was leaning against some beams and planks that were used in construction. He was looking down at the ground. Then with a preoccupied impatient air, he lifted his head and addressed General Eblé, 'It is taking a very long time, General! A very long time!' 'You can see, Sire,' [replied Eblé] 'that my men are up to their necks in the water, and the ice is delaying their work. I have no food or alcohol to warm them with.' 'That will do,' the Emperor replied. He stared at the ground but, a few moments later, he began complaining again, seemingly forgetting what the General had just told him.[439]

To facilitate approaches to the bridges, Eblé's men prepared and laid out dozens of fascines on the half-frozen marshes along the riverbank. Small wooden rafts were quickly assembled to put up trestles in the middle of the river. Still, many *pontonniers* had to work up to their chest in the icy waters, surrounded by large sheets of ice floating in the river. To allow the army to secure a bridgehead across the river, the *pontonniers* concentrated their efforts on the bridge for infantry and completed it around one o'clock in the afternoon.[440] The finished bridge was about 100 metres long and some 4 or 5 metres wide. It consisted of twenty-three trestles of varying height (between 1 and 3 metres) and placed at

2.5– to 5–metre intervals. Longitudinal stringers running between the peaks of the trestles supported planks laid across the width of the bridge. Limited in the choice of material, the *pontonniers* utilized all available woods, including fragile roof slats that were 'four or five *lignes* [1–1.25cm] thick' from nearby houses, and so had to place double and triple layers of planks, which were then covered with bark, hay or branches.[441] The *pontonniers* struggled to place and keep the trestles steady and Bourgogne tells us that 'it was a painful and difficult piece of work, as the trestles sank continually in the mud'. Napoleon's *Mamluk* Louis Etienne St Denis described seeing 'the roadway not more than a foot above the water, [which] did not seem to me very strong, especially as it had to resist a great quantity of ice blocks, which the river was bringing down pretty rapidly'. Borcke also confirms that the roadway was

> 'very close to the surface of the river' and notes that 'minor things, such as the breaking of individual surface planks, caused major delays and crowding, with people pressuring forward and to the side, which tripped many into the water …'[442]

As soon as the bridge was ready, Oudinot's corps was sent across the river. Chapelle and Chapuis tell us that 'Napoleon, who had not left the banks of the Berezina since early morning, now stood next to the bridge and watched the crossing of the II Corps, whose regiments were all in perfect order and full of ardour.'[443] Seeing Oudinot, the Emperor called out to him, 'Do not cross yet, you might be taken.' But Oudinot pointed to the men drawn up behind him and answered, 'I fear nothing in their midst, Sire!'[444] The first to cross were the Polish cavalry (2nd and 7th Lancers), followed by the 8th Chevauléger and Castex's light cavalry, the 23rd (some 500 men led by Colonel Marbot) and 24th Chasseurs. Then came the divisions of Legrand (26th Light, 19th, 56th, 128th Line, 3rd Portuguese), Maison (11th Light, 2nd, 37th and 124th Line) and Merle (some 800 men from 123rd Line, 3rd Croat, 1st, 2nd, 3rd and 4th Swiss regiments). One gun and a howitzer (*obusier*) with caissons were carefully transported in their wake as well. Towards 5 p.m. Dąbrowski's division began crossing the river. By early evening, Napoleon had moved some 6,000–9,000 men to the western bank.[445] While crossing the bridge, Gaspard Schumacher (of the 4th Swiss) saw Napoleon 'dressed in a grey overcoat and a fur cap' and surrounded by Murat, Berthier and other senior officers. Captain Rey and Jean-Marc Bussy, also Swiss, and the Italian Laugier, described how the troops, seeing Napoleon standing near the bridge, became inspired by his presence and began yelling 'Vive l'Empereur!' while crossing the bridge. As his regiment approached the bridge, Thomas Legler heard continuous shouts of 'Vive l'Empereur':

The Battle of the Berezina

When our turn came and we had to halt near the bridge, some words from the Emperor to General Merle reached our ears. 'Are you pleased with the Swiss, General?' he asked. 'Yes, Sire. If the Swiss attack as sharply as they know how to defend themselves, Your Majesty would be content with them.' 'Yes, I know they are good men.'

After reaching the opposite bank, Legler writes, 'we sent up a ringing cheer for the Emperor'.[446] The Allied troops then turned left and attacked Russian forces led by Kornilov, who slowly retreated on Stakhov. Pils described,

> As soon as the whole of the first brigade had reached the Minsk road, [Oudinot] ordered it to halt and wait for the rest of Legrand's division; he placed himself in observation with General Albert, following the movements of a strong party of Cossacks. At that moment two round shots flew by to his right: one of them knocked General Albert over, who, however, jumped up at once and exclaimed, 'These *canailles* do not even have any good powder or I would have been cut in two.'[447]

According to Arnoldi, Oudinot's attack began in earnest 'shortly after noon' and Kornilov's men, facing Oudinot in the front and bombarded from across the river, retreated for the next three hours before being reinforced by Czaplic, halfway between Brili and Stakhov. The latter had been 'twelve *verstas*' from Brili when he heard of the Allied crossing and hurried back at once.[448] Vaudoncourt described Czaplic's men being 'attacked in the wood that intersects the two roads from Zembin to Wesselovo and Borisov, and, after a smart contest, driven behind Brilova'.[449] The II Corps had thus established itself in position before Brili, where it could cover the passage of the rest of the Grand Army. At the same time, a small detachment – some 100 troopers from the 1st Polish Chasseurs and the 7th Polish Lancers, led by Konstantin Przebendowski and some fifty troopers under command of Bronikowski (whom Napoleon had just berated for his actions at Minsk and Borisov) – was sent towards Zembino. A Cossack outpost, deployed there, failed to destroy the local bridges and wooden causeways running through the marshes and across the Gaina rivulet, although these were already prepared for destruction. As Chambray explained, 'Nothing was more important than to occupy the road to Zembino because one and a half *lieue* [~6km] from Studyanka it crosses marshy woodland, impracticable for vehicles except when frozen hard or in very hot weather.' Wilson confirms: 'Had the Russians burnt or destroyed these bridges, the route would have been irreparably closed against the enemy's progress.'[450] But the Russian outposts failed. Later that day Przebendowski reported to Ney that he had 'arrived at Zembino without encountering anyone. All Cossacks retreated [...] Everyone assures me that there is no enemy on the road to Vilna [...] The bridges and dams are in good condition'. Ney forwarded the news to headquarters and Berthier, after reading the report, supposedly declared: 'We have won. We now have a completely clear route to advance on.'[451]

Reaching the front line, Czaplic stopped his troops on the edge of the Stakhov woods, so as not to expose them to enemy artillery fire, but was soon attacked by II Corps, which sought to prevent the Russians from threatening the crossing. Otroshenko remembered 'a bitter firefight in which we were driven to the woods. We gradually received reinforcements, but these were insignificant. Both sides fought relentlessly in this combat ...'[452] Not far from Stakhov Arnoldi finally found a position to deploy his twelve-gun battery and 'began to fire in every direction as rapidly as it was possible, which continued for some three hours'. He noted that 'only through the efforts of artillery and the incredible gallantry of the infantry, together with the dismounted Cossacks and part of cavalry was the enemy contained and not an inch of ground was surrendered despite the enemy's superiority in numbers'.[453] Malinovski recorded that 'our horse artillery pieces could not remain in position for long and only the Jägers, who took advantage of the woods, managed to contain enemy attacks, defending their positions the entire day and night, preventing the enemy from

Estimated Crossing Timeline, 26 November

8–9 a.m.	Jacqueminot forded the river to secure a bridgehead
1 p.m.	First, 'infantry' bridge was completed
1.15 p.m.	2nd and 7th Polish Lancers began crossing, followed by Castex's Brigade (23rd and 24th Chasseurs) and Przebendowski's Polish troops
2 p.m.	Oudinot's II Corps began crossing
	Legrand's division
	Maison's Division
	Merle's Division
4 p.m.	Second, 'artillery' bridge was completed
4.15 p.m.	II Corps' artillery began crossing, followed by portions of the Guard Artillery
5 p.m.	Dąbrowski's Polish infantry began crossing
8 p.m.	Second bridge collapses, artillery crossing interrupted
10 p.m.	III Corps began crossing on the first bridge, followed by Doumerc's cavalry division and V Corps
11 p.m.	Second bridge repaired and artillery crossing resumed.

capturing the heights'.[454] The Russians also began receiving reinforcements as the 38th Jägers and Tverskii and Kinburnskii Dragoons (led by Major Generals Laskin and Umanets) reached the battlefield. According to Russian sources, a battalion of the 38th Jägers, led by Major Tiratskii, made a successful bayonet attack, while the dragoons effectively engaged Oudinot's cavalry before being driven back by his cavalry and artillery. Czaplic then moved the dragoons back to protect the guns, while the Cossacks – Pozdneev's, Dyachkin's and Melnikov's – and the Pavlogradskii Hussars maintained pressure on the enemy.

The Russians enjoyed superiority in artillery (twelve against two) and Arnoldi commented that the Russian success in halting the enemy was

> largely due to enemy's lack of artillery, which could not be moved [in large numbers] across the river before the [second] bridge was completed in the early hours of the 15th [27 November]. We, on the other hand, had twelve guns which inflicted considerable casualties.

Oudinot certainly realized the danger and sought to mitigate it. His troops made several attacks against the battery and Arnoldi acknowledged:

> There were moments when our infantry retreated beyond the line on which our artillery was deployed in the woods and the French skirmishers approached in throngs, maintaining a strong fire against the cannon. Only the flashes of their muskets showed us where to direct the canister fire, which alone allowed our infantry to drive the enemy back beyond our front line. One moment the skirmishers attacked in a very large number and rushed yelling towards our battery, which was fortunately protected by two squadrons of the Kinburnskii Dragoons, which just arrived from Borisov. I shouted to them to dismount, which they accomplished at once and opened a battalion fire, while I directed my guns to fire canister, which halted the enemy, who tried to capture the guns at any cost.[455]

Towards the evening, Czaplic received the Kolyvanovskii and Kozlovskii Infantry Regiments (some 900 men with twenty-four guns) sent by Langeron from Borisov.[456] Major Naumov led a battalion of the Kozlovskii Regiment to reinforce the Russian right flank along the river, where he successfully counter-attacked and gained ground. Still, the French and Poles kept attacking in the centre and left flank until late evening. Oudinot described the enemy taking positions 'behind a ravine, where he has placed some more cannon, over and above those he had shown during the day'. Both sides suffered considerable losses and Larrey estimated up to 600 wounded among the Franco-Polish troops. Oudinot reported that his men lost 'a few killed, but considerable wounded', among whom was Dąbrowski (lightly injured) and 'the intrepid' General Legrand, who was seriously wounded.[457] The Marshal asked Napoleon to replace the latter with General Albert, 'the most capable of the officers of his rank'. Doumerc's cuirassiers, who had crossed the river late in the evening, played no role in this action and Oudinot complained to Berthier that 'If I had had cuirassiers, we would have achieved something outstanding today.' He also warned the Chief of *Etat Major* that: 'if we get engaged on the Minsk road, which is a continuous defile through forests, we shall absolutely lack for everything, and the enemy will be able to hold us up at each step.'[458]

On the Russian side, Czaplic claimed in his initial report that his losses were insignificant (compare to Larrey's far-fetched claim of 3,000 Russian POWs) and his memoirs refer to 380 men captured, including eight officers and a captain of the Imperial Guard. In his report to Chichagov, Czaplic complained about 'the enemy cannon, deployed on a very advantageous position [across the river]' that maintained fire on the Russian-occupied road, 'which had woods on both sides and the swamps extending to the river itself [...] All of this now makes it impossible for us to break through to Zembino'. He also informed Langeron of 'the enemy holding an excellent position and building two bridges under the protection of thirty guns'.[459] Trying to explain this first setback to Emperor Alexander, Chichagov took responsibility on himself:

> The battlefield was covered with bodies but, as it often happens, it was impossible to prevent an army, five times larger than mine and protected by artillery, from crossing the river. I must admit, Your Majesty, that even if I had guessed correctly and organized a more effective defence, the affair would have still resulted in the enemy's crossing. [Napoleon] had superiority in numbers and, occupying this point, he could not only set up a bridge upstream but also attack us in the flank and possibly inflict greater casualties.

Chichagov also tried to spread the responsibility to his fellow army commanders, who should have been assisting him in entrapment but instead were far from the banks of the Berezina: 'Besides, throughout all this time,' he advised Alexander, 'I had received no news of the arrival of our forces [Wittgenstein and Kutuzov] and Napoleon thus could bear down on us with all his strength before we received any kind of assistance.'[460] Langeron (and partially Czaplic) were as guilty of ineffective leadership as Chichagov. Russian historian Vasiliev has recently noted:

> Czaplic well understood that he should not leave the Veselovo-Zembino-Studyanka region, yet followed orders while Langeron, despite intelligence

giving him the right not to follow the order to recall Czaplic back to Borisov […] still followed through with it, and then, after hearing of [Czaplic's] situation, he dispatched only two regiments to Stakhov instead of marching with all his forces there.[461]

The assessment seems to be harsh, since one must consider Langeron's concern that Napoleon might be attempting a diversion while the real attack would be delivered at Borisov proper. And so he kept most of his forces to counter such a move. His decision, however, proved consequential: 'When Langeron arrived at Czaplic's position,' writes one participant

> it was already impossible to inflict losses on the enemy, and even less so to prevent his crossing: a large part of Napoleon's army was on this side of the river and, deploying columns and batteries, fought us without a pause, driving our small detachment so far back that we had no opportunity to harm the enemy troops crossing the river.[462]

By four o'clock in the afternoon, the second bridge, which was built for wagons and cannon, using trestles, beams and planks of larger dimensions, was completed. Due to the lack of planks, the *pontonniers* used, as Chapelle, Chapuis and Laugier attest, 'logs of 15–16 feet length and 3–4 inches wide'. Lacking men, General Aubry sent for more troops from several infantry regiments to make fascines to support the bridge's table, which was then covered with straw and mud to smooth the surface. Around 4.15 p.m., the artillery (some forty guns and 100 caissons) of II Corps crossed over to the western bank, followed by that of the Guard. General Neigre directed the passage of the 'grand artillery park' and as Fain describes, it contained some 250 artillery pieces with caissons. In addition, hundreds of other transports were gathered on the bank waiting their turn to cross.[463] St Denis described

> several generals, sword in hand, were holding back the multitude who were pressing forward at the approaches to the bridge; the Grand Equerry [Caulaincourt], who had charge of policing the crossing, sent across in an orderly manner and successively the transport of the Emperor's household and the artillery, directing the drivers to go slowly and at some distance apart in order not to strain the bridge. At the same time he made the grenadiers and *chasseurs* of the Old Guard march on either side of the vehicles …'[464]

Yet, the sheer number of transports presented an enormous logistical problem in the crossing. To start with, the movement of so many artillery pieces, caissons and transports had softened the soggy swamps, frozen by early frosts, delaying the movement of heavy transports, which sank deep into the mud. Furthermore, the hastily-erected structure could not withstand the weight of so much traffic and gave way under the weight.

During construction, the *pontonniers* faced a problem with the trestles sinking too deep into the mud and, having no time to use pilings to further support the trestles, they had to make them tall enough to be pounded deep into the riverbed without excessive settling. During the crossing, Chapelle and Chapuis tell us, some coachmen, eager to reach the perceived safety of the western bank, bounced and bumped their transports across the bridge too quickly, causing some trestles to sink deeper into the mud, warping the bridge's table. Around 8 p.m., the bridge collapsed when three trestles subsided too deep into the muddy bed of the river. The heroic men who built the bridge – Fain refers to 'our *pontonniers*, our marines, our sappers' – were resting around the fires, warming themselves and drying their soaked clothes, and now they had to lower themselves again into the frigid water, struggling to repair the bridge in the darkness. Standing on the shore, General Eblé directed the works, appealing to the *pontonniers'* sense of 'l'honneur et de la patrie'. With thermometer rapidly falling, the officers organized large bonfires and divided their companies into two groups, each working in the icy water for fifteen minutes at a time. Fain noted in his journal:

> Braving the cold, fatigue, exhaustion, even death, they were working ceaselessly, water up to their shoulders. The death they must find under the ice-floes is not less the death of brave men for that.

After three hours of agonizing labour, the bridge was repaired by 11 p.m. but at two in the morning (27 November) three more trestles, in the deepest part of the river, collapsed. Once again the *pontonniers* were called upon to wade out – some on rafts – into the freezing water, and, after four hours of work, they fixed the bridge by 6 a.m. on the 27th.[465]

Meanwhile, Chichagov still remained south of Borisov. During the night of 26 November, he received a new letter from Kutuzov, who again directed the Admiral's attention south. The Russian Field Marshal suggested that Napoleon, if unable to clear his way to Minsk via Borisov, would most certainly turn towards Pogost and Igumen. He then informed Chichagov of the location of the main Russian army, which, indirectly, revealed to the Admiral that he could hardly hope to receive any help from the Field Marshal. The letter further strengthened Chichagov's conviction that the Grand Army would seek escape in the south. In the morning of 26 November, the Admiral, however, began receiving conflicting reports. First came word from Cossack outposts near

The Battle of the Berezina

Ushkevichi, concerning an attempt by the enemy to build a bridge at Ukholody. Concerned by this development, Chichagov decided to move his army up and dispatched General Rudzevich with the 10th and 22nd Jäger Regiments, Aleksandriiskii Hussars and one light artillery company to take a position at Gliven, on the road to Borisov, with orders to prevent enemy crossings in the vicinity.[466] But he barely began making arrangements for the march from Zabashevichi when new intelligence arrived, revealing that the enemy bridging at Ukholody was, in reality, another diversion – the 'French' had abandoned the material on the riverbank and disappeared. The Cossacks, who dared to ford the river and reconnoitre, learned from the locals that the enemy force had quickly moved northwards.[467]

Then, around 10 a.m., Chichagov began receiving messages (as previously mentioned) from Czaplic and Langeron on the concentration of enemy forces at Borisov and 'immense enemy columns' moving further to the north, where artillery fire could be heard that morning. Langeron concluded that the enemy was probably attempting 'to cross the river 20–30 *verstas* north of Borisov in order to march [...] [towards] Vilna'.[468] Later, Czaplic informed the Admiral of the enemy attacking his detachment near Brili. Khrapovitskii maintains that 'Chichagov continued to hesitate, uncertain what was going on and whether the recent news was simply a diversion with which the enemy wanted to deflect his attention from the real crossing site.'[469] Simultaneously, O'Rourke reported that his scouts crossed the river and found no major enemy forces as far east as Pogost, but on their return, they captured forty Poles from the 15th Lancers. While rummaging through the documents of their squadron commander, Suliakowski, the Russians found a copy of the order that revealed Napoleon's intention to break through north of Borisov.[470] 'This officer's evidence,' writes Khrapovitskii, 'has finally revealed to us that we had been deceived and confused by the enemy's diversion and while all our attention was directed to the Nizhneye Berezino, the enemy was in reality seeking his escape north of Borisov.'[471]

Realizing the seriousness of the situation, Chichagov made arrangements to counter Napoleon's moves. He advised Langeron:

> If you are informed by Czaplic that the enemy is attempting to cross the river anywhere along his position, you must, without awaiting *any further permission* [my emphasis] from me, hurry there at once, leaving one battalion with artillery at the *tête-de-pont* to wait for Major General Rudzevich. Advise Czaplic that he must proceed to the enemy crossing site and seek to prevent it by all means.

The Admiral then ordered Count O'Rourke to leave one grenadier battalion with two guns at the village of Berezino and march with the rest of his men northwards. Major General Rudzevich was instructed to proceed without delay to Borisov: if he found Langeron already departed to assist Czaplic, then Rudzevich was to leave one battalion with two guns at the *tête-de-pont* and advance with the remaining troops to the enemy crossing site.[472] Colonel Lukovkin was told to remain with his regiment on the road to Igumen to watch out for enemy movements to the south. To improve communications, he instructed Czaplic (already in the midst of battle) and Cossack General Grekov VIII to establish a 'flying post' system between Zembino, Borisov and Nizhneye Berezino.[473] Chichagov himself planned to march with the army from Zabashevichi to reach Borisov by nightfall or at least to have a break at Gliven.

O'Rourke also dispatched Major Jason Khrapovitskii to Kutuzov with the urgent news. Khrapovitskii, having crossed the river at Berezino, rushed to Pogost, where he encountered Count Ozharovsky, who was moving with his detachment from Mogilev. Ozharovsky initially was sceptical of Khrapovitskii's account and delayed him for some time before finally dispatching another messenger to Kopys, who finally, on 28 November (!), informed Kutuzov of the developments at Studyanka.[474]

Back at the Berezina, Chichagov's orders could not be executed with sufficient speed. The main forces of the 3rd Western Army had to make an arduous march back from Zabashevichi, delayed by its own transports and artillery. By 10 p.m. on 26 November, only one division was able to reach Borisov, while the rest of the army was en route. O'Rourke, further to the south, received orders late that day and his detachment joined the army on the morrow. Still concerned about the enemy presence at Borisov, Langeron initially dispatched two regiments to reinforce Czaplic and led the rest of his forces northwards only late in the evening, when the initial combat between Oudinot and Czaplic was already over. By then, Czaplic lamented:

> It pains me that I lost all advantages that I had available before and, although I could not prevent the enemy from setting up the crossing since the position on the opposite bank is rather advantageous, I would have made them pay dearly for it. Yet, now I have nothing left to do, neither with cannon nor cavalry, except try to inflict some damage.[475]

Wittgenstein's Misjudgment

In the meantime, Napoleon was still concerned that Wittgenstein might appear from the north-east and would have been undoubtedly thrilled to know there was no immediate threat from that direction. By late 25 November, Wittgenstein's corps had concentrated at Barany (some 35km from Borisov), with a newly-enhanced advance guard of Vlastov moving to Kostritsa and a detachment under Colonel Albrecht at Yanchin.[476] Although in hindsight,

Wittgenstein should have acted more decisively, Carl von Clausewitz, who served on Wittgenstein's staff, tried to justify his actions by noting that the General was still concerned that Napoleon might turn north and break through near Lepel. Besides, he 'had lately had two French marshals oppose him, whose united strength he reckoned nearly equal to his own', and available intelligence indicated that Napoleon still had considerable forces with him. 'The last official accounts received of the enemy's strength dated before the actions near Krasnyi,' Clausewitz explained

> It had then been much overrated by Kutusow [*sic*], and it was impossible to estimate with accuracy its losses in these actions. Observation by reconnaissance was very difficult for it was impossible to distinguish in the moving mass those still bearing arms from others. In short it is both conceivable and excusable, that in Wittgenstein's headquarters it should have been supposed, that a mass of 90,000 to 100,000 men was in their front; whereas we now know that it consisted of about 30,000 men.[477]

Thinking that he could expect no help from Chichagov, Wittgenstein chose to act cautiously. He planned to reach Kostritsa by the 26th and, depending on circumstances, to march either to Borisov or Veselovo. He was convinced that Victor's retreat through Batury and Loshnitsa only further indicated Napoleon's intention to cross the river either at or below Borisov.[478] His conviction was reinforced on the 25th when Ataman Platov informed him that he was 'closely' pursuing the Grand Army along the main route and planned to be at Borisov by 26 November. More importantly, Colonel Albrecht, sent to reconnoitre routes to Loshnitsa and Borisov, reported 'a large concentration of enemy forces at Borisov while one mile to the left from it, a bridge is being constructed at Ukhalovichi (i.e. Ukholody)'. Albrecht obviously could not observe all of this in person so he relied on hearsay, which he then conveyed to his superior. As the reader already knows, it was Oudinot's diversion aimed at Chichagov but it now misled Wittgenstein as well. The Russian commander decided to march directly on Borisov and catch Napoleon between two armies and the river. On 26 November, Wittgenstein marched with his corps towards Kostritsa (arriving by evening), while a small Cossack detachment was sent to reconnoitre the road to Zembino via Veselovo, where the Grand Army was already quietly building bridges. Esaul Zolotarev was unable to accomplish this mission after encountering enemy troops at Podberezie. He reported that the locals heard the sound of construction and gunfire further south at Studyanka.[479] When General Diebitsch informed Wittgenstein of this important intelligence and suggested attacking at once to pin down Napoleon, Wittgenstein dismissed it, commenting, 'Let Chichagov deal with it. When the enemy leaves his tail on this side of the river, I will announce myself.' Despite Diebitsch's attempts to convince him, Wittgenstein stubbornly stuck to his position. Flügel Adjutant Sergei Volkonsky, who witnessed the scene, later noted that Wittgenstein did announce himself when he attacked Partouneaux's division, but that was indeed just the tail of Napoleon's army.[480]

Had Wittgenstein marched directly on Veselovo and Studyanka on 25 or 26 November, Napoleon might have found himself in a grave situation, since his army was still stretched out between Studyanka and Loshnitsa. Mikhailovsky-Danilevsky and Buturlin justified Wittgenstein's actions by noting that 'the road from Kostritsa to Studyanka was impassable to artillery'.[481] But there were other routes Wittgenstein could have used to reach Veselovo. Clausewitz acknowledges that Wittgenstein 'might have been beaten by Buonaparte, but he would have hindered his passage for a day, and perhaps for two. But this self-sacrifice for the general good, which sounds so well in books, is nevertheless not be reckoned on in the practice of the world'. Furthermore, upon arriving at Kostritsa, Wittgenstein learned from his scouts that the Grand Army was organizing a crossing at Studyanka. The Russian general initially thought it doubtful since, as far as he knew, the region between Borisov and Zembino was occupied by Chichagov. Nevertheless, he decided to move towards Borisov on the 27th and 'attack the enemy in their rear, while he was occupied by [Chichagov] in front'. Clausewitz admitted that he could not understand the reason

> why Wittgenstein marched not on Studyanka, but on the Smolensk road, while he knew that the former was the point selected by the enemy to cross. Unquestionably this exhibited certain timidity, a too great anxiety to preserve his corps from all injury, and on this occasion, General Wittgenstein cannot be acquitted of a certain share in the escape of Buonaparte.

Volkonsky thought 'either Wittgenstein's personal resentment of Chichagov or his anxiety of being subordinated to the Admiral saved Napoleon and the French army from capture'.[482] Wittgenstein's arrival at Studyanka undoubtedly would have been decisive. It would have forced Napoleon to delay his crossing and allowed Chichagov to gather his forces at Brili, while Platov and Miloradovich could have exerted pressure from the east.

By the evening of the 26th, the Grand Army was still relatively scattered on both sides of the Berezina. Oudinot, with his corps (7,000 men) and the Polish division (1,300 men),[483] was between Brili and Stakhov on the western bank, but the rest of the army was still on the eastern bank. The Guard (about 6,400 men) reached Studyanka in the afternoon. The VIII Corps was initially ordered to follow the IX Corps but Junot, after waiting several hours for news from Victor, decided to march towards Studyanka at 3 a.m. on the 27th.[484] The survivors of the III and V (Polish) Corps (Zajączek and Claparède's division), had arrived at Studyanka in the afternoon of the 26th;[485] the III Corps and Claparède began crossing the river around 10 p.m., followed by the Poles (16th and 18th Divisions, plus Malinowski's 15th Polish Regiment) around midnight. With Oudinot already protecting the road from Brili, Napoleon instructed Ney to take position on the nearby heights, with the Poles moving deeper into the woods. Ney was also instructed to deploy guards at both bridges to prevent anyone from crossing to the other side.[486] Like the rest of the army, Ney's troops were exhausted. Finding a few minutes spare while awaiting his turn to cross, Fezensac, in charge of the 4th Line, decided to count his effectives since after Smolensk he had had 'neither the time nor the courage to study my regiment's destruction'. His notes are quite revealing about the state of the Grand Army by November 1812. Assembling his unit, Fezensac mustered it according to the list he had brought from Moscow:

> Alas! What changes had taken place since then! Out of seventy officers scarcely forty remained, and of these the greater part were inefficient from either sickness or fatigue [...] Almost all the company cadres had been destroyed at Krasnyi, which rendered the maintenance of discipline a still more difficult matter. Of the remaining soldiers I formed two *pelotons*, the first consisting of grenadiers and *voltigeurs* while the second was from the centre companies. I selected the officers to command them and ordered each of the others to take a musket and always march with me at the head of the regiment.

Fezensac had lost all his possessions, as had Marshal Ney, while his aides-de-camp 'were starving'.[487] The V Corps was in no better condition, with officers and soldiers sick and hungry. When the wounded Poniatowski's carriage reached the camp, his adjutant Kicki appealed to the Polish troops for some provisions for the weakened General. As Krasinski recalled, the troops pooled whatever they had and gave the General 'some bread and a few hot potatoes with some grease from our pot'.[488]

At the same time, Victor (10,000 men) still kept two divisions at Borisov and another division supporting Viceroy Eugène (1,200 men) at Nemanitsa. On 25 November, Berthier advised him that his 'principal goal is to prevent General Wittgenstein from attacking' the army and instructed him to 'send several officers to keep us informed of your position several times per day'. Later that day, however, Victor was reprimanded for removing his rearguard from the Lepel road, which exposed Borisov; Berthier again reminded him: 'I reiterate to you the order of the Emperor, which is for you to attack the enemy. This is of the greatest importance [...] The crossing of the river is expected tomorrow morning.' The following morning, at 4 a.m., Berthier again wrote to Victor: 'The Emperor wishes that, while passing Borisov, you shall halt there to regroup and to see whether the enemy makes any demonstration at this point. Then, you will continue your march on Studyanka.' This order was hardly issued when another was sent in its wake, this time Napoleon wanted Victor to 'rest at Borisov to form the rearguard of the army'. By then, Victor reported that Fournier's four regiments of light cavalry remained on the heights near Borisov to observe the approach of the enemy, while Partouneaux's 12th Division was left near Loshnitsa.[489]

Further east were the remnants of IV and I Corps. Around 6.30 p.m. on the 26th, Eugène received Berthier's letter informing him of the bridges being

The Grand Army on the Eve of the Crossing

Unit	Chambray	Wilson	Fain	Gourgaud
Old Guard and Guard Cavalry	4,900	5,500	4,880	8,500 (with Col. Daulancourt's dismounted Guard cavalry)
Young Guard	1,500	3,000	2,200	2,200
I and IV Corps	2,400	3,100	9,000 (with VIII Corps)	~8,600 (with all of artillery)
II Corps (with Dąbrowski's Division)	7,000	7,800	9,300 (with Doumerc)	9,300
III and V Corps (with the Vistula Legion)	3,000	3,400	5,400	5,400
IX Corps	10,800	13,200	10,000	11,000
TOTAL	29,600	36,000	40,780	45,000

completed at Studyanka and Napoleon's intention to 'immediately carry out the crossing with a sharp force'. The IV Corps was told to be ready to follow the rest of the army. Eugène replied that he had left his position at Nacha and arrived at Loshnitsa, where he found Partouneaux and Fournier, who had orders to wait for Davout's corps. Awaiting further news of the crossing, Eugène halted his forces 'behind Loshnitsa, halfway to Borisov'. He complained that 'with each passing day the number of combat-ready troops decreases remarkably fast'. The IV Corps reached the crossing by the 27th. At the same time, Davout, with about 1,000 men from I Corps, departed from Krupki and, protected by Fournier's cavalry, also arrived to Loshnitsa. Partouneaux's division, supported by Delaitre's cavalry brigade, allowed the IV and I Corps to pass and assumed the function of rearguard, covering the road to Borisov.[490] The VIII Corps, which was reorganized into a 400–man strong battalion one week earlier, had suffered further losses that all but destroyed it. On 23 November, Junot informed Napoleon that 'I barely have any infantry left in the VIII Corps, I do not have a single cannon and my cavalry has hardly one hundred horses left.' According to Lossberg, the Westphalian Light Cavalry Brigade, led by General Hammerstein, had only 120 men by late November.[491] Depending on the source, Napoleon had between 30,000–35,000 fit troops, with probably as many stragglers tagging along.

To deal with the present danger, Napoleon chose to delay moving more troops across the river so as to counter Wittgenstein if he appeared. The Emperor also instructed the rearguard to decelerate its withdrawal, so as to keep Kutuzov's advance guard further from the crossing.[492] Yet, fearing Chichagov's attack against Oudinot's isolated corps, Napoleon ordered Ney to concentrate and move his troops across the river sometime after 10 p.m. To guard the approaches to the bridges, initially there was a semi-circle of *gendarmes* posted around each entrance. They were still dressed in their regulation uniforms, and blocked passage to any units not bearing their weapons. Caulaincourt wrote that: 'The Emperor inspected the marshland along the other bank of the river, and in the afternoon took careful observations of this position. It was long past nightfall when he returned to Studyanka.'[493]

27 November: The Crossing, Day 2

The night of 27 November proved unusually quiet: 'The calendar shows it is the Day of Repentance and Prayer today …' noted Otto Raven, a young officer from Mecklenburg. On the western bank, Louis Bégos and his comrades from the 2nd Swiss Regiment prepared for the night inside

> the forest of full grown trees, rather dense, both the ground and the pines being thick with snow. The bivouac did little to restore us, since we had not

eaten anything all day long [and] the Russians were so close. At nightfall, each soldier took his pack as a pillow and the snow for his mattress, with his musket in his hand. An icy wind was blowing hard. To keep each other warm, our men lay closely huddled together. The biggest pines were not shedding their snow, and under this kind of umbrella we suffered less. Our *vedettes* were at their posts and the officers, most of them leaning against a tree for fear of a surprise, did not get any sleep all night.[494]

Not far from them, the men of the 1st Swiss Regiment also settled for the night, 'breathing more freely having crossed the Berezina and driven back the enemy'. Still, they had suffered losses and Legler counted only 300 fit men in his unit. The troops were particularly upset about leaving the sick Colonel Raguettli at Borisov:

Several of us had offered to stay behind and help him, but he had rejected all such offers. 'Gentlemen, other duties call you. You must attend to them first, and if you manage to get across – as I hope you will – we will soon see each other again.'

With two senior officers present, it was decided that Commandant Blattmann would assume Raguettli's authority, while Commandant Zingg would remain in the rear.[495] The *chasseurs* were suffering from cold and hunger as well. Sitting around a bonfire, Sergeant Major Calosso saw a wounded and dishevelled Italian soldier, wearing a filthy uniform and wrapped in burnt furs, trying to find a spot near the fire. Calosso's comrades tried to drive him away but then noticed the bullion of his sword-knot and, after inquiring, learned that he was colonel of one of the Italian Royal Guard regiments.

On the eastern bank, as the winter darkness settled, Lieutenant Albrecht von Muraldt of the 4th Bavarian Chevaulégers (from Ornano's light cavalry brigade) saw terrain

covered as far as the eye could see with cannon, caissons and all kinds of vehicles, where fires had been made up, and a variegated mass was crowding together. Among this mass of troops of all ranks and arms one seldom saw anything reminiscent of a complete uniform.

Muraldt and his comrades found shelter in a half-demolished barn and spent the night defending themselves against 'those outside, who were trying to carry away the beams still left, to keep up their fires'.[496] Earlier in the day, Raven and his comrades from the Mecklenburg Battalion saw some pigs being shot by starved troops but despite their efforts they could not get any meat for themselves.

The Battle of the Berezina

Similarly, the Westphalian Jakob Walter, who had not eaten for the past few days, was able to get some 'raw bran in which there was hardly a dust of flour'. That night he obtained a place at the fire by contributing some wood and began mixing snow with bran:

> I kneaded it together into a lump about the size of my fist, which because of its brittleness fell into three or four pieces again in the fire. I allowed it to heat red on the outside in order to obtain something like bread from the inside [and] ate it all with the heartiest appetite.[497]

Captain Franz Roeder (of the Hessian Foot Guards) seemed more fortunate, since his company still had some meat and flour, but, with only one cooking pot, they took turns preparing food, which meant Franz never got his turn. With thousands of starving men roaming around, theft and marauding became widespread. As Roeder lay down to sleep, 'my greatcoat was stolen from me by one of my batmen, my jar of honey was pilfered by another and my coffee got left behind'. Another French officer

> passed the night in trying to bring something like order into our arrangements for crossing, sending the ammunition wagons first, and repairing the bridges where they had given way under the weight of the artillery. It was a very dark night, and many French, Dutch, Spanish, and Saxon soldiers fell into the wells of the village and were drowned. Their cries of distress reached us, but we had no ropes or ladders with which to rescue them, and they were left to their fate.[498]

During the night and early morning, the bridges suffered recurring problems that delayed the crossing. As previously mentioned, the transport bridge collapsed around 8 p.m. on the 26th and was reopened by 11 p.m. The artillery of V Corps began crossing around midnight but the movement seems to have been slow and frequently interrupted. Meanwhile, the delays created serious problems for the Allied forces on the western bank. Around 1 a.m. on the 27th, Oudinot informed Berthier that 'the enemy has placed six more guns in front of his position' and complained of interruptions in the flow of supplies, which were depriving his units of ammunition. Heavy caissons could not be brought in, since 'the main bridge has not been completely repaired yet'. A similar observation was made by the Russian officer Arnoldi, who argued that Czaplic's detachment held ground

> against the numerically superior enemy because they lacked artillery, which could not be moved across the river due to unreliable bridges before the dawn of 15th [27 November.] We, on the other hand, had twelve guns

inflicting considerable damage on the enemy, which allowed us to remain in position until late night.[499]

Oudinot noted that 'the forest, where we hold positions, is rather sparse, which obliges me to extend my troops further to the right and left'. He asked for more reinforcements, since his troops had suffered considerable losses in the day's fighting. Merle's division had less than 800 men under arms.[500]

Around two in the morning, the transport bridge caved in again, as three more trestles, this time in the deepest part of the river, collapsed. Once again the gallant *pontonniers* had to wade into the freezing water. They worked tirelessly for four hours and the bridge was operational by 6 a.m.[501] And yet, the bridge was still not strong enough and, when Boulart and Pion des Loches led their Guard artillery batteries across at dawn, they found it 'not very solid' and noticed Eblé's indefatigable *pontonniers* 'having the courage to put themselves into the water and working despite the bitter cold; they behaved admirably'.[502] The steady flow of supply wagons, caissons and carriages kept moving across until the bridge broke again at 4 p.m. It took the *pontonniers* two hours to repair the two broken trestles and the movement resumed after 6 p.m. Nevertheless, as Belliard recorded in his journal: 'The crossing progresses extremely slowly [...] On the entrance and exit from the bridge, there are dense marshes, which greatly delay the movement of artillery and baggage train.'[503]

The crossing was a messy and confusing affair. The surface of both bridges was covered with debris and corpses, both animal and human. According to Chapelle and Chapuis:

> The right bridge, where the infantry and cavalry was crossing, suffered no collapses, but it required constant maintenance of its table, which consisted of triple layers of old, rotten planks removed from village houses; they were not securely fixed and got dislodged easily.

Many surface planks were damaged and horses frequently broke their legs after falling through the gaps, plunging attached vehicles into the water. These pitiful creatures were then shot or trampled by the endless column of transports. Judging from Pion des Loches' memoirs, some Guard artillery companies crossed the river in the morning, when their commanders had pushed ahead, leaving carriages behind to clutter the approaches. Thus, Pion des Loches was incensed by Antoine Drouot ('the sage of the Grand Army' as Napoleon described him), who was among the first to cross, leaving some of his carriages in Pion's care. With another artillery company (led by Boulart) preceding him, Pion des Loches could not move his men fast enough and had to withstand pressure from soldiers of the Imperial train and gunners trying to get over.[504]

The Battle of the Berezina

Meantime, the Grand Army continued its passage. The Vistula Legion, which arrived at daybreak, was the first to cross around 10 a.m. The wounded Brandt, from the Vistula Legion, described 'battalions drawing up alongside one another in battalion columns'. Nearby, he could see Napoleon surrounded by a group of generals and

> deep in discussion with one of them who stood before the Emperor with his hat in his hand. It was the heroic General Eblé. Napoleon's face was as unreadable as ever. He was wearing a great fur coat which was unbuttoned and revealed his habitual uniform beneath. Murat never allowed circumstances to prevent the wearing of the most outlandish costumes and was today attired in a fur cup surrounded by a huge plume [...] A scar on his face from a sabre wound he had received at Aboukir and which was not normally visible, had been accentuated by the cold and was now rather obvious [...] Berthier and the Viceroy [Eugène] were wearing fur coats. Ney, easily recognizable by his reddish features and lively manner, wore a dark green overcoat. I also recognized Mortier, who stood out from the rest because of his height, Narbonne, with his hair powdered and in a queue just as it would have been at Versailles, Duroc, one of the Emperor's most faithful companions ...[505]

The Young Guard was to follow the Vistula Legion, but Napoleon gave instructions to 'delay this movement to allow the Viceroy's [Eugène] troops to arrive and out of concern of Wittgenstein's sudden appearance on this bank'.[506]

Early that morning Victor led his troops out of Borisov, where Colonel Griois witnessed 'unimaginable disorder'. He described 'stragglers, carriages, horses jamming the streets. Victor's troops had to fight their way through crowds. People were shoving each other, curses and expletives could be heard from all directions.'[507] By noon, Victor arrived with two divisions (Girard's 28th and Daendels' 26th) at Studyanka, while Partouneaux's division, with Delaitre's cavalry, remained near Borisov. Alexander Bellot de Kergorre, a young *commissaire des guerres*, admired Victor's 'guns and ammunition wagons drawn by fine horses, their harness in good condition. It was a long time since we had seen anything of the kind. Our own few caissons and baggage wagons were drawn by wretched little horses with their ragged rope harness'.

At various moments throughout the morning, Napoleon personally directed the crossing. Thus, Louise Fusil, an actress travelling in a marshal's carriage, was able to

> examine him closely standing at the entrance to the bridge. To me he seemed as calm as at a review at the Tuileries. The bridge was so narrow

Campaign Chronicle

Estimated Crossing Timeline, 27 November

12–3 a.m.	Portions of Ney's Corps, followed by the Poles (16th and 18th Divisions, plus Malinowski's 15th Polish Regiment) crossed the river on the infantry bridge
	Artillery of the V Corps moved across the transport bridge
2 a.m.	Transport bridge collapsed
3–7 a.m.	'Infantry' bridge remained deserted
6 a.m.	Transport bridge repaired. Crossing resumed with the Guard foot artillery
10 a.m.	The Vistula Legion began crossing on the infantry bridge, while its trains moved to the transport bridge
12 p.m.	Young Guard began moving across the river
1 p.m.	Napoleon moved across the river, followed by the Old Guard
2 p.m.	Guard Foot Artillery still crossing the bridge, followed by the Imperial train
4 p.m.	Transport bridge collapsed again
5 p.m.	Daendel's Division crossed the river
6 p.m.	Transport bridge repaired
8 p.m.–through the night	IV and I Corps crossing the river, followed by IV Reserve Cavalry Corps

our carriage almost touched the Emperor. 'Do not be afraid,' Napoleon said. 'Go on, go on. Do not be afraid.'

Soon, Fusil could see Murat

holding his horse by the bridle, his hand posed on the door of my calèche. He looked at me and said something polite. To me his costume seemed utterly bizarre for such a moment and in minus 20 degrees. His neck was open. His velvet mantle was flung negligently over one shoulder […] His black velvet toque was adorned with a white feather. All of this gave him the air of a hero in some melodrama. Never before had I seen him at such close quarters and I could not take my eyes off him. When he was some distance behind the carriage I turned round to look him in the face. He noticed it and saluted me graciously with his hand. He was a flirt [coquet] and liked when women noticed him.[508]

Later that morning Fain, Napoleon's trusted secretary, saw Marshal Lefebvre working tirelessly at getting his troops across: 'This old warrior, who had not shaved for several days, was adorned with a white beard and leaning on a traveller's stick, which in his hands had become a noble marshal's baton.'[509]

Eyewitnesses tell us that 'until the evening of the 27th, there was no particular obstruction to the crossing because the stragglers had not arrived in large numbers yet'. But this changed that evening as thousands of hungry and exhausted men and women reached the crossing site, bringing a large quantity of horses and carriages with them: 'Their disorganized march caused such confusion that only through infinite struggle and great danger was it possible to reach the bridges', lamented Chapelle and Chapuis. Private carriages, wagons and other transports converged towards the bridges in '30–40 columns', blocking all approaches and inciting tensions and quarrels. A Polish officer from Girard's division was stunned to see 'huge disarray and countless crowds with thousands of coaches and carriages of all sorts. These transports were full of spoils, many wounded, sick and hungry'. Men were fighting for places and the weak were trampled. The approaches to the bridge were 'covered with corpses over which people marched to get onto the bridge'.[510] According to Labaume:

> The crowd was so great and the approaches were so dangerous that on reaching the river the multitude got wedged into a mass, unable to move. In spite of these difficulties, however, those on foot managed, by great exertions, to save themselves.

Raven also speaks of an 'immovable mass' of people and 'carriages, loaded with belongings and valuable possessions'. As the number of people seeking to cross the river increased, Napoleon ordered the *gendarmes* to allow only battle-ready troops across the river. According to Muralt:

> A few elite *gendarmes*, who still had horses, had been ordered to turn away non-combatants (a description applicable to almost everyone) as they pushed forward so that the Guard could pass unhindered. A task they flung themselves into heart and soul, without distinction of person or rank, receiving anyone who tried to push forward with violent blows of the flats of their swords.[511]

In this turmoil, there were still glimpses of humanity. Dominique Larrey, the Surgeon General of the Grand Army who was idolized by the troops for his work, was also trying to cross the river and found himself in the midst of a furious struggling crowd. He was on the point of being crushed to death when the soldiers recognized him. They carried him across the river in their arms with the cry, 'Let us save him who saved us!'[512]

Hundreds of carriages were discarded and the wounded had to walk or be carried across. But, as Brandt observed:

the *gendarmes* had not finished. Only combatants can cross, they told us, blocking our way forward. 'This is absurd!' I cried, 'you cannot confuse wounded with stragglers, damn it.'

Fortunately for Brandt, a senior officer came to his aid by pointing out that he belonged to the corps that was crossing over. As he slowly moved across the bridge, Brandt noticed that 'the planks of the bridge were by no means even and some of them were already missing, especially as we drew closer to the far bank. There the entire bridge was below the water level and we had water up to our ankles'. Fusil also noticed that

many senior officers were leading their horses by the bridle, because no one could cross this bridge on horseback. It was so fragile, it trembled under the wheels of my carriage. The weather, which had grown milder, had somewhat melted the ice on the river, but that only made it more dangerous.[513]

Members of the Sacred Squadron were ordered to cross individually and rally on the opposite bank. Colonel Victor Dupuy followed Squadron Leader Officer of the 1st Carabineers, who was riding a large, powerful horse and was able to clear his way with it. 'Rather slowly, amidst curses and shouts flung at us, we managed to reach the bridge to safety,' Dupuy recalled. 'The access to the bridge was blocked but [the bridge] itself was almost entire free. Near it and on either side many unfortunates were struggling in the river and it was impossible to help them.' Among thousands surrounding him, Heckens saw

several women crossing over with their infants and I recognized some of them from the theatre in Moscow. They would have done better to have stayed in Moscow instead of following the army. The Russians would not have avenged themselves on them for Emperor Napoleon's mad enterprise.[514]

Some generals tried using their authority to get their possessions across, which only infuriated the Emperor, who ordered the burning of General Marchand's carriage as an example to other senior officers. Still, as people became anxious to escape, hundreds of wagons and carriages logjammed on the approaches to the bridges, many of them abandoned as people left whatever possessions they had, in hope of getting across the river. At this difficult moment, the lowest human traits revealed themselves and looters killed, robbed and despoiled the weak and destitute. From the once mighty Grand Army, François Dumonceau could see only

> a compact conglomeration of thousands of men of all arms, soldiers, officers, even generals, all mixed up, covered in the filthiest rags and grotesquely disposed to protect themselves against the freezing weather, swarming with vermin [...] Their faces [were] downcast by exhaustion, pale, sinister, smoke-blackened, often mutilated by frostbite, the eyes hollow, extinct, hair in disorder, the beard long and disgusting.[515]

On the western bank, as Mikhailovsky-Danilevsky described:

> everyone remained in the same position in which the cold darkness and windy night found them. At dawn, our officers, and those of the French, deployed skirmishers as if on the training field, without any hostile actions. Both sides then spent the day quietly and without firing a single shot. Neither was willing to resume battle. Our troops could not attack because they were numerically inferior and awaited the arrival of the army from Borisov. The French, meantime, had no reason to renew the fighting, delighted by the Russian inactivity, which allowed them to complete the crossing.

And so, Pils writes, 'the day passed in great tranquillity and the army continued its crossing ...'[516]

Around 1 p.m. Napoleon, followed by the Young and Old Guard crossed to the western bank but Victor, Davout and Eugène, with the great mass of stragglers and transports, remained on the eastern bank. According to a Mecklenburg officer, 'the first to cross were the [Guard] musicians still carrying their instruments when many troops did not carry their weapons anymore. They were followed by officers and infantry moving orderly and calmly ...'[517] The Imperial Suite had to wade through the masses blocking the approaches and some participants (i.e. Mailly-Nesle) saw its members, including Caulaincourt, being pushed and shoved around. While crossing, Napoleon came across Major de Grünberg, from the Württemberg Chasseurs, who 'was holding a little greyhound bitch that was shivering piteously under his coat'. Seized by compassion, Napoleon, 'this great captain who sent thousands of men to their death', offered to buy the dog. The Major replied that:

> this small animal has been my companion through all sufferings of this campaign; I want to keep her with me in memory of everything I saw and experienced. But, if Your Majesty wishes, I will place it at your disposal.

The Emperor, visibly moved, told him to keep it: 'I would not want to deprive you of it.'[518] Reaching the opposite bank, Napoleon was soon joined by the Sacred Squadron, Old Guard and the Imperial train, which, in addition to imperial possessions, also transported the wounded officials, including General Ornano and General Intendant Daru. After crossing, the train was immediately dispatched, under escort, towards Vilna.

The Lancer Brigade was among the Guard units crossing in Napoleon's wake. Dumonceau, leading his company of the 2nd Guard Lancers, remembered

> the mob of disbanded men creating an obstacle by turning up from all quarters, interfering everywhere, encumbering the terrain over a considerable extent and refusing to let us through. The detachments of *pontonniers* and *gendarmes* at the bridgeheads were struggling violently with them to contain and regulate their passage. This only resulted in shouts, vociferations and terrible commotion.

He had his troopers dismount and, to avoid shaking the bridge, cross individually, leading their mounts by the bridle. The bridge

> had no rail, was almost at water level, covered with a layer of horse dung. It was already badly damaged, dislocated, in parts weakened and swaying in every direction. Some *pontonniers*, in the water up to their shoulders, were busy restoring it. Among them were some Dutchmen who welcomed us and made haste to ease our passage by tossing into the river a broken cart, some dead horses and other debris of all kinds that were obstructing it.[519]

Still struggling to get through, Dumonceau's men had to 'resort to force' and, drawing their sabres, 'knocked down anything in our way and striking out with [the] flats [of our blades], thrust back anyone who, pushed by the multitude in the opposite direction, were hemming us in from all sides as in a wine press'. To ease their crossing, Captain Załuski's men from the 1st Polish Guard Regiment remained on their horses, turned their lances downward and 'by dealing out harmless blows to right and left', slowly moved across the river.[520]

After reaching the western bank, Napoleon, surrounded and guarded by the Sacred Squadron as Heckens and Dupuy tell us, examined Oudinot's position near the settlement of Zanivki, where his headquarters was established in a small house with only two rooms:

> The inner one has been reserved for the Emperor. The other was instantly occupied by his suite. There we lie down pell-mell on top of one another, like a flock herded together in the narrowest of sheepfolds.[521]

The Battle of the Berezina

The Sacred Squadron surrounded the house while the Guard was moved towards Brili. Later that afternoon Napoleon returned to the bridges, where great confusion reigned. 'It was impossible to cross the river that day,' recalled Karl von Suckow, a Württemberg officer:

> I became convinced of this after seeing what was happening on the approaches to the bridge, and on the bridge itself. There was a mass of destitutes who were trying to reach the opposite bank. Blasphemies, insults and shouts shook the air. Those who had walking sticks used them mercilessly on those in front, all just to move forward by a few steps.[522]

Le Roy saw men 'come rushing in a mob at the bridgehead as everyone wanted to get across at once. They were shoving and crushing each other. It was the beginning of that disorder that reigned and would only get worse the following day'.[523]

In the afternoon, news of the appearance of Russian troops from the northeast only increased the confusion. One of Wittgenstein's detachments, led by Esaul Gordeev, was reconnoitring the area when he came across 'a Guard cavalry regiment and some five hundred infantrymen' not far from Veselovo and attacked them. After a short combat, he reported capturing over fifty men and killing or wounding up to 200; this might be the attack recorded in the memoirs of Captain de Monceau, who commanded the 6th Company of the Red Lancers of the Guard: 'about the middle of the day, a light alarm was caused by the appearance of some Cossacks and we ran to our weapons; but this alarm lasted only moments and then [we] returned to rest, but ready to ride out at the first signal'.[524] After interrogating the prisoners, Gordeev informed Wittgenstein of Napoleon's passage of the Berezina over two bridges and promised to attack in the direction of Studyanka.[525]

In the meantime, Eugène's and Davout's corps reached the crossing site at Studyanka, occupying the heights on the eastern bank. Around 4 p.m., Cesare Laugier and his comrades – who were resting from a long march – were called to arms when another Russian detachment, with 'a few guns', appeared on the road to Dubenka: 'We rushed to our arms,' Laugier described, 'and charged the enemy, driving him back after a brief but fierce combat that claimed the lives of many brave men. Corporal Paganello charged with his comrades towards the enemy guns but they all paid with their lives for this audacity …'[526]

Late in the evening, IV corps finally got its turn to cross and Eugène, accompanied by some 500 survivors of his Royal Guard, was first to move over the bridge around 8 p.m. Napoleon instructed Eugène to 'bivouac at the burned village in rear of the Young Guard'.[527] Laugier saw Eugène instructing General Theodore Lecchi 'to leave an officer at the bridge to show Broussier's and

Pinot's divisions the route to follow, so as to reach that burning village. In my capacity of adjutant-major, I have been detailed by that general for this painful task'. Standing on the bridge, Laugier saw the '1st and 2nd Division arriving together. They crossed by sections of five to six men abreast, and after a quarter of an hour, during which the bridge was free, Pino's division arrived as well.'[528] But Labaume claims that 'many in the IV Corps could not tear themselves away from the fires they had lighted, arguing that it was just as well to wait until next day, when the bridges would be clearer of people'. We may assume that a portion of the IV Corps remained on the eastern bank or crossed in groups together with Davout's units, which began crossing the river late at night. Eugène and his suite, meanwhile, settled into a burnt-out village located on marshy ground:

> The wind, bitter and blowing with violence, drove against our faces great flakes of icy snow. Most of the officers, to avoid being frostbitten, raced or walked rapidly to and fro, stamping their feet [...] Firewood was so scarce that a fire could hardly be made for the Viceroy, and to obtain some faggots it was necessary to remind the Bavarian soldiers that Prince Eugène had married the daughter of their King![529]

Eugène was followed by Davout's I Corps and Latour-Maubourg's survivors of the once dashing IV Reserve Cavalry Corps. Napoleon advised Davout to 'pass tomorrow morning at the sound of artillery and also take position behind the burned village'.[530] Captain Coignet of the Guard described:

> The Emperor sent for Marshal Davoust [sic], and I was appointed to guard the head of the bridge, and allow only the artillery and ammunition to go over. The Marshal was on the right side and I on the left. When all the ammunition had gone over, the Marshal said to me, 'Come on, my brave fellow; let us rejoin the Emperor.' We crossed the bridge and the frozen marsh; it was strong enough to bear our ammunition, without which all would have been lost.[531]

Thus, by midnight on 27 November, Napoleon had moved most of his army – I, II, III, IV (partially) and V Corps plus the Imperial Guard – safely across the river. The two divisions of IX Corps and Fournier's cavalry arrived at Studyanka around noon on the 27th and, on Napoleon's orders, remained on the eastern bank 'to guard the bridges and Studyanka, send out patrols so as not to be surprised by the enemy and ensure the best possible order in the passage of the bridges'. The Emperor also specified that Victor should 'take a good position near the village, on the heights, with his infantry, artillery and cavalry, in order to be able to defend it for several days while all wagons, baggage and other unspecified transports pass'. The Emperor was satisfied with the progress despite, as he wrote to Maret, 'plenty of floating ice that threatened the security of our bridges[…] excessive cold […] [and] the army's extreme fatigue'. But he was displeased with the actions of the Austrian corps, which was supposed to pin down the 3rd Western Army but instead let it reach the Berezina. As Napoleon wrote: 'One wonders what is Prince Schwarzenberg doing?'[532]

While the Grand Army gradually passed over the river, tens of thousands of stragglers remained on the opposite bank, hoping to cross the following day. Spread over several miles, this herd of unfortunates settled for the night among woods and marshes as the snow began falling heavily. Very few appear to have attempted to cross. Many were in the same condition as Suckow – frostbitten and unable to walk. Knowing how difficult it would be to cross the following day amid an unruly mob, he still chose to remain near the fire in the company of some Frenchmen: one of them was so grateful of Suckow's assurance that Napoleon would not march on St Petersburg in the spring, that he gave his most precious possession – half a piece of bread.[533] Some participants note in their memoirs that the bridges were open but deserted during the night of 28 November and thousands missed this unique opportunity to save their lives: 'We were quiet when night came, everyone in his bivouac, and no one came to cross the bridge during the night of the 27th–28th, a most astonishing thing,' writes Bourgogne, who, suffering from fever, awoke at dawn and went up to the bridge, where he 'met no one but the *pontonniers*, who camped on the two banks to repair the bridge in case of any accident'. Many stragglers simply became complacent and, as Le Roy put it, were 'loath to cross during the night'. Upon approaching the bridge, the Polish officer Turno 'heard only the monotonous bumping together of ice-floes carried along by the Berezina. No one was going over it'.[534] Marbot left one of the most vivid accounts, observing that

> much has been said of the disasters which took place at the Berezina but what has never yet been said is, that the greater part of them might have been saved if the headquarters staff had understood its duties better, and taken advantage of the night of 28 November to get all the baggage and, still more, the thousands of stragglers who next day blocked the way across the bridges.

After establishing a bivouac at Zanivki, Marbot noticed the absence of the packhorse carrying his regimental cash-box and account-books, so he returned to find them. To his great surprise, he found the bridge completely deserted: 'At that moment,' he remembered years later, no one was crossing, while a hundred paces away I could see by the bright moonlight more than 50,000 stragglers and soldiers separated from their regiments – *rôtisseurs* as they were called. These men, sitting calmly in front of enormous fires, were grilling horseflesh without a notion that they had in front of them a river, the passage of which would cost many of them their lives on the next day, while they could at the present time cross it without hindrance in a few minutes, and finish preparing their supper on the other bank. Not one officer of the imperial household, not one aide-de-camp, not a single marshal, was there to warn those poor wretches, and, if necessary, to drive them to the bridges …

Marbot claims that he succeeded 'partly by persuasion, partly by force' in making several hundred stragglers cross to the right bank before he had to rejoin the regiment:

As I passed by the headquarters staff and Oudinot's staff I called attention to the empty state of the bridges, and the ease with which the unarmed men could be brought across at a moment when the enemy was not trying to do anything. But it was in vain; I only received evasive answers, and each man left the task of directing the operation to his colleagues.[535]

As the stragglers settled down by their fires, some collapsed with exhaustion, others tried to find morsels of food, and a few sought to exploit an opportunity to enrich themselves. Castellane complained of increased thievery:

Our men developed a horrible tendency to steal things. At our bivouac someone stole Chabot's hat. He had his head lying on it. A fur had been taken from one of my horses. More than one officer, believing his horses were following him, arrived here with only its cut reins around his arm. If he turned around, he saw his horse already killed, cut up and shared.[536]

Yet, in the midst of this hostile environment, there were also moments of altruism and humanity. Thus, Louise, the pregnant *cantinière* of the 7th Light, had gone into labour that evening: 'The entire regiment was deeply moved and did what it could to assist this unfortunate woman who was without food and without shelter under this sky of ice,' described Sergeant Bertrand,

Our Colonel Romme set the example. Our surgeons, who had none of their ambulance equipment, abandoned in Smolensk for lack of horses, were given shirts, kerchiefs and anything people could come up with. I had noticed Marshal Victor's artillery park not far away and ran over to it, purloining a blanket thrown over the back of one of the horses. I rushed back as fast as I could to bring it to Louise. I had committed a sin, but I knew that God would forgive me on account of my motive. I got there just at the moment when our *cantinière* was bringing into the world, under an old oak tree, a healthy male child, whom I was to encounter in 1818 as a child soldier in the Legion of the Aube.[537]

Napoleon's success in moving most of his men across the river was largely made possible by Russian inactivity. Chichagov reached the crossing site in the evening of the 27th and, even then, most of his army was still en route. According to Malinovski, Chichagov's army

> stopped for the night near the Borisov fortification while the advance guard reinforced Major General Czaplic, who, having already fought the enemy the previous day, sought to prevent the enemy from occupying the heights and reach the road leading to Zembino. The enemy, after crossing the river, occupied the low laying fields along the river. Major General O'Rourke was ordered to march to Stakhov as soon as he could and, by midnight, he reached Yushkevichi, where his completely exhausted men required rest.[538]

Arnoldi noted that no major actions took place on the 27th because 'neither side had the desire to resume fighting: we were too weak to attempt this, even after some regiments arrived from Borisov, while the French hurried to complete the crossing and were delighted that they were not disturbed'.[539]

Chichagov, meantime, rode ahead of the army and reconnoitred Napoleon's position, which was covered by a 'tall pine forest'. The road running north through the woods and across the rolling terrain was 'sufficiently wide to deploy a battery of 8 or 10 guns in line'. There were also two smaller paths, the right descended to the swamps along the river, while the left passed Napoleon's right flank as it led to the village of Likov. Chichagov understood the difficulties of his position and noted that he could not take advantage of his superiority in artillery (100 guns) and cavalry (some 9,000 men). He also knew the limitations of his own foot soldiers. Thickly wooded terrain meant the infantry would have to attack in open order: 'The Russian infantry, when deployed in line, is unbeatable,' Chichagov commented, 'but when attacking in open order, where each soldier must act independently and adjust to terrain, it lacks the necessary ingenuity and agility, shown by other European armies, especially the French and particularly the élite soldiers standing in front me.'[540] Still, he believed that urgent action was required to prevent Napoleon escaping. In the evening, Arnoldi tells us, Chichagov summoned a council of war, which decided to attack the following day.[541] Czaplic suggested harassing the enemy positions until 2 p.m.

before making a general attack: 'If we had succeeded, we would have gained great advantages,' Czaplic explained. 'Otherwise we did not risk much, since we would have fought for just a couple of hours and the woods would have facilitated our withdrawal.'[542] Chichagov agreed and advised his generals to prepare for the battle. Czaplic was also instructed to deploy a small detachment to observe the Zembino road and, if necessary, cut Napoleon's line of retreat. Towards midnight, Major General Lanskoy was tasked with this mission and led a cavalry detachment with six guns towards the village of Lyakhovka, south-west from Brili.

Chichagov was made furious by the failure of his fellow Army commanders to support him:

> Neither Wittgenstein nor Kutuzov arrived [...] They abandoned me with my meagre forces to face Napoleon, his marshals and an army that was three times larger than mine, while Schwarzenberg and the Polish rebels threatened me from behind. Our planned juncture, aimed at delivering a decisive blow to our enemy, had obviously failed. While Napoleon finished constructing [his] bridge and moved his forces across, I had nothing else to do but gather my troops, which I had deployed along the Berezina, and to reorganize the corps that suffered losses in the battle of 14 [26] November. I wanted to gather all my forces to attack Napoleon during his retreat and inflict as much damage as possible; or, [if Napoleon turned south] to defend the route to Minsk by all means possible [...] My forces had not concentrated yet and required the entire day, 15th [27], to accomplish this. Consequently, I had slim hopes of succeeding even if I had attacked upon my arrival. This would have been a senseless decision, which could have led to the destruction of my troops. Yet, by waiting for a few hours, I could hope for support from Kutuzov or Wittgenstein, both of whom I eagerly expected ...[543]

The Battle of Stary Borisov: Wittgenstein Arrives and Partouneaux Surrenders

We have seen that Wittgenstein reached Kostritsa by 26 November and made a consequential decision to proceed to Borisov instead of Studyanka, where his scouts reported the enemy crossing. His arrival at Studyanka on the 26th would have probably played a decisive role. Napoleon would have been forced to keep more troops on the eastern bank to deal with the new threat, weakening his forces on the western bank, where Chichagov had concentrated his army late on the 27th. We can only speculate on the outcome of the subsequent battle, but it is not far-fetched to assume that Napoleon would have been in extremely perilous circumstances. Nevertheless, Wittgenstein chose to proceed to Borisov. Kharkevich is probably right when he explains that the possibility of meeting Napoleon face to face, without any hope of support from Platov or Yermolov, had a profound impact on Wittgenstein. The fear of defeat guided his decision, which little corresponded to circumstances and produced far meeker results but was much safer.[544]

On the morning of 27 November, Wittgenstein issued his new orders. Vlastov, who had sent at least two reports advising Wittgenstein of the enemy crossing at Studyanka throughout the night,[545] was instructed to move from Zhitkovo to Stary Borisov. He was followed by Generals Berg and Steinheil with their respective forces (personally led by Wittgenstein), while Major General Fock remained with the reserves at Kostritsa. Wittgenstein also received reinforcements as Seslavin's and Chernozubov's flying detachments joined him and were also diverted to Borisov. Wittgenstein informed Platov, Miloradovich and Yermolov of his decision and urged them to hurry to Borisov.[546]

Approaching Stary Borisov between 2–3 p.m., Vlastov encountered the survivors of the Grand Army marching towards Studyanka.[547] Lieutenant Colonel Antropov quickly deployed artillery (six heavy and four light guns) to bombard the enemy, while the replacement battalions of the 11th, 18th and 36th Jäger Regiments were deployed in open order. The enemy was driven in the direction of Studyanka, pursued by Cossacks and two squadrons of the Combined Hussar Regiment.[548] Wittgenstein soon joined Vlastov at Stary Borisov. According to Buturlin:

a large number of the retreating French [stragglers] moved towards Veselovo, while the rest dispersed in the woods. The Grodnenskii Hussar Regiment pursued the enemy on the road to Borisov while the Cossacks, assisted by the Combined Hussar Regiment, pursued the enemy fleeing towards Studyanka.[549]

The prisoners soon informed the Russians that an entire French division was still at Borisov. With the Russians at Stary Borisov, Partouneaux was effectively isolated from the Grand Army and had no choice but to fight his way through. Wittgenstein and Vlastov (Steinheil was en route) began preparing an attack and deployed their troops in strong positions around Stary Borisov. Vlastov's main forces were north of the settlement, holding positions on the heights overlooking the narrow valley in which Stary Borisov was located. Lieutenant Colonel Neidhardt, of the Imperial Suite, occupied the village with the Combined Jäger Regiment and a battalion of the 25th Jägers. An artillery battery was deployed behind the settlement while two more light guns, commanded by Staff Captain Fedorenko and protected by the Sevskii Infantry Regiment and a battalion of the 25th Jägers (led by English officer, Dörnberg), were set up next

Mikolai Bronikowski. *Author's Collection*

Grigory Maximovich Berg. *Author's Collection*

Pavel Vasilievich Chichagov. *Author's Collection*

Yefim Ignatievich Czaplic. *Author's Collection*

Jan Henryk Dąbrowski. *Author's Collection*

Antoine Baudouin Gisbert van Dedem
van de Gelder. *Author's Collection*

Fedor Fedorovich Ertel. *Author's Collection*

François Fournier-Sarloveze. *Author's Collection*

Karl Osipovich Lambert. *Author's Collection*

Mikhail Illarionovich Kutuzov.
Author's Collection

Louis Alexander Andrault Langeron.
Author's Collection

Michel Ney. *Author's Collection*

Joseph Kornilovich O'Rourke.
Author's Collection

Nicolas Charles Oudinot.
Author's Collection

Pavel Petrovich Pahlen. *Author's Collection*

Louis Partouneaux. *Author's Collection*

Ivan Vasilievich Sabaneyev.
Author's Collection

Alexei Grigorievich Sherbatov.
Author's Collection

Claude Victor-Perrin. *Author's Collection*

Egor Ivanovich Vlastov. *Author's Collection*

Peter Khristianovich Wittgenstein.
Author's Collection

Retreat to the Berezina (Maurice Orange). *Author's Collection*

Burning the Colours (Juliusz Kossak). *Author's Collection*

Construction of the Berezina bridges, as recorded by Grenadier Pils. *Author's Collection*

Eblé inspires his troops, as recorded by Grenadier Pils. *Author's Collection*

The Berezina bridges. *Author's Collection*

Passage of the Berezina (Juliusz Kossak). *Author's Collection*

Passage of the Berezina (F. de Myrbach). *Author's Collection*

Passage of the Berezina (January Suchodolski). *Author's Collection*

Partouneaux Surrenders – lithograph of 1814. *Author's Collection*

Swiss Troops at
the Berezina by
Karl Jauslin.
Author's Collection

Battle of the Berezina by Peter Hess. *Author's Collection*

Battle of the Berezina by Jan Hoynck van Papendrecht. *Author's Collection*

On the banks of the Berezina, as recorded by Christian G. von Faber du Faur.
Author's Collection

The Berezina between Brili and Borisov as seen today. *Author's Collection*

The view from Brili to the Berezina. *Author's Collection*

The view from
the monument
at Brili to the
Berezina.
*(Photo © Sergei
Kabrusev.)*
Author's Collection

The Berezina near
Studyanka.
Author's Collection

The Berezina's
western bank
at Brili.
Author's Collection

The Berezina's western bank, north of Brili. *Author's Collection*

One of the wooden posts marking the entrance to Eblé's vanished bridges. *Author's Collection*

Monument to the Grand Army's Fallen. (*Photo © Sergei Kabrusev.*) *Author's Collection*

The 1962 monument erected on the supposed entrance to the infantry bridge on the eastern bank. (*Photo © Sergei Kabrusev.*) *Author's Collection*

Monument built by Ivan Kolodeyev, who lived in Borisov and spent years researching the Berezina crossing. Demolished in 1962, the monument was restored by the Byelorussian government on the 190th anniversary of the battle in 2002. (*Photo © Sergei Kabrusev.*) *Author's Collection*

Monument commemorating the 150th Anniversary of the crossing. (*Photo © Sergei Kabrusev.*) *Author's Collection*

Memorial, designed by N. Ryzhenkov in 1962, to commemorate 'the destruction of the remnants of the Napoleonic aggressors'. (*Photo © Sergei Kabrusev.*) *Author's Collection*

to the main road south of the village. Vlastov himself deployed two infantry battalions (with two guns) 'on an advantageous position' not far from the main road.[550]

The 12th Division of General Louis Partouneaux was probably the best preserved of the three divisions in Victor's corps. A graduate of the Louis le Grand College, the 42–year-old Partouneaux had been in military service since volunteering in 1791. Two years later he had fought at Toulon (where Napoleon earned his fame) and later served in the Army of Italy. In 1799 he was promoted *general de brigade* and fought the Austro-Russian forces led by Alexander Suvorov. In the decisive Battle of Novi in August 1799, the French Army was defeated and Partouneaux was wounded and captured by the Russians. After being released in late 1800, he served in various military districts before earning promotion to *general de division* in 1803. He spent the next nine years in Italy, earning the reputation of an efficient commander. One of the marshals later characterized him as 'a distinguished officer who deserves benevolence from the Emperor; His Majesty does not have a subject more loyal and devoted to him'.[551] In March 1812, Napoleon rewarded Partouneaux's service with command of the 12th Division. The division saw virtually no fighting in the first ten weeks of the campaign in Russia, but then went into action against Wittgenstein's forces. Now, in late November, Partouneaux was tasked with the crucial mission of protecting the Grand Army: but one wonders if he was ready for it? Partouneaux was a brave, fastidious and efficient commander, but of an average talent, rarely rising above his peers. Furthermore, the Russian campaign had a profound impact on him. In mid-November, Victor advised Berthier that Partouneaux was 'in such a state that he is unable to continue fighting any more. In addition to old wounds he had sustained, he has attained a disease which requires immediate rest and assistance'. It is unclear what disease Victor referred to but Partouneaux also wrote to Berthier, asking to be relieved of his command: 'Until now courage and zeal have kept me going,' he explained, 'but my physical strength has abandoned me. I can no longer stand up to the pains being caused by the rigour of the season and my wounds. The very service of the Emperor may be compromised by my no longer being able to be as active as before.' His request was ignored and less than two weeks later, this half-broken man was given the task of protecting the Grand Army's retreat.

Partouneaux was assisted by three brigade commanders, Generals Pierre Joseph Billard (aged 40), Louis Camus (aged 52 and a veteran of the Revolutionary Wars, whom Partouneaux described as 'a brave man who has performed well in war') and Marie Pierre Blanmont (aged 42). The 12th Division began the campaign with some 12,500 men and twenty guns, but, as Partouneaux himself noted, 'it was made up of young soldiers, many of them refractory conscripts'. During the campaign it had lost a considerable number of men: in mid-October, it listed 9,000 men on the rosters, but only some 3,200 had survived by late November; they were supported by two cavalry regiments (some 500 Saxon and Berg horsemen, who were provisionally united into a brigade) led by Delaitre.[552] Partouneaux reported that his men were 'in excellent shape, but suffered greatly from fatigues, privations and combat'. Less than two weeks later, a Russian officer confirmed: 'Partouneaux's division was in the best possible state: the cavalry from Saxony and the Grand Duchy of Berg was striking.'[553]

On 26 November, Partouneaux's division was at Loshnitsa and, after Davout and Eugène passed the town by late afternoon, it assumed the function of rearguard, slowly retreating to Nemanitsa and Borisov, where it arrived around noon on 27 November.[554] After Victor's corps moved to Studyanka, Partouneaux received a series of orders that ultimately resulted in the destruction of his division. As he later described, his mission was to protect Borisov as long as possible, to delay the Russian arrival at Studyanka, to prevent the establishment of direct communications between Wittgenstein and Chichagov, and to protect the stragglers still passing through the town.[555] On 25–26 November, the defence of Borisov was of great importance to the Grand Army, which was still largely on the eastern bank and vulnerable to any attacks from the rear. But Borisov's importance diminished by 27 November, when most of the army had moved across the Berezina, although thousands of stragglers were still on the eastern bank.[556] But Partouneaux seems to have remained in Borisov longer than expected. After the campaign ended, contemporaries debated whether Partouneaux had acted on a specific order to stay in Borisov or simply took the decision himself. Partouneaux defended his actions in a booklet published in 1815, in which he described the arrival of an officer – Colonel d'Ambrugeac – with instructions from Berthier to remain at Borisov; a similar account is given in Ségur's famous history of the 1812 Campaign, and Sous Lieutenant Beulay, who served in Partouneaux's division, noted the arrival of Berthier's messenger at 4 p.m. on 26 November. Berthier usually acted as a conduit for Napoleon's will and participants argued that the order must have been issued by the Emperor himself; Partouneaux's first report to Victor simply notes Berthier's order to remain at Borisov while his letter, written in 1821, notes that d'Ambrugeac 'delivered the orders of the Emperor'.[557] Gourgaud, Napoleon's ADC who later made a habit of duelling critics of the Emperor, categorically denied any such orders being made. Napoleon himself certainly seemed surprised by Partouneaux.[558] Considering participant testimonies, it is possible that Berthier misunderstood Napoleon's intentions and acted on his own in sending an officer with an order to Partouneaux to remain near Borisov to cover the Grand Army's movement, protect stragglers and divert Chichagov's attention if possible. Victor's letter of 28 November seems to support this notion, since it refers to Berthier's order to

Partouneaux to remain at Borisov.[559] Yet, a prolonged stay in Borisov proved fatal for the 12th Division.

Partouneaux spent most of the morning of the 27th waiting for stragglers to pass through Borisov. Both he and Delaitre described 'immense columns of stragglers' delaying the division's advance. The 12th Division finally entered Borisov around 3 p.m. and rested for one and a half hours to allow the stragglers to depart from Borisov. Dutch Captain Wagevier, who commanded a grenadier company of the 2nd Battalion of the 125th Line, described his troops looking forward to reaching the crossing, but they were exhausted by their march and were 'falling down from fatigue or under the weight of spoils'. Partouneaux kept Camus' brigade in town and had the remaining brigades of Billard and Blanmont on the Orsha road covering Borisov's approaches.[560]

Camus' brigade, according to Delaitre, 'had one battalion deployed in column in the street adjacent to the bridge, which was already protected by a cavalry squadron, and two more battalions at the nearby square. The two other battalions were employed to restore order in the city which was in a complete disorder'. Thousands of stragglers, many of whom still believed in Oudinot's feint bridging at Ukholody, had massed in and around Borisov. Beulay found it difficult to convince these people to evacuate Borisov, where 'they had been retained by hope of sleeping in the warm under a roof'. The roads were cluttered with wagons, carriages and people – camp-followers, straggling soldiers, fugitives from Russian towns, all choking the road. Delaitre observed that:

> The stragglers filled all the houses: patrols could hardly tear off and force them to continue their march. The enemy easily noticed this tumultuous state of affairs and so his forces had been successively increased, waiting for a favourable moment to attack.

As one historian ably described:

> Even more harrowing than the misery and hideous aspect of the fugitives was their utter apathy and helplessness. The crowd heaved itself sluggishly along the tracks in whatever direction it chanced to take or was pushed by moving troops. Most of the wretches who composed it seem to have lost their senses no less than their appearance as more or less civilized human beings. The instincts of comradeship and humanity were almost extinct, and progress was constantly retarded by the brawling and fighting ...[561]

Not far from Borisov, one participant described:

several wagons filled with gold and silver coins had been abandoned, either because their horses had been killed or because the Emperor, afraid his military treasure might profit the enemy, had preferred everyone to take a fistful as he passed by.

Seeing so much wealth, 'even men who could not drag themselves along became agile like monkeys, and strong as dogs disputing a bone; there was a senseless scuffle, a general battle'.[562]

In the late afternoon, Chichagov attempted to threaten the Grand Army's flank by moving his troops across a hastily-repaired bridge at Borisov. Russian Major Khrapovitskii criticized the Admiral for wasting time on this attack instead of marching towards the crossing at Studyanka. But Chichagov was naturally concerned about the presence of enemy forces at Borisov, where, he believed, they might attempt forcing the river. So, 'moving on planks of the damaged bridge', Khrapovitskii described, 'our Jägers crossed the river and attacked the enemy'.[563] According to Camus, the combat began around 4.15 p.m. and his brigade held ground before being assisted by Blanmont's troops.[564] The 125th Line led the charge and Captain Wagevier later remembered that the town presented a terrible sight:

> Imagine a place burning brightly and two armies fighting in the midst of it. Burning houses falling in a terrible noise, the thunder of muskets and guns, moans of the wounded and no hope for mercy: the merciless enemy was in front, behind and all around us.[565]

Partouneaux drove the Russians across the river and then kept Billard and Camus inside the town while Blanmont's brigade served as a rearguard covering the road from Orsha.

By then, Partouneaux was alarmed to hear the sound of guns from the direction of Stary Borisov. Partouneaux and his generals admitted the possibility of the enemy intercepting their line of retreat, but they also believed that the Grand Army would take 'certain measures to prevent this and ensure our retreat'.[566] The appearance of Russian troops spread panic among hundreds of stragglers moving along the main route. Some of them fled – abandoning their possessions and dozens of wagons – in the direction of Studyanka but others, as Delaitre and Ségur described, retreated to Borisov and 'apprized Partouneaux that he was separated from the rest of the army'. The General realized how desperate his position was. He was isolated from his corps by several miles of woods and swamps; Wittgenstein had occupied Stary Borisov in the north, Chichagov's men were in the west and Platov and Miloradovich were expected to appear from the east at any moment. In fact, according to Beulay, the

Cossacks were already harassing the rearguard: 'The passage had to be forced,' writes Delaitre, 'Partouneaux made that resolution at once and communicated it to generals and officers under his command. This feeling being unanimous, the arrangements for advance were made at once.' Gourgaud noted that

> Partouneaux had reason to hope that he could force the [Wittgenstein's] corps to open a passage, for this corps was between two fires [the Grand Army at Studyanka and Partouneaux at Borisov].[567]

Partouneaux marched northwards around 5 p.m.[568] One of Delaitre's light cavalry regiments was tasked with supporting Camus' brigade, which spearheaded the offensive; the other regiment was to cover the right flank and the rear of two other brigades against the Cossacks. Partouneaux left behind one battalion from Blanmont's brigade with instructions to destroy the bridge across the Skha to delay Platov's advance.[569] The Allied troops marched on 'a slippery road, crowded with baggage and runaways, a violent wind blowing directly in [their] face, and a dark and piercing cold night'. Beulay complained that

> The cold was becoming intolerable [...] Our men could hardly load their weapons so painful was the contact with the iron. It was snowing. Great flakes were swirling round our faces and blinding us. We could not see so much as 50 metres ahead of us.

As Sous-Lieutenant Wolf described:

> two cavalry regiments remained close to Borisov to gather the few detachments which still remained behind. When it was our regiment's turn to march, we could clearly see the proximity of the enemy from the fires surrounding us. Our weak and exhausted horses could hardly support themselves on the ground [...] The previous days had been so distressing for us that we were in a true physical and moral torpor. In this state of total exhaustion, we could hardly perform as cavalry, although we were not afraid of the prospect of fighting our way through.[570]

Delaitre wrote:

> At the first signal, the battalions advanced in tight columns along the road. Neither difficult terrain, nor the number and strong position of the enemy or the arrival of [Russian] *parlementaire* could delay the advance of soldiers whose devotion and bravery deserved the best success possible.

The Battle of the Berezina

The Russian *parlementaire* delivered Wittgenstein's request for Partouneaux's surrender, to which the French General supposedly responded: 'I am not turning back and you are about to witness our efforts that will force you to let us through.' The French General detained the messenger and resumed the march.[571]

In these difficult circumstances, Partouneaux made a fateful mistake. Moving by forced march, his troops approached a crossroads not far from Borisov where two tracks led north. That to the left skirted the bank while the right led to the north-east through Stary Bykhov, now occupied by the Russians. With the road to the left full of stragglers, Partouneaux turned to the right, believing it would take him directly to Studyanka: instead, as Labaume explained, 'this mistake took the division right into the middle of Wittgenstein's entire corps'.[572] Murat's aide-de-camp, Rossetti, made the same mistake the day earlier and his account helps us understand Partouneaux's error. About an hour's journey from Borisov, Rossetti wrote:

> the road divided and as the Berezina flowed on my left I did not hesitate to take the road on that side. But after marching for a while I noticed that this road was not trampled down and that the snow covering it was virtually intact. So I turned back and took the right-hand route. The night was very dark; yet I had noticed that it was insensibly bending to my right and that I had necessarily turned my back on the river.

Unable to figure out the direction, Rossetti stopped his 'little column'. Around 2 a.m., an artillery park from IX Corps appeared behind him. Its colonel studied the map before departing and insisted that the right-hand road was the right one – he later stumbled upon the Russians. Rossetti was not convinced and, at dawn, he marched back to the Berezina, where he followed the original path.[573] Alas, Partouneaux's division made the same 'cruel mistake' – in the words of the 29th Bulletin – on the 27th and stayed true to the course. Only one battalion, the 4th of the 55th Line, commanded by Major Joyeux, who had been charged with the destruction of the bridges on the Skha, avoided this blunder.[574] On leaving Borisov, he also reached the crossroads but turned left from the main road. Marching along the swampy banks of the Berezina, Joyeux passed the village of Maly Stakhov, where he took a guide who safely led the battalion to Studyanka. On hearing of its arrival, Napoleon assumed it was Partouneaux's entire division and ordered Gourgaud to greet it. Meeting Joyeux, Gourgaud inquired if the division was far off, and was surprised to hear the Major's reply: 'It can only be ahead of me, I am its rearguard.'[575] It was obvious that something had happened to the 12th Division and, as the 29th Bulletin recorded, 'some uneasiness [about its fate] was conceived'. Gourgaud informed the Emperor of this unpleasant development, causing him to exclaim: 'Why, just when by a miracle everything had seemed to be saved, does this have to come and spoil it all?'[576]

So what happened to the 12th Division? Approaching Stary Borisov, Partouneaux's division had Camus' brigade, supported by Chef de Bataillon Sibille's four light cannon (ten others were with Daendels' division), and Delaitre's horsemen moving ahead: 'I supported them with the 3rd Brigade while General Blanmont received orders to capture the heights on our flank,' reported Partouneaux. Camus described: 'I advanced with my *voltigeurs* in front of me. Some three and half *verstas* from the bridge, passing on a sunken road at the bottom of a chain of hillocks, we encountered the enemy …'[577] These were the Cossacks and Grodnenskii Hussars dispatched by Wittgenstein towards Borisov. Seeing 'a major troop movement straight in front of us' the Allied troops hoped it was Victor. Alas, writes Beulay, 'It was the Russian artillery taking up position to bar our path.'[578] But the Russian fire 'did not cool the ardour of the brave men I commanded,' claimed Camus, 'Colonel [Jean-Chrysostôme Bruneteau de] St Suzanne swept the heights with two battalions of his regiment [29th Légère]. I supported him at once with the remainder of my brigade, which probably comprised six hundred combatants; I then proceeded along the road leading to [Studyanka].'[579]

The Allied troops 'attacked with great resolution', notes Chambray, but were repeatedly repelled. 'In spite of the audacity and determination of these attacks, which were made and renewed at different points, we gained no ground against stronger enemy forces,' concluded Delaitre. The Russians 'had superior troops and artillery on the road and they soon stopped our advance with intense musket fire and an overwhelming quantity of round shots and canister', reported Sibille.[580] By this time, Vlastov's forces, on the right flank behind the village and covering the road to Studyanka, were reinforced by the newly-arrived corps of Steinheil, which occupied the centre and left flank, while Lieutenant General Berg's corps was kept in reserve. Partouneaux initially attacked Vlastov's positions and Steinheil's right flank, engaging the Navaginskii Infantry Regiment and two *opolchenye druzhinas* (the 7th of St Petersburg and the 4th of Novgorod), which were supported by Major General Heilfreich's 4th HAC.

The advancing French and Dutch troops suffered frontal and flanking fire from the Russian batteries but some units, notably the 44th Line, managed to break into Stary Borisov, where they fought a close-quarter combat with the Russians.[581] Observing the enemy positions, Camus believed that 'there could be three thousand [enemy] infantrymen in the first line alone; I also noticed the second line, stronger than the first, with approximately two thousand horsemen and ten cannon'. To deal with the Russian artillery, Sibille deployed two of his 6–pounder guns on a small hill in the woods, which perfectly exposed the enemy:

The Battle of the Berezina

I fired some thirty rounds of grapeshot at a distance of some fifty *toises* [100m], which caused heavy casualties to the enemy and forced him to retreat in disorder, and allowed our lead troops to march to the edge of the wood.[582]

According to Camus:

> The fighting intensified as we engaged the enemy, who turned to bayonets [...] I must note that stragglers limited our actions in this battle. Their crowds mingled among us, cluttered the road and thwarted our manoeuvres. General Blanmont, seeing me in the heat of action, had to resort to bayonets to get rid of these poor wretches and arrive to my support in time.[583]

Stary Borisov changed hands several times and Camus and Billard attacked the Russian positions on both sides of it. At one moment, they even managed to capture a Russian battery west of the village.

The numerical superiority of the Russians soon tipped the scales. Vlastov counter-attacked with the Azovskii and Navaginskii Regiments, supported by the 25th Jägers and *opolchenye* (4th and 6th *druzhinas* of Novgorod, 2nd, 3rd and 7th *druzhina* of St Petersburg).[584] The fighting was fierce and the Russian *opolchenye* records offer interesting insights. Colonel Pogrebov, commanding the 4th Novgorod *druzhina*, was wounded eight times and later died as a result (Zauryad-Major Fetsov took over the command of the *druzhina*). Lieutenant Korsakov, a *sotnya* commander of the 7th St Petersburg *druzhina*, was seriously wounded in the neck. Cornet Trusevich, who was earlier sent on a reconnaissance mission, used his newly-gained knowledge of the terrain to move the 3rd St Petersburg *druzhina* unnoticed through a ravine and turn Partouneaux's right flank. The 2nd St Petersburg *druzhina* was deployed in an open order and, facing an enemy attack, Major Goroshevskii 'led the second line of skirmishers to support the first which already engaged the French, driving the enemy out of the woods and pursuing them all the way to their baggage train'. Several officers were commended for 'bravely charging with the reserves when the enemy column tried to turn the right flank of our skirmishers'. During one such attack, Colonel Chemiot, commanding the 7th St Petersburg *druzhina*, led his men 'in a closed column to reinforce the 1st Battalion of the Navaginskii Infantry Regiment, deployed on the right flank in front of the village'. The 7th *druzhina* and the 1st Battalion later coordinated a bayonet attack that drove back the French and inflicted 'heavy losses in killed and wounded'.[585] General Camus also acknowledged that the 'Cossacks and the Russian infantry threatened our rear; they captured our baggage and that of Colonel St Suzanne, one of our pieces of artillery, and a few prisoners. Commandant Sibille was wounded by a bayonet to the hand defending his artillery piece'. Despite a disabled right hand, Sibille 'advanced with my artillery and placed it so as to open a passage for us. Both sides maintained an intense cannonade for nearly two hours, during which we fired more than 400 rounds and a huge quantity of grapeshot, which inflicted heavy losses on the enemy ...' As more and more gunners died and were wounded, Captain Levasseur 'appealed to the stragglers to come and man the pieces, but none of them did, unwilling to expose themselves to danger'.[586]

In the midst of the battle, Partouneaux received two important messages. Unbeknown to him, Colonel Alexander Seslavin's flying detachment raided Borisov late in the evening, capturing two guns and up to 3,000 stragglers.[587] While expecting the arrival of Platov's Cossacks, Seslavin was supported by Chichagov, who sent one infantry regiment across the hastily-repaired Borisov bridge. The loss of Borisov meant that the 12th Division had no place to retreat and was exposed from the rear, forcing it to fight on two fronts at once.

Of equal importance was the (erroneous) news that the bridges at Studyanka were burning. Camus' report mentions that 'a fire which burst in this moment on the river, greatly alarmed me and I communicated my concerns to the general of division'. Although Camus does not specify, Partouneaux's report leaves no doubt that it was 'the bridge on which we were to pass' across the Berezina. Ségur also tells us that Partouneaux's 'aide-de-camp named Rochex [...] asserted that he had seen the bridges at Studyanka on fire'. It is unclear what Rochex or Camus might have seen and some sources suggest that, with darkness descending, they might have confused the burning bridges over the Skha River, which were set alight on Partouneaux's own orders, or they might have been misled by the bonfires of stragglers warming up at Studyanka.

Thinking he was abandoned, Partouneaux decided 'to try to slip between the enemy units under cover of darkness'.[588] Partouneaux later argued that he informed his subordinates, particularly General Blanmont, of his plans to scale the heights and break through the Russian defences, and Colonel Boyer, chief of staff of the 12th Division, delivered this information. Camus' report does mention Partouneaux suggested to him of his decision 'to try breaking through to right or left' and 'attempt either fording or swimming across the Berezina; Partouneaux himself intended to go to the right'.[589] In his after-action report, however, Marshal Victor blamed Partouneaux for 'not informing his generals about the orders he had received and the direction that his division was to follow to rejoin the army'. In 1821, General Blanmont, who read an article Partouneaux published to justify himself in *Le Moniteur Universel*, wrote to the editor of *Constitutionnelle* that he 'had not received any orders to ascend the heights from Boyer'. Instead, Partouneaux's ADC, Gaille, requested that I sent a battalion from my brigade, and rejoin promptly the division with the remainder of my troops; this order was carried out to the letter; the battalion that I dispatched had ascended the heights without encountering the enemy or General Partouneaux. It, thus, reached the bridges over the Berezina, where it rejoined the Grand Army. I wish I had received the order [from Boyer]: I would have carried it out the same way I executed the one brought to me by Gaille […] And I would have avoided a serious wound and twenty-one months of captivity …[590]

This criticism stung Partouneaux, who responded in the March 4 issue of the *Constitutionnelle*: 'As for the order disputed by Blanmont,' observed the General, 'at Vitebsk, in the presence of several senior officers, the chief of my staff [Boyer] had confirmed he had delivered the order directly to Blanmont; these witnesses are still alive and reside in Paris; besides, I possess incontestable materials that will be produced if needed.' Partouneaux accused Blanmont of lapsed memory and confusing orders he had received:

> [Blanmont] might have misunderstood the order or confused it with another I sent with my ADC Alguay; that order instructed him to leave one of his battalions to burn the bridge over the Skha and serve as a rearguard; this provision was in accordance with the order which had been given to me by Victor to burn the bridges upon withdrawal.[591]

Partouneaux then highlighted similarities between Blanmont's account and the actions of the 4th of the 55th Line, which was tasked with burning the bridge over the Skha.

Whoever was right, by late evening, the 12th Division was scattered across the battlefield and Partouneaux himself rallied some 400–600 survivors of the 3rd Brigade. Wittgenstein sent another officer with an offer to surrender but Partouneaux detained him to gain time. Under cover of darkness, he led his men onto the steep and woody heights on his right, hoping to pass through Wittgenstein's positions unnoticed. He tried breaking through in several places but each time he ran into Russian defences. Partouneaux seems to have lost his way in the darkness and, at one moment, found himself marching on a half-frozen bog, falling through the ice and almost drowning before his troops saved him. By midnight, Partouneaux again approached the Russian positions, where he was surrounded by Chernozubov's Cossacks. With his men exhausted from fighting, cold and hunger, Partouneaux decided to surrender. At 11 p.m. Steinheil received a messenger who informed him of the surrender offer. In the early morning on 28 November, the Russians brought in 'General de division Partouneaux, General de brigade Billard, two colonels, thirty officers and 600 soldiers'.[592]

Campaign Chronicle

Meantime, Camus,

made arrangements for the execution of the new order, but I was no more fortunate in it than in the earlier one. Everywhere I tried I found superior enemy columns above us and I could not pass. During this combat, which lasted three hours, we received no news from the bridges [at Studyanka] and no reinforcements came to our help. We, however, had to leave the valley where we were located; it was probably around 7 p.m.

Camus summoned a brief council of war and, together with Blanmont and Delaitre, made a decision to retreat 'to the heights some three-quarters of [a] *lieue* from Borisov, the only strong position in the vicinity'. It was during this movement that Blanmont was wounded by a musket ball in his right knee and Delaitre slightly injured in his left arm: 'The number of killed, captured or wounded among officers and soldiers soon rose to two-thirds of the effective force. It was necessary to put an end to this unequal combat,' reported Delaitre.

Camus now took over the command of nearby units and retreated towards Borisov, which he found occupied by the Russians. 'During this rather difficult march,' writes Camus,

We were accompanied by stragglers, at least 7,000 strong, who spread great confusion in our ranks and made it impossible for us to conduct orderly manoeuvres. Our small *pelotons* seemingly floated amidst their multitudes and suffered from the enemy, who occupied the heights [...] At last, we reached the heights, where I formed my infantry in three columns and Delaitre flanked them with his cavalry.

Camus was still regrouping his forces when the Russian cavalry (probably from Seslavin's detachment and Platov's Cossacks) appeared from Borisov and charged them: 'We met it with volleys,' describe Camus, 'but the enemy counter-attacked at once with canister fire. This combat lasted half an hour before the enemy withdrew out of our range, and we remained under arms, in this position on the road, for the rest of the night.'[593] The regimental histories describe the 125th and the 44th Line forming a square to face the Russian charges and suffering heavily from artillery fire. Captain Wagevier recalled:

It was impossible to do anything in that tempestuous night and we were not bothered any more. But we did not know at that time that we were surrounded by the Russians. We laid on the ground without leaving our positions in the square and got closer to each other to warm up. I lay next to the drummers and sappers on the snow in the middle of the square.

When I decided to get up, I discovered that my coat was frozen to the ground and I struggled to get it off without ripping it. The most depressing thoughts about my future filled my soul …[594]

Another participant (Beulay) remembered the survivors gathering in a ravine behind a small wood, which shielded them from the Russians. The 4th Battalion of the 36th Line remained on the plateau to keep the Russians at a distance. At about 10 p.m., Beulay's battalion commander ordered him to find the commanding general and tell him the regiment was suffering losses, had run out of ammunition and could not hold ground any more. Reaching the safety of the ravine, Beulay was stunned by 'the senseless disorder reigning at its bottom; it was impossible to rally any unit whatsoever, regiment or battalion …' Many officers were killed or wounded and 'we no longer had any generals or colonels; from that moment it was some rare commandants and captains who took over their functions'.[595]

The Russians maintained fire throughout the evening, inflicting heavy casualties: 'It was a veritable butchery!' writes a French participant, stunned by 'the horrible uproar, the cries of the wounded, the rattle of the dying, the whistling of musket balls, the snorting of roundshots and the roaring of the guns'.[596] To stop this bloodbath, Wittgenstein finally ordered a ceasefire and sent a flag of truce, informing the survivors that Partouneaux and the 3rd Brigade had already surrendered. As Camus described (and Delaitre confirmed): 'around 10 p.m., an officer of the 126th Line, who was captured, came to inform me that Partouneaux, his entire staff, General Billard and his brigade, Colonel St Suzanne and part of his two battalions [29th Légère], were all made prisoners, and that Wittgenstein had sent him to demand my surrender as well.' But, 'no one believed that our divisional general had capitulated', Beulay recalled, 'so, without listening to him any longer, the Russian officer [who probably accompanied the French one] was sent back'. Appreciating their reckless bravery, Wittgenstein seems to have dispatched another messenger, inviting the French to send someone to verify the fact that the 3rd Brigade had indeed surrendered. Camus convened a council of war, which selected Chef de Bataillon Landevoisin for this task, with instructions to 'scrupulously observe' Russian forces and to prolong negotiations until dawn. Camus then selected three officers to ford or swim across the Berezina and seek orders and reinforcements from the main army. Instead of crossing the Berezina, these officers found a small path leading to Victor's camp by dawn.[597] But it was too late to save Camus' men.

Camus and Delaitre spent the entire night sending out many detachments and officers to all points on the Berezina to find a passage: 'The river from Borisov until the position occupied by the enemy was covered on the edges with a thick crust of ice and thawed out in the middle,' described Delaitre. 'It was not fordable at any point. Several troopers drowned while trying to reach the opposite bank, which was continuously traversed by Cossack parties. Attempting to break through to the right [towards Stary Borisov] presented even fewer chances of success; Wittgenstein's army covered all the passages ...'[598]

Meantime, as he travelled to the Russian camp, Landevoisin seems to have been accompanied by grenadier Lieutenant Taillefer (at least Beulay claims so). Escorted to the Russian headquarters, Taillefer found Partouneaux 'in a state of utter despondency'. Wittgenstein talked to the grenadier, 'threatening to kill every man to the last' unless the remaining troops surrendered at once.[599] Around 8.30 a.m. on 28 November, Landevoisin returned to his brigade with devastating news:

> Wittgenstein has a corps of 45,000 men; 15,000 men with fifty guns are ahead of the bridge, and 20,000 men are on our right flank. Chichagov has 15,000 men on our left. Platov, with approximately 25,000 men, including 10,000 horsemen, has occupied Borisov at night and is in our rear. I walked all night long and saw enemy lines – the forces that I told you are not exaggerated. I also saw Partouneaux and Billard, both are captives.

Camus was now convinced that further resistance was futile and surrendered around 9 a.m. Later that morning, Steinheil described the Grodnenskii Hussars escorting the prisoners, which included 'Generals Camus, Blanmont and Delaitre, three colonels, fifteen lieutenant colonels, some 150 officers and up to 4,500 soldiers, with three guns and numerous wagons and horses'.[600] The Berg Lancers tried to avoid surrender and a few dared to swim across the river but floundered under ice and drowned; so their commanding officer, Count Nesselrode, led the survivors to the nearby heights, from which Partouneaux had previously failed to find an escape route. Finding Russian forces in position once more, the remaining 164 lancers could do nothing but surrender.[601]

Overall, the Russians captured over 5,000 men, but some estimates go as high as 8,000–9,000; General Berg referred to four generals, fifty officers and 6,000 soldiers captured.[602] Of these, probably up to 2,500 men were from the 12th Division and the rest were stragglers from various units caught up in the fighting. Napoleon's 29th Bulletin referred to the loss of '2,000 infantry, 300 cavalry and three guns captured' but failed to account for dead, wounded and stragglers. The division also lost two eagles from the 44th and 126th Lines. The famous *Victoires, conquêtes [...] des Français* estimated the loss at '3,000 infantry, two weak cavalry regiments and three cannon'.[603] Scholars still disagree on the precise losses of that day, some acknowledging combatant losses but ignoring the thousands of stragglers captured that day. Edward Foord and David Chandler believed that only 160 men out of Partouneaux's 4,500 escaped, and this estimate is repeated in later works. A recent

The Battle of the Berezina

Russian study (I. Vasiliev) refers to some 7,400 captured, including over 200 officers and three guns. In his massive study of Napoleonic battle casualties, Digby Smith cites 264 officers (including four generals) and 7,800 men captured, and these numbers most certainly include stragglers as well. The *Encyclopedia of the Patriotic War of 1812* (2004) estimated the casualties of the 12th Division at 1,614 infantry and 300 cavalry captured, with three guns and two eagles.[604]

Partouneaux himself reported that 'the division has suffered very high casualties relative to its strength; by the end of the day it was reduced to less than half of its strength'. Delaitre estimated that some 1,500 men survived the battle, while '4,000–5,000 stragglers fell to the enemy; most wounded died during the night'. Camus reported that on 27 November he had 1,130 combatants in his brigade, but the following morning only 291 were present: 'The brigade of Blanmont also suffered great losses,' he wrote, 'and it had less than 300 men. Sibille had only fifteen gunners remaining out of forty he had the day before.' Sibille himself reported that 'only eighteen gunners survived out of forty-two, the rest were killed or wounded'.[605] Martinien's study reveals fifty-three officers lost in the 29th Light, twenty-nine in the 44th Line, twenty-seven in the 126th, sixteen in the 51st Line, twelve in the 36th Line and twelve in the 10th Light. The regimental history of the 125th Line shows that only 120 men survived the battle and thirty-three officers were killed, mortally wounded or became so weak that they died days later. The regimental histories of the 36th and 51st Line note that less than 200 men survived in these units. Oleg Sokolov estimated the loss of 1,896 men in the 12th Division and showed 102 casualties in the 10th Light, and over 830 men in Camus' brigade. Andolenko refers to 439 men (out of 749) lost in the 44th and cites Colonel Dumoulin's letter showing the loss of 206 men (out of 346) in the 126th Line; the latter regiment counted 1,887 men in Smolensk.[606]

As Boniface de Castellane remarked, 'Luck, one has to admit, seems to have abandoned these poor fellows.'[607] Indeed, some men in the 12th Division had only recently been released from prison hulks in England after being captured at Saint Domingue in 1801. Now they faced another long imprisonment. A Russian officer thought 'The prisoners of this division suffered much from the hardships of life [...] The Saxons [from the Prinz Johann Chevauléger Regiment] despaired when parting with their horses and one old sergeant cried bitterly at the thought of giving up his horse.' Among the anguished Saxons was Sous-Lieutenant Wolf, who described a 'heart-wrenching scene' of surrendering horses to the Grodnenskii Hussars. The prisoners seem to have been abused and robbed in the first few hours of captivity.[608] One of them, Captain Wagevier, left an interesting account of his experiences in Russian custody:

Since we knew we were prisoners now, we laid down our arms, sorrowfully awaiting our fate. [Russian] officers, who spoke fluent German and French, approached us from time to time. They were mostly friendly to us and tried to soothe us by saying that such were the fortunes of war and we should not lose our spirits. But these pleasing words hardly helped us [...] I was in the hands of several rough Russians, who searched me, took my watch and purse and then left me cursing [for not having more]. I had to tolerate this quietly since any opposition was futile. I saw how one colonel from the 44th Line was stabbed for resisting. My poor horse was taken from me [...] Some time later another group surrounded me, tore off my epaulettes and medal, and ripped my collet. I silently endured this abuse [...] and was glad to escape with only a few shoves and pushes. But I later suffered the most humiliating abuse, which deeply affected me. A Russian grenadier approached me with a loaded musket, stopped in front of me, tore a scarf off my neck and seeing that I had no other possession left, he spat in my face and called me a 'French dog'. He then ordered me to remain in place and proceeded to another victim. Thus, deprived of everything, I no longer feared any examinations and was left alone. But even in such dramatic circumstances the spirit of the French Army remained alive: to prevent our colour from falling into enemy hands and becoming a trophy, some soldiers from our regiment concealed the colour and the eagle so thoroughly that the Russians could not find it.[609]

The news of Partouneaux's surrender stunned and infuriated Napoleon. This was the second time a major Allied unit surrendered during the 1812 Campaign – eighteen days earlier General Jean Pierre Augereau's brigade (1,700 men) surrendered to the Russians at Lyakhovo. On hearing of Partouneaux's fate, Napoleon declared:

> If generals have not the courage to put up a fight, they can at least let the grenadiers do it! A drummer could have saved his comrades from dishonour by sounding a charge. A *cantinière* could have saved the division by shouting 'Every man for himself' instead of surrendering.

Besides losing an entire combat division, a major blow in itself, the Emperor had spent the entire day (the 27th) waiting for Partouneaux, which forced him to defend the crossing on the 28th as well. The Grand Army could have used this time to break away from the pursuing Russian armies. Instead, it remained on the banks of the Berezina and had to fight a bloody engagement on two banks at once and ultimately abandon thousands of stragglers.

Partouneaux spent over a year in captivity and returned to France in the summer of 1814. By then, his reputation was undermined by the 29th Bulletin and Napoleon's harsh assessment. On 2 February 1813, he wrote from captivity:

'It is in the middle of misfortunes caused by captivity that we have just read the 29th Bulletin reprinted in all the newspapers. Everything related to the 12th Division and me is based on the falsest reports.'[610] He sought to clear his name but the damage to his reputation was already done. In 1815, during the Hundred Days, Napoleon refused to accept him back into service and Partouneaux wrote to him in an attempt to clear his name:

> You were quite unjust towards me in your bulletin, which was a major blow to me: people who were unaware of the orders that I had received, the obstacles that I had faced, accused and condemned me; the brave men who knew me did not support me but they feared for me; I did not complain at the time about your extreme injustice. But every day I still feel the need of explaining this cruel and unfortunate affair.

Partouneaux's 'Addresse', published in 1815, contained various documents, including the reports of Partouneaux, Camus, and Delaitre, relating to the events at Stary Borisov. Partouneaux also wrote extensively to various journals to defend his actions during the battle. Thus, in August 1817, he told the editor of the *Journal Annales Politiques, Morales and Literréraires* that the recently-published history of the Russian campaign by Ségur was 'greatly inaccurate' when describing the battle at Stary Borisov. He declared Ségur biased and claimed that Soult, Davout, Clarke and St Cyr all spoke against the official version recounted in the 29th Bulletin.[611] Four years later, Partouneaux again turned to his quill, writing to the editor of *Le Moniteur Universel*, criticizing the newly-released volume XXI of *Victoires, conquêtes [...] des Français* for its 'very laconic' (the battle was described in ten lines) and 'erroneous' description of the battle. In March, he published another piece in response to an article by General Blanmont, which questioned some of Partouneaux's arguments (see above). He also argued that 'If I had left Borisov earlier, perhaps I would have reached the bridges on which the army crossed the river; but I had specific orders from the Emperor and had to follow them ...'[612]

28 November: The Crossing, Day 3

The dawn of the new day proved foggy and cold: 'The sky was sombre' recalled Dumonceau. 'The snow had been falling so thickly that the daylight had been obscured by it,' wrote another officer. 'The paths traced yesterday by the infantry and artillery have been covered over again to a depth of a foot and a half.' Wilson thought that

> This frost was 'a mingled yarn of good and ill' for Napoleon. Good, as it hardened the surface of the marsh beyond, and assured practicable transit

when reached; bad, as it augmented the general distress, and added intensely to the labour and suffering of the workmen toiling day and night in the ice-binding stream.[613]

Russian Plans for Attack

For the Russians, the victory at Stary Borisov was twofold. First, they had destroyed a major enemy division, captured thousands of troops and liberated Borisov. Besides the military significance, the victory also had great propaganda value. Second, the advance guard commanders of Wittgenstein, Chichagov and Kutuzov finally established direct communications. Malinovski described that 'around 11 p.m. the main field army's advance guard, under the command of Ataman Platov and MG Yermolov, arrived and the Admiral's army completed the construction of the pontoon bridges at Borisov by dawn'.[614] Important as it was, direct contact caused new problems. Among these commanders, Chichagov was senior in rank and Wittgenstein now had to fall in line. But the 'saviour of St Petersburg' had no such intentions. Thus, Prince Golitsyn, Kutuzov's orderly, overheard the Field Marshal complaining about Wittgenstein undermining the Russian operation 'out of sheer pride and unwillingness to subordinate himself'.[615]

Seslavin, who acted on behalf of Wittgenstein, reached the headquarters of the 3rd Western Army around 10 p.m. on 27 November. Chichagov recalled that Seslavin

> asked me what I intended to do, but his tone revealed at once that Wittgenstein considered himself completely independent and intended to act on his own discretion. Thus, besides the fact that [Wittgenstein's] support was belated, a petty vanity now interfered and harmed coordination of our actions.

Chichagov explained to Seslavin that the council of war, held earlier that evening, decided to attack the Grand Army along the western flank and 'invited' Wittgenstein to launch a simultaneous attack on the eastern bank. He also requested two infantry divisions as reinforcements. Mikhailovsky-Danilevsky described Wittgenstein agreeing to three key provisions: the Army of the Danube would engage the enemy at Stakhov, Platov and Yermolov would cross to the western bank and support Chichagov, while Wittgenstein's corps would attack in the direction of Studyanka.[616] But as Chichagov noted, Wittgenstein 'did not respond to my request for reinforcements but promised to attack at dawn, which he then failed to do'. That same night Chichagov also met Kutuzov's messenger, Flügel Adjutant Mikhail Orlov. The Admiral was stunned to hear that instead of being in the immediate vicinity of Borisov, Kutuzov was,

The Battle of the Berezina

Estimated Crossing Timeline, 28 November

12–7 a.m. (?)	Bridges were deserted; stragglers were urged to cross but very few did
From 8 a.m. through most of the day	Stragglers and transports slowly crossed, but bridges collapsed on a few occasions, interrupting passage
~ 9 p.m.	The IX Corps began crossing; Fournier's cavalry and the Poles were the last to cross at dawn of 29 November

in fact, 'six marches away'. Chichagov commented sarcastically: 'This reveals how "relentlessly" he pursued the enemy. This is called to "follow at the heels of the enemy from a reasonable distance."'[617]

On Chichagov's orders, several messengers crossed over to Borisov to meet the arriving advance guards of the main Russian army. Passing through Borisov full of stragglers, Lieutenant Martos proceeded along the Smolensk road, finding Platov, whom he advised to accelerate the movement. Turning to the Orsha road, Martos set out to find Yermolov's advance guard:

> It was a windy and cold day; all roads were covered with snow. Crowds of Frenchmen wandered in nearby fields, setting up fires, slicing horse meat and gnawing at bones, frying or eating raw meat. I soon came across ice-covered corpses and freezing men. These images would never fade from my memory. I shuddered looking at them but kept going. The road lined with the bodies of dead warriors and horses showed me the way [...] Some 17 *verstas* from Borisov, I finally met Yermolov.[618]

By then, Chichagov's other adjutant, Lieutenant Lisanevich, also reached Yermolov, who had 'bivouacked near Loshnitsa, the last post station before Borisov'.[619] Lisanevich asked Yermolov to hasten to Borisov, to which he agreed: 'As I sent the adjutant back,' Yermolov remembered, 'I gave him a report to the Admiral and asked that he be informed that my troops, although having just completed an arduous march, were ready to make another one. I still thought it necessary to give them four hours to prepare porridge, repair their shoes and rest [...] The troops marched quickly, burning with the desire to fight, and they entered Borisov long before noon [on 28 November].' Arriving at Borisov, Yermolov first met Platov, who told him of Chichagov's repeated requests to hurry across the river.

By dawn

several pontoon bridges were built, covered with straw and drenched with water which had frozen in the cold. The infantry passed over without difficulty, and the artillery and ammunition caissons were also transported without problems. The exceptional ability and adroitness of the Cossacks overcame all hurdles; fords were discovered and two cuirassier regiments crossed the river at once.

Yermolov then met Wittgenstein, who had also established his headquarters at Borisov. The meeting is interesting because it again highlights the existing enmity among the Russian commanders. 'As an old acquaintance,' Yermolov wrote,

Wittgenstein received me with particular attention and I found in him all the traits of a knight, not the least of which was pride. It was evident in his discussion of the plans and actions he had carried out, the many battles he had won and the courage of his troops. He told me that Admiral Chichagov, although having the means to prevent the enemy crossing or decisively defeat the army of Napoleon, had only left a weak detachment under General Czaplic and moved his remaining troops a considerable distance away.

Although true on the surface, such a claim was misleading and injurious to Chichagov, especially since Wittgenstein knew the real reasons for Chichagov's redeployment of the army. Talking to the Count, Yermolov realized that

Wittgenstein was already aware that the main reason why the Admiral had marched towards Igumen was because of the Field Marshal [Kutuzov] as he had heard unsubstantiated information about Napoleon seeking a crossing site there.

Nevertheless, Wittgenstein refused to accept Chichagov's authority and, although promising to help him, failed to act upon it. Some of Wittgenstein's senior officers were upset by this. Yermolov described finding Major General Ivan Begichev, the duty general at Wittgenstein's headquarters and a 'strict and demanding' officer, who complained about discord: 'We are acting like children who ought to be whipped with birches.'[620]

Operations on the Western Bank: Battle of Stakhov-Brili
With the arrival of Wittgenstein, Platov and Yermolov, Napoleon faced the dire prospect of being entrapped. Chichagov had some 34,000 men, Wittgenstein

about 36,000–38,000 and Yermolov and Platov some 12,000, which meant that the Russians had some 84,000 men in the immediate vicinity of Borisov and Studyanka. But less than half of them would be engaged in the battles of 28 November. The effective strength of Chichagov's forces committed to the battle at Stakhov was probably around 23,000–25,000 men, Wittgenstein diverted only 14,000–15,000 men to Studyanka (the rest remained at Stary Borisov and Borisov) while Platov guarded the Minsk road and Yermolov's detachment (exhausted by a long march) was kept in reserve. Some authors, especially Francophiles, tend to exaggerate the Russian numerical superiority and often refer to some 120,000–150,000 men seeking to entrap Napoleon's depleted Grand Army. But these numbers are incorrect, since they count Kutuzov's army, which was days away from the Berezina and played no role in the fighting.

Late on 27 November, Chichagov informed Czaplic of the arrival of reinforcements. He urged him 'to attack the enemy tomorrow. I will follow you at once, and Count Wittgenstein will attack the enemy crossing [from the east]'. The following morning, Czaplic, reinforced by Jäger detachments from Pahlen's advance guard, moved towards the positions held by Oudinot's II Corps around 5 a.m. Chichagov promised to support his attack with all available forces when time permitted and, in the meantime, as Czaplic described, the Admiral 'placed several more regiments under my disposal, pledging to deploy the remaining forces of the corps in such a manner so they can follow me in columns'.[621] At dawn, Platov's Cossacks were the first to cross to the western bank and Yermolov's detachment followed shortly afterwards. Chichagov suggested moving some cavalry to the left flank, where they could break through to the Zembino swamps and destroy the wooden causeways to cut Napoleon's line of retreat. For this mission, he selected 'all cavalry except for five regiments'.[622] However, to accomplish this, the cavalry (mainly Cossacks) first had to cross the Gaina River. Colonel P. Kaisarov led them to reconnoitre the area and find fords across the river. Davydov and Yermolov both agree that the Cossacks found the river 'not frozen yet and, although the creek was shallow everywhere, it was impossible to approach to within less than 30 *sazhens* from it because of impassable swamps, in which our horses got stuck'.[623] One wonders what would have happened if the Cossacks had successfully raided Zembino and destroyed the causeway and bridges there? Napoleon might have attempted rebuilding them while repelling attacks from Chichagov and Wittgenstein; or, as Yermolov argued, he might have attempted to 'seize the road to Minsk, where he would have found abundant supplies, could rest his army, call in reinforcements from Lithuania and restore order'.

As the first sunrays pierced the morning mist, Czaplic deployed his forces in four groups. MG Rudzevich led the 10th and 22nd Jägers in the centre, supported by MG Kornilov's 7th, 12th and 28th Jägers inside the woods on the right flank and MG Mesherinov's 27th, 32nd and 38th Jägers in the woods on the left. Arnoldi's 13th HAC moved behind the infantry and was protected by the Pavlogradskii Hussars and two dragoon squadrons (unclear which units). Colonel Krasovskii led the 14th Jägers, two dragoon (?) and Cossack regiments and four guns along the riverbank, protecting the extreme right flank. The signal for attack was a salvo by two guns of Arnoldi's company.[624] Chichagov, who reached Stakhov around 8 a.m., organized reinforcements from the 9th and 18th Divisions, which he moved in support of Czaplic by 9 a.m. Behind Czaplic's position the Admiral 'came across an elevated terrain, with a stream flowing in front of it', where he deployed a reserve artillery in anticipation of any enemy breakthroughs or to provide cover for an orderly withdrawal.[625]

Expecting the enemy assault, Napoleon arranged his forces in a four-line-deep position. The first line included the II Corps: Albert's division (~1,200 men) was on the left side of the road while Maison (~2,000) and Merlet (~800) took up positions to the right; a thick chain of skirmishers was deployed in front of them. Behind them was the second line under Ney; in the centre, along the road, stood a few hundred survivors of the III Corps and the remnants of the V Corps, supported by Edward Zołtowski's brigade and Malinowski's 14th Polish Regiment.[626] The 17th Division (~850 men) was on the left side while the Vistula Legion (~1,800 men) was on the right flank. Dąbrowski's eight guns were placed on a hill not far from the road. The third line served as reserves and included Doumerc's cuirassier division, and the light cavalry brigades of Castex and Corbineau. Napoleon kept the Imperial Guard (Mortier's Young Guard, Lefevbre's Old Guard, and Bessières' Guard Cavalry) as main reserves near Zanivki. The I and IV Corps were slowly moving towards Zembino, accompanying the train and wounded and securing the defiles and bridges across the marshes. Victor's IX Corps still remained on the eastern bank. It is difficult to determine the strength of these units, since most were undermanned, and some presented only shadows of their former strength. Thus, Ney's III Corps counted around 400 men and the 25th Division, which officially included six infantry and four cavalry regiments, had only 150 survivors. The strength of the Grand Army varies depending on the source and most numbers cited are 'guesstimates'. It is possible that the total number of combatants was around 40,000 men with over 250 guns. The cavalry was decimated by the elements and fighting and probably still counted some 5,000–5,500 men. Most of this force – around 20,000 men – was concentrated on the western bank and thus faced Chichagov's army. The number of stragglers accompanying the army but still stranded on the western bank probably approached 30,000 men.

The Allied soldiers naturally expected the assault: 'In advance we could calculate that the Balance of Victory would, for us, tip on the side of Misfortune,' wrote Tellegen of the 128th Dutch Regiment. 'Our situation was most fatal:

The Battle of the Berezina

The Allied Forces in the Battle of Stakhov-Brili (according to O. Sokolov)[627]

First Line	
Oudinot's II Corps	4,000 men
Remnants of Ney's III Corps	400 men
Second Line	
17th Division	850 men
Remnants of the V Corps	600 men
Zołtowski's brigade	1,000 men
Malinowski's detachment	1,000 men
The Vistula Legion	1,800 men
Reserves Doumerc's cuirassier division	1,200 men
Corbineau and Castex's cavalry brigades	800 men
Polish cavalry	1,100 men
Main Reserve Young Guard	1,500 men
Old Guard	3,500 men
Guard Cavalry	1,200 men
TOTAL	18,950 men

starving, shivering with cold, an enemy before us ten times stronger than we ...'[628] At dawn, Oudinot gathered his staff officers for a breakfast of onion soup: 'Each of them was required to contribute something so that the cook could do his business. One supplied bread, another the onion, the third the fat.' As they sat to enjoy this hot meal around 7 a.m., Captain de Cramayel 'arrived at gallop to warn us that the enemy was attacking and that the Cossacks were already at blows with the outposts'.[629] Indeed, the Russians launched the attack around 6 a.m. and – at least initially – it unfolded successfully. Czaplic reported that his men drove the 'French' skirmishers back for 3 *verstas*. Encouraged by this success, he kept attacking, believing that Chichagov's main forces were en route. But the tide of battle soon turned. The Russians, moving along the road 'surrounded, both on right and left, by thick and tall forest', had to proceed in open order because 'this was the only tactic [*genre de combat*] which local terrain permitted'. Langeron acknowledged that in such fights 'the French soldiers had an advantage over ours since they acted without orders, were accustomed to acting alone and shot better'.[630] Furthermore, the Russians could not deploy more than two guns at once on the road, which meant they were continuously outgunned. After the first salvo, Arnoldi describes:

the enemy columns dispersed and skirmishers and two unlimbered guns, deployed only a pistol's shot away from us on the road, quietly turned back and retreated to join their reserves in the woods. I fired several rounds of canister, instead of solid shots, and, having reloaded, I ordered my guns to move forward. Beyond the point, where the French skirmisher reserves were located, the road made a right turn and ran straight to the position that I occupied with my four guns in the morning of 14 [26] November where the crossing began. There, straight in front of the crossing, there was a small sandy hill […] Until reaching the above-mentioned turn, our lines faced no fire and therefore moved rather rapidly. But barely had we made the turn when we were showered with cannonballs fired from a nine-gun battery deployed in three levels on that sandy hill; there were three guns on each level and, exploiting the height, they were firing over each other. I could not return fire with my light 6–pounders and simply kept moving forward to reach a distance where I could fire effectively. But covering half a *versta* under a hail of cannonballs is easier said than done. Before I passed this distance or, one may say, endured this terrible torture, I lost one-third of my men and horses, one officer and one caisson, which exploded.[631]

Despite the losses, Arnoldi managed to deploy his guns where he wanted and 'through this tenacity, inspired our infantrymen, who seeing the battery advancing on the road, rushed forward with yells towards the woods and forced the enemy line back'. According to Dąbrowski: 'The enemy attacked forcefully […] The combat was tenacious on both sides and neither prevailed.'[632] At the same time, Colonel Krasovski, advancing along the river, 'reached the position where he could activate his battery and fire upon the area adjacent to the bridge. This fire inflicted considerable damage on the enemy'.[633] Around 8 a.m., Oudinot counter-attacked with Merle's division, the Swiss infantry at its head.[634] As the 1st Swiss prepared to enter the fray, Legler was reminded by Commandant Blattmann of his favourite song, 'Our Life is but the Journey' and asked him to sing it for him: 'I started to sing at once,' Legler recalled, 'and when I finished, Blattmann heaved a deep sigh, "Yes, Legler, that is how it is. What splendid words!"' Other officers and soldiers took up singing and marched into the fray.

The four Swiss regiments were supported by 'a few small Polish infantry units, a squadron of *chasseurs* and one of lancers', as well as the Dutch 123rd and 124th Line Regiments.[635] In the charge, they recovered the lost ground. The Swiss, especially the 2nd Regiment, led by Commandant von der Weid (Vonderweid), fought vigorously but soon exhausted their ammunition. Several messengers dispatched to get cartridges were either killed or wounded in the midst of 'murderous firing'. Legler witnessed as

The Battle of the Berezina

General Amey and a few staff officers had been wounded and several killed, among them Commandant Blattmann who was shot in the head. General de Brigade Candras and his adjutant had fallen too; a roundshot had taken off the latter's head.

By now, hundreds of Swiss troops (Legler estimated up to 300) lacked ammunition and stood idle behind pine trees; to officers' calls to fight, they simply responded 'gebt uns Patronen [give us cartridges]'. Seeing General Merle in the distance, Legler hurried to ask his permission to charge, to which Merle agreed. Returning to his regiment, Legler urged the drummers to lead but 'they all refused it'. So, in the heat of the moment, he seized 'the first one at hand – a Swiss lad by name Kundert, from the Glarus canton, something I did not notice then – by his collar and threatened to run my sword through him if he did not follow me'. Legler then ran forward, 'dragging Kundert behind me to the front line, while he beat the attack with one hand. Just as I let go of him, a bullet struck him in the right jawbone'.[636] The Swiss attack was supported by lancers but it was repelled and the Russians counter-attacked with numerous infantry and dragoons. Legler described:

> We were swept up in the flight of the lancer squadron on our right flank. Looking back as we ran, we saw Russian dragoons at our heels, and some enemy infantry advancing with them. I called at the troops to halt and form up. Those who heard me did as I had ordered and our well-aimed shots at the closest dragoons, some of whom fell from their horses, had such a good effect that the others galloped back, leaving the infantry standing.

Cartridges had arrived at last and, after distributing them, Legler realized that there was not enough to keep up a heavy fire. So another bayonet charge was made against the enemy and both Legler and Bégos testify that the Russians retired for several hundred 'paces'.[637] During this fighting, the 'intrepid' von der Weid of the 2nd Swiss was mortally wounded after a musket ball went through his throat. Falling into the hands of Louis de Bouman, he whispered his last words: 'I have died here as a Christian.' The savagery of the fighting can be seen from the fact that only twelve soldiers and two officers survived from the entire 2nd Swiss.[638]

The memoirs of Jean-Marc Bussy, a soldier of the 3rd Swiss Regiment, provide additional details on the Swiss participation:

> We fought for a long time without gaining any ground. It seemed to us that the enemy was receiving reinforcements since his fire intensified [...] Suddenly, we were pushed back for some fifty steps. Then our chiefs

shouted: *En avant!* The charge overwhelmed the enemy [...] who withdrew slowly and kept firing. Soon our advance was checked by the charging enemy cavalry [...] Our battery and that of 4th Regiment destroyed the Russian battery, which was then abandoned on the road.[639]

Czaplic, meantime, anxiously awaited reinforcements and was delighted to hear that the Admiral had dispatched the 9th (Voinov) and 18th (Sherbatov) Divisions to help him. Resuming attacks, the Russians gradually gained ground: 'We exchanged some fire,' writes Bégos,

> but twenty minutes later they recovered their earlier advantages and sought to throw us into the Berezina. Then I ordered [a] new attack and our bayonets pushed them back again. Seven times we were attacked with vigour, and seven times we covered the ground with their dead and wounded. In spite of these partial successes, I remained very anxious about the fate of our colour: twice the officers who carried it had become casualties [...] Although our men were very tired and had not eaten anything all day, not one of them uttered a single complaint and they always charged vigorously with the bayonet.[640]

Oudinot, observing the losses his corps suffered, ordered Merle to move to the cover of the woods on its left flank while two more guns were moved into position. By now a thick smoke, mixed with falling snow, only worsened battle conditions and Pils noted that 'we could not see farther than thirty paces for the snow'. Thus, before the gun crews managed to unlimber, one of the guns was carried off by the Russians who were closer than expected. Another participant described:

> For a while the fight was sustained; under pressure from superior forces, the II Corps finally began to give way. Our reserves, hit by roundshot at ever closer range, fell back. This movement occasioned the stragglers in the woods to fly for safety to the bridge ...[641]

Oudinot did his best to rally his forces and hold ground. Tellegen recalled the Marshal motivating his troops: 'The safety of the Emperor and the rest of the army depended on this battle [but] we were in shreds, all but annihilated.' The 123rd Line, less than 100 men strong, was extended on the left flank, fighting alongside the Swiss.[642] D'Auzon de Boisminart, commanding the regimental artillery of the 124th Line, recalled that only some 100 men, led by Captain van Zulekom, Adjutant-Major Herr and Lieutenants Wagener, Sangnié and Hoffmann, survived in the 124th Dutch Regiment; all officers massed together while the 'peloton de l'Aigle', led by Lieutenant Colonel Mouchet, was moved to the rear to avoid the loss of the Eagle.[643] At the same time, after Brigade General Moreau was wounded and the colonel of the 56th Line was killed, Tellegen, who already led the 128th Line, had to take command of this regiment as well:

> The blade of my sword was shot in half. I had already received several bullets through my clothes and not long afterwards, a bullet through my left breast, breaking two ribs ...

Forced to leave the battlefield, Tellegen came across Oudinot. The Marshal, convinced that his infantry could no longer defend positions, had already decided to call up heavy cavalry and dispatched his last surviving aide-de-camp, de la Chaise, to General Doumerc with orders to attack with his 4th, 7th and 14th Cuirassiers. Seeing Tellegen, he addressed him before being suddenly hit by a musket ball (or shell splinter) – his twenty-second wound![644] Pils, who struggled to extract his boot from the stirrup to assist Oudinot, watched in horror as the Marshal fell and, his foot also caught in the stirrup, was dragged with his head on the ground by the startled horse.[645] Fortunately, Pils was helped by a 'young *voltigeur* whose right fist had been shattered ...' Tellegen speaks of two cuirassiers assisting the Marshal. These men rushed to the Marshal's aid but 'the illustrious wounded man gave no more sign of life', so they took him into the woods where they prepared a stretcher out of pine branches.[646] According to Fain, Napoleon, who travelled to observe the battlefield, 'reached an opening in the woods just in time to see the wounded duc de Reggio [Oudinot] being carried off'.[647] According to Pils, however, the Emperor was a cannon shot away, 'standing on foot at the forest fringe on the right of the road, surrounded by his staff. Behind him the Imperial Guard, drawn up in battle order'. Informed of Oudinot's wound, he sent his own carriage but the Marshal refused because he could not stand the jolting. As the officers carried Oudinot before him, Napoleon approached the Marshal to inquire about his health but Oudinot passed out. Turning to his best physicians, Corvisart, Desgenette and Larrey, Napoleon told them to take care of him.[648] As Oudinot's wife later described:

> the Marshal refused to be bound down. Pils gave him a napkin to bite into and the operation commenced. In vain the knife probed to a depth of six or seven inches, it could not reach the bullet, which was never extracted. The sufferer had not given way either physically or morally. He heard all that was whispered about him and notably Dr. Desgenette's remark: 'If he vomits, he is a dead man.' This did not take place, and at last they were able to apply a bandage.[649]

In the meantime, Napoleon put Ney in command of Oudinot's forces with orders to hold the Russians back at all costs, in order to cover the retreat of the rest of the army. General Bonneval, dispatched to deliver the order to Ney, found him 'on a little white horse, surrounded by his staff [...] Each time a musket ball or a roundshot whistled nearby, he shouted, "Fly past, rascals [*coquins*]!"' Later, one of Ney's officers proudly proclaimed: 'This illustrious soldier, who had saved the III Corps at Krasnyi, now saved the whole army and the Emperor himself on the banks of the Berezina.'[650]

As the Russian attacks intensified, Ney rallied II Corps and, calling up some of his own troops as well as the Vistula Legion and then the V Corps in support, checked Czaplic's advance and began driving him back upon Stakhov. One French officer described:

> Around noon, Marshal Ney arrived, followed by his staff, to talk to the Duke of Trévise [Mortier], and, in his usual habit of audaciously exposing himself in the most dangerous place, he put himself in the middle of the main road. Marshal Mortier, whose composure was tested in twenty battles, could not show himself as less intrepid than the Prince of Moscow so he joined him in that spot. All divisional and brigade generals now considered it a matter of personal honour to imitate this example and so a whole group of illustrious men gathered together at the same spot. In addition to two marshals, one saw Generals Delaborde, Roguet, Berthezène, Doumerc, Dutch General Tindal, Prince Emile of Hesse ...[651]

The Vistula Legion spent the entire morning on the extreme right flank, where 'the wind brought the sound of distant cannon, the noise of which resembles trees falling in a forest'. Henryk Dembinski, an officer in the 5th Polish Chasseurs à Cheval and future hero of the 1831 Polish Uprising, remembered that his brother had stored a few ounces of barley flour and he and his comrades cooked it that morning. They had barely begun eating when 'drums called to arms and our men hastily deployed'.[652] Around noon, the legionnaires saw 'wounded men drifting back from the fighting and learnt that the struggle was at its height. News was slow in coming and we were prey to all-consuming fears'. Soon after, Ney reviewed the Vistula Legion and ordered it into action. The Legion passed in front of the Emperor, who congratulated it on its fine appearance and warlike attitude: 'Those who are about to die salute you!' sardonically commented Brandt.[653] Dembinski described General Zajączek, 'the Nestor of the Polish Army'[654] who had defended Praga against the Russians in 1794 and now commanded the V Corps in place of the wounded Poniatowski, walking with his sword in hand at the head of the Polish troops. Not recognizing him, Napoleon took him for Dąbrowski and loudly encouraged him 'Forward

The Battle of the Berezina

Dąbrowski, go and take your revenge!' When the adjutants conveyed these words to Zajączek, Zajączek allegedly responded: 'I will indeed go and take revenge for Dąbrowski.'[655]

Kniaziewicz's 18th Division moved to the left while the rest of the V Corps remained on the right side of the road, supporting the survivors of II Corps. The combined efforts of Poles, Swiss and French succeeded in stemming the enemy assaults as they took advantage of the wooded terrain, which prevented the Russians from utilizing their superiority in artillery and cavalry. But, in such circumstances, the fighting soon turned into close-quarter combat and losses mounted on both sides. Dembinski's brother, an officer in the 12th Polish Regiment, described his regiment fighting in open order and halting 'twelve Russian battalions attacking in columns [...] One-third of our generals were wounded'.[656] Brandt, who was wounded and left behind, also heard that 'most of the Vistula Legion's officers had been killed or wounded. Captain Rakowski, the wizard, was amongst the killed [...] Not long after, we saw Major Regulski arrive accompanied by Claparède. Both had been lightly wounded. Their presence here did not bode well for the fate of the rest of the Legion'. Indeed, Marbot notes that 'the Russians renewed their attack and broke the Polish Vistula Legion'.[657] The officer losses continued to mount. In the Vistula Legion, Colonel Kasinowski was killed and senior regimental officers Bielinski, Mieroslawski, Regulski and Schutz wounded.[658] Lieutenant Colonel Jerzmanowski, commanding the 8th Polish Regiment, was seriously wounded and replaced by Captain Porczynski, who was killed moments later. Commanders of the 1st (Malachowski), 3rd (Blumer) and 6th (Sierawski) Polish Regiments were all wounded. Among the French casualties were General Moreau and many senior officers in the 19th Line, 26th Light and 37th Line. In the heat of the battle, Dąbrowski was also wounded in the hand but continued fighting until loss of blood forced him to quit. He handed over command to General Kniaziewicz, who was put out of action soon after and replaced by Krasinski. General Zajączek then briefly commanded the V Corps, 17th Division (plus the 14th Polish regiment) and cavalry and, as Dąbrowski reported: 'these units fought with great vigour encouraged by his example, repelling several vigorous enemy attacks'. Davout later praised Zajączek for his 'devotion and courage'.[659] Zajączek, however, was severely injured when a cannonball shattered his leg. According to Larrey, he had 'his right knee smashed to pieces by a roundshot, which almost ripped the leg apart'. The physician ordered amputation, which he performed at once 'under the enemy gun fire, in the most rigorous cold and on snow'.[660]

As the battle continued, the 2nd and 12th Polish Regiments managed to break through the Russian line but, appearing on a small opening in the woods, they suffered from the Russian battery, which Chichagov deployed on an elevation behind his lines. The Kozlovskii and Kolyvanskii Regiments then charged the Poles, driving them back into the woods. The Russian Jägers seem to have used a clever tactic during the fighting inside the woods. Josef Szymanowski, commanding the 2nd Polish Regiment, described repelling one of the Russian attacks and seeing 'many enemy soldiers falling to the ground as if killed or wounded'. When the Poles advanced, Szymanowski tried to warn his comrades to check on the lying Russians as they bypassed them but it was too late. When the Russians counter-attacked, the 'dead' Russians grabbed their weapons and opened up, so the 2nd Polish found itself between 'two fires'.[661] The Russians tried capturing the regimental eagle but Jozef Szuchalski, himself wounded, carried it to safety: 'We fought as in a confined mountain battle,' described a Russian officer. 'Both sides employed artillery and skirmishers; if the lines thinned out, reinforcements were committed at once. Our losses mounted and the enemy suffered as well, but we could not advance [...] I personally witnessed how entire regiments were spread out in skirmisher lines and mixed among themselves.'[662]

The 13th HAC, deployed on the main road, suffered greatly from the Polish counter-fire and was repeatedly charged. The intensity of the battle is well reflected in its commander's memoirs:

When attacked, I stopped firing on the enemy guns and kept turning my guns in both directions, firing roundshot and canister into the enemy masses on the edge of the woods. Several times they gathered in large groups in troughs along the road and retaliated for my murderous fire. I had already considered myself a doomed man and, despite being almost surrounded, I continued to fire one round after another at the enemy masses and, I think, my decisiveness to hold my position, even though the enemy skirmishers were already upon it, was a major reason why our infantry held ground [...] In three hours of the battle, my artillery company could no longer operate after losing more than half its men and horses killed and wounded and had nine caissons and two limbers destroyed; three officers were wounded, one of whom lost his leg above the knee. I had three horses shot under me and my coat looked like a sieve from bullet holes. The place where my company stood on the road was narrower than the one where the French artillery was deployed. So my company endured this hellish torture in six shifts, that is, two guns operated no more than half an hour, usually ending up completely destroyed.[663]

After his entire company was devastated, Arnoldi requested reinforcements. Around 11 a.m., two guns, commanded by Staff Captain Czartoryski, from Lieutenant Colonel Lev Pashenko's 34th Light Company[664] were first to arrive, but they were destroyed within fifteen minutes; still Czartoryski seems to have damaged two enemy guns and a few caissons, since he was commended in after-battle reports. Pashenko's remaining guns arrived in turns. The first two to arrive were led by Sub-Lieutenant Leonov (wounded), then the remaining ones under Feurwerker 1st Class Shemenin, but they all suffered the same fate as Czartoryski's guns. Next arrived cannon from Lieutenant Colonel Adam de Barbiesch's 38th Battery Company, which lasted for two and a half hours before being shattered; Lieutenant Yuriev's two guns were credited with damaging two enemy guns, Sub-Lieutenant Firgin's cannon destroyed one gun and a caisson and Ensign Timashevskii was praised for effective fire. Finally, in the evening, Arnoldi received the 11th Light Company of Lieutenant Colonel Adolf Prebsting with which he finished the battle.[665]

By noon,[666] a dramatic development took place that turned the tide of battle and entered the annals of the Napoleonic wars. Following Ney's order,[667] Doumerc advanced with his cuirassier regiments (4th, 7th and 14th, up to 400 men in total), supported by Dziewanowski's Polish lancers (2nd, 7th and 15th, some 700 men).[668] Although it involved a variety of regiments, this charge is primarily known for the cuirassiers whom Napoleon later praised in his 29th Bulletin. Despite popular perception, the cuirassiers were not entirely French and the 14th Cuirassiers, in fact, consisted of Dutch horsemen led by Colonel Albert Dominicus Trip van Zoudtlandt, who would later distinguish himself fighting the French at Waterloo. According to the 29th Bulletin, Doumerc ordered a charge 'at the moment when the Vistula Legion was engaged in the woods, to pierce the enemy's centre'. Marbot observed that: 'As the forest was rather sparse the cavalry could move between the trees without difficulty.' Meanwhile, Legler could see 'the brave cuirassiers of the 4th and 7th Regiments, who were standing only 1,000 paces away from us'. He soon heard the word of command: 'Squadrons, by the left flank, march!' and the cuirassiers went into the attack.

The charge of these 'iron men' wrought great havoc, since the Russians were in open order and failed to rally. This was the result of a major mistake made by a Russian commanding general. Chichagov lamented that Czaplic was 'supposed to be supported by a reserve column of eight regiments, which I dispatched with Sabaneyev. Unfortunately, the latter spread his units out on the left flank. The enemy exploited this mistake at once'.[669] Czaplic, who eagerly expected the reinforcements, was 'bewildered to hear drums beating and see some troops spreading as skirmishers'. He rushed to see who these were and urged local commanders to rally their troops and form columns, which they refused to do because of 'existing orders'. Exasperated, Czaplic went to Voinov, informing him 'about disadvantages resulting from such inept orders'. Voinov simply shrugged his shoulders, pointing to General Sabaneyev, Chichagov's chief of staff, as the source for these instructions. Unable to get to Sabaneyev and seething with anger, Czaplic returned to his troops.

At this moment, Sabaneyev effectively commanded the troops. As some contemporaries noted, this was the first major land battle for Chichagov (not counting his hasty retreat on the 23rd) and he chose to remove himself from command. One particular rumour claimed that the Admiral told Sabaneyev: 'Ivan Vasilievich, I do not know how to command troops during the battle, so take command of them and attack the enemy.' [670] Participants, including Czaplic, attest to the fact that it was Sabaneyev, not Chichagov, who issued orders during the battle itself. But Sabaneyev committed a grave mistake in the first minutes of the attack when he deployed all his forces in open order, thus reducing their effectiveness; years of service in Jäger units certainly had shaped Sabaneyev's mindset, predisposing him to light infantry tactics, which he now utilized to spread out eight regiments! Buturlin notes that 'since his units moved through the wooded area, Sabaneyev thought it better to spread most of his men as skirmishers…'[671] Czaplic, whose memoirs are full of criticism of this manoeuvre, suggests that Sabaneyev, by spreading the troops and beating drums, 'thought to deceive the enemy into thinking that we had numerically superior forces […] But I cannot think of any circumstances when one should disperse reserves to frighten the enemy'.[672] Furthermore, Czaplic later learned that Chichagov specifically instructed Sabaneyev to keep the troops in columns and 'had this order been carried out, the consequences would have been outstanding for us'. But the opportunity was lost. The newly-arriving Russian divisions were spread out in skirmisher order, unprepared to face Doumerc's 'iron men'.

Doumerc began the first charge with the 7th Cuirassiers, under Colonel Dubois, while the 4th Cuirassiers moved to the left of the road and the 14th Cuirassiers was kept in reserve, followed by the Polish cavalry. Dubois' men – 'striking with the speed of lightning' as one Russian historian described[673] – broke through Czaplic's skirmishers and rode down the dispersed units of the 18th Division, which was 'one of the best in the army, with excellent generals, but was completely surprised by this ferocious attack'.[674] Langeron described the cuirassiers 'emerging from between the trees and undergrowth, joining other cuirassiers at the edge of two small plains, forming up in a flash and charging our columns'. Doumerc praised the 14th Cuirassiers for 'making successive charges', which prevented the Russians from reforming.[675] As they fled, the Russian soldiers spread further confusion among their comrades in the rear. This allowed the Allied soldiers to gain some ground. As soon as the cuirassiers charged, Legler's Swiss regiment 'ran forward with a single shout: "The cuirassiers are attacking the enemy in the wood to our left! Forward at the bayonet!" Some were shouting "Vive l'Empereur!" and I myself, "Long live the brave men from Polotsk!"'[676]

The Battle of the Berezina

'This cavalry charge,' writes Czaplic, 'had a tremendous effect, especially since the soldiers, who were supposed to support me, were scattered [by Sabaneyev] all around the woods and, in the confusion, began firing in my rear so I found myself between fires. This only increased the commotion among our troops.' Rochechouart, who earlier marched with the 22nd Jägers, accompanied Langeron to 'occupy a wood with two grenadier battalions and a regiment of Don Cossacks. When we reached the verge of the wood, three cuirassier squadrons charged us; they sabred and put to rout our grenadiers, but our Cossacks stood their ground [!], and enabled us to rally …' According to Martos:

> The French had driven our first division onto the second one [...] MG Lieders led the 9th Division to replace Prince Sherbatov's 18th Division, which fled back. Lieders rushed forward with bayonets, disorganized the French and forced them to fall back. Then our infantry began to regroup once more but, except for Lieders' men, it still acted indecisively and timidly. Napoleon soon broke through our centre [...] and drove back our dragoons. But Czaplic rushed with his hussars to their assistance and halted the enemy's daring attack …

Yermolov noted that 'there was not a clearing in the woods where enemy cuirassier detachments did not attack and disorganize our infantry'. The cuirassiers' attack was 'quite unexpected', Czaplic acknowledged, and it almost succeeded in capturing some Russian senior officers. Fighting their way out, Voinov was seriously bruised while Czaplic suffered a sabre cut to the head: both had horses shot under them. General Sherbatov was surrounded and 'almost dragged off the horse by his uniform' when he was saved by the timely arrival of the Pavlogradskii Hussars.[677]

It seems some Russian units managed to organize resistance since Doumerc reported about attacking 'a 4,000–5,000–man square' but Russian sources are silent on this count. It does seem implausible that a square of that size could have been rapidly formed by dispersed troops and then broken and routed by a few cuirassier squadrons. Nevertheless, in the 7th Cuirassiers, which lost eighteen officers, Chef d'Escadrons Delavillasse was credited with being the first to break into the square, although he was wounded in the process. He was supported by Captain De Lamoussaye, who 'demonstrated extreme bravery and was wounded twice by a bayonet'. Adjutant-Major Duguen also fought inside the square, had his horse killed and suffered three wounds. He was joined by cuirassier Foelinger, who 'set great example for his comrades and was among the first inside the square, where he was wounded multiple times by a bayonet'. Sous-Lieutenant Morando was commended for 'always leading charges', and Lieutenant Treca was noted for 'exceptional [*trés brillante*] bravery' as he rushed towards the enemy and 'killed an enemy commander and captured four officers'. Sous-Lieutenant Pagani was 'a young man of bravery and composure [*sang-froid*] in all trials, demonstrating dashing bravery in all charges'. Colonel Dubois was praised for his leadership and Napoleon promoted him to *general de brigade*, and awarded twenty-six Legions d'Honneur to the regiment.[678] In the 14th Cuirassiers, Captain de Tuil de Seroskerken, Adjutant Major van Campen, and twenty other cuirassiers were commended for their exploits.[679] The 4th Cuirassiers lost fourteen officers and the after-action report acknowledged Chef d'Escadron Chatry de la Fosse, Adjutant-Major Simon and nineteen other officers for their courageous actions during these attacks.[680] The cuirassiers were supported by the Polish light cavalry, which dispersed the Russian infantry and pursued it through the trees. On the edge of the wood, the Allied cavalrymen were charged by Russian horsemen and the 7th Cuirassiers became disorganized. Noticing this, Doumerc led the 14th Regiment in four successive charges, gaining enough time for the 7th Regiment to regroup.[681] The Russian hussars were soon reinforced by the St Petersburgskii, Kinburgskii, Starodubskii and Tverskii Dragoons. The St Petersburgskii Dragoons, led by MG Manteuffel, moved to the left flank, where they charged the 14th Cuirassiers. In the ensuing mêlée, the dragoons and hussars drove the cuirassiers back and Pierre Guildenhof managed to snatch the Dutch regimental *étendard*.[682] To the left of the road, some of Castex's regiments were also involved in occasional charges. Marbot described his friend Alfred de Noailles, Berthier's aide-de-camp (a man 'of virtue and fine character' in Lejeune's opinion), being surrounded by a group of Cossacks, who 'threw him from his horse and dragged him along by the collar, striking him as they went'. Marbot immediately sent a squadron to his assistance but the effort was fruitless.[683]

The Russian cavalry counter-attack bought precious time and allowed the Russian infantry to reorganize. The Allies also received reinforcements. General Berthezène's brigade of the 1st Division of the Young Guard, supported by Prince Emile of Hesse's horsemen, drove back the Russian right flank.[684] According to Legler (in the 1st Swiss), the initial cuirassier charge was

followed by a calm that lasted for a quarter of an hour at least. Now, at last, our other column, the Poles, advanced, and we received cartridges, which had finally arrived in sufficient quantity. The oddest thing about this bayonet attack was that, although we had lost many dead and wounded during the firing, we ourselves hardly lost anyone at all. The enemy's second line, which now engaged us, had not been firing at us for half an hour before the Poles were forced back on top of us. We absorbed them into our line and resumed firing. We were amazed how accurate the enemy shots were …[685]

The Battle of the Berezina

According to Bégos:

> The first Swiss regiment, which was not far from us, set the example of intrepidity [...] During one of the Russian attacks, Captain Rey ordered the drums to beat for a bayonet attack; but all drums were already damaged, so he took one of them and began to beat the charge with redoubled blows.[686]

Bussy, from the 3rd Swiss, describes the chaotic mêlée that ensued following the cuirassier charge:

> We cannot fire with so many troops intermingling. So a bayonet and the butt of the rifle are used to parry and deliver blows [...] We still manage to gain considerable ground but cannot regain our initial position. We can see men lying on the snow and realize that our ranks have been depleted while the enemy is receiving reinforcements. It is with our force that we must compensate for numbers [...] It is worse than butchery. There is blood everywhere on the snow, which is beaten up by constant advancing and retreating [...] While reloading my rifle, I see a Russian who aims at me. I say, 'If you miss me, I will not miss you!' Indeed, he misses his shot and I do not even hear the musket ball. I rest against a small fir tree: Fire! I see a man falling down [...] One starts to think of things [...] One does not dare any more to look on the right or left, fearing not to see his friend, his comrade any longer. Our ranks are tightened, our line shortened and courage redoubles. Our wounds are taken care of. We do not lack ammunition; our *gibernes* are filled [...] One fights always a little more closely. We charge with bayonets. Terrible clash, which we sustain with unusual intrepidity! Horrible carnage! To get to the bridges, the enemy must pass through us first but we fight to the last! And we keep shouting, 'Vive l'Empereur!'[687]

In the afternoon, Wittgenstein, who earlier promised to send reinforcements to Chichagov, crossed the river to meet the Admiral in person. Chichagov was not at all amused to see 'Wittgenstein arrive, alone, without any troops, at 2 p.m.' He told him 'about our situation and again asked for reinforcements, which, however, could not arrive on time'. Remarkably, Wittgenstein responded, 'But what do you intend to do? The enemy would fire until darkness and would then, as usual, retreat.' Despite Chichagov's attempt to convince him to make a wholehearted effort to defeat Napoleon, the General 'remained with a large part of his forces [at Borisov] and uncaringly observed the battle that was deciding the fate of the French army'. Years later, Chichagov was still fuming about Wittgenstein's actions: 'Promising to attack at the same time as we did at 5 a.m., he launched an attack only at 10 a.m. and failed to dislodge Victor from his positions for the entire day. He only committed 14,000 men, although he had 45,000 under arms, and at the same time, he refused to reinforce me with two divisions. And so, most of his forces stood idle at a distance.'[688]

As the battle continued, the Russians exploited their numerical superiority to slowly push the Allied forces back but made small headway. After recalling his horsemen, Doumerc deployed cuirassier squadrons behind infantry regiments and occasionally counter-attacked through the intervals between the units. The fighting was largely conducted inside the woods and was rather chaotic, which complicates its precise reconstruction. The Russian regimental histories reveal that both sides exchanged repeated attacks before the front line stabilized. The Kostromskoi, Tambovskii and Apsheronskii Regiments made several charges only to be repelled and attacked in turn: the latter unit alone withstood four major cavalry charges, losing some 100 killed and wounded; the Kostromskoi Regiment suffered similar losses.[689]

The fighting continued until late evening when it gradually died down in the darkness. The Polish artillery performed exceptionally well and Czaplic complained about its 'hellish fire that devastates everything, destroying trees and sending splinters everywhere, which inflicted serious injuries on our men'.[690] According to Langeron, 'The fire of these guns was so continual and so devastating that it became very difficult for generals and their aides-de-camp to cross the road without exposing themselves to a great danger.'[691] Marbot states that 'the enemy's artillery was thus prevented from getting a good sight of our troops, so that its volleys did not touch us; but as the shot flew over our heads they broke off branches thicker than a man's body, which killed and wounded many of our people and many horses in their fall'. Bourgoing noted that some cannonballs flew over the first three lines and claimed lives among the Portuguese cavalrymen guarding Marshal Mortier. Bégos confirmed that

the cannonade did not cease for a moment. Inside the woods, enormous trees fell with a crashing noise. It was augmented by the cries of the wounded and the terror of those who survived after seeing cannonballs striking their neighbours; yet moments later, as they thought they had escaped the danger, they themselves were mortally wounded. One must see a horrible spectacle such as this with one's own eyes to truly believe it.

'The French fought resolutely,' praised Sherbatov. 'Their cavalry distinguished itself with gallantry and efficiency. Operating in thin woods, it inflicted heavy casualties on us and delayed our advance until night.'[692]

'I must give credit to the skill with which Doumerc managed to exploit forest openings for his cavalry attacks,' Chichagov admitted. 'We continued fighting until night and held ground but could not advance.' Indeed, Doumerc's attack, in which most of the cuirassiers perished, played a key role in saving the day for Napoleon. It blunted the Russian attacks on the western bank and inflicted significant losses on the enemy. Doumerc's men captured hundreds of Russians but their precise number is still debated. Many Allied participants describe, like Dumonceau and Coignet, 'long lines of prisoners', who were 'all covered with blood, and pitiful to see', marching from the front line. Davout described 'that beautiful charge of the cuirassiers that produced 3,000 prisoners, who were paraded in front of the French army. This success decided the day and, consequently, the passage as well'. The 29th Bulletin praised 'The brave cuirassiers [who] successively pushed in four squares of infantry, and put to rout the enemy's cavalry, which came to the assistance of his infantry.' It also claimed 6,000 Russian prisoners (!), two guns and six flags.[693] The Bulletin exaggerated, as usual. The Russians could not have lost so many men, since that would have been half of the engaged troops. Langeron refers to 'no less than 600 killed and as many captured', while Rochechouart notes (implausibly) that the 22nd Jägers alone lost 1,200 men captured, who then escaped three days later. Chichagov, in his memoirs, made a very interesting statement: 'As for the prisoners captured by Doumerc, I could not get the precise number of them because of false reporting, which has become so widespread in the Russian army.'[694] Most Russian studies acknowledge up to 600 prisoners and 1,500–2,000 killed and wounded.

The Allies paid a steep price for this success and probably lost up to 5,000 men, including a couple of hundred captured. But as the survivors prepared for the night, their shattered ranks still held their own and their courage and devotion had saved the Grand Army: 'they shed blood as soldiers protecting the honour of their arms and saving thousands of victims', noted Dedem. 'How much more unfortunate were those incalculable warriors who perished in the river or were crushed under the feet of the horses and the wheels of the carts!'[695] Many Allied generals and senior officers were wounded. General Canderas was killed, while Generals Legrand, Dąbrowski, Zajączek, Claparède, Kniaziewicz, Albert, Amey, Moreau and Groigne (died on 29 December) were wounded. The Swiss regiments, which listed up to 4,000 men in the days before, now counted some 300 men: the 2nd Swiss had virtually been destroyed.[696] But the Swiss distinguished themselves and Bégos proudly observed that '28 November will always be a memorable day for the glory of the Swiss'. His comrade-in-arms, Bussy, wrote: 'What a terrible battle! What carnage! What a day for the Swiss! Yesterday, we had eighty-seven *voltigeurs* in the company; today, only seven of us are healthy and sound.' Another Swiss participant, Jean-Pierre Maillard, commented: 'It was during this brilliant day that many of our brave Swiss men succumbed. The majority preferred to die on the battlefield, rather than surrender.'[697] The Poles also suffered heavy losses and according to Polish historian Bielecki's estimate, the 15th Polish Regiment lost half its strength, while the two battalions of the 14th Regiment lost over 350 men (out of 1,000).[698] Hundreds of wounded (some estimates show up to 2,000 men) were abandoned on the battlefield and froze to death during the cold night.

The fighting was mostly done by non-French forces, mainly Swiss, Dutch and Poles. Their role, however, was often overlooked and their success was (and is) usually described as 'French'. Maillard complained that 'our beautiful regiments were destroyed that day but few histories mention this'. Reading Thiers' account of the Berezina, one Polish officer could not hide his indignation that the author failed to mention the Polish contribution: 'There were no French soldiers in this combat but rather Polish troops led by the Polish generals Dąbrowski, Zajączek and Kniaziewicz [...] But Thiers mentions none of them in his romance [sic].' Upset by such treatment, Andrzej Daleki, a Pole, observed that the French claimed credit for the Polish exploits: 'Wherever the French faced difficulties, they sent us, the Poles, to resolve them. When it was necessary to lead the attack, we were sent ahead; when the army had to retreat, we were placed in the rear to cover it.'[699]

The Russian losses were equally heavy. Lambert estimated 3,000–4,000 killed and wounded in this 'poorly conceived and badly commanded battle' and Chichagov acknowledged up to 5,000 casualties. Among these were the wounded generals Voinov, Sherbatov and Czaplic as well as dozens of regimental commanders and senior officers. 'We attacked too early and did not sufficiently coordinate our actions with Count Wittgenstein,' concluded a British officer.[700] Meanwhile, a contemporary Russian historian commented that

> Only half of the Army of the Danube participated in the battle, and even then it was spread out in skirmisher lines. There were no manoeuvres, flanking or movements in columns. The rest of the army and cavalry [...] and the detachments of Count Platov and Yermolov, which crossed the Berezina at Borisov, were not committed in the battle and remained in the reserves at Stakhov. The wooded terrain prevented Admiral Chichagov from exploiting his numerical superiority in cavalry which meant that only infantry skirmishers and [artillery] were engaged ...[701]

Chichagov kept his forces in position inside the woods between Stakhov and Brili while Yermolov and Platov bivouacked at Stakhov.

Operations on the Eastern Bank: The Battle of Studyanka

As the fighting raged at Stakhov, another battle began across the river, where Wittgenstein attacked Victor's corps. On 27 November, Victor received imperial orders instructing him to guard the bridges and 'occupy a strong position on the heights in front of the village in order to be able to hold ground for several days …' Still awaiting news from Partouneaux, Victor dispatched 'Fournier with his two cavalry regiments and General Damas with his Berg Brigade to support the 12th Division'.[702] Fournier and Damas soon came across the Russian forces and 'a very lively fusillade ensued', which ended with the Allied retreat. Victor, after Partouneaux's surrender, had only Girard's division left to occupy a defensive position near Studyanka and Napoleon, intending to preserve the bridges for another day, reinforced him with Daendels' division, which crossed back to the eastern bank by dawn on the 28th; but a large portion of divisional artillery had to be left on the western bank due to congestion at the bridges.[703] Expecting the Russian attack, Victor took position almost perpendicular to the river, just south of Studyanka, on the plateau behind the marshy stream running into the Berezina. He deployed his troops in an advantageous position, the infantry being mostly withdrawn behind the crest, which was occupied by a line of sharpshooters. On the right, close to the river, there was a thick cluster of trees defended by Hochberg's Badenese brigade (1st and 3rd Regiments, Baden Jäger Battalion), supported by the 4th Battalion of the 55th Line;[704] Carl Sachs recalled that some Badenese troops 'changed position several times before they settled down on the heights near Studyanka and were allowed to stack their muskets into a pyramid'.[705] Next on the left stood the Berg Brigade (1st, 2nd, 3rd and 4th Regiments) of General Damas. Further in line were Girard's 4th, 7th and 9th Polish regiments, with the Saxon brigade beyond them. As the Baden Captain von Zech described, the guns (fourteen pieces) were placed at advantageous positions on the heights to command the approaches.[706] In addition, over thirty guns, manned by Polish crews led by Captain Koryzmy, were deployed near Brili, on the other side of the Berezina, to protect Victor's right flank.[707] Victor placed the few surviving horsemen, amounting to no more than 400 men from two Baden and Hesse regiments led by Fournier, on the extreme left to prevent his flank from being turned. In all, Victor commanded '7,000 men, 400 horsemen and fifteen guns'.[708]

After accepting Partouneaux's surrender that morning, Wittgenstein left Steinheil at Borisov to disarm the prisoners and led the rest of his army upon Studyanka. Vlastov spearheaded this advance, and LG Berg and MG Fock were not far behind him. Wittgenstein himself remained at Borisov.[709] Around 9 a.m. the Russian advance guard drove back Victor's outposts near the village of Bychi and observed the main line of IX Corps. Sachs described how his comrades from the Badenese Brigade were boiling some meat when a 'swarm of Cossacks appeared, quickly followed by the Russian Jägers'.[710] These were the opening salvos of Vlastov's attack. After reconnoitring Victor's position, the Russian commander deployed his Jägers on the left and centre and sent his regular cavalry (with Cossacks) to the right. He also set up his batteries (Berg refers to twenty-four guns),[711] which began shelling Victor's left wing and the area behind it where a dense mass of people congregated in the hopes of crossing the river. Hochberg could see 'the enemy occupying the heights with numerous cannon; a lively artillery fire soon began …' Sachs confirms that artillery fire began almost as soon as the Russians appeared.[712]

The Russian cannonade spread panic among the wild crowds, which surged around the entrance to the bridges as cannonballs rained down. Chapelle and Chapuis described a massive crowd of '600 to 700 *toises* [1,200–1,400m] wide and 150 to 200 [300–400m] *toises* deep' forming in front of the bridges so that 'the entire expanse in front of the village of Veselovo [Studyanka] was covered with the multitude of people on foot and on horse, and carriages …' According to Laugier:

> Up to then, the crossings over the bridges had been made with the greatest regularity. But as soon as the guns were heard […] and it had become known that Partouneaux's division had fallen into the enemy's hands and that Wittgenstein was advancing, then men, women, baggage, light carriages, guns, ammunition wagons, heavy coaches, all rushed toward the bridges' narrow approaches.[713]

One can only imagine the panic and chaos reigning there. Driven by self-preservation, men fought their way forward by any and every means. The onslaught of such a mass of people proved too much for the fragile crossing. Labaume described a horrifying state of affairs:

> after the bridge reserved for the vehicles broke down, the baggage train and artillery advanced towards the other and attempted to force their way across. A frightful struggle immediately took place between the infantry and horsemen. Many perished by mutual slaughter; a greater number still were suffocated towards the entrance to the bridge, and the bodies of men and horses blocked the approaches to such an extent that in order to reach the river it was necessary to climb over the corpses of those who had been crushed. Some there were who still breathed, and who struggling against the horrors of death, endeavoured to raise themselves by seizing those who were trampling on them. While this appalling struggle was in progress, the multitude which followed, like an angry sea, continually engulfed fresh victims.

Across the river, Dumonceau could see the entire intervening plain:

The Battle of the Berezina

At first, as yesterday, a compact crowd had accumulated at the bridges and was causing a dreadful tumult without being able to cross in an orderly manner. All the while it was being swollen by a broad column intermingled with carriages or carts, which we saw still turning up over the hills. Behind it Marshal Victor's IX Corps, our rearguard, its right leaning on a wood which it doubtless still occupied throughout its entire extent, and its left extended by some cavalry squadrons in the direction of other woods [...] Now our eyes were being drawn to this line, now to the bridges. Through the smoke we struggled to make out the former's movements, marked by the direction of the firing, at times flinging itself down the reverse slope in front of some enemy assault; then having repelled it, returning to reoccupy its former position.[714]

For Bourgogne,

we were a medley of Frenchmen, Italians, Spaniards, Portuguese, Croats, Germans, Poles, Romans, Neapolitans, and even Prussians. I saw some canteen men whose wives and children were in great despair, weeping. We noticed that the men seemed to suffer more, both morally and physically, than the women. The women bore their sufferings and privations with an astonishing courage, enough to reflect shame on certain men, who had no courage and resignation to endure their trials. Very few of these women died, except those who fell into the Berezina in crossing the bridge, or some who were suffocated.

According to Kergorre:

The enemy was aiming at this mass, but, true to his habit, he aimed too high. Indeed, these projectiles constituted little threat, and nobody paid any attention. The most appalling danger was the one we were creating ourselves. For a distance of more than 200 paces the bridge was ringed around by a semi-circle of dead or dying horses and by several layers of trampled men. One could not afford to make a false step because once you had fallen, the man behind you put his foot on your stomach and you would add yourself to the number of the dying ...

But some Russian shots did find their target and Suckow witnessed as one round smashed a horse (pulling a carriage with a mother and two children) to pieces:

The mother jumped out of the carriage, and holding her two little ones in her arms begged people passing by to help her. She prayed, she wept, but none of these fugitives prey to terror, listened to her. [Moments later] she and her children had disappeared; or rather, she had been knocked down and crushed by the human flood ...

Captain Kurz saw as a young woman, with a toddler, had her thigh ripped away by a cannonball. Realizing this was the end, she kissed her daughter tenderly before strangling her; clutching her in her arms, she then lay down to await death.[715]

Marbot could never forget seeing how

the masses of unattached men – who had had two nights and days to cross the bridges, and who, in their apathy, had not taken advantage of them because no one compelled them to do so – wanted to cross all at once as soon as Wittgenstein's cannonballs began to drop among them. The vast multitude of men, horses, and wagons got completely clubbed at the entrance of the bridges, blocking them without being able to reach them [...] As a crowning disaster, one of the bridges broke under the weight of the guns and ammunition wagons. All then made for the other bridge, where the confusion was already so great that the strongest could not withstand the crush, and a great number were suffocated. Seeing the impossibility of crossing the encumbered bridges, many of the wagon drivers urged their horses into the stream. But this method of crossing, which would have been very useful if it had been carried out in an orderly way two days before, was fatal to almost all who attempted it, because, pushing wildly forward, they hustled and overturned each other. Still, some reached the opposite bank, but as nothing had been done to prepare a landing by sloping away the banks – as the staff ought to have done – few vehicles succeeded in getting up, and many people perished there also.

Polish Captain Turno was appalled to see 'whole ranks of desperate men, being pushed onwards by masses of other unfortunates coming on behind' and to hear 'their piercing screams'. Similarly, Captain François (of the 30th Line) was horrified by the scene of 'a terrible struggle among the despairing men'. It was around 10 a.m., recalled Bourgogne, 'when the second bridge, built for the cavalry and artillery, had broken in under the weight'. As everyone rushed for the remaining bridge, it became 'an absolute impossibility to get across [...] and everyone mingled in frightful disorder, crushed against each other'.[716]

In the midst of this chaos, the *gendarmes* tried to regulate the passage and Marshal Lefebvre stood at the entrance to keep as much order as possible. But they were 'swept on with the others and forced to cross, to avoid being suffocated or crushed to death'. Remarkably, as the world came tumbling down around them, the heroic *pontonniers* were still faithfully at work repairing the broken trestles and sacrificing their lives to save others. General Eblé tried in vain to establish a little order. Placing himself at the head of the bridge he addressed the multitude but it was only by means of the bayonet that some women, children, and wounded were saved. Others were less fortunate. Sergeant Bertrand (of the 7th Light) was among a group of soldiers trying to cross amidst 'this spectacle of horror, with scattered heads, arms, legs, a bloody slush'. As his group progressed, Bertrand

> heard my name being called out, and in this sad confusion saw the wife of one of the regiment's NCOs, holding her dying child in her arms. This sight made the most atrocious impression on me I have ever felt. I shall always remember the expression on this mother's face, with her lost and beseeching look. But my duty as a soldier, though it tore my heart, came before all feelings of commiseration ...

Reaching the bridge at last, Betrand 'marched along a very steep slope since the flooring gave way on one side. Several of us fell into the water and some went under enormous ice-floes ...'

Meantime, the battle progressed near Studyanka. Vlastov's first attacks concentrated on the Baden Brigade, commanded by the 20-year-old Count Wilhelm von Hochberg, the future Margrave of Baden. Shortly after 10 a.m., the Russian 25th Jäger and the Combined Jäger Regiments crossed the ravine and attempted to occupy small woods in front of the Badeners. After a brief fight, the Baden Jägers and a battalion of the 55th Line exhausted their ammunition and were driven back, but the Russians were stalled by flanking fire from the battery established on the other side of the river. Hochberg took advantage of this to counter-attack with the 2nd Battalion of the 3rd Baden Regiment and reoccupy the original position.[717] Dumonceau observed from a distance as

> the Emperor ordered a battery of the Imperial Guard [...] to aim its fire across the river [...] It took the enemy battery on the other bank obliquely, thus forcing it to withdraw to a distance. At the same time, it turned back a column that was preparing to deploy from the wood on which IX Corps' right was resting. We saw infantry skirmishers who had just been driven out of the wood return with élan [and] throw out the enemy ...

The battery belonged to Boulart, who 'was ready for anything, though not without turning over sad thoughts in my mind. The Emperor was near my artillery almost throughout the day'. Sachs described the Badenese charging the Russians, who 'stood and let themselves be shot without inflicting much damage to us'.[718] The Russians soon received reinforcements and, hearing the rolling 'hurrah, hurrah', the Badenese braced for the attack: 'we opened such devastating fire,' wrote Sachs, 'that the enemy could hardly advance for a hundred paces.' And so the Russians 'doubled up their fire' and Badenese casualties began to mount. With several NCOs shot around him, Sachs suffered a musket shot to his right shoulder blade: 'Feeling warm blood running down my back,' Sachs asked Oberleutnant Bressle to check the wound. Bressle recommended Sachs to go to the rear but the gallant officer chose to remain with his company. But not for long. Moments later another musket ball shattered his right arm, forcing Sachs to drop his sword. As he drifted into unconsciousness from blood loss, his comrades brought him to the rear and, in the process, discovered several more bullet holes in his uniform.

The Russians soon tried to flank the right flank of the Badenese Brigade and '[Major General] von Lingg rushed a grenadier company from the left to halt the enemy.'[719] The fight on the left flank continued for about two hours, Vlastov reported, before Fournier's cavalry threatened his right flank and drove back Rodionov's Cossack Regiment. Rapp, whom Napoleon dispatched to the left bank to check on the status of the IX Corps, reported: 'I saw brilliant charges of infantry and cavalry; those which General Fournier conducted were particularly conspicuous by their synchronization and impetuosity. But the disproportion was immense and we were forced to give way.'[720] On the Russian side, Vlastov described:

> The gallant Colonel Gerngross charged fearlessly with the Combined Hussar Regiment, routed the enemy and pursued him to the very batteries and infantry, where he suffered a canister and heavy musket fire. He retreated in orderly fashion and occupied the heights, which later turned ruinous for the enemy. With this attack, Colonel Gerngross, threatening the enemy flank, helped to halt the enemy attacks in the centre and left flank.[721]

Vlastov also deployed additional batteries to bombard Victor's positions. Lieutenant Colonel Antropov's battery supported Gerngross on the right flank, while Diebitsch commanded thirty-six guns in the centre against the Berg Brigade.

By noon, Victor's corps suffered heavy losses from artillery fire and Captain von Zech speaks of 'gaps opening in the position'.[722] So Victor ordered Damas to attack to gain time to regroup and force the Russians to remove their artillery. The Berg Brigade, arranged in two columns covered by skirmishers and supported by the Baden Hussars, first descended into the ravine with a shallow stream, which sheltered them from the Russian batteries on the heights.[723] One column then remained in the gully while the other engaged the Russian Jägers and drove them back for a few hundred paces before suffering from the canister fired by the 1st HAC and 27th Battery Company. General Damas was wounded in the chest and Badenese General Michel Geither (Kaitter) lost his hand.[724] Zech describes the Berg troops making at least two attacks.[725] Wittgenstein's report notes that the Berg brigade attacked 'spreading most of its men as skirmishers throughout the bushes', and Mikhailovsky-Danilevsky admits that 'Vlastov had to retreat'. But the first units from LG Berg's brigade arrived in time to support him. General Berg reported that Vlastov

> asked me to hurry up with my corps so I dispatched the 24th Jägers to his right flank, and having joined the advance guard, deployed twelve guns of the 5th Battery Company on the advantageous position, in front of the enemy battery that defended the road leading to the crossing.[726]

The Permskii Infantry Regiment reinforced the centre. The Sevskii Infantry Regiments, the 10th *druzhina* of the St Petersburg *opolchenye*, the 4th *druzhina* of the Novgorod *opolchenye* and the 1st Marines were deployed on the left flank, under the leadership of Privy Councillor Alexander Bibikov, who had been wounded at Smolyany and commanded the troops from his sledge. MG Fock moved his forces to the right flank, where he supported Gerngross' cavalry with two squadrons of the Combined Cuirassier Regiment and the 23rd HAC.[727]

The Russians soon counter-attacked and, as Wittgenstein reported, 'in a bayonet charge, the 24th Jägers drove the enemy across the stream which divided the two positions and our skirmishers pursued him to his very cannon. Yet, the enemy's advantageous position and superiority in infantry [!] spoiled our attack'.[728] Hochberg acknowledged that the Berg troops retreated in disorder and confused the second column, awaiting them in the ravine. The Russians exploited their superiority in artillery to continue heavy bombardment of Victor's positions. Gerngross' cavalry kept up pressure on the right flank as well. To turn the tide of the battle, Victor promptly ordered Girard's Polish division to charge the Russian positions:[729] 'En avant, brave Poles!' Victor encouraged them in person. The Badenese seem to have charged the left flank, where they encountered the Sevskii Regiment and the 1st Marines, while the Poles, with Girard personally leading them, fought the 24th Jägers, Permskii, Nizovskii and Voronezhskii Regiments in the centre. General Berg described:

> The enemy again tried attacking our right flank but this attack was also unsuccessful. Our gallant Nizovskii and Voronezhskii Regiment and the replacement battalions of the Count Arakcheyev's Grenadier, Pavlovskii and Ekaterinoslavskii Grenadier Regiments used bayonets to force the enemy to give up this intention; equally unsuccessful was the enemy cavalry

attack, but the enemy position was still formidable and it was impossible to cross the stream without suffering heavy losses.

To stem the enemy attack, LG Berg and Vlastov concentrated the fire of the 1st HAC, 9th Light and 14th and 27th Battery Companies:[730]

'My brigade came under an intense firefight,' wrote Hochberg, who commanded the Badenese troops. 'The fighting was still continuing on my right flank and I had to dispatch reinforcements to that battalion [2nd of the 3rd Regiment] after it exhausted its ammunition. Captain Woldeck, who commanded a company in my [3rd Baden] regiment, was ordered to bring cartridges. As he approached the caisson, located behind my brigade, a roundshot smashed his head and we lost a very courageous officer. Moments later I saw how a grenade killed Lieutenant Oehl and wounded seven men, while a roundshot sheared Captain Mahler's leg.

After the attack was repelled, Hochberg was observing Russian cannonballs falling amidst the crowds near the bridges when he suddenly noticed a column approaching his position: 'It was overcast,' he recalled,

I could not distinguish what troops these were, but seeing their white shakos I thought they were Poles. Moments later I realized they were firing at us; to avoid any mistakes, I went towards them, shouting to them to stop firing, and only then I realized these were the Russians. I ran immediately to my brigade and ordered it to meet the enemy …

The enemy column was part of the Russian attack carried out by the Voronezhskii and Nizovskii Infantry Regiments against the Berg Brigade, which had not yet recovered from the previous assault. And so Victor turned to Fournier, who attacked with the Baden Hussars in the first line and Hesse Chevaulégers in the second line; they were supported by a couple of hundred horsemen (mostly Poles) from Latour-Maubourg's IV Reserve Cavalry Corps, the 8th Lancers (Lubienski) and a few Guard Chasseurs à Cheval.[731] Wittgenstein reported that 'the enemy, after being twice repelled, moved back the 4th [Reserve Cavalry] Corps and part of the Guard'.[732] In his history of the campaign, Ségur wrote that Latour-Maubourg 'was passing the bridges with his cavalry when he perceived the danger and immediately retraced his steps'. After the book was published in the early 1820s, General Amable-Guy Blancard, who served as a colonel of the 2nd Carabiniers in 1812, disputed Ségur's account and wrote a long letter explaining what happened: 'At Smolensk, I took command of a regiment made of the survivors from the two carabinier and one cuirassier regiments,' he wrote. 'At the Berezina, during the first two days of the passage, we remained in position north of the bridges, covering the approaches to them.' On the 28th, General Latour-Maubourg decided to cross over the river and, after struggling in the crowd, he managed to get across. Blancard and his men were still on the eastern bank when Wittgenstein's troops engaged Victor. He described seeing widespread confusion and 'a multitude of soldiers fleeing along the bank' and 'great disorder near the bridges'. Hearing the gunfire, Blancard chose to remain on the eastern bank and was regrouping his men when 'seven to eight Russian squadrons, in very good order, appeared on the plain ready to charge towards the bridges but they stopped after observing us'. In a daring move, Blancard charged with his fatigued men and was perplexed when the Russians withdrew: 'I could not comprehend what compelled the commander of the Russian cavalry to hesitate in front of a much weaker enemy ...' he noted years later. As he rallied his men once more, Blancard was joined by numerous soldiers, officers and even generals who fell behind their unit: 'among these were some 100 Prussians from various cavalry units and Murat's old aide-de-camp Major General Beaumont, whom I offered to take command, which he refused, noting that he wanted to share our fortune as a volunteer'. Blancard remained on the eastern bank for a couple of hours longer before finally crossing the river.[733]

Meantime, Fournier's charges unfolded. Captain Roland Warchot, of the 8th Polish Lancers which remained 'in the rearguard all day long on the 28th', described:

> I had some 500 horse under my orders. Against me I had perhaps about 10,000. But the accidents of the terrain were making it impossible for the Russians to deploy their lines, obliging them, much to their annoyance, to group near the timber road paved with transversely laid tree trunks or risk being stuck in marshes [...] The Russians in front of me did not bother me since my detachments, deployed in twelve to sixteen files, could contain them and bar their passage. Up to now they had not had any guns with them and I was not afraid of their charging me as long as I did not find myself obliged to beat a retreat. But from the moment I had to retire, and thus lose some ground, I suffered considerable losses. Generally, the Russians are terrible the moment one no longer stands one's ground. They fall on you like madmen. When I ascertained that my regiment moved across the Berezina and that our six guns were safe, I persuaded our gallant Colonel Lubienski to leave [...] I still had some 300 horses left and made several charges to cover the retreat but lost many men with each attack. My horses were poorly shod or not shod at all so many riders fell off them and were killed getting up from the ground.

Warchot, with twenty or thirty lancers, was soon surrounded by the Russians and managed to parry a few lance stabs before one of them went through his chest and 'came out between my shoulders'. He lost consciousness and was captured.[734]

General Fournier was also wounded at the very start of the charge but Colonel Laroche and his men 'executed a brilliant charge'.[735] In what became known as the 'Charge of Death', the brave Hessians and Badenese first attacked the Russian 24th Jägers, which many Allied participants (and later historians) confuse with the 34th Jägers.[736] The charge seems to have been very effective, since French and German participants refer to some 500 Jägers captured. The horsemen then fell on the Nizovskii and Voronezhskii Regiments: 'The Russian right wing, already victorious, was obliged to halt; it was attacking, but [the cavalry] forced it to defend itself, and the enemy's ranks were broken by a sanguinary charge,' described a participant.[737] Bogdanovich acknowledged that 'the enemy steadfastly pursued and broke through our centre'.[738] But the Allied cavalry then suffered from the canister fire of the 23rd HAC and the 6th and 11th Light Companies and was counter-attacked by two squadrons of the Combined Cuirassier Regiment,[739] and the replacement battalions of the 1st Grenadier Division.[740] 'Encouraged by personal example of their commanders,' Wittgenstein reported, 'these battalions charged with bayonets and routed the advancing enemy, driving it across the stream to its original position.'[741] In the heat of action, Colonel Laroche tried rallying his Baden Hussars against the cuirassiers but was overwhelmed and almost captured.[742] In a wild mêlée, Sergeant Major Martin Springer, although already wounded by sabre cuts and bullets, fought his way to save Laroche. As the Allied horsemen were fighting the cuirassiers, they were taken in flank by a Russian hussar regiment, which sealed their fate. Hochberg described (and Zech confirmed):

> The hussar regiment was almost destroyed in this honourable combat. Only about fifty horsemen out of 350 returned over the Berezina. It was a stroke of destiny that these two fine regiments were able to close their battlefield careers with such a fine action, which saved the lives of so many of their comrades by their sacrifice, in this campaign where the deprived cavalry, in the bitter climate, faced its end.

By the close of the battle, the Hessian Chevaulégers counted only twenty-five to thirty men of some 200 they had in the morning.[743]

The survivors of Fournier and Latour-Maubourg's cavalry retreated behind the infantry and later crossed the river piecemeal. A few dozen continued fighting until late at night and were seen protecting the Saxon Regiment deployed in square. LG Fock sent the Combined Cuirassier Regiment and the Mogilevskii Infantry Regiment, supported by the 23rd HAC, to turn the enemy left flank, which Victor was forced to pull back towards the bridges; with his forces in a semi-circle, he continued to hold ground. Laugier described some stragglers joining Victor's troops to fight off the Russian attacks: 'Our brave comrades, Pieroni, Tiraboschi, Pizzoni, Menegatti and other good Italian officers and soldiers who separated from their units, sought it their duty to participate in this fight …'[744] According to Wittgenstein: 'The darkness did not allow us to pursue and attack the enemy any more, especially since the strong cannonade, which could be heard from Chichagov's side all day long, ceased in the evening.' Mikhailovsky-Danilevsky acknowledged that

> had all of Wittgenstein's forces coordinated their actions, the destruction of Victor would have been imminent. But the forces of our corps were dispersed: Count Steinheil remained all day long at Stary Borisov, disarming Partouneaux's division […] Of the two columns entrusted to Berg, only one took part in the battle while the other long remained behind due to confusion, which often occurs during war; it arrived at Studyanka only after the battle was over.[745]

The Russian artillery, however, continued firing on the Allied positions. Rafail Zotov, an ensign in the St Petersburg *opolchenye* described:

> We stood on the heights under cover of the twelve-gun battery of General Fock and observed from afar the unsteady masses of the enemy, thronging on the bank and pushing towards the bridges. In front of these masses stood a few French columns, which repelled with remarkable bravery all our attempts to reach the crossing. Finally, either because of our bombardment or the weight of rushing people, one of the bridges collapsed and the crossing ended. The crossing might have been over but the scene of horrors, mourning and desperation was just opening …[746]

Across the river, Borcke saw

> huge numbers of people, carts and horses intermingled and pushing themselves in confusion on the bank, which was being bombarded by enemy roundshot. Many tried to walk over corpses and rubble but, missing the entrance to the bridges, they jumped into the icy water and tried to swim across. In the middle of the bridge, a life-and-death struggle developed in a terrible clash …[747]

'Many soldiers and officers have been killed or wounded,' Victor wrote to Berthier late that night. 'The losses to the enemy are considerable as well. The numerous columns sent against us were beaten by the well-directed fire of our artillery and infantry. We have captured some 400–500 men.'[748] But IX Corps suffered between 3,000 and 4,000 casualties in the process.

On 30 November, Victor reported that 'the 26th and 28th Divisions have a combined total of 4,000 men, including 1,400 Badenese, 600 Berg troops, 1,200 Poles and 800 Saxons'. In the 28th Division, the 4th Polish Regiment had seven officers and 438 men, the 7th Regiment counted nine officers and 224 men, while the 9th Polish Regiment had eighteen officers and 420 men. According to Victor, in the Saxon Brigade, the Low Regiment had 137 survivors while the Rechten Saxon Regiment counted only 115 men.[749] However, some sources disagree with Victor's assessment. Bielecki argues that IX Corps lost over 4,200 men, while Hochberg specifically notes that Berg Brigade had only sixty survivors.[750] Marshal Victor suffered a contusion, Daendels was bruised after falling off his horse, and Generals Damas, Geither, Lingg, Girard and Fournier were all wounded. But their sacrifice paid off and these officers and their troops had bought the much-needed time required of them.

Although Wittgenstein enjoyed a threefold numerical superiority, not all his forces were engaged in the battle. As mentioned above, Steinheil was left to deal with the prisoners and Berg was able to bring only half (1st Line) of his corps. However, the Russians utilized irregular troops, whose role is often overlooked in this battle. Vlastov had the 1st, 4th, 5th, 6th, 10th, 13th, 14th and 15th *druzhinas* of the St Petersburg *opolchenye* and the 2nd, 4th, 6th and 14th *druzhinas* of the Novgorod *opolchenye*. Some of these were kept in reserves but others – the

Losses of the IX Corps (based on Bielecki and Hochberg)

Unit	Losses	Survivors
4th Polish Regiment	?	445
7th Polish Regiment	~700	233
9th Polish Regiment	?	438
Saxon Brigade	~900	109
Baden Brigade	1128	~700
Berg Brigade	~1150	60
Fournier's cavalry	~250	~100
4th batt of the 55th Line	~120	~100
Artillery	~20	~100
TOTAL	~4268	~2285

4th and 6th Novgorod *druzhinas* – were used to defend batteries and as skirmishers [*v strelkakh*].[751] *Zauryad*-Major Fetsov, who commanded the 4th *druzhina* of the Novgorod *opolchenye*, reported the loss of twenty killed, eighty-nine wounded and thirty missing. Captain (2nd class) Brovtsyn acknowledged thirteen killed, forty wounded and twenty-five missing in his 6th *druzhina* of the Novgorod *opolchenye*.[752] Wittgenstein's official report cites the loss of 800 killed and up to 1,200 men wounded but the numbers are most certainly reduced. Most Russian historians agree that Wittgenstein probably suffered between 4,000 and 5,000 casualties.

Wittgenstein's actions during the battle at Studyanka are quite puzzling. He acted half-heartedly, failed to utilize his superiority and seemed reluctant to assist Chichagov. Rumours of his vacillation spread quickly and Joseph de Maistre soon reported to the King of Sardinia that Wittgenstein hesitated to act despite repeated pleas from Chichagov. Furthermore, as the battle wound down, Wittgenstein made a contentious decision – he informed Chichagov of his intention to stop the pursuit and remain in position the following day:

> I was involved in a heated action until late at night. My casualties and those of the enemy are considerable. The enemy is dislodged from the first position but now occupies a second, more advantageous position some three *verstas* from the first one [...] Since the enemy is still in force, I intend, if the enemy does not retreat tonight, which I consider likely, to remain in position and quit attacking tomorrow. As Your Excellency knows, we are receiving reinforcements from the main army on a daily basis. In addition, we should give more time to General of Cavalry Count Platov to intercept the enemy's line of retreat.[753]

Once again, Chichagov was left alone to deal with the Grand Army ...

Burning the Bridges

As darkness descended on the battlefield, Victor received new orders shortly after 7 p.m.:

> Now that the fighting is over, you must surely move your artillery across the bridge in order to clear the village of Studyanka. Any transports you will not be able to move across must be set on fire. Your rearguard should evacuate the left bank by 5 a.m. [Once this is accomplished] your rearguard and General Eblé's *pontonniers* must burn both bridges.

Victor began to withdraw around 9 p.m.[754] The survivors of the 26th Division covered the retreat and remained in position until late at night. Despite cold and exhaustion, Hochberg, who now led the division, was finally able to rest and enjoy a small 'feast': his hunting dogs captured a hare in the midst of the battle and his cook now prepared it. The hungry soldiers spent the night rummaging through abandoned carriages for some food and drink.[755] Towards midnight, Victor ordered Hochberg to clear the bridge and Captain Zech was dispatched with the grenadier company of the 1st Baden Regiment to accomplish this. The area around the bridges was packed with thousands of fugitives trying to escape. The approaches were blocked by heaps of broken vehicles and dead or dying people and animals piled one upon another in the bloodstained snow and mud, through which it was impossible to make way. Eblé, who had barely slept for six (!) days, and the surviving *pontonniers* continued to work courageously on the bridges, trying to keep them standing, clear the rampart of corpses, dead horses and carriages, and regulate the passage of the despondent mob.[756] They did their best to remove obstacles for the retreating IX Corps but Hochberg's men still had to fight their way through this mass of people. In the dreadful nocturnal scramble, Colonel von Dalwigk, commander of the Hessian Guard Chevaulégers, got separated from his men and pushed into the icy river, barely surviving death. A Hessian driver recognized the Colonel by his white greatcoat and pulled him out. Hochberg described:

> Captain Zech made an incredible effort to keep the bridge open for the troops. At times, some [artillery] carriages took up to a quarter of an hour to pass over the bridge. No one was allowed onto the bridge during this time. We heard appeals from all sides and the Poles especially begged me to let the infantry pass before the artillery. I refused them. Besides, I still waited for the 2nd Battalion of the 1st Regiment, which was still defending the foods we captured from the Russians.[757]

Around 1 a.m., the 26th Division moved to the infantry bridge but found it damaged, since, as Johann Moritz (one of the few *pontonniers* who survived the ordeal) later remembered: 'there was a terrible rush towards the bridges as everyone wanted to be first across the river'.[758] While the *pontonniers* were feverishly working to repair it, Hochberg led his men towards the artillery bridge, leaving a rearguard composed of the survivors of Girard's division. It was not until dawn on the 29th that IX Corps was at last across and Fournier's cavalry, mostly Baden Hussars, were the last to cross. The bridges were left open for the benefit of stragglers but the artillery bridge having collapsed under the weight of transports, only the infantry bridge remained operational. Around 7 a.m., Napoleon finally ordered the destruction of the bridges. Eblé placed inflammable material on the bridges' transverse logs but delayed the fire, hoping to save more lives. He personally urged the stragglers to cross while they still had time, setting several carriages alight in order to provoke a movement, but it produced little effect. Other officers also tried to convince people to move but their 'appeals, threats or orders were in vain', writes Soltyk. 'No one stirred. Most had fallen into such apathy that they listened indifferently to the words being addressed to them.' According to Colonel Griois: 'We no longer knew how to appreciate danger and we did not even have enough energy to fear it.' Colonel Séruzier, whom Eblé had ordered 'to break the bridges and blow them up' put 'all possible firmness and haste' in getting the remaining transports across:

> 'We knew the Russians were getting close,' the Colonel writes, 'but I could not get the drivers of the baggage, *cantinières* or the *vivandières* to listen to reason. In vain I told them everyone would be saved if only there was a little order; that their safety depended on crossing at once, and that our troops' salvation would depend on the bridges being broken. Only a few crossed with their light vehicles. The greater number lingered on the left bank ...'

After waiting more than an hour, and with the Russian cavalry, especially Cossacks, dangerously close, Eblé finally gave Séruzier the order to destroy the bridges between 8.30 and 9 a.m.[759]

The destruction of the bridges set the stage for the final act of the Berezina tragedy: 'Perhaps no other event in history has so completely embodied every element of misery,' observed one historian.[760] Indeed, seeing their only hope for safety on fire, thousands of stragglers, as if awakened from slumber, made a desperate attempt to run through the flames, others jumped into the freezing water to wade or swim to the opposite shore: 'I saw them all in the water up to their shoulders,' remembered Bourgogne. 'Overcome by the terrible cold, they were all perishing miserably.'[761] Even years after the event, Louise Fusil, who, in 1812, was travelling on the Zembino causeway a few miles from the crossing, could still hear

> a scream, a single cry from the multitude. Indefinable, it still resounds in my ears every time I think of it. All the unfortunates who had been left on the other bank were falling, crushed by the Russian Army's grapeshot. Only then did we grasp the extent of the disaster.

Tascher described finding

> the disorder and congestion terrible. Several times I managed to avoid being suffocated, and struggled across after waiting for four hours. Half an hour afterwards, the enemy started to fire and the crossing turned into a massacre.

Campaign Chronicle

According to Bourgogne:

> The greatest disorder prevailed at this place. All the men who had not taken advantage of the night to cross had thrown themselves in a mass onto the banks of the river as soon as they heard the artillery, in order to cross by the bridges [...] To complete our misery, snow began to fall and a cold wind blew. This dreadful state of things lasted all day and through the next night, and all this time the Berezina became gradually filled with ice, dead bodies of men and horses, while the bridge got blocked up with carts full of wounded men, some of which rolled over the edge into the water.

For Vossler, 'This day and the cruel spectacle of it all is something I shall never forget as long as I live.' He described how

> around one o'clock the cry went up, 'The Cossacks are coming!' Those on the periphery knew they would be the first victims. Any speeding up of the movement towards the bridge seemed utterly impossible but the cry electrified the rabble and spurred everybody to a final effort. Groups of cavalrymen closed ranks and ruthlessly rode down everything in their path. At the approaches to the bridge all semblance of order had ceased. Officers and orderlies had either fled before the raging mob or, if they stood their ground, had been cut to pieces. By now there were many trying to swim the river but few succeeded: most perished in the icy water. The fight for a passage reached its ultimate horror when the Russian guns began to find the range of the milling mass, spreading death and destruction. From now on it was a fight of each man against his neighbour. The stronger trampled their weaker comrades to the ground and struggled on until they, in turn, found their match in others stronger still. This ghastly scene ended only with the approach of darkness, when a detachment of French engineers on the far bank dismantled their end of the bridge, leaving what remained behind – men, horses, guns, and wagons of every description – at the Russians' mercy.

According to Colonel Séruzier:

> The Cossacks flung themselves on these people who had been left behind. They pillaged everything on the opposite bank, where there was a huge quantity of vehicles laden with immense riches. Those who were not massacred in this first charge were taken prisoner and whatever they possessed fell to the Cossacks.

213

The Battle of the Berezina

Le Roy thought a skilful painter could have painted a beautiful [vivid?] picture out of this tragedy:

> He would have painted a still-life. Trees laden with hoar frost, snow and icicles. In the foreground the village of [Studyanka]. In the background, between white-powdered conifers, would be seen perfidious Bashkirs, waiting keenly for a favourable moment to throw themselves on their prey. The river itself would play the chief role and could represent Acheron, the river of Hades in the [Greek] myths. The damned on the left bank. The elect on the right.[762]

Louis de Rochechouart, serving in Chichagov's army, was deeply shaken by the sight revealed to him on 29 November:

> There could be nothing sadder, more distressing! One could see heaps of bodies, of dead men, women and even children, of soldiers of every formation, of every nation, frozen, crushed by the fugitives or struck down by Russian grapeshot; abandoned horses, carriages, cannons, caissons, wagons. One would not be able to imagine a more terrifying sight than that of two broken bridges and the frozen river [...] I saw an unfortunate woman sitting on the edge of the bridge, with her legs, which dangled over the side, caught in the ice. She held to her breast a child which had been frozen for twenty-four hours. She begged me to save the child, not realizing that she was offering me a corpse! She herself seemed unable to die, despite her sufferings. A Cossack rendered her the service of firing a pistol at her ear in order to put an end to this heartbreaking agony ...

Nearby, Martos saw

> a woman who had collapsed and was gripped by the ice. One of her arms had been hacked off and hung only by a vein, while the other held a baby which had wrapped its arms around its mother's neck. The woman was still alive and her expressive eyes were fixed on a man who had fallen beside her, and who had already frozen to death. Between them, on the ice, lay their dead child.

In 1817, the Württemberg surgeon Huber wrote a letter to his friend Henri de Roos describing a heartbreaking scene he had witnessed:

> [I saw] a beautiful woman of twenty-five, wife of a French colonel who had been killed a few days ago. Indifferent to everything happening around her,

she seemed to devote all her attention to her daughter, a very beautiful child of four [...] Several times she tried to reach the bridge, and each time she failed. A grim despair soon overcame her. She was not weeping. Her eyes fixed now on the sky, now on her daughter, and I heard her say, 'O God, how unhappy I am now not even to be able to pray!' Almost instantly her horse was hit by a bullet and another shattered her left thigh above the knee. With the calm of silent despair, she took her crying child, kissed her several times and then with her bloodstained skirt, which she had taken off her broken leg, she strangled the poor little girl; and then, hugging her in her arms and pressing her to herself, she sat down beside her fallen horse. She reached her end without uttering a single word as she was trampled by the horses of those pressing forward onto the bridge.[763]

Visiting the riverbank, Langeron described the numerous vehicles abandoned by the Allies:

All the riches of Moscow were collected in this park, and one saw more than ten thousand, including magnificent carriages, berlines, calashes, phaetons, drozhkys, etc. taken in the capital, in the noble estates or in the workshops of harness-makers – all trophies the French had intended to carry to Paris. These carriages, wagons and carts were laden with articles of great value: rich jewellery, superb furs, pearls, diamonds in profusion, sacred goblets from the churches of Moscow, the gilded cross from the Church of St John the Great, collections of engravings, many books from the superb libraries [...] silver dishes, even porcelain. For several days everything was scattered and plundered, yet it was impossible to remove a hundredth part of the treasures abandoned by the enemy. A large part was thrown into the river, and when the spring came the local peasants and the Jews, who never missed such opportunities, rushed from every corner of Poland, fished out the treasures, and made off with an immense haul.

Nevertheless, when a Prussian officer, Major Blesson, visited the Berezina in 1822, he recorded: 'Halfway to Studyanka already we spotted – just think of it, ten years after the catastrophe – a mass of leather ware, strips of felt, scraps of cloth, shako covers, etc. strewn on the ground and fields. As one approached the river, these melancholy relics lay thicker and even in heaps, mingled with the bones of human beings and animals, skulls, tin fittings, bandoliers, bridles and suchlike. Scraps of the bearskins of the Guard had survived ...'[764]

Aftermath

The loss of life at the passage of the Berezina will never be exactly known but the battle probably ranks among the bloodiest of the Napoleonic Wars. It practically put an end to the Grand Army as an organized fighting force. Considering cold and starvation, the army possibly lost some 20,000–25,000 men on the banks of the Berezina. In the combats of 26–28 November, the II and IX Corps, which bore the brunt of the fighting, probably lost half their effective strength. On 30 November, Victor reported that the 28th Division counted thirty-four officers and 1,082 soldiers, while the two Saxon cavalry regiments listed 252 men. On the same day, Napoleon acknowledged that his army was reduced to 7,000 infantry and 6,000 cavalry. However, according to Chambray, three days after the crossing, the Grand Army comprised only 8,800 men: 3,200 men in the Old Guard, 800 in the Young Guard, 2,100 men in Victor's corps and just 400 in the I and IV Corps. Ney led some 2,300 survivors, including 200 men in the Vistula Legion, 800 in Dąbrowski's division, 323 in V Corps and 500 men in II Corps. On 2 December, Ney himself reported that the Vistula Legion counted only 200 men, the 16th Polish Division 190 men, the 17th Division 800 men, the 18th Division 133 men, and all three divisions of III Corps had only 500 survivors. If these figures are correct, then the Grand Army had lost up to 21,000 combatants between 26 November and 2 December.[765] Wittgenstein reported that his forces alone captured one lieutenant colonel, thirty-six officers and 2,000 soldiers on 25–26 November, and five generals, five colonels, fifteen lieutenant colonels, 254 officers, 8,800 soldiers, four guns and two colours on 27 November: a total of 11,116 men in three days. For 28 November, Wittgenstein lists twelve guns seized: 'numerous people drowned and several thousand privates and many officers captured'. The *Journal of Military Operations* recorded Wittgenstein's report of 'thirteen guns and up to 1,500 soldiers captured, with numerous officers who are still being brought in'. At the same time, Chichagov captured fifty-two officers and over 2,284 men, seven guns and one 'flag' on 21 November and another 3,000 men on 27 November. These reports alone suggest that the Russians captured at least 16,452 men and the final number of prisoners most certainly exceeded 20,000. The official

Aftermath

Estimates of the Grand Army losses at the Berezina

Author	Year	Casualties	
		Combatants	Non-Combatants
Chambray	1823	~20,000	?
Scott	1832	~36,000 killed	
Mikhailovsky-Danilevsky	1839	'many thousands killed and drowned, up to 20,000 captured'	
Thiers	1856	?	7,000–8,000
Bogdanovich	1860	20,000–25,000	Up to 25,000
Bingham	1884	28,000: 12,000 killed, 16,000 captured	
Leer	1893	Over 25,000 men	
Stschepkin	1906	20,000–25,000	?
Foord	1915	20,000–25,000	'enormous'
Bodart	1916	20,000	?
Herold	1963	>25,000	
Chandler	1966	20,000–30,000	~30,000
Marshall-Cornwall	1967	25,000	
Haythornthwaite	1996	20,000–30,000	'untold number of stragglers'
Gates	1997	?	~30,000
Schom	1997	?	>36,000
Sokolov	1999	25,000 (half of them stragglers)	
Rothenberg	1999	50,000	
Encyclopedia of the Patriotic War of 1812	2004	25,000–40,000 (half of them non-combatants)	
Pigeard	2004	23,000	?
Zamoyski	2004	~ 15,000	~10,000
Connelly	2006	?	~10,000
Franceschi & Weider	2008	?	25,000–30,000
Palmer	2003	over 13,000 killed	
Stone	2006	'tens of thousands' killed	
Shishkov	2006	'enormous losses' 23,392 prisoners	

Journal of Military Operations records that the Russians captured five generals, 427 officers, 23,500 soldiers, twenty-two guns and four colours between 28 November and 2 December.[766]

The Battle of the Berezina

The loss of life among the non-combatants must have been enormous: 'The banks of the Berezina are covered with corpses,' Chichagov wrote to Kutuzov on 30 November. MG Foerster, who visited the crossing days after the battle, reported that 'the area between the bridges, the nearby plains and the river itself is so packed with human and animal corpses that in some places it is possible to walk across the river'. Captain François also recorded that the Berezina was full of dead human bodies, animal corpses and transports.[767] Thousands died of cold, starvation and violence between 26–28 November and thousands more were captured on the 29th. It is usually estimated that between 5,000 and 10,000 stragglers still remained on the eastern bank when the bridges were destroyed. The Russian troops had little to spare for these captives and the Cossacks quite often stripped them of their last possessions. Joseph de Maistre, citing the January 27 issue of the *Gazette de la Cour*, referred to 30,105 human and horse cadavers gathered on the banks of the Berezina in the spring of 1813 but the newspaper did not specify the precise number of human losses.[768] The immensity of losses was still evident even ten years after the event. Blesson, who visited the river in 1822, recorded:

> Where the main bridge had been, an island close to the bank divides the river into two arms. This island owes its origins to the vehicles and bodies which fell off the bridge, and to the corpses which were carried down to this point and then covered with mud and sand ...[769]

The Allied officer corps was particularly hard hit. Despite its shortcomings, Martinien's famous study of the Napoleonic officer corps remains an invaluable source for officer losses and it reveals that some 1,600 officers were killed and wounded on the Berezina; hundreds more were captured. Martinien estimated that the Grand Army lost a total of 9,380 (2,965 killed and 6,415 wounded) officers during the entire Russian Campaign and the losses at the Berezina represented over 17 per cent of total Allied officer corps losses in Russia. One may compare this to 1,928 officers and forty-nine generals, as Zemtsov calculated, killed and wounded at Borodino on 5–7 September, or 2,414 officers and sixty-six generals (Rothenberg's estimate) lost at Leipzig in 1813. The fighting of 28 November claimed the greatest share (over 1,250 men) of these casualties while some sixty officers were killed or wounded on the 26th, over 200 on the 27th and forty on the 29th. With respect to branches, almost 1,000 officers were lost in infantry, up to 300 in cavalry, over 100 in auxiliary (*pontonnier*, engineer and train) regiments, and some eighty in artillery. Among senior officers, Marshal Oudinot was wounded and Victor seriously bruised. Thirty-two generals were casualties: twenty-five, among them nine generals of division and sixteen generals of brigade, were wounded, one general (Candras) was killed; and

Aftermath

five generals (Partouneaux, Delaitre, Camus, Blanmont and Billard) were captured.[770] This was one of the Grand Army's highest senior officer losses of the Napoleonic Wars. For comparison, fourteen generals were killed and wounded at Austerlitz, twenty-three at Eylau, eleven at Friedland, thirty-nine at Wagram, forty-nine at Borodino, sixty-six at Leipzig and thirty-five at Waterloo. Other senior officer losses at the Berezina included one Imperial ADC (Rapp), seventeen *adjoints* and thirty ADCs of the *Etat Major*.

Top 15 Regiments with Heaviest Officer Losses (based on Martinien's studies)

Units	26 Nov	27 Nov	28 Nov	29 Nov	Total
29th Légère	–	53	1	–	54
123rd Line	–	–	44	–	44
3rd Infantry Regiment of the Portuguese Legion	–	–	39	–	39
4th Swiss	–	–	38	1	39
125th Line	–	38	–	–	38
44th Line	–	30	–	–	30
126th Line	–	30	–	–	30
1st Infantry Regiment of the Vistula Legion	–	–	28	–	28
129th Line	–	–	26	–	26
124th Line	–	–	22	–	22

Top 15 Cavalry Regiments with Heaviest Officer Losses

Units	26 Nov	27 Nov	28 Nov	29 Nov	Total
2nd Berg Chevaulégers	–	–	23	–	23
7th Cuirassiers	–	–	20	–	20
14th Cuirassiers	–	–	18	–	18
4th Cuirassiers	–	–	16	–	16
6th Saxon Regiment (de Rechten)	–	–	12	1	13
7th Polish Lancers	8	–	4	–	12
Lithuanian Chasseurs à Pied	–	–	12	–	12
Lithuanian Gendarmerie à Cheval	–	–	10	1	11
Baden Hussars	–	–	10	–	10
11th Hussars	–	–	9	–	9
8th Saxon Regiment (de Low)	–	–	9	–	9

The Battle of the Berezina

The Russian losses are less well known due to sketchy reporting and only general estimates could be made. Napoleon claimed up to 6,000 Russian prisoners, two guns and eight colours but no Russian source supports this claim and the number seems unfeasible. On the other hand, Kutuzov claimed that the Russians suffered only 4,000 casualties, which also seems improbable.[771] Most scholars agree that the Russians lost some 10,000–15,000 men in these actions.

The End of the Campaign: 30 November–31 December 1812

'After the crossing of the Berezina, all faces brightened,' recalled Caulaincourt. 'The men embraced, congratulating each other as though we had crossed the Rhine, from which we were still four hundred leagues away,' wrote Bourgogne. 'We felt that we had been saved, and giving vent to less selfish instincts, we pitied and regretted those who had had the misfortune of being left behind.'[772] As the battles raged on the 28th, Napoleon ordered Eugène, Davout and Junot to march on Zembino.[773] The full importance of Czaplic's failure to break down the long wooden bridges over the marshes now became apparent. The marshes were hardly as yet solid enough to bear vehicles, and had the bridges been destroyed nothing could have passed, effectively entrapping Napoleon's army. Before daylight on the 29th Napoleon started with the Guard, followed by Victor and Ney, but the passage over the long narrow bridges was so slow and the road so packed with men and transports that by the end of the day Ney was only at Zembino, a few miles from the crossing. Eblé and the surviving *pontonniers* marched with the rearguard and after the last troops had passed, they destroyed sections of the bridges to check the pursuit.[774]

The weather rapidly deteriorated starting on 30 November: 'An icy wind came in from all sides,' recalled Constant, Napoleon's valet, and the temperature gradually declined. Charles-François Minod, of the 2nd Swiss Regiment, described:

> The severity of the cold increased daily, while the difficulty of obtaining provisions and fodder became a constant worry [...] With the cold increasing, the brave warriors, who had faced a thousand perils in so many battles, were forced to follow the torrent of a most distressing retreat.[775]

The increasing cold rapidly shattered any remaining semblance of organization and the number of men actually with the colours dwindled fast. On 1 December Ney sent the eagles of the III Corps with their guards and the regimental officers to take refuge with the headquarters and the few thousand troops who still marched with it. Ney himself led a rearguard of a few hundred men. The Grand Army's retreat to Vilna contains little of military interest since it was nothing short of a flight of the mass of fugitives trailing mechanically along the road,

Aftermath

constantly followed and attacked by Cossacks. The remains of the army marched – in the words of Captain Coignet – 'like prisoners, without arms or knapsacks. There was no longer any discipline or any human feeling for one another. Each man looked out for himself …'

Chichagov's army, exhausted by the fighting the previous day, rested on the 29th but Czaplic's advance guard pursued the retreating enemy as far as Kabinskaya Rudnya, where he was delayed due to a destroyed causeway over the marshes. Still, the Russian pursuit produced hundreds of prisoners. On 29 November, MG S. Lanskoi, whose flying cavalry detachment was tasked with intercepting the Grand Army,[776] attacked the village of Pleshenitsy on the Allied line of retreat, nearly capturing the wounded Marshal Oudinot, whose staff heroically defended the house in which he lay. Oudinot had been evacuated to this place under the guard of a small escort. While having his wound dressed, the village was occupied by Lanskoi's detachment. Half-naked and brandishing a brace of pistols, the Marshal made a successful dash for a nearby house, containing General Pino and a handful of Italian grenadiers. There the small party held out against repeated attacks, although Oudinot was wounded again.[777] During their raid, Lanskoi's men captured 'General Kamienski, two colonels, two lt. colonels, two majors, twenty-four officers and 217 soldiers'.[778] Czaplic, after crossing the Zembino marshes by strengthening the ice with planks and brushwood, also pursued the Grand Army and captured seven guns and up to 300 stragglers by 30 November. Over the next two days, as the *Journal of Military Operations* recorded, Czaplic's pursuit resulted in the capture of another 'five cannon, seven officers and over 500 privates. The road, on which the enemy is retreating, is covered with dead human and animal corpses, up to thirty caissons and numerous transports'. Platov's Cossacks soon joined Czaplic and together the two generals captured up to 1,000 stragglers in early December. Platov's report spoke of the capture of Bavarian General Preysing, three colonels, thirty officers and over 2,000 privates. On the next four days there were further rearguard actions, all much alike and all resulting in the loss of guns and prisoners.

The march to Vilna proved to be the most devastating of the campaign. The weather began to deteriorate again and the temperature dropped below zero: 'The sky showed a still more dreadful appearance,' wrote de Ségur:

You might see icy particles floating in the air; birds fell from it quite stiff and frozen. The atmosphere was motionless and silent: it seemed as if everything which possessed life and movement in nature – the wind itself – had been seized, chained and as it were, frozen by a universal death.

Lejeune remembered: 'We were all covered with ice. Our breath, looking like thick smoke, froze as it left our mouths and hung in icicles from our hair, eyebrows, moustaches and beards, sometimes quite blinding us.' Blindness, caused by snow, ice and the smoke from fires, became prevalent and von Roos recorded how 'he saw men dragging their comrades along by sticks, like beggars'. The army suffered greatly from the lack of supplies and rumours of cannibalism and horror stories of men reduced to drinking their own blood, sapped the moral strength of even the strongest. According to Marbot:

> one of the stoutest and bravest officers in my regiment was so distracted by what he had seen in the last few days that he laid himself down on the snow and no persuasions being able to make him rise, died there. Many soldiers of all ranks blew out their brains to put an end to their misery.

Poor nutrition also led to dysentery which, according to Lejeune, 'worked terrible ravages amongst us […] its victims, with their dry and livid skin and emaciated limbs, looked like living skeletons'. In addition, many had suffered frostbite: 'Lack of sound and suitable footwear cost thousands of lives …' commented Vossler. 'In many cases extremities simply broke off, in others fingers and toes, and often whole arms and legs had to be amputated.'

Thus the Grand Army, losing hundreds of men every day, slowly progressed to Vilna. According to Löwernstern:

> The war has essentially ended for the lack of enemy combatants. It is true that the soldiers were plundering the abandoned French transports, but we no longer took prisoners and the extreme cold claimed these unfortunates. The road was covered with corpses […] Over one *versta*'s distance, I counted seventy-six frozen horses and 148 human corpses […] and the rest of the road to Vilna represented a similar poignant picture.

Tyrconnell counted over 600 bodies over 16 miles and saw 'piles of dead bodies next to every building, with a few survivors crawling out to beg for bread …'[779] Another participant described that

> anyone who has not witnessed the pursuit simply cannot imagine the horrors that we saw at every step on the route from the Berezina to Vilna. This dreadfulness only increased as we approached Vilna. The road was covered with corpses, which, in some places, were used to fill up ditches for the artillery to pass, dead horses, abandoned cannon, caissons, transports, etc. We had to clear the path for our army while the road was lined up with throngs of half-frozen and almost naked French …

A similar account also exists in Khrapovitskii's memoirs:

Aftermath

The road was covered with dead and dying [...] Every knoll on the road was packed with transport, cannon, regimental and artillery vehicles; every bivouac resembled the field of bloody battle or the Valley of Josaphat,[780] the Valley of Wail and Sorrow.

Having led the Grand Army across the Berezina – its last major obstacle before the Polish frontier – Napoleon's job as a commander was largely done and he decided to return to Paris to retrieve the reins of power, which had been shaken by a recent coup attempt by General Malet. On 5 December, Napoleon appointed his brother-in-law, Marshal Murat, commander of the army and left for Paris. Many viewed his departure as a betrayal and, according to Marbot, this 'produced a great effect on the troops'. Pion, of the Guard artillery, went so far as to declare his emperor 'the greatest fool in the world' and claimed that the soldiers 'cursed Napoleon at the tops of their voices'.

On 8 December, the survivors of the Grand Army straggled into Vilna, where they initially found large supplies of food and ammunition. But in the ensuing chaos, supply stores were ravaged and many stragglers trampled to death. The following day, Russian troops under Colonel Seslavin engaged Ney's rearguard, comprising the survivors of the 34th and 20th Divisions, and briefly seized one of the suburbs of Vilna. Murat, instructed by Napoleon to rest troops in the city, became concerned about the proximity of Russian forces and ordered the evacuation of Vilna on the night of 9 December, abandoning thousands of wounded in the hospitals. On 10 December, MG Orlov-Denisov's detachment, supported by Platov's Cossacks, attacked the outskirts of Vilna, capturing some 2,000 men and forcing Ney's rearguard to withdraw to the Ponarskaya Hill, some 4 miles west of Vilna. Ney deployed his troops (some 4,000 men) at the bottom of the hill and, after a brief combat with Cossacks, withdrew towards Kovno. At the same time, the detachments of Czaplic, Golenischev-Kutuzov and Borozdin attacked Vilna from different directions and captured the town. The precise number of casualties in Vilna is difficult to verify but Russian reports reveal some 14,000 Allied soldiers, including seven generals, 242 staff officers and over 5,000 sick soldiers. As they mounted their pursuit, the Russians also captured some 100 guns on the road to Ponarskaya Hill.

By 31 December, the last remnants of the Grand Army, including Macdonald's corps, crossed the Nieman and the Russian Campaign was over. On 17 February 1813, Emperor Alexander proudly proclaimed:

Soldiers! The year has ended – a year forever memorable and glorious – one in which you have trampled in the dust the pride of the insolent aggressor. The year has passed, but your heroic deeds survive. Time will not efface their trace. They are present to your contemporaries – they will live with their posterity. You have purchased at the price of your blood the deliverance of your country from the hostile powers leagued against its independence.

Conclusion

T he Berezina came very close to being a landmark. Had the Russians succeeded in their entrapment of Napoleon, European history would have recorded a different 'Waterloo' and its course might have developed in a different direction. One may envision Napoleon killing himself with a poison, which he had carried since Maloyaroslavets in order to avoid capture, or being indeed captured and imprisoned in a dark cell of the St Peter and Paul fortress in St Petersburg. With Napoleon gone, a different 'Congress of Vienna' might have been summoned in 1813, where Russia would have been in the dominant position. Presumably some kind of European balance of power would have emerged, though probably more tentative than was the case in 1814–1815. Would the Bourbons have returned to France? Would Prussia and Austria have recovered their territories? One wonders how the Napoleonic Legend would have developed without the 'Flight of the Eagle' in 1815 or Napoleon's 'martyrdom' on St Helena? Possibilities seem infinite, but none of them came to realization. The Russians failed at the Berezina and Napoleon escaped: 'Berezina! Fateful name, fateful river where the misfortunes of mankind could have ended, but did not end, continuing for three more years!' lamented one German participant. 'Fateful place where the most terrible blunder was made, a blunder for which Europe paid with hundreds of thousands of lives on the fields of Lützen, Bautzen, Dresden, Kulm, Leipizig, Troyes, Ligny, Waterloo, with long years of devastation and war.' A British participant, while admiring the Russian patriotism, devotion and gallantry, also commented, 'the fact that Bonaparte escaped [...] will forever stain their achievements'.[781]

Much has been said about the outcome of the battle and campaign in general. 'Napoleon, unconquered of man, had been vanquished by the elements,' proclaimed William Napier, essentially ignoring Russian war efforts.[782] Adolphe Thiers thought that the passage of the Berezina was 'the immortal event [...] one of the most tragic to be found in history and a fitting end to this campaign'. Historians often praise Napoleon for his actions and describe the success on the Berezina as a result of his brilliant strategic mind: 'At this desperate crisis Napoleon's genius [was] revived' notes a modern historian. 'He laid an elaborate

Conclusion

trap' that deceived the Russians and the subsequent battle was 'one of the most remarkable feats in the history of warfare' believe other historians. 'In the realm of military art,' proclaims one study, 'the crossing operation over the Berezina must be considered as a masterwork of genius. Executed under such adverse conditions, it merits admiration.'[783]

But it is hard to embrace such wholehearted admiration of the success obtained at a very high price. Although the core of the army escaped, tens of thousands were killed in the battle, trampled in the rush for the bridge, drowned in the icy waters or captured. Certainly, we may agree with a French historian's assessment that it was 'une victoire militaire' but some may also concur with another historian's opinion: 'If getting the remnant of the Grand Army across the Berezina with very heavy loss, through the enemy's commander-in-chief mismanaging badly, be a masterpiece, what epithets are to be attached to Austerlitz and Friedland?'[784] The crossing had a devastating effect on the Grand Army. After the Berezina, 'one could assume that the French army ceased to exist', noted one participant, while in a modern historian's assessment, 'the passage of the Berezina was the swan song of the Grande Armée'.[785] The army, which Napoleon shaped into one of the most devastating military machines in European history, had met its demise in the snowy fields of Russia. For the Russians, it was a sweet retribution for the past defeats and, writing to Chichagov a few days after the crossing, Czaplic described the events on the Berezina as the long-awaited revenge for Austerlitz.[786]

At the Berezina, Napoleon escaped from what Clausewitz described as 'one of the worst situations in which a general ever found himself'. Was it a victory for Napoleon? Yes, it was, since he achieved his primary goal of breaking through enemy forces and leading his army out of Russia. Furthermore, he saved most of his officer corps, all marshals and the nucleus of his Guard. It cost him dearly, but the greater part of casualties fell on non-combatants and stragglers. Russian historian Modest Bogdanovich emphasized that

In the end, about 2,500 officers of the [Imperial] Guard and the corps of Davout, Ney and the Viceroy managed to cross over the Nieman and over 1,800 of them returned to the service. If Napoleon had been unable to save them, then he would have been unable in four months to organize a new army, capable of successfully operating against the eminent armies of Russia and Prussia. Had Napoleon finished his career on the banks of the Berezina, the fields of Germany and France would have never been coloured with blood in 1813, 1814 and 1815. That is why the crossing of the Berezina, despite the enormous success we achieved and considerable losses Napoleon suffered, was justly perceived by the people as a failure that shattered our hopes and earned more honour to the vanquished, than the victors.[787]

But the success was not due to Napoleon's genius but rather a combination of factors. In analyzing this battle, three key factors for Napoleon's success can be emphasized: the role of dedicated and skilled troops, good Allied leadership at corps and regimental level *and*, most crucially, the lack of Russian military initiative.

In discussions of the first factor, scholars often refer to the Berezina as a 'French victory'. It might be a matter of 'semantics' but such a description seems to be misleading. A large portion (if not the majority) of troops involved in the actual fighting on the banks of the Berezina were foreigners. The Dutch built the bridges, which were defended by the Polish, Swiss, Dutch, Illyrian, Portuguese, Berg, Baden and Saxon troops. Naturally, French units were involved in combat as well, but the brunt of the fighting was sustained by foreigners; as one historian calculated, out of 20,000 Allied troops who fought on the Berezina, the French probably accounted for only 5,000 men.[788] Thus, the success at the Berezina was an Allied one, not French. Overall, the Allied troops performed well and the surrender of the 12th Division at Stary Borisov is often considered the only setback for Napoleon in the entire Berezina operation. But in reality, the 12th Division probably saved thousands of lives, since Wittgenstein had to leave half his corps to secure the prisoners while attacking Victor's IX Corps with the remaining half. This allowed Victor to defend his position for the entire day and cover Napoleon's retreat. Notwithstanding their ethnic background, the troops of the Grand Army showed remarkable resilience, steadfastness and gallantry. But above them all stands the sacrifice of those who built and maintained the bridges, who continued working when exhausted, repeatedly immersed in icy waters with little chance of warmth or dry clothing.

The good leadership of the Allied forces played a key role in the battle. 'Napoleon and the marshals had done the impossible,' observes one prominent historian, 'if, during a bitter retreat, the crossing of the Berezina still *was* a victory.'[789] In the eyes of another historian, the Berezina was 'as audacious as it was desperate' and Napoleon's men 'made up with deception, skill and spirit what they lacked in numbers and equipment, outwitted, outmanoeuvred and outfought' the Russian armies.[790] Yet, we probably should put a certain qualification on this argument. Overall, the corps, division and regimental commanders performed rather well, showing the skills and talents that earned them their fearsome reputations. Marshals, especially Oudinot, Ney and Victor, served well and further proved their merits. As Clausewitz justly observed, 'the military virtues of [Napoleon's] army, which not even its calamities could quite subdue, were destined here to show themselves once more in their full lustre'.

Conclusion

Napoleon certainly gets 'much of the credit for his coolness under such potentially disastrous conditions', as one biographer argues,[791] and the participants, almost unanimously, note how important the Emperor's presence was for the army's morale. Nevertheless, Napoleon can be criticized on several accounts. He effectively endangered his forces when he allowed his pontoon train to be burned while a large portion of the private baggage train remained intact. He did not conceive the crossing, nor did he choose the site at Studyanka, relying on reports from his subordinates on the practicality of bridging the river. His marshals and generals did this for him. Once across the river, Napoleon made no real steps to supervise the crossing personally, which resulted in great confusion: 'It cannot be said that Napoleon showed to any advantage at the Berezina,' observes one historian. 'The selection of the point of passage was due to the skill and energy of Oudinot; the credit for the resistance on the 28th is to be attributed to Ney and Victor; while the true heroes of the episode were General Eblé and his *pontonniers*.'[792] David Chandler agrees that the success at Berezina was more the results of 'the devoted service of three of [Napoleon's] subordinates. Eblé, the selfless bridge-builder; Oudinot, the selector of the crossing place [...] and Victor, commander of the intrepid rear guard'.[793]

Had the Russians destroyed the causeway leading from the Berezina, the outcome would have been very different. 'And the fact that the success or failure of the entire French operation depended on this single causeway demonstrates what a gamble Napoleon was undertaking,' argues a prominent British historian.[794] This point is better elaborated by another early twentieth-century historian:

> Much praise has been lavished on the skill and courage exhibited by Napoleon at the Berezina, but most of it is ill applied. His 'unerring sagacity' in selecting the right point at which to break through the enemy was merely the very ordinary good sense of not rejecting the only chance of escape. The information given to him was conclusive as to the impossibility of effecting a passage at or below Borisov: no great skill was therefore required in deciding to try higher up. Studyanka was chosen as the exact spot, not by Napoleon, but by Oudinot, and happened to combine every advantage for the purpose, the one drawback of marsh on the right bank being neutralized just in time by the renewed frost. Excellent use was indeed made of the favourable conditions on the ground, but all would have been unavailing but for Chichagov being misled into going south of Borisov. Courage indeed there was of the highest order, but it was the courage of the soldiers, who succeeded in holding off a superior enemy, still more of the sappers who died to make a means of escape for the rest ...[795]

The Battle of the Berezina

This brings us to the last and, in this author's view, the most important factor in Napoleon's success at Berezina. The Russian indecision and mismanagement were undoubtedly the single most important factor in deciding the outcome of the entire operation. If the three Russian armies had operated in unison and converged on the Berezina as originally envisioned, the Grand Army's chance of escaping would have been very slim. The great Russian historian Eugène Tarle commented that

> perhaps even Napoleon's genius would not have sufficed to save him in these desperate, utterly hopeless circumstances, if a single will had reigned in the Russian camp, or, more accurately, if the will upon which everything in the Russian camp depended had actually been intent upon surrounding and capturing the French Emperor.[796]

Wittgenstein and Chichagov were both troubled by his presence and neither was anxious to come to close quarters with Napoleon. Bogdanovich argued that although the Grand Army was weakened and on the verge of collapse, it still presented a great threat because Napoleon commanded it: 'The hearsay increased its size up to sixty, even eighty, thousand men and neither Wittgenstein nor Chichagov had correct information on the incredible disorder in the Grand Army [...] and so both desired to avoid direct confrontation with Napoleon.'[797] Historian Eugène Stschepkin is partly right in noting that: 'The Emperor owed his deliverance, above all, to the magic of his name and the prestige of his arms.'[798]

The discussion on who was to blame for Napoleon's escape began almost as soon as the crossing was over. 'By night, everything calmed down,' wrote Rafail Zotov, serving with Wittgenstein's troops,

> Our entire corps gathered around bivouacs and as bonfires ignited, reflections, debates and speculations poured at once. What did the events of the day mean? How and why was Napoleon allowed to cross? Why was he even allowed to build the bridges? Why had not Chichagov's army trampled him back into the river when the crossing began? Why did not Kutuzov follow on Napoleon's heels to destroy him on the riverbank? These thoughts kept us guessing all night long. Of course, we first deplored Chichagov, then Kutuzov and finally even our own Wittgenstein. The whole Berezina affair seemed to us as pathetic and suspicious.[799]

Much blame was (and still is) assigned to Admiral Chichagov, who 'apparently understood nothing of what was happening', as one modern writer proclaimed.[800] Similar sentiments can be found in many other works but, as previous comments

Conclusion

in this book reveal, this charge is misplaced. Chichagov was not an army commander and Tyrconnell was right when he noted that 'the [Russian] government must be held responsible for appointing an admiral, instead of a general, to handle such an important mission'. Chichagov's brash treatment of subordinates only complicated this task. Tyrconnell also observed that the officers of the 3rd Western Army 'do not trust their commander, who is not a military man and who mistreats many of them, shows indecisiveness in planning and always blames his mistakes on them'.[801] Bogdanovich justly observed:

> Contemporaries blamed Chichagov exclusively for the failure [on the Berezina] which is hardly surprising: Prince Kutuzov was the man who liberated Russia from the invasion of Napoleon and his hordes; Count Wittgenstein was the defender of our northern capital, who inspired people with his victories at a time when our misfortunes seemed to be everywhere. They both stood so highly in public opinion that no one could dare to question their actions.[802]

The Admiral, on the other hand, had neither military experience nor reputation.

Chichagov did make a few mistakes during the campaign. In early November, he spent days vacillating on his course of action, a time he could have used to reach and fortify Borisov. He was accused of failing to properly defend Borisov on 23 November but the Russians' loss of this town gave little advantage to Napoleon. Chichagov still controlled the western bank and had Wittgenstein approached from the north and Kutuzov from the east, the Grand Army still would have been trapped. Chichagov's most important mistake was in diverting most of his army south of Borisov. But he did not make this decision on his own whim, and it was not caused solely by Napoleon's 'elaborate trap'. Rather, Chichagov's decision was based on the misleading intelligence and instructions provided by Wittgenstein and Kutuzov; the French diversions simply reinforced it. Without these instructions, one might wonder if the Russians would have fallen for the diversions alone and moved so *many* troops *so far* to the south? Besides, after Wittgenstein and Kutuzov failed to arrive on time, Chichagov had limited resources to effectively guard a long riverbank with several fords. There are many examples throughout history – one may recall the crossings of Alexander the Great, Hannibal, Caesar, or even Napoleon himself in 1796 and 1809 – that show how the passage of rivers may be won even in the presence of the enemy forces. In his *Military Instructions*, Frederick the Great, one of the pre-eminent practitioners of military art, argued that

> nothing is more difficult, not to say impossible, than to defend the passage of a river, especially when the front of attack be of too great an extent. I

would never undertake a commission of this kind, if the ground which I had to defend was more than eight German miles in front, and unless there were two or three redoubts established on the bank of the river within this distance; neither should any other part of the river be fordable ...[803]

Chichagov had none of these factors on his side in 1812. Instead, he had to monitor a 40–mile stretch of river, which could be forded at several points. If facing Chichagov alone, Napoleon would have crossed the river without difficulty. His task was made easier by mistakes committed by the Admiral and his lieutenants. On 21–22 November, Chichagov ignored the evidence of the Grand Army's approach to Borisov, which resulted in the defeat of his advance guard and a hasty retreat across the river. After moving to Zabashevichi, the Admiral also vacillated upon receiving intelligence on the enemy bridging attempts in the north. His lieutenants made their share of mistakes as well. Langeron ignored crucial intelligence on the enemy bridging north of Borisov and insisted on implementing orders when circumstances required him to improvise. Sabaneyev selected ineffective tactics during the fighting on the 28th, which resulted in missed opportunities and high casualties. Czaplic, whom Kutuzov cursed as a 'stupid cow [sic!] and fool'[804] probably committed one of the gravest mistakes by failing to destroy the wooden causeways and bridges over the Zembino marshes. Had these been burnt, Napoleon would not have had any escape route to the north and would have had to fight his way through Chichagov's army to Minsk. Mikhailovsky-Danilevsky notes:

> Napoleon would have had to turn left towards Minsk ... In this direction, he would have had to move through marshes and thick woods, while Chichagov could take up a very strong position not far from Stakhov, behind the Brodni Rivulet, which had vast marshes in front of it.[805]

Forster, who examined the Zembino causeways for a special report for Alexander, summarized: 'the narrow paths and unstable bridges, surrounded by marshes, would have contributed to almost complete annihilation of the enemy if only the *defile* were properly reconnoitred and the bridges destroyed'.[806] Similar conclusions can be found in the works of many Allied soldiers.[807]

Without absolving Chichagov of his faults, this writer believes that Wittgenstein and Kutuzov should share the blame. Before the Berezina, the former's pursuit of Victor and Oudinot was unenergetic, often influenced by the professed fear of Napoleon moving in his direction. This allowed Victor to retreat to Borisov unmolested until 27 November. 'We should not be surprised of his cautiousness,' writes one Russian historian, 'he did not want to threaten the fame he earned in previous victories.'[808] Wittgenstein, when told about the

Conclusion

enemy crossing near Studyanka, ignored such reports and proceeded towards Stary Borisov, giving Napoleon additional time to save his army. Mikhailovsky-Danilevsky, the court historian, admitted that 'had Wittgenstein arrived two days, or even a day, earlier and attacked the rear of the enemy army, Napoleon's crossing would have turned disastrous'.[809] Arriving at Borisov, Wittgenstein expressed hesitation at the prospect of being subordinated to Chichagov, which hampered coordination of Russian actions during the combats of 28–29 November and the subsequent pursuit. Even Dmitri Buturlin, who tried his best to justify Wittgenstein's actions, found it 'very strange that Wittgenstein was unable to drive into the river Victor's weak corps, which instead resisted for an entire day'. Joseph de Maistre's letter reflects what some in Russian society thought about the Russian General's actions:

> In his report, the honourable Count wrote, 'I forced the enemy to cross the river at Studyanka.' Some justly observed that this statement means that he in fact was fighting against Chichagov, whose mission was to prevent such a crossing in the first place.

According to Golitsyn: 'Kutuzov said that Wittgenstein's certain actions could not be justified but they could be forgiven because of his fame and for the sake of the expulsion of the enemy out of Russia [...] and that God would finish what certain Russian generals could not.'[810]

Kutuzov's role in the events of the Berezina is complex and, depending on the study, he is either absolved of all responsibility or held chiefly culpable for the Russian mismanagement. Thus, Kutuzov's most recent Russian biography exonerates him of any responsibility, blaming Chichagov instead. 'His confusing orders to his colleagues,' concludes David Chandler, 'were largely responsible for the loss of an apparently inevitable and complete success.'[811] As we have previously discussed, Kutuzov did not pursue the Grand Army vigorously, causing many participants to wonder about his intentions. While the outcome of the campaign was decided at the Berezina, Kutuzov was miles away slowly moving westward. It took the Russian main army eleven days (19–30 November) to cover the distance between Krasnyi and the Berezina, while the Grand Army did it in six days (19–25 November)! Some Russian scholars defend this slow advance by noting the need to 'preserve the men and wait for supply trains that lagged behind by several marches'.[812] On a personal level, Kutuzov desired the destruction of the enemy and, in a private letter of 1 December, he acknowledged, 'I cannot say I am cheerful since not everything is going as well as I desire. Bonaparte is still alive ...'[813] But his political considerations dictated a different set of actions. Kutuzov knew well that the 1812 Campaign had effectively ended at Smolensk and Napoleon was simply trying to get out of

Russia. Therefore, he looked beyond strictly military factors and believed that it was not in Russia's political interests to eliminate Napoleon: 'I am by no means sure that the total destruction of Napoleon and his army would be such a benefit to the world,' Kutuzov told the British commissioner. 'His succession would not fall to Russia or any other Continental power, but to that which already commands the sea [Britain], and whose domination would then be intolerable.' Kutuzov was convinced of the importance of preserving the Russian military, since Napoleon's defeat could no longer be doubted and winning one more battle was not as important as Russia's role in future political developments in Europe, which might require military confrontation with rival powers.

One may justify Kutuzov's actions in the light of these considerations. But it is more difficult to excuse his deliberate attempts to undermine Chichagov and blame him for the failure at the Berezina. Denis Davydov provides a damning assessment:

> Kutuzov avoided the enemy and, remaining in one place, he was constantly far behind the enemy. This, however, did not prevent him from informing Chichagov that the main army was closely pursuing the enemy. *These letters were backdated and delivered late to the Admiral* [my emphasis]. Chichagov often reprimanded couriers for being late but they explained that they were sent much later than the dates indicated on letters.

It is quite surprising to hear of a commander-in-chief intentionally distorting intelligence that his fellow commander utilized to engage the enemy. One modern Russian historian observes: 'Kutuzov most likely had neither a definitive plan of action [against Napoleon] nor desire to interfere in events, preferring to let everything resolve itself. But at the same time he took every precaution to protect himself from any criticism, which required finding a convenient target for attacks.'[814]

Wittgenstein was a difficult target to assail, since he had won the Battle of Polotsk and was hailed as the 'Saviour of St Petersburg', riding a wave of popularity in the army and society. Chichagov, on the other hand, was a more convenient scapegoat because he was unpopular among officers and generally less well known. Besides, Kutuzov had personal scores to settle with him and Lev Chichagov, the Admiral's descendant, believed that 'Kutuzov's bitterness about being replaced in the Army of the Danube' was the cause. Martos, who served under Chichagov, notes that 'the old man [Kutuzov] mercilessly took revenge on Chichagov, intending to ruin us ...'

Kutuzov learned of Napoleon's escape while on the march to the Berezina: 'He was very upset,' remembered Golitsyn, but unaware of details, he continued to issue orders to pursue the enemy to the Nieman [...] When the details of all our commanders' actions were revealed, Kutuzov blamed Chichagov the least of all, but still held him responsible for wasting time on his march to Borisov [...] On Kutuzov's calculations, Chichagov could have been on the Berezina five days earlier and this time would have sufficed to reconnoitre all points at which the French army could organize a crossing, to construct fortifications and observe the road from Borisov to Bobr and further [...] He tried to justify Chichagov [...] and often commented mockingly that, if for no other reason, Chichagov could be forgiven because he was a sailor unaccustomed to land and it was the Emperor's fault, since he entrusted such an important task to a man who was inexperienced in the military art ...[815]

But as reports of the Russian failure on the Berezina poured into the main headquarters, Kutuzov also began covering up his role in it while blaming his rival, Chichagov. Despite Wittgenstein's disappointing actions, Kutuzov congratulated him on 'a victory that Your Excellency gained over the enemy during the crossing of the Berezina, I must thank you for your proficient contribution to the enemy's defeat'.[816] Chichagov received a quite different letter: 'Yesterday I received the news that Napoleon supposedly crossed the Berezina with his army near Veselovo. I cannot believe this [...] I request you to explain what measures and directions you undertook ...'[817] In his report to Alexander, the Field Marshal emphasized the 'crucial mistakes of Admiral Chichagov' and listed some of the most damning ones:

1. Instead of occupying the advantageous right bank of the Berezina, he moved part of his forces to the left bank and set up his headquarters at Borisov, located in a depression surrounded by heights on all sides. The inevitable consequence of this would have been, and was, the sacrifice of many courageous warriors of Your Imperial Majesty and the loss of the entire baggage train ...
2. The tall and narrow bridge and a dam on the Zaika Rivulet [a tributary to the Gaina River] were not destroyed, even though the Admiral's forces reached the Berezina four days before the enemy.
3. The enemy built the bridge and began and continued the crossing one day before the Admiral even knew about it, although he had to guard no more than 20 *verstas* of riverbank. After learning about the crossing, he marched to that site, but encountered enemy skirmishers and failed to attack in large numbers, but only limited himself to fighting with two guns and skirmishers ...[818]

The Battle of the Berezina

A closer look at Kutuzov's arguments reveals that some stretched the truth, while others plainly lied. In hindsight, Chichagov did make the mistake of moving his army across the river on 22 November but one must remember that he acted in accordance with instructions he had received from Alexander and Kutuzov. He did not have four days to set up defences. Lambert's advance guard stormed Borisov on 21 November, Chichagov's main forces reached it on the 22nd and Oudinot's drove them out on the 23rd. Kutuzov fails to mention that the Admiral acted in an information vacuum and was unaware of the Grand Army's approach, which Kutuzov should have warned him about. The third argument also stretches the truth. It makes no mention of Kutuzov's own misleading instructions to Chichagov on Napoleon possibly moving to Igumen, which made the Admiral shift his forces. Besides, Kutuzov's assessment of '20 *verstas*' or 13 miles is plain wrong. The distance between Veselovo and Borisov alone is over 10 *verstas* (7 miles), while the Berezina flows for some 50 *verstas* (33 miles) before reaching Berezino, where O'Rourke's detachment was sent to guard the road to Igumen, where Kutuzov thought Napoleon was heading. Chichagov, explaining his actions to Alexander, noted that 'Zembino is 30 *verstas* away from Borisov, which I had to defend in addition to the entire distance of the Berezina.' After learning of the crossing, Chichagov indeed marched to Stakhov but, contrary to Kutuzov's claim, he attacked with available forces and requested reinforcements from Wittgenstein, Platov and Yermolov. Chichagov might be criticized for his failure to attack on the 27th but we must remember that his army was still *en route* and Borisov was still occupied by the 'French' who, in Chichagov's mind, could have forced a passage there.

Chichagov knew that he would be held responsible for the Berezina: 'I think I will be reproached for not capturing Bonaparte and his army,' he wrote to Alexander on 29 November,

> I will be criticized for not guessing his direction and placing my corps to cut that route. I am, however, convinced that a corps, which, for example, I could have sent to Zembino, would not have produced any better results than the one that defended the site where the enemy sought to cross. The river is fordable in many places and it is possible to move, under protection of a strong battery, a considerable number of men to an opposite bank in a short period of time. I have only 16,000–17,000 infantry, which alone cannot be considered useful in given circumstances, since the cavalry is completely useless [...] I did my best to fulfil my mission, but I now understand well the impregnable obstacles that reality puts in front of us ...

Anticipating that 'deceitful assertions' could influence Alexander, Chichagov dispatched General Sabaneyev to St Petersburg. Sabaneyev reached the capital on

Conclusion

6 December but was not received by Alexander. Was the Emperor already swayed? Probably. But Countess Edeling was also struck by 'the Admiral's eccentricity' in selecting 'his fiercest enemy, General Sabaneyev to deliver his report to the Emperor; Sabaneyev, of course, had no interest in defending him'.[819]

The army and society was soon saturated with stories of Chichagov's incompetence and mismanagement, which 'saved' Napoleon. Kutuzov's family members and supporters only fanned the winds of gossip. Already on 1 December, Kutuzov's son-in-law wrote: 'The Gentlemen has escaped. Chichagov will be the cause of the bloodshed still to come ...' The Russian Commander-in-Chief's wife, Princess Ekaterina Kutuzova, publicly commented that 'Wittgenstein saved St Petersburg, my husband Russia, and Chichagov – Napoleon.'[820] 'It is impossible to describe the common loathing felt against Chichagov. Everyone suspects him of treason,' wrote a contemporary. Vasily Zhukovsky, one of the first Romantic poets in Russia, was completing his famous poem *A Bard in the Camp of the Russian Warriors*, when he heard of the events on the Berezina and 'threw out' as he wrote, an entire section dedicated to Chichagov. Gregory Derzhavin, another famous Russian poet, wrote a sharp epigram praising Kutuzov for 'tying up a deadly net around the French' and condemning the 'amphibious [*zemnovodnii*] general' who 'slithered in to unravel it'.[821] General Dokhturov complained that 'our *admiral* [original emphasis] scatters everything to the winds', while Robert Wilson heard the rumour that 'the enemy found a bridge over the Berezina [abandoned by Chichagov] and simply built another bridge for infantry to accelerate the crossing ...'[822]

Yermolov met Kutuzov before he reached Vilna: 'I immediately went to see him,' the General recalled,

> and he questioned me rigorously about the battle on the Berezina. I managed to explain to him that Chichagov had not been as guilty as many had desired to portray him. I did not justify his erroneous movement on Igumen, but similarly I did not hide the mistakes committed by Wittgenstein. I easily perceived the depth of Kutuzov's antipathy towards the Admiral. He was not pleased that I dared defend him. However, it was difficult to disregard my testimony considering my high rank and Kutuzov was reluctant to sway me away from the facts I had seen with my own eyes. He pretended to be extremely satisfied to learn the truth and assured me (although I was not convinced) that he would now look upon the Admiral in a different light and that up to now he had been determined to treat him unfavourably.[823]

By 13 December, Kutuzov reached the Lithuanian capital, where he finally met the man he so despised. Major Khrapovitskii, who served as the provisional commandant of Vilna, greeted the Field Marshal with a large escort and took him to the Governor's residence. 'Around 8 p.m.,' Khrapovitskii remembered,

> Prince Kutuzov entered the town and, after hearing my report, he asked about the Admiral. I told him that he would have the honour to appear in a short while. I immediately rushed to the Admiral, informing him of [Kutuzov's] arrival. I found him ready, but not in naval but a parade uniform. When the carriage arrived, he asked me to travel with him. As soon we entered the hallway [in Kutuzov's residence] we heard much pacing. Inside the hall we found the Prince himself, walking towards us surrounded by at least thirty, if not more, generals and staff officers.[824]

Kutuzov's orderly Golitsyn, based on the testimony of an eyewitness, adds an interesting note about this meeting. As they greeted each other, Kutuzov sarcastically told Chichagov that the baggage train and silverware that the Admiral lost at Borisov were recovered and offered to return them. The Admiral, 'with a sly smile', responded in French, 'If you are hinting that I have nothing to eat on, then, on the contrary, I want to assure you that I can treat you and even provide all essentials if you decide to give a banquet.'[825] Khrapovitskii writes that

> The two commanders embraced each other and, taking hands, went into the farthest room. I, as an official who accompanied the Admiral, followed them there. Passing two rooms, they halted in the fireplace room. [Kutuzov] set the Admiral next to himself and [...] told him, 'I would like to congratulate Your Excellency on the victories you have gained over the enemy, and thank you for all your efforts.' It struck me that Kutuzov raised his voice when speaking those last words. Without delay, the Admiral responded in a firm and loud voice, 'The glory and honour belong to you alone, Your Highness. Everything was accomplished on your orders, and therefore all victories belong to you as well.' Having exchanged such compliments, both sat quiet. Tea was served at once and a typical conversation resumed. After half an hour, the Admiral stood up, bid farewell and Prince Kutuzov escorted him to the hall.[826]

It was probably the same evening that Yermolov found Kutuzov conversing with Chichagov and Wittgenstein:

> Wittgenstein was describing several battles he had won in such a bragging tone that it seems the main army's role had only consisted of winning some small, insignificant actions. Even Kutuzov's finesse was not enough to hide

his indignation and he showed it, although he treated the Admiral with more attention and he was content with such respect. The relationship between Chichagov and Kutuzov seemed courteous, but that did not prevent Kutuzov from doing harm to the Admiral, something noted by many.[827]

With Emperor Alexander expected to arrive at Vilna, the town was flooded with courtiers, adventurers and people seeking favours. In such an atmosphere, gossip and intrigue was rife: 'As soon as the news of the French defeat and its devastating retreat reached St Petersburg,' writes Martens,

> Incalculable numbers of *kamer-junkers*, adjutants and various adventurers, all seeking to benefit from the campaign, rushed to [Vilna] enlisting in the army as majors and colonels. They were appointed commanders of the Cossack detachments and they then received medals for capturing half-frozen Frenchmen, or the [Order of] St George for seizing cannon that were already stuck in the snow: 'We will show the French who the Russians are,' they said at every opportune moment, showing off the epaulettes and crosses that they had received for their exploits ...

These newly-minted heroes surrounded Kutuzov, lavishing praises on him while condemning Chichagov. Kutuzov himself avoided open attacks on the Admiral but his cynical remarks often did the work. At one dinner, as the guests drank a toast to the 'victor's health', Kutuzov supposedly raised his glass with the words, 'Alas, not everything was accomplished! If not for the Admiral, a simple Pskov gentleman could have said, "Europe, you can now breathe freely."'

Alexander, who reached Vilna on 22 December, knew Kutuzov's faults well. Wilson claims that the Emperor told him:

> I know that the Marshal has done nothing he ought to have done – nothing against the enemy that he could avoid; all his successes have been forced upon him. He has been playing some of his old Turkish tricks, but the nobility of Moscow support him, and insist on his presiding over the national glory of this war.[828]

And so, although Alexander privately rebuked Kutuzov for his inactivity, he publicly praised the Field Marshal and rewarded him with the prestigious Order of St George (1st class). General Rayevsky, the hero of Borodino, was blunt in one of his private letters: 'Kutuzov openly lied about our last battles. He claimed credit for them and garnered the St George order.' Another officer commented:

The Battle of the Berezina

Awards were lavishly distributed according to Kutuzov's nominations, which were not always impartial and had often been made without serious deliberation. Soon, the court was organized, with its inseparable factions and gossip; so there was an extensive field for intrigue, where Kutuzov, well known for his cunning, was constantly in the lead. Here at least he was an invincible opponent.[829]

Before Alexander's arrival, Yermolov presented Kutuzov with his secret report on Chichagov's actions on the Berezina:

> [Kutuzov] told me that he was ready to look on Chichagov without hard feelings. In the opinion of many, Chichagov's fault consisted of the fact that he managed to see through and completely understand Kutuzov! The Field Marshal could not ignore my report (coming from the chief of staff of the 1st Army), in which I described myself as an actual witness, whose troops comprised the reserves and had not fired a single shot.

By then Chichagov was already on the move, leading his army towards the imperial borders: so 'it is more likely,' continues Yermolov, 'that Kutuzov took advantage of the Admiral's absence to describe Chichagov's actions on the Berezina to the Tsar, no doubt defending him against all those unwarranted accusations'. But others were not so sure. Davydov believed that Yermolov's report, 'which completely exonerated Chichagov was probably intentionally lost by Kutuzov'. General Fedor Orlov, Alexander's Flügel Adjutant, believed that 'had Admiral Chichagov received the necessary support [from Wittgenstein and Kutuzov], not a single Frenchman would have escaped'. The Berezina was not a major river, certainly not as wide or deep as the Danube, Elbe, Nieman or Vistula, and so 'Napoleon did not have to possess special sagacity or skill to accomplish the crossing'. Yermolov felt 'with indignation how powerless my evidence is against the charges made against Chichagov'. Arnoldi, who fought at Stakhov and Brili, believed that

> if anyone decides to condemn Chichagov for letting the French cross the Berezina, such a charge would be misplaced since, as an eyewitness, I can testify that it was impossible to prevent it. [Chichagov] had some 22,000 men under arms on the Berezina and had to defend the river over an area of over 100 *verstas*, while as many enemy combatants were trying to cross it. Besides, are there any examples in history where one army desired to cross and someone prevented it? And it would have been even less feasible against Napoleon.

Conclusion

Still, Arnoldi argued that Napoleon could have been cornered and defeated but Wittgenstein and Kutuzov had to fully commit to this mission, and they did not.[830] Countess Edeling wrote in her memoirs that

> Chichagov was deceived by incorrect information and let Napoleon across the Berezina, which bought widespread condemnation upon him. Although he tried his best to undo the damage and pursued the enemy with incredible speed, his efforts remained unappreciated.[831]

Alexander, upon his arrival at Vilna, did not reprimand Chichagov, who received 'a most kind and warm reception' from the Sovereign.[832] But the Admiral's enemies spread gossip that essentially destroyed Chichagov's reputation. Politically, Chichagov was not well connected and he belonged to no court factions that could have defended him. His closeness to, and influence over, the Emperor caused great jealousy and earned him many powerful enemies who now turned popular opinion against him. A descendant of the Admiral later grumbled:

> The same public opinion, which in the beginning of the war forced the appointment of Kutuzov as the Commander-in-Chief, now impertinently blemished Chichagov, blaming him for the mistakes of other generals. Ministers and courtiers, although they knew deep in their hearts that the Admiral was not so guilty, also understood that it was in their interest to overthrow him from his pedestal and separate him from the Emperor. The Admiral had no sympathy for dishonesty and obtusity.

Chichagov was vilified as the man who single-handedly undermined the Russian effort and saved the 'Corsican Ogre'. De Maistre reported to the Sardinian court that 'everyone condemns him on all sides as an abominable traitor ...'[833] The Russian fabulist, Ivan Krylov, the famous follower of the traditions of Aesop and Lafontaine, ridiculed Chichagov in a popular fable, *The Pike and the Cat*, portraying the Admiral as the Pike, thrust out of his element and failing to rise to the occasion. The fable held its place among other items of popular culture criticizing the Russian Admiral. Thus, a popular cartoon represented Kutuzov holding one end of a long net, Napoleon, in the form of a hare, slipping out at the other end, which was held by Chichagov, who was shown exclaiming: 'I'll save you!' In later years, when the famous War of 1812 Gallery was established at the Hermitage and included over 330 portraits of generals who served against Napoleon, Chichagov's portrait was not included.

In early 1813, Chichagov requested leave from the army for 'health' reasons. But, in reality, it was due to constant sniping and attacks: 'I left the army not because of extreme sensitivity, but rather to avoid harming our cause due to Kutuzov's endless fault-finding [*pridirok*] against me,' Chichagov wrote in a private letter on 25 May 1813,

> [Kutuzov] sought to undermine everything I did, even if it would have added to his fame [...] I am accused of numerous mistakes, but what are they? No one can explain them to me. A major charge accuses me of not capturing Napoleon, but have I ever promised to do that? Was I ordered to do it? Was it my task? Was it even possible to do it?

Chichagov quietly endured the popular anger. De Maistre described him,

> suffering these injustices with his usual dignity, honour and firmness. He wanted to induce the Emperor into defending him and giving him due recognition. But it was impossible for the Emperor to do this, since it would require demolishing a common idol [Kutuzov] and affronting Wittgenstein ...[834]

'The crowd is blind, but it is even more so in our country because it is less educated and lacks the ability to use reason. This means it can be easily deceived and manipulated. But what should we think about those who, knowing the truth, still tolerate falsehoods and slander?' Chichagov wrote to Semen Vorontsov in September 1813. Unwilling to embroil himself in public debates, Chichagov vented his anger in private: 'My greatest fault is that I reached the position set by the Emperor, while others [Wittgenstein and Kutuzov] did not, but yet proved to be right ...'[835] It is still unclear why Chichagov, who was so convinced of his innocence, decided not to press for an investigation or inquiry into the events. Vorontsov certainly suggested something along these lines:

> Before leaving the army, you should have travelled to the headquarters in Kalisch, asked for an audience with the Emperor, insisted on Kutuzov's presence, and then explained to them everything you have accomplished, showed all correspondence and orders, explained that you are being accused of letting Bonaparte escape and that your honour is too precious not to demand a council of war to investigate you. I am convinced that Kutuzov would have been forced to defend you and admit, in the Emperor's presence, that you have done nothing wrong. Afterwards, they would have had to reward you for your service and the same people who tormented you, would have had to eat their own words [...] I am surprised you did not choose to act as you should have ...

Conclusion

The lives of the three Russian commanders involved in the Berezina operation went in separate ways. Kutuzov, already an old man, became sick and died in April 1813. He remains one of the most popular and celebrated Russian commanders. As it often happens with national heroes, Kutuzov gradually became larger than life, a hero who was credited with saving Russia. Later, Soviet leaders exploited his personality for even more grandiose schemes, forcing many Soviet historians to distort historical facts to create a mythical figure of the Field Marshal.

Wittgenstein enjoyed a rather successful career. After the death of Kutuzov, he assumed command of the Russian Army on 25 April 1813 but his limitations as a military commander were quickly revealed as he mishandled his command at Lützen and Bautzen. After these defeats he resigned but continued to command a corps for the rest of the Napoleonic Wars, distinguishing himself at Dresden, Leipzig and Bar-sur-Aube. After the war, he commanded the 2nd Army and served in the State Council, earning promotion to general field marshal in 1826. During the Russo-Turkish War of 1828–1829, Wittgenstein became Commander-in-Chief of the Russian Army and was virtually ignored by his General Staff, led by Ivan Diebitsch, which operated independently from him and led to his dismissal due to 'poor health'. He spent the next decade at his estate of Kamenka in the Podolsk province; in 1834, King Frederick William III of Prussia conferred upon him the title of prince for his role in the 1813 Campaign. While travelling to recuperate in Europe, Wittgenstein died at Lvov in June 1843.

Chichagov's life was the most tragic of all. After leaving the army, he remained in Russia until 1814 when, tired of continued public recriminations, he requested imperial permission for an unlimited furlough to recuperate abroad. He travelled to England, where his three daughters lived with their grandparents. The Admiral knew that he was leaving Russia for good and took with him the ashes of his beloved wife, burying them in a small church at Beddington, where he had married her in 1799; the 1844 history of the town mentioned 'an attractive memorial, in a Grecian style of design [...] commemorative of Elizabeth, daughter of Chas. Proby of Chatham, and wife of Paul Tchitchagoff'.[836] The Admiral spent the rest of his life in England and travelling throughout Europe. He resigned from all posts in Russia but remained a member of the State Council for the next twenty years. He socialized with the English nobility and tried to clear his name; in his letter of July 1814, Jeremy Bentham described Chichagov holding an evening reading of General Frédéric-François Guillaume de Vaudoncourt's account of the crossing of the Berezina that justified the Admiral's actions.[837] In 1816, Chichagov began writing his own memoirs and, the following year, published a booklet, *Retreat of Napoleon*, which defended his actions. In 1822 he bought a small château at Sceaux, near Paris, where he settled down. In 1834, he disregarded Emperor Nicholas' decree that Russian subjects could not remain abroad more than five years and was severely penalized for it: he was officially dismissed from the State Council and his property was requisitioned. In response, Chichagov mailed his orders and awards to Nicholas and accepted British citizenship in 1836, forever breaking ties to his motherland. In 1842, Chichagov, by now almost blind, sold his château and moved to live with his daughter Catherine Naudet du Bouzet in Paris. He died there in September 1849 and was buried next to his brother Vasily at a local cemetery at Sceaux. His reputation never recovered and popular opinion continued (and still does) to hold him responsible for the Russian failure on the Berezina.

Notes and Sources

1. Peyrusse (1894), 125; Vaudoncourt (1815 (b)), 1.
2. Berthezène, II, 172; Jomini (1894), 127.
3. Leo Tolstoy, *War and Peace*, trans. by Nathan Dole (New York, 1889), III, 211.
4. Jonathan North, 'The Beresina Bridges', *Military Heritage*, 1999 1(2), 60–67, 95; Brian C. Kelly, 'Conquest Kept Joyless', *Military History*, 1993 10(5), 50–57; Ira Meistrich, 'Berezina', *MHQ: The Quarterly Journal of Military History*, 1990 2(3), 94–106.
5. Chambray, II, 78.
6. Barrau, 91; Mailly, 72; Bourgogne, 56; Griois, II, 82.
7. Laugier, 118–119.
8. Rapp, 221–222; Charles Tristan Montholon, *Mémoires pour server a l'Histoire de France sous Napoléon, écrits a Sainte-Hélène* (Paris, 1823), II, 104.
9. Dorokhov to Konovnitsyn, No. 64, 21 October 1812, *M.I. Kutuzov: sbornik dokumentov*, IV, part 2, 57–58.
10. Griois, II, 89.
11. Wilson, *Narratives*, 234.
12. Kutuzov to Alexander, 25 October 1812, 21 February 1813, *M.I. Kutuzov: sbornik dokumentov*, IV, part 2, 98, 110.
13. Mailly, 78; Fezensac, 77–78; Caulaincourt, II, 110–112.
14. Dumonceau, II, 190–191; Fezensac, 76.
15. Klinkhardt, 61; Claude-François de Méneval, *Memoirs illustrating the History of Napoleon I from 1802 to 1815* (New York, 1894), III, 71.
16. Dumas, II, 405.
17. Dumas, II, 409.
18. Kutuzov to Alexander, 18 November 1812, *Kutuzov: sbornik dokumentov*, IV, part 2, 308; *Journal of Military Operations between 15 and 19 November*, in ibid, 318. On 21 November, Kutuzov wrote that 'the captured alone include six generals, 190 staff and junior officers, 19,170 rank-and-file, ninety-seven guns in addition to 112 pieces that [the French] abandoned upon departure from Smolensk'. In a letter to Wittgenstein, he repeated the same numbers but added that 'six flags and field marshal's baton, entire train and treasury' were also captured. Prince Kutuzov to General Kutuzov, 21 November 1812, No. 477; Kutuzov to Wittgenstein, 22 November, No. 480, in Kharkevich (1893), 29, 32–33.
19. Thiers, XIV, 580f.
20. Zhilin, 297.
21. Kutuzov to Chichagov, 18 November 1812, No. 449, in Kharkevich (1893), 1–2.
22. Alexander to Kutuzov, 11 November 1812, Dubrovin, 303.
23. *Arkhiv Rayevskikh* (St Petersburg, 1908), I, 183.
24. Eyler, 361.
25. Yermolov, 202; Davydov (1962), 541–42.

26. Wilson, Narrative, 319; Wilson to Alexander, 19 November 1812, in Dubrovin, 326.

27. Caulaincourt, 220.

28. Kutuzov to Ozharovsky, No. 438; Kutuzov to Seslavin, No. 442, 16 November 1812, RGVIA, f. VUA, op. 16, d. 3521, l. 63b–64.

29. Puibusque, 146–147.

30. Eugène of Württemberg, 'Vospominania o kampanii 1812 g v Rossii', *Voennii zhurnal*, 3 (1849): 131; Wilson, *Invasion*, 234; A. Voyeikov, 'General Graf Leontii Leontievich Bennigsen', *Russkii Arkhiv*, 59 (1868), 1857.

31. Kutuzov to his wife, 26 November 1812, *Kutuzov M.I. Sbornik Dokumentov*, IV, part 2, 385.

32. *Writings of John Quincy Adams*, IV, 395; Ker Porter, 101; Maistre to Blacas, 14 September 1812 (Addition à la dépêche), in *Correspondence diplomatique de Joseph de Maistre (1811–1817)* (Paris, 1860), I, 181.

33. Emperor Alexander to Chichagov 13 September 1812, RGVIA, d.3546, l.6–9b; Alexander to Tormasov, Wittgenstein and Steinheil, 13 September 1812, in *General Staff Archive*, XVIII, 210–212; Alexander to Kutuzov, 13 September 1812 in Bogdanovich, II, 344–345; 605–614.

34. Barclay de Tolly to Chichagov, 12 August 1812, *General Staff Archive*, XVII, 168.

35. Alexander to Chichagov, 13 September 1812, in Bogdanovich, II, 607; *General Staff Archive*, XVIII, 211; *M.I. Kutuzov: Sbornik dokumentov*, IV, 463–465.

36. Michael Oginski, *Denkwürdigkeiten über Polen, das Land und seine Bewohner* (Constance, 1843), III, 169.

37. Toll, *Denkwürdigkeiten*, II, 190; Bogdanovich, II, 346.

38. Tarle, 266.

39. RGVIA, f.846, op.16, d.3597, l.1; Wilson, *Narrative*, 131, Mayevsky, 8 (1873), 153.

40. Langeron, 9 (1907), 569–571.

41. Anne Louise Germaine de Staël, *Dix années d'exil* (Paris, 1904), 369.

42. Maistre to Rossi, 9 May 1812, *Correspondance diplomatique de Joseph de Maistre*, I, 100. Even State Secretary Shishkov was not privy to the appointment and learnt about it after overhearing a Swedish general.

43. Chichagov, 9 (1870), 15–16.

44. For details on early life see Leonid Chichagov, 'Admiral Pavel Vasilievich Chichagov. Zapiski o sobytiyakh ego zhisni (epokha imperatora Pavla)'. *Russkaya starina*, vol. 38, 1883, 487–506. For a revisionist biography of Chichagov (in Russian), see Vladimir Yulin, Admiral P.V. *Chichagov–Istinnyi patriot Otechestva: Novoye v traktovke ego roli v istorii Rossii* (Moscow, 2002), http://www.museum.ru/museum/1812/Library/Chichagov/index.html.

45. Shishkov, 66; Toll, *Denkwürdigkeiten*, II, 353.

46. Maistre to King Victor Emmanuel I, *Arkhiv knyazya Vorontsova* (Moscow, 1880), XV, 491–492.

47. Toll, *Denkwürdigkeiten*, II, 353.

48. *Arkhiv admirala P.V. Chichagova* (St Petersburg, 1885), 29.

49. Tolstoy, 44–45.

50. Maistre to King Victor Emmanuel I, *Arkhiv knyazya Vorontsova*, XV, 492.

51. *Mémoires politiques et correspondence diplomatique de J. de Maistre*, 304; *Arkhiv admirala P.V. Chichagova*, 27–28.

52. Shishkov, 111.

53. Alexander to Kutuzov, 13 September 1812, in Bogdanovich II, 613–614.

54. Shishkov, 126.

55. *Feldmarshal Kutuzov: Dokumenty, dnevniki, vospominaniya* (Moscow, 1990), 210.

56. *Arkhiv Chichagova*, I, 23–25.

57. Shishkov, 66.

58. Langeron, 1–2.

59. Chichagov to Alexander, 17 November 1812, in *Sbornik Russkogo istoricheskogo obschestva*, VI, 49.

Notes and Sources

60. Toll, *Denkwürdigkeiten*, II, 354.

61. Tyrconnell to Cathcart, 26 November 1812, in Dubrovin, 346.

62. Dmitrii Bantysh-Kamenskii, *Slovar dostopamiatnykh liudei Russkoi zemli* (St Petersburg, 1847), I, 284–285.

63. *Deyania Rossiiskikh polkovodtsev i generalov oznamenovavshikh sebya v dostopamyatnuyu voinu s Frantsiyei v 1812, 1813, 1814 i 1815 godakh* (St Petersburg, 1822), II, 143–144.

64. Aleksey Djivegelov et al. *Otechestvennaya voina i Russkoye obshestvo* (Moscow, 1912), III, 106f.

65. The data on military service is skewed due to the prevailing practice in the Russian Army of enlisting children at a young age.

66. Mikhailovsky-Danilevsky, *Imperator Aleksandr I i ego spodvizhniki*, vol. III, 'Lambert', 8.

67. *The English Historical Review*, 12 (1897), 379; Baron Müffling, *Memoirs of the Campaign of 1813 and 1814* (London, 1853), 64.

68. A. Brikner. 'Zapiski grafa Lanzherona o russkom voiske (1796–1824).' *Russkaya mysl*, 9 (1896), 29–42; 'Memuary Lanzherona o kampaniyakh 1812–1813–1814 gg.' *Istoricheskii vestnik*, 93 (1903), 1100–1104.

69. Mikhailovsky-Danilevsky, *Imperator Aleksandr I i ego spodvizhniki*, vol. II, 'Langeron', 12.

70. Bantysh-Kamenskii, II, 263.

71. Tyrconnell to Cathcart, 30 November 1812 in Dubrovin, 354.

72. Mikhailovsky-Danilevsky, *Imperator Aleksandr I i ego spodvizhniki*, vol. II, 'Sabaneyev', 2.

73. Filip Vigel, Zapiski (Moscow, 1928), I, 265; Mikhailovsky-Danilevsky, *Imperator Aleksandr I i ego spodvizhniki*, vol. II, 'Sabaneyev', 10; *Pushkin v vospominaniyakh sovremennikov* (Moscow, 1974), I, 373; Langeron, *Zapiski*, 10 (1908), 269.

74. Chichagov to Kutuzov, No. 1790, 2 November 1812, in *Sbornik istoricheskikh materialov*, X, 102–103.

75. 'Zhurnal voyennikh deistvii …' in *The Buturlin Papers*, RGVIA, d.3479, ll.22–29; Ferdinand von Funck, *In Russland und in Sachsen*, 1812–1815 (Dresden, 1930), 181–203; Vasiliev (2001), 121–125; Finley, 361–368.

76. Napoleon to Berthier, 6 October 1812, *Correspondance de Napoleon*, XXIV, No. 19,258, 254.

77. Dąbrowski to Victor, 5 January 1813, RGVIA, d.3479, l.45ff.

78. Napoleon did order two divisions from Augereau's XI Corps to march to Bronikowski's help but they could not arrive in time. Bogdanovich, III, 221.

79. Victor to Dąbrowski, Victor to Bronikowski, Dąbrowski to Berthier, 28 October–16 November 1812, in Fabry, 119–120, 152, 178; Dąbrowski to Victor, 5 January 1813, RGVIA, d.3479, l.49b.

80. Vaudoncourt (1815(b)), 22–24; Kołaczkowski (1901), 69–70.

81. Chichagov to Alexander, 17 November 1812, RGVIA, d.3700, l.313; Chichagov to Kutuzov, No. 1897, 19 November 1812, RGVIA, d.3503, l.45. Chichagov reported that during their advance his troops seized up to 6,000 prisoners, including eighty officers; Kossecki's detachment alone yielded over sixty officers, including one lieutenant colonel and several majors. Also see *Journal of the Advance Guard of the 3rd Western Army*, 325–326; *Journal of Military Operations of the 3rd Western Army*, 217–218; *Journal of Military Operations of the Main Army*, in Kutuzov: *sbornik dokumentov*, IV, part 2, 418; Buturlin, II, 206; Laffitte to Berthier, 18 November 1812, in Fabry, 189; Vaudoncourt (1817), 285–286; Vaudoncourt (1815(a)), 19–24; Bogdanovich, III, 222–225; Bielecki, 16–17; Otroshenko, 546; Nawrot, 641–644; Pradzynski, 59–61.

82. Dąbrowski, 'Tableau des militaires le tout grade … proposes pour la decoration de la Legion d'Honneur', RGVIA, d.3479, l.42.

83. Laffitte to Berthier, 18 November 1812, in Fabry, 189.

84. Bronikowski to Bassano, Bronikowski to Berthier, 15–17 November 1812, in Fabry, 173, 180.

85. Dąbrowski to Berthier, 16 November 1812, in Fabry, 178 ; Chuquet (1912), I, 159–160. The

report of Colonel Lalance of the 7th Württemberg Regiment provides a few interesting insights. Pfister, 147–148.

86. Rochechouart, 162.

87. *Journal of the Advance Guard of the 3rd Western Army*, 326; *Journal of Military Operations of the 3rd Western Army*, 218; Chichagov to Lambert, Chichagov to Czaplic, 17 November 1812, RGVIA, d.3517, ll.47, 49; Chichagov to Kutuzov, No. 1897, 19 November 1812, RGVIA, d.3503, ll.45–45b; Vaudoncourt (1815(a)), 25; Cate, 362; Bogdanovich, III, 226.

88. Chichagov to Alexander, 17 November 1812, RGVIA, d.3700, ll.313–313b.

89. Mikhailovsky-Danilevsky, IV, 118–119.

90. Berthier to Victor, 19–20 November, in Chambray, II, 213–214.

91. Kutuzov to Chichagov, No. 428, 15 November 1812; Kutuzov to Alexander, No. 437, 16 November 1812, *Kutuzov: sbornik dokumentov*, IV, part 2, 282–283, 292.

92. Rochechouart, 163.

93. Czaplic, 514.

94. Chichagov to Ertel, 11, 13 and 19 November 1812, Nos. 1091, 1095, 1103, and 1138, RGVIA, d.3517, ll.39b–40, 41–41b, 45, 55; Bogdanovich, III, 226.

95. Chichagov to Alexander, 17 November 1812, RGVIA, d.3700, l.314.

96. Chichagov to Tuchkov and Ertel, 19 November 1812, RGVIA, d.3517, ll.53b, 55; Tuchkov to Chichagov, 26 November 1812, RGVIA, d.3518/2, ll.110–111. Tuchkov was later dismissed for plundering Prince Radziwiłł's estate. Bronevskii, 564.

97. Domergue, II, 282–283.

98. Joseph de Maistre to the King of Sardinia, 14 July 1813, *Russkii arkhiv*, 1 (1912), 56.

99. Yermolov, 208.

100. Tyrconnell to Cathcart, 18 November 1812, in Dubrovin, 322, 324.

101. Orders to Lambert, Langeron, Lukovkin, Czaplic, Liders, Voinov, Knorring and Chernishev, 18–21 November 1812, RGVIA, d.3517, ll.49b–56b; *Journal of the Advance Guard of the 3rd Western Army*, 326; *Journal of Military Operations of the 3rd Western Army*, 219–220.

102. Chichagov to Lambert and Langeron, 18 November 1812, RGVIA, d.3517, ll.49b–50; Kharkevich, 69; Vasiliev, 132–133; Bogdanovich, III, 229.

103. Berthier's Note (with Itinerary), 24 November 1812, in Fabry, 218; *Voyennii entsiklopedicheskii leksikon*, II, 432.

104. Vistitsky III to Barclay de Tolly, 8 October 1810, with attached report 'O Krepostyakh, vremmennykh ukrepleniyakh, lagernykh mestakh i voyennykh postakh v Byelorussikh i Minskoi guberniyakh 1810 g.' in *General Staff Archives*, I, 251; J.L. Stephens, 'Incidents of Travel in Greece, Turkey, Russia, and Poland' in *The Universal Library: Voyages and Travels* (London, 1853), I, 112.

105. Barclay de Tolly to Opperman, 3 April 1810; Opperman to Barclay de Tolly, 27 March 1810, *General Staff Archives*, I, 28, 45.

106. Wilson, *Narrative*, 299.

107. Napoleon to Davout, 11 July 1812, *Correspondance de Napoleon*, No. 18,944, XXIV, 48.

108. Dąbrowski to Berthier, 24 November 1812–5 January 1813, in *The Buturlin Papers*, RGVIA, d.3479, l.49b–50; Foerster's Memo, RGVIA, d.3701, l.2; Oudinot to Berthier, 22 November 1812, 6 a.m., SHAT 2C 133; Berthier to Oudinot, 22 November 1812, in Chambray, II, 268; Kołaczkowski (1901), 69–70; Kukiel, 406; Bielecki, 38–41.

109. Brandt, 241.

110. Brandt, 241. Brandt also claimed Bronikowski was appointed based on an embellished recommendation by Marshal Suchet.

111. Bronikowski to Berthier, 18–20 November 1812, in Fabry, 189–190, 196.

112. There is dispute over which French regiment was present. Kukiel refers to the 95th Line while Bielecki to 93rd Line. The 95th Line consisted of five battalions (plus a depot batt.) in

Notes and Sources

1812 and the 5th and depot battalions were deployed in Maastricht. This leaves the 6/93rd Line as the only possibility, although its regimental history is silent on this. *Historique de 95e Régiment*, 92. Lalance's report notes that the Württemberg Regiment was weakened by campaigning and counted some 484 men (Pfister, 147–149).

113. Dąbrowski to Berthier, 24 November 1812, Khakervich, Annex, 54. A Russian officer, who served with Lambert, claimed there were six guns in the *tête-de-pont*. Anonymous, 140.

114. Vaudoncourt (1835), 140; Kołaczkowski, 258; Wilson, *Narrative*, 299.

115. Foerster's Memo, RGVIA, d.3701, l.2.

116. Lalance's report in Pfister, 149; Kukiel, 406; Dziewanowski, 75–76; Vasiliev, 135–136; Bielecki, 38–42; Bogdanovich, III, 230–231.

117. Dąbrowski to Berthier, 24 November 1812, RGVIA, d.3479, l.50; Mycielski, 152.

118. Rochechouart, 164.

119. *Journal of the Advance Guard of the 3rd Western Army*, 326–327.

120. Raven referred to first shots made around 5 a.m. and Dąbrowski and Sukhetsky both note that the attack began at 6 a.m. so the Russian movement should have started earlier than that. Raven, 135; Dąbrowski to Berthier, 24 November 1812, RGVIA, d.3479, l.50; Sukhetsky, 3.

121. Otroshenko (1877), 547548; Vaudoncourt (1815(b)), 36; Pfister, 149.

122. In his recommendation, Dąbrowski referred to Malachowski's thirty years of service and distinction at Bobruisk, Borisov and Berezina. RGVIA, d.3479, l.42.

123. Bielecki, 46–47; Bogdanovich, III, 232.

124. Rochechouart, 164.

125. Mikheyev to Lambert, 28 November 1812, in Kharkevich, 52; *Journal of the Advance Guard of the 3rd Western Army*, 327.

126. Mikheyev to Lambert, 28 November 1812, in Kharkevich, 52–53.

127. Dąbrowski to Berthier, 24 November 1812, in *The Buturlin Papers*, RGVIA, d.3479, 1.50.

128. Vaudoncourt (1815(b)), 37–38.

129. RGVIA, d.3479, 1.42.

130. Rochechouart, 164–165.

131. Bielecki, 49; Dąbrowski to Berthier, 24 November 1812, RGVIA, d.3479, 1.51.

132. Dąbrowski to Berthier, 24 November 1812, RGVIA, d.3479, l.50–50b; Kołaczkowski (1901), 70.

133. *Journal of the Advance Guard of the 3rd Western Army*, 327; Kukiel, 408.

134. Vaudoncourt (1815(a)), 30–31; Vaudoncourt (1835), 142.

135. Sukhetsky, 3.

136. Mikhailovsky-Danilevsky, *Imperator Aleksandr I i ego spodvizhniki*, vol. III, 'Lambert', 6–7.

137. Bielecki, 52. Gugenmus and Captains Weisslog and Riedel were nominated to the Legion d'Honneur for their actions at Borisov. Dąbrowski, 'Tableau des militaires le tout grade ... proposes pour la decoration de la Legion d'Honneur', in *The Buturlin Papers*, RGVIA, d.3479, 1.43.

138. Dąbrowski to Berthier, 24 November 1812, RGVIA, d.3479, 1.50b.

139. *Journal of the Advance Guard of the 3rd Western Army*, 328; *Journal of the Military Operations of the 3rd Western Army*, 220; Bogdanovich, III, 234–235. Raven noted that Dąbrowski abandoned town around 4 p.m. Raven, 135. Sukhetsky writes that while some Russian troops pursued the Poles, others began to plunder houses in Borisov. Sukhetsky, 3. The Poles took up a position behind Borisov, protected by the high grounds of a nearby rivulet. Vaudoncourt (1835), 144.

140. Foerster's Memo, RGVIA, d.3701, l.2; Kharkevich, 82; Vasiliev, 143; Dąbrowski to Berthier, 24 November 1812, RGVIA, d.3479, l.51.

141. Dąbrowski to Berthier, 24 November 1812, RGVIA, d.3479, 1.50b; Vaudoncourt (1817), 290; Chambray, II, 273, 273f.

142. Langeron to Wittgenstein, 21 November 1812; Chichagov to Kutuzov, 27 November, Kharkevich, 59, 60–61; Wittgenstein to Alexander I, No. 73, 24 November 1812, RGVIA, d.3490, ll.71b; Wittgenstein to Kutuzov, No. 178, 23 November 1812; Chichagov to Kutuzov, No. 1909, 27 November 1812, RGVIA, d.3503, ll.42b, 45b; Kutuzov to Alexander, No. 569, 1 December 1812, RGVIA, d.3521, ll.90b–91. The official *Journal of Military Operations* recorded that between 14 and 22 November, Chichagov's troops captured some 11,000 men and twenty-four guns.

143. Bielecki, 54–55; Kukiel, 408–409; Pfister, 149.

144. Caulaincourt, 233. According to Chambray, upon hearing the news of the loss of Borisov, Napoleon grumbled, 'il est donc décidé que nous ne ferons que des sotises'. Chambray, II, 269.

145. Chichagov, *Mémoires*, 143.

146. Anonymous, 140.

147. Langeron to Wittgenstein, 22 November, Kharkevich, 60.

148. *Official Journal of Incoming Correspondence*, RGVIA, d.3503, ll.30b–45.

149. Rochechouart, 162.

150. Malinovskii, 90–91. The *Journal of the Advance Guard of the 3rd Western Army* refers to some 40,000 men, including Ertel's corps which took no part in the events on the Berezina.

151. Chichagov, *Mémoires*, 144.

152. *Journal of the Military Operations of the 3rd Western Army*, 221; Chichagov to Lukovkin, 23 November 1812, RGVIA, d.3517, l.54–54b.

153. Chichagov to Kutuzov, 27 November 1812, Kharkevich, 61.

154. RGVIA, d.3385, ll.42–42b.

155. Langeron, 52.

156. Khrapovitskii, 114.

157. Czaplic to Chichagov, N0.344, 22 November 1812, RGVIA, f.VUA, op. 16, d.3518, ll.37–38.

158. Chichagov to Alexander, November 1812 [no date], in *Sbornik Russkogo istoricheskogo obschestva*, VI, 52; Chichagov, *Mémoires*, 145.

159. Khrapovitskii, 114; O'Rourke, 122.

160. Malinovskii, 90.

161. Lorencez to Ségur, 8 May 1823, SHAT, 1M 2138; Oudinot to Berthier, Victor to Berthier, 16 November 1812; Victor's *Circulaire*, 18 November 1812, in Fabry, 175–178, 186–187.

162. Napoleon to Berthier, 19 November 1812, *Correspondance de Napoléon*, XXIV, No. 19,342, 361–362.

163. Order to the II Corps, Victor to Berthier, Oudinot to Dąbrowski, 10–21 November 1812, Fabry, *Campagne de 1812*, 198, 203–204; Oudinot to Berthier, 20 November 1812; Lorencez to Ségur, 8 May 1823, SHAT, 1M 2138; Oudinot to Dąbrowski, 21 November 1812, *Journal de Pils*, 320.

164. According to Wilson, General Pamplona informed Oudinot of the loss of Borisov. *Narratives*, 301. According to Vaudoncourt, he encountered Oudinot's artillery park at Nachi and was surprised to find it virtually unguarded from the direction of Borisov. He informed General Merle of the loss of Borisov but the news had no visible effect on the general, who paid no attention to the news, claiming he had heard no gunfire and preferred to wait for Oudinot. Vaudoncourt sarcastically noted, 'If he was not commanding the French, I would have wished Chichagov to appear at that moment – we would have had a jolly affair.' Vaudoncourt (1835), 145–146.

165. Oudinot to Berthier, 21 November 1812, in Fabry, 203; Ségur, II, 256.

166. Szymanowski, 95–96; Marbot, III, 183.

167. Vaudoncourt (1835), 146.

168. Oudinot to Berthier, 22 November 1812, 6 a.m., SHAT 2C 133. The letter is dated '3 a.m.'

Notes and Sources

in *Journal de Pils* (320–321), Fabry's *Campagne de 1812* (206) and in a copy in SHAT, 1M 2138.

169. Oudinot to Berthier, 22–23 November 1812, SHAT 2C 133; Lorencez to Ségur, 8 May 1823, SHAT, 1M 2138; Dąbrowski to Berthier, 24 November 1812, in *The Buturlin Papers*, RGVIA, d.3479, l.51; Bielecki, 71.

170. Corbineau to Oudinot, 22 November 1812, SHAT 2C 133; Corbineau, *Passage de la Bérézina*, 43–51; Oudinot to Berthier, 23 November 1812, in Journal de Pils, 322; Bielecki (1984): 28; Ségur, II, 266; Chambray, II, 289–290; Beaulieu, 244–247; Załuski, 273–274.

171. Berthier to Oudinot, 22 November 1812, Chambray, II, 276–278.

172. Oudinot to Berthier, 22–23 November 1812, SHAT 2C 133; Order to the II Corps, 23 November 1812, in Lorencez, 72.

173. *Journal of the Military Operations of the 3rd Western Army*, 221; Falenberg, 202; Malinovskii, 91; Buturlin, II, 234f; Anonymous, 140.

174. Tyrconnell to Cathcart, 30 November 1812, Dubrovin, 343.

175. Oudinot to Berthier, 23 November 1812, SHAT 2C 133.

176. Marbot, III, 184.

177. Dąbrowski to Berthier, 24 November 1812, in *The Buturlin Papers*, RGVIA, d.3479, l.51b; Dąbrowski, 'Tableau des militaires le tout grade […] proposes pour la decoration de la Legion d'Honneur', in *The Buturlin Papers*, RGVIA, d.3479, ll.42b–43.

178. Anonymous, 140; *Journal of the Military Operations of the 3rd Western Army*, 221; Chichagov to Alexander, November 1812 [no date], in *Sbornik Russkogo istoricheskogo obschestva*, VI, 52.

179. Tyrconnell to Cathcart, 30 November 1812, Dubrovin, 344.

180. Langeron, 53.

181. Buturlin, II, 234–235ff.

182. Chichagov, *Mémoires*, 146.

183. Rochechouart, 169–170; O'Rourke, 123. The regimental history of the Apsheronskii Infantry Regiment (naturally) has no mention of this incident. L. Boguslavskii, *Istoriya Apsheronskogo polka, 1700–1892* (St Petersburg, 1892), I, 324.

184. Scheltens, 156.

185. Sherbatov, 54; *Journal of the Military Operations of the 3rd Western Army*, 222; Malinovskii, 91; Khrapovitskii, 114.

186. Arnoldi, 101–102; Rochechouart, 168.

187. Tyrconnell to Cathcart, 30 November 1812, Dubrovin, 343; Martos, 497.

188. Rochechouart, 168–169.

189. Falenberg, 203.

190. Langeron, 53.

191. Marbot, III, 184–187.

192. Rochechouart, 170.

193. Marbot, III, 186–187.

194. Foerster's Memo, RGVIA, d.3701, l.2. Some participants refer to the bridge being destroyed in three places.

195. Tyrconnell to Cathcart, 30 November 1812, Dubrovin, 344; *Journal of the Military Operations of the 3rd Western Army*, 223.

196. The 29th Bulletin, 3 December 1812, in *Les Bulletins François, concernant La Guerre en Russie pendant l'année 1812* (London, 1813), 100; Dąbrowski to Berthier, 24 November 1812, in *The Buturlin Papers*, RGVIA, d.3479, l.51b; Marbot, III, 187; Oudinot to Berthier, 23 November 1812, SHAT 2C 133; *Victoires et Conquétes*, XXI, 273; Beaucour, 27.

197. Curély, 311–312.

198. Oudinot to Berthier, 23 November 1812, *Journal de Pils*, Appendix XXV, 323; Lorencez to Ségur, 8 May 1823, SHAT, 1M 2138; Lorencez, 73.

199. Anonymous, 141.

The Battle of the Berezina

200. Wittgenstein to Alexander I, No. 68, 18 November 1812, RGVIA, d.3490, ll.68–68b; Wittgenstein to Kutuzov, No. 168, 18 November 1812, RGVIA, d.3503, l.41; *Journal of Military Operations between 13 [25] and 16 [28] November 1812*, XIII, 64.
201. RGVIA, d.3385, l.42b; Kharkevich, 106.
202. Oudinot to Berthier, 24 November 1812, SHAT 2C 133.
203. Berthier to Oudinot, 23 November 1812, Chambray, II, 281–282.
204. I am grateful to Mark van Hattem and Mariska Poole of the Legermuseum (Netherlands) for sending me a copy of Tellegen's memoirs.
205. Chambray, II, 288; Lorencez, 73; Beaucour, 27.
206. Velichko, *Voyennaya Entsiklopediya*, IV, 493.
207. Oudinot to Berthier, 23 November 1812, SHAT 2C 133.
208. Oudinot to Berthier, 24 November 1812 (5.30 a.m.) SHAT 2C 133; 'Rapport de Bordesoulle', 'Rapport de Falkowski', and 'Croquis et rapport envoyés à Maison' in Chuquet (1912), III, 66–68; Lorencez to Ségur, 8 May 1823, SHAT, 1M 2138; Lorencez, 73–74.
209. Oudinot to Berthier, 23 November 1812, SHAT 2C 133; Lorencez to Ségur, 8 May 1823, SHAT, 1M 2138.
210. Ségur to Lorencez, 26 April and 14 May; Lorencez to Ségur, 8 May 1823, SHAT, 1M 2138.
211. Lorencez, 73f; Lorencez to Ségur, 8 May 1823, SHAT, 1M 2138.
212. Order to the II Corps, 24 November 1812, in Fabry, 219–220. The 5th Light Cavalry Brigade, the 2nd and 7th Polish Lancers and the 6th Division (with Bronikowski's troops) would start the march around 6 p.m., followed by the 9th Division (with reserve artillery) and 8th Division (with its artillery park), followed by the 3rd Chevaulégers; Dąbrowski's men were assigned to protect artillery.
213. Pils, 139; Lorencez to Ségur, 8 May 1823, in Pils, 313.
214. *The Dutch in Time of War*, 73.
215. Aubry to Oudinot, 25 November 1812, SHAT 2C 133; Chambray, II, 291.
216. Oudinot to Berthier, 24 November 1812, Lorencez, 75.
217. Oudinot to Berthier, 24 November 1812 (5.30 a.m.), SHAT 2C 133.
218. Oudinot to Berthier, 24 November 1812, SHAT 2C 133. A slightly different text of this letter is published in Fabry (220) and *Journal de Pils* (325).
219. Ségur, II, 267; Khrapovitskii, 116.
220. *Journal of the Military Operations of the 3rd Western Army*, 223.
221. *Journal of the Military Operations of the 3rd Western Army*, 223.
222. Malinovskii, 92; Arnoldi, 102; Kharkevich, 122; Vasiliev, 156.
223. O'Rourke to Chichagov (No. 3), Grekov to O'Rourke (No. 655), 24 November 1812, RGVIA, d.3518, 11.11.60–60b, 62; Arnoldi, 102.
224. Chichagov to Alexander, 30 November 1812, *Sbornik Russkogo istoricheskogo obschestva*, VI, 61.
225. Wittgenstein to Chichagov, No. 490, 23 November 1812, in Kharkevich, 69.
226. Kutuzov to Chichagov, No. 485, 23 November 1812, RGVIA, d.3521, l.75–75b; Chichagov to Alexander, 30 November 1812, *Sbornik Russkogo istoricheskogo obschestva*, VI, 61.
227. Tyrconnell to Cathcart, 30 November 1812, in Dubrovin, 344–345.
228. Czaplic, 'Remarques sur la campagne de 1812', RGVIA, d.3385, ll.43–43b.
229. Chichagov to Alexander, 30 November 1812, *Sbornik Russkogo istoricheskogo obschestva*, VI, 61.
230. Mikhailovsky-Danilevsky, IV, 188; Langeron, 55.
231. Martos, 499.
232. Rochechouart, 172.
233. Vaudoncourt (1815(b)), 51f.
234. Khrapovitskii, 114.
235. Khrapovitskii, 116.

Notes and Sources

236. Voenskii, *Napoleon i borisovskie evrei v 1812 g.*, 195–198. The locals were Movsha Engelhardt, Leiba Beninson and a third man whose name is lost to history. After the battle, Chichagov had all of them executed as traitors. The descendants of Movsha Engelhardt were later forced to change their name to Engelson – local tradition claims that, after the war, a certain General Engelhardt, related to MG Engelhardt who died leading a charge on the Borisov *tête-de-pont*, had visited the town to gather information about his ancestor's death. Unknowingly, he interviewed Movsha Engelhardt's son, Morduch, and, after learning his last name, became so incensed that he petitioned Emperor Nicholas to have his name changed because it 'stained' the general's family name.

237. Chichagov, *Mémoires*, 152–153.

238. Chichagov to Alexander, 11 November 1812, in *Sbornik Russkogo istoricheskogo obschestva*, VI, 60–62.

239. Chichagov, *Mémoires*, 154.

240. Tyrconnell to Cathcart, 30 November 1812, in Dubrovin, 349.

241. O'Rourke's forces were earlier distributed as follows: Grekov VIII, with one battalion of the Volynskii Uhlans, Grekov's and Barabanshikov's Cossack regiments and two squadrons of the Mariupolskii Hussars, was watching the area between Gury-Ushkevichi and Borisov; Lukovkin, with one battalion of the Volynskii Uhlans, Lukovkin's and Isaev II's Cossack regiments, was between Glinik (Gliven) and Usha, with outposts as far as Nizhneye Berezino. O'Rourke himself was at Gury-Ushkevichi. O'Rourke to Chichagov, No. 3, 24 November 1812, RGVIA, d.3518, ll.60–60b.

242. Orders to O'Rourke, Rudzevich, Langeron, Grekov VIII, Lieders, and Czaplic, 25 November 1812, RGVIA, d.3517, l.57b–59b, 60b–61.

243. O'Rourke to Chichagov, Nos. 11–12; Lukovkin to O'Rourke, No. 802; Malinovskii to Chichagov, No. 8, 25 November 1812, RGVIA, d.3518, l.64, 78–79, 81–81b; Khrapovitskii, 114; Bogdanovich, III, 259; Rochechouart, 173.

244. *Journal of the Military Operations of the 3rd Western Army*, 224.

245. Knorring to Chichagov, 23–24 November 1812, in Kharkevich, 85–86; RGVIA, d.3518, l.59.

246. Wittgenstein to Chichagov, No. 498, 24 November 1812, RGVIA, d.3518, l.75.

247. Chichagov, 'Pereprava cherez Berezinu …' 1158–1159.

248. Chichagov to Czaplic, Nos. 1165 and 1170, 25 November 1812, RGVIA, d.3517, ll.58b–60; Czaplic to Chichagov, No. 347, 25 November 1812, RGVIA, d.3518, l.71.

249. Chichagov to Langeron, No. 1171, 25 November 1812, RGVIA, d.3517, l.60b.

250. Esaul Lyutenskov to Langeron (No. 860), Esaul Lyutenskov to Chichagov (No. 861), in Kharkevich, 88.

251. Arnoldi, 102.

252. Falenberg, 204.

253. Langeron, xlviii–xlix.

254. Langeron, 64–65. This author could not find any of Langeron's letters to Czaplic among the archival documents from RGVIA, and Kharkevich, who faced a similar problem when writing his definitive study, also noted that these messages are only mentioned in Czaplic's and Chichagov's memoirs while the originals are missing. Kharkevich, 141.

255. Langeron to Chichagov, No. 947, 26 November 1812, RGVIA, f. 846, op. 16, d.3518/2, ll.94–94b; Langeron to Chichagov, 26 November (9.30 a.m.), in Kharkevich, 96.

256. Chichagov to Langeron, No. 1173, 26 November 1812, RGVIA, f. 846, op. 16, d.3517, l.61.

257. A. Apukhtin, 'Berezinskaya operatsia', in *Otechestvennaya voina i Russikoye obshestvo* (Moscow, 1911), IV, 249; Vasiliev, 188–189; Kharkevich, 141–142.

258. Bogdanovich, III, 261; Cate, 369.

259. Vasiliev, 186.

The Battle of the Berezina

260. Chichagov, 'Pereprava cherez Berezinu ...' 1160–1161.

261. Chambray, II, 302.

262. Czaplic, 509; Czaplic to Chichagov, No. 344, 22 November 1812, in Kharkevich, 57–58.

263. Kharkevich, 140; Apukhtin, 249; Chambray, II, 302; Foerster's Memo, RGVIA, d.3701, 1.2.

264. Czaplic, 509.

265. Arnoldi, 102.

266. Ségur (1825), II, 242; Rossetti, 173.

267. *Vedomost o raschilesnii 1-go korpusa ...*, 16 October 1812, RGVIA, d.3558, ll.67–69.

268. Wittgenstein to Alexander I, No. 51, 31 October 1812, RGVIA, d.3490, 1.55b.

269. *Précis de la Campagne du 1er Corps de l'armée pendant l'année 1812*, RGVIA, d.3558, ll.171–172b; Wittgenstein to Alexander I, Nos. 52, 57, 60–62; 9–13 November 1812, RGVIA, d.3490, ll.56, 57b, 59–62; Wittgenstein to Kutuzov, Nos. 60, 156, 160, 8–12 November 1812, RGVIA, d.3503, ll.35–37; *Journal of Military Operations between 7 [19] and 13 [25] November 1812*, XIII, 58.

270. Napoleon to Berthier, 7 November 1812, *Correspondance de Napoleon*, No. 19326, XXIV, 351.

271. Eidahl, 316–319; Despiques, 54; The 28th Bulletin, 11 November 1812, in *Les Bulletins François*, 98.

272. Wittgenstein to Alexander I, Nos. 65–66, 13–17 November 1812, RGVIA, d.3490, ll.65–66b; Wittgenstein to Kutuzov, No. 172–175, 20 November 1812, RGVIA, d.3503, ll.39–39b; *Précis de la Campagne du 1er Corps de l'armée pendant l'année 1812*, RGVIA, d.3558, ll.177–178; Lorencez to Ségur, 8 May 1823, SHAT, 1M 2138.

273. Wittgenstein to Alexander I, No. 58, 7 November 1812, RGVIA, d.3490, ll.59–59b; Wittgenstein to Kutuzov, No. 160, 12 November 1812, RGVIA, d.3503, l.37; *Zhurnal vkhodyashikh bumag 1-go otdel.Korpusa*, RGVIA, d.3522, l.133.

274. 'Rapport succinct du general de Lorencez, chef d'état-major des 2e et 6e Corps, sur les opérations militaires depuis l'arrivée du maréchal Oudinot (9 novembre) jusqu'au 19 du meme mois', in *Journal de Pils*, 136–138; Lorencez to Ségur, 8 May 1823, SHAT, 1M 2138; Victor to Berthier, Oudinot to Berthier, 16 November 1812, in Fabry, 175–178.

275. Ameil, 730; Lorencez to Ségur, 8 May 1823, SHAT, 1M 2138.

276. 'Notes et observations sur les operations du 9e corps ...' cited in Weinzierl, 326; Oudinot to Victor, 15 November 1812, in *Journal de Pils*, 318–319.

277. Wittgenstein to Alexander I, Nos. 68, 70, 18–22 November 1812, RGVIA, d.3490, ll.68–68b, 69b–70; Wittgenstein to Kutuzov, No. 168, 18 November 1812, RGVIA, d.3503, l.41.

278. Kutuzov's headquarters received Wittgenstein's orders in the following order (journal entry codes in parenthesis): Nos. 160 (574), 175 (598), 172 (602), 168 (618), 169 (621), 178 (632), *Official Journal of Incoming Correspondence*, RGVIA, d.3503, ll.37, 39–39b, 41–41b, 42b.

279. Kutuzov to Wittgenstein, No. 426, 15 November 1812, RGVIA, f. VUA, d. 3515, l.260.

280. Victor's Orders to the IX Corps, Victor to Partouneaux, Victor to Girard, 19–20 November 1812, in Fabry, 193–195, 197.

281. Napoleon to Berthier, 19 November 1812, *Correspondance de Napoleon*, No. 19342, XXIV, 361–362; Victor to Dąbrowski, Victor to Berthier, 20–21 November, in Fabry, 198, 204–205; Lorencez to Ségur, 8 May 1823, SHAT, 1M 2138.

282. Ameil, 730; Victor to Berthier, 21 November 1812, in Fabry, 204–205. The regimental history of the 125th Line states that the 12th Division, which was 12,000–men strong upon departing from Smolensk in early November, counted only some 4,000 troops by the end of the month. Lt. Col. Roulin, *Le 125e Régiment d'Infanterie* (Orleans, 1890), 119.

283. Beulay, 63.

284. Markgraf von Baden (1864), 60; *Geschichte des 1. Badischen Feldartillerie-regiments Nr. 14*, 89; Sauzey, *Les Allemands sous les aigles francaise*, 185; Steinmüller, 154; Holzhausen, 90.

285. Wittgenstein to Alexander I, No. 71, 22 November 1812, RGVIA, d.3490, ll.70–70b.

Notes and Sources

286. Langeron to Wittgenstein, Vlastov to Wittgenstein, 21–22 November 1812, Kharkevich, 59–60, 64; *Zhurnal vkhodyashikh bumag 1-go otdel.Korpusa*, RGVIA, d.3522, l.134; Wittgenstein to Alexander I, No. 73, 24 November 1812, RGVIA, d.3490, l.71b.

287. Victor's Order, Deployment of the Troops of the IX Corps, 22–23 November 1812, in Fabry, 208, 212.

288. Vlastov to Wittgenstein, 23 November 1812, Kharkevich, 65–66. Vlastov claimed over 200 French were killed and over 330 men captured, including a colonel of the 126th Line. Wittgenstein reported that, in two days of pursuit, his troops captured thirty officers and over 1,000 men. Wittgenstein to Yermolov, No. 508, 25 November 1812, RGVIA, d.3503, 1.42b.

289. *Zhurnal vkhodyashikh bumag 1-go otdel.Korpusa*, RGVIA, d.3522, 1.134; Wittgenstein to Kutuzov, No. 178, 23 November 1812, RGVIA, d.3503, l.42b.

290. Victor to Berthier, 25 November (10 a.m.) 1812, SHAT 2C 133.

291. Kutuzov to Wittgenstein, 18 November 1812; Yermolov to Wittgenstein, 23 November 1812, Kharkevich, 73. Kutuzov's letter reached Wittgenstein only on 24 November.

292. Wittgenstein to Alexander I, No. 73, 24 November 1812, RGVIA, d.3490, l.71b.

293. Wittgenstein to Kutuzov, 23 November 1812, Kharkevich, 68. Wittgenstein also argued that his and Chichagov's forces should make a concentrated attack on Victor and the advance elements of the Grand Army, after which, remarkably, Wittgenstein wanted to return to the Baltic provinces to 'clear that region […] by driving out Macdonald'.

294. Wittgenstein to Chichagov, 23 November 1812, Kharkevich, 69.

295. When Chichagov informed him about the disastrous combat at Loshnitsa, where Pahlen's advance guard was routed, Wittgenstein was surprised to read the admiral referring to the united forces of Victor and Oudinot. He concluded that Chichagov was mistaken and could not have fought Victor since Wittgenstein's own advance guard was pursuing them near the Dolgoye Lake. He assured Chichagov that Oudinot could not have more than 10,000 men. Chichagov to Wittgenstein, Wittgenstein to Chichagov, 23–24 November 1812, Kharkevich, 71–72.

296. Victor to Berthier, 24–25 November 1812, in Fabry, 221, 224–225. The *Journal of Military Operations* claimed the Russians captured over 2,000 prisoners, including thirty officers, in two days of fighting around Batury on 23–24 November. *Journal of Military Operations between 13 [25] and 16 [28] November 1812*, 64.

297. Steinmüller, 154–155.

298. *Zhurnal vkhodyashikh bumag 1-go otdel.Korpusa*, RGVIA, d.3522, l.135.

299. Vlastov to Wittgenstein, 13 November (three letters) 1812, Kharkevich, 75–76.

300. Neidhardt to Diebitsch [n.d.], Raginevich to Gerngross, 23 November 1812, Kharkevich, 78; Auvera, *Geschichte des Kgl. Bayer. 7. Infanterie-regiments*, 497.

301. Platov to Wittgenstein, 24 November 1812, Kharkevich, 79.

302. Wittgenstein to Yermolov, 25 November 1812, Kharkevich, 79–80; Wittgenstein to Kutuzov, No. 181, 25 November 1812, RGVIA, d.3503, l.45. Wittgenstein informed Kutuzov that his troops had captured thirty-seven officers and some 2,000 soldiers between 23 and 25 November.

303. Victor to Berthier, 24 November 1812, in Fabry, 219–220.

304. Ségur (1958), 241.

305. Holzhausen, 90; Hochberg, 170; Steinmüller, 155.

306. Steinmüller, 155.

307. Victor to Fournier, 25 November (9 p.m.) 1812; Victor to Berthier, 26 November (3 a.m.) 1812, in Fabry, 225–226.

308. Ségur (1840), II, 214–215.

309. Chłapowski, 290.

310. Bourgogne, 122–123; Coignet, 337–338; Caulaincourt, 222–223.

311. Larrey, IV, 94.

312. Castellane, I, 189–190.

313. Pastoret, 481; Walter, 71; Peyrusse (1869), 121.

314. Jomini to Berthier, 17 November 1812, in Chuquet (1912), I, 148; Pastoret, 480–481; Ségur (1840), II, 217.

315. Quintin, 25.

316. Data compiled based on Martinien's *Tableaux [...] des officiers tués et blessés*.

317. Prince Kutuzov to General Kutuzov, 21 November 1812, No. 477; Kutuzov to Wittgenstein, 22 November, No. 480, in Kharkevich (1893), 29, 32–33.

318. Lecointe de Laveau, 140.

319. Yelin, 128.

320. Boulart, 274; Roos, 192–193.

321. Thirion de Metz, 239.

322. Thirion de Metz, 235–237; Saint-Elme, 152; Bertin, 284; Ségur (1840), II, 218; Coignet, 338.

323. Yermolov, 204.

324. Fain, II, 314–315.

325. Berthier to Junot, 17 November 1812, 8 p.m., Lyadi, in Gourgaud, 321.

326. Bourgogne, 124; Laugier, IV, 63; Lossberg, 261.

327. Griois, II, 141.

328. Ségur (1840), II, 217.

329. Walter, 72–73; Dedem, 284.

330. Griois, II, 140; Ségur (1840), II, 216; Chambray, II, 215–216. For contrasts between Murat and Berthier, see Hogendorp, 337.

331. Griois, II, 144.

332. Maag, 222; Schaller, 128.

333. Laugier, IV, 64; Ségur (1840), II, 217; Zajączek to Berthier, 17 November 1812, in Chuquet (1912), I, 150–151.

334. Sanguszko, 112.

335. Pastoret, 483–484.

336. Girod de l'Ain, *Grands Artilleurs*, 323; 'Notice historique sur le Ponts militaires: Passage de la Bérézina', *Journal des Sciences Militaires des Armées de terre et de mer*, XXI (March 1838), No. 61, 389–390.

337. Gourgaud, 237; Caulaincourt, 224–225; Ségur (1840), II, 246, 255; Castellane, I, 191.

338. Caulaincourt, 226–227, 230.

339. Caulaincourt, 229.

340. Caulaincourt, 232; Ségur (1840), II, 215, 266; Chambray, II, 166–167.

341. Caulaincourt, 232–233.

342. Caulaincourt, 235.

343. Castellane, I, 192; Fain, II, 327.

344. Chambray, II, 269.

345. Caulaincourt, 235.

346. Ségur (1840), II, 248.

347. Bogdanovich, III, 238–239.

348. Ivan Herman's Survey, 9 [20] February 1797, *State Council Archives*, II, 269–270.

349. *Voyennii entsiklopedicheskii leksikon*, 880.

350. *Voyenno-statisticheskoye obozreniye Rossiiskoi imperii*, XI, Part 4, 23.

351. Thiers, XIV, 596.

352. Jomini earlier advised Berthier about local routes. Jomini to Berthier, 22 November 1812, in Chuquet (1912), I, 190–191.

353. Ferdinand Lecomte, *Le général Jomini* (Paris, 1860), 108–109; Vovsi, 74; Thiers, XIV, 596–597; Bogdanovich, III, 241–242.

Notes and Sources

354. Berthier to Oudinot, 22–23 November 1812, Chambray, II, 277, 281–282.

355. Order du jour, 22 November 1812, *Correspondance de Napoléon*, No. 19346, XXIV, 313.

356. Napoleon to Berthier, 23–24 November 1812, *Correspondance de Napoléon*, Nos. 19348, 19350, XXIV, 314–315.

357. Chambray, II, 283–286; Grouchy, III, 56; Dedem, 283; Chuquet (1911), 263–266.

358. Dedem, 286.

359. Ségur (1840), II, 248; Bourgogne, 130.

360. Bourgogne, 127–128.

361. Vossler, 77; Borcke, 206–208; Thirion, 238.

362. Berthier to Eblé, 24 November 1812, in Girod de l'Ain, *Grands Artilleurs*, 459–460; *Historique du 1er Régiment de Pontonniers*, 105; Chuquet (1912), II 156; Chambray, II, 284. The organization of the *équipages de pont* was set in August 1812. Napoleon to Berthier, 10 August 1812 in Gabriel Fabry, *Campagne de Russie, 1812* (Paris, 1902), III, 543–545.

363. Caulaincourt, 240–241.

364. Ozharovsky to Kutuzov, Nos. 23–25, 20–21 November 1812; Seslavin to Kutuzov, 22 November 1812; Platov to Kutuzov, Nos. 195–196, 21 November 1812; Yermolov to Kutuzov, 21 November 1812; Davydov to Kutuzov, 21 November 1812, RGVIA, d. 3503, ll.36b–39; Bogdanovich, III, 239; Buturlin, II, 232.

365. 'Otchet o deistviyakh intendantskogo upravleniya v voine protiv frantsuzov v 1812, 1813 i 1814 godakh', in *Kutuzov: sbornik dokumentov*, IV, part 2, 703.

366. Chicherin, 63.

367. Uxküll, 100; Mitarevskii, 141–142, 148–149.

368. Karpov, 222; Radozhitsky, 238; Muravyev-Apostol, 36–37.

369. Zhirkevich, 664.

370. Radozhitsky, 282–284.

371. Muravyev-Karskii, 390; Bronevskii, 565.

372. Platov to Kutuzov, Platov to Wittgenstein, 24–25 November 1812, in Kharkevich, 78–79, 102, 104–105.

373. Alexander to Kutuzov, 12 November 1812, RGVIA, d.3572, ll.35–35b; Alexander to Kutuzov, 13 November 1812, in *M.I. Kutuzov: Sbornik dokumentov*, IV, part 2, 322f. As State Secretary V. Marchenko noted, 'Ambiguity of Kutuzov's intentions and unfavourable news about him almost convinced the Emperor to recall Barclay de Tolly.' 'Avtobiograficheskaya zapiska' in *Russkaya Starina*, 3 (1896), 103.

374. Kutuzov to Platov and Seslavin, 19 November 1812, Nos. 455, 458, RGVIA, d.3521, ll.67b–68b.

375. Yermolov, 205.

376. Bennigsen, 11 (1909): 374; 'Kutuzov v 1812 godu: Istoricheskaya kharakteristika D.P. Buturlina', *Russkaya starina*, 12 (1894), 139, 146; Bogdanovich, III, 287; Buturlin, II, 238–238f, 270.

377. Jomini was already sick and soon developed pneumonia. He attended Napoleon and assisted Eblé on 26 November but was too weak to stand on 27 November and was laid down on the straw in one of the huts. Lecomte, 111; Charles Augustin Sainte-Beuve, *Le général Jomini* (Paris, 1869), 125; Jean-Jacques Langendorf, *Krieg führen: Antoine-Henri Jomini* (Zurich, 2008), 49–50.

378. Napoleon to Murat, 25 November 1812, *Correspondance de Napoléon*, No. 19353, XXIV, 317; Chambray, II, 294; *Historique du 1er Régiment de Pontonniers*, 105; 'Notice historique sur le Ponts militaires: Passage de la Bérézina', *Journal des Sciences Militaires*, XXI (March 1838), No. 61, 390.

379. *Historique du 1er Régiment de Pontonniers*, 105; Lecomte, *Jomini*, 110; Chambray, II, 294.

380. Lorencez to Ségur, 8 May 1823, SHAT, 1M 2138.

381. Caulaincourt, 244; Corbineau, 48–49.

382. Curély, 312–314.

383. Napoleon to Maret, 27 November 1812, *Correspondance de Napoléon*, No. 19358, XXIV, 320; Wilson, *Narrative*, 323.
384. Chasseloup to Gassendi, 10 February 1822, in *Avenir Militaire*, 13 March 1894; Fain, II, 375; Chapelle and Chapuis, 227–228; Chambray, II, 294; Benthien, 151–152.
385. Chambray, II, 296.
386. Pils, 141.
387. Marbot, III, 195; Benthien, 153; Caulaincourt, 245.
388. SHAT, C2 286; Derrêcagaix, 516.
389. Chasseloup to Gassendi, 10 February 1822, in *Avenir Militaire*, 13 March 1894; Gourgaud, 250; Chambray, II, 295; Pils, 140–141; *Historique du 1er Régiment de Pontonniers*, 106; Jongh, *Hollandse infanterie bij de bruggen over de Berezina*, 17; Eugéne Lomier, *Bataillon des Marins de la Garde* (Saint-Valery-sur-Somme, 1905), 374. Eblé and Chasseloup were assisted by a group of officers, which included Colonel Chapelle, Chefs de bataillon Chapuis, Zabern and Delarue, Captains Joffre, Benthien and Boulanger, Aides-de-camps Braun, Busch, Baillot, Gauthier, Dorimon, Pichon, Andrieux, etc. 'Notice historique sur le Ponts militaires: Passage de la Bérézina', *Journal des Sciences Militaires*, XXI (March 1838), No. 61, 390–391.
390. Lejeune, II, 236; Pils, 140.
391. Rossetti, 171; Chambray, II, 293–294, 296; Caulaincourt, 245; Beaucour, 28.
392. Legler, 198.
393. Caulaincourt, 244.
394. Chambray, II, 295; Bielecki, 112.
395. Legler, 200.
396. Larrey, IV, 98–99.
397. Rosselet, 265.
398. Poniatowski to Berthier, 6 November 1812, in Chuquet (1912), I, 117.
399. Chambray, II, 295–296.
400. Pastoret, 494.
401. Pils, 142–143.
402. Rapp, 246 (similar account in Rossetti, 172).
403. Legler, 201.
404. Rapp, 246–247; Rossetti, 173.
405. Chapelle and Chapuis, 228.
406. Chambray, II, 298; Caulaincourt, 245.
407. Benthien, 150, 151f; Hoof, 84.
408. Chapelle and Chapuis, 228; Vlijmen, 185; Roguet, IV, 531; Zamoyski, 466; Beitzke, 356; 'Na beregakh Bereziny', *Moskovskie vedomosti*, 212 (1903); Foerster's Memo, RGVIA, d.3701, l.2b.
409. Arnoldi, 102–103; Czaplic, 'Remarques sur la campagne de 1812', RGVIA, d.3385, 1.45; Tyrconnell to Cathcart, 29 November 1812, in Dubrovin, 348.
410. Arnoldi, 102–103.
411. Foord, 359–360.
412. Six, I, 420–421; Girod de l'Ain, 242–322.
413. Thiers, XIV, 605.
414. Jongh, *Hollandse infanterie bij de bruggen over de Berezina*, 17–18.
415. Pradzynski, 63–65; Bielecki (1984), 41–45.
416. Benthien, 153; Bourgone, 206; Vlijmen, 322; Jongh, *Hollandse infanterie bij de bruggen over de Berezina*, 18.
417. Raven, 142.
418. Rybinski, 100.
419. Chuquet (1994), 96; Laugier, IV, 229; Davout to Vaudoncourt, 22 November 1814, in Blocqueville (1887), 112.

Notes and Sources

420. Benthien, 152–153.

421. Wilson, *Narrative*, 328.

422. Oudinot (1896), 177–178.

423. Constant, IV, 6; Gourgaud, 245; Castellane, I, 192; Walter, 81; Pils, 143; Bourgogne, 206; Borcke, 217; Tellegen, 63; Baudus, II, 274; Dumonceau, 220; Laugier, IV, 229–230.

424. Boulart, 275; Ségur (1840), II, 263–264.

425. Arnoldi, 103.

426. Rossetti, 173.

427. Rapp, 247.

428. Caulaincourt, 245.

429. Chłapowski, 136; Pradzynski, 63–64; Rossetti, 173; Gourgaud, 249; Bielecki (1984), 34; Vasiliev, 192; Marbot, III, 197–198; Curély, 315.

430. Załuski, 273; Rossetti, 173; Kukiel, 428.

431. Rossetti, 173.

432. Gourgaud, 249.

433. Marbot, III, 197–198; Caulaincourt, 245.

434. Dumonceau, 220.

435. Arnoldi, 103–104.

436. Lassus-Marcilly, 87–88.

437. Thiers, XIV, 606–607; Kharkevich, 148; Bielecki, 123.

438. Rosselet, 266; Roguet, IV, 531.

439. Bégos, 189–190; Rey to Bégos, 3 February 1839, in Chuquet (1912), II, 179–181.

440. Fain, II, 377; Chambray II, 301; Chapelle and Chapuis, 229; Bielecki (1984), 37; *Historique du 1er Régiment de Pontonniers*, 107.

441. Benthien, 153; Chapelle and Chapuis, 229; Hermann Haupt, *Military Bridges* (New York, 1864), 256–257; Vlijmen, 322.

442. Bourgogne, 206; Borcke, 218; St Denis, 35; Brandt (1877), 319.

443. Chapelle and Chapuis, 229. Similar description in Chambray II, 301.

444. Pils, 144.

445. Oudinot to Berthier, 27 November 1812 (1 a.m.), in Fabry, 238; Chambray II, 301; Chapelle and Chapuis, 229; *Historique du 2e Régiment d'infanterie*, 34; *Historique du 37e Régiment d'infanterie*, 178–179; *Livre d'or du 56e Régiment d'infanterie*, 52; Schumacher, 95; Fain, II, 378f; Pradzynski, 63–64; Bielecki (1984), 37; Nafziger, 318.

446. Schumacher, 95; Rey to Bégos, 3 February 1839, in Chuquet (1912), II, 180; Laugier, IV, 230–231; Legler, 202.

447. Pils, 144.

448. Arnoldi, 103–104; Mikhailovsky-Danilevsky, IV, 163–164.

449. Vaudoncourt (1815(b)), 52.

450. Chambray II, 301–303; Soltyk, 443; Bielecki, 127.

451. Przebendowski to Ney, 26 November 1812, in Chuquet (1911), 246–247; Bielecki, 128–129.

452. Otroshenko, 552.

453. Arnoldi, 104.

454. *Journal of the Military Operations of the 3rd Western Army*, 224.

455. Arnoldi, 104.

456. Langeron to Chichagov, 26 November (3 p.m.), RGVIA, d.3518/2, l.102; Langeron, 67.

457. Larrey, IV, 102; Oudinot to Berthier, 26 November 1812, in Fabry, 236; Roguet, IV, 532; Caulaincourt, 245.

458. Oudinot to Berthier, 26 November 1812, in Fabry, 236.

459. Czaplic to Chichagov; Langeron to Chichagov, 26 November (3 p.m.), RGVIA, d.3518/2, l.102–104.

460. Chichagov to Alexander, 11 December 1812, in *Sbornik Russkogo istoricheskogo obschestva*, VI, 62–63.

461. Vasiliev, 195.

462. Falenberg, 204.

463. Fain, II, 378; Chambray II, 306; Chapelle and Chapuis, 229; Laugier, IV, 231–232; *Historique du 1er Régiment de Pontonniers*, 107.

464. St Denis, 35.

465. Fain, II, 379; Chapelle and Chapuis, 229–230; Chambray II, 308, f308; *Historique du 1er Régiment de Pontonniers*, 107.

466. Chichagov to Langeron, Voinov and Rudzevich, Nos. 1173, 1176–1178, 26 November 1812, RGVIA, d.3517, ll.61, 62–62b.

467. Esaul Lutenskov to Chichagov, Nos. 860–864, 26 November 1812, RGVIA, d.3518/2, ll.97–98.

468. Langeron to Chichagov, 26 November 1812, Kharkevich, 95–96.

469. Khrapovitskii, 116.

470. Malinovskii to O'Rourke, No. 9; O'Rourke to Chichagov, No. 14, 26 November 1812, RGVIA, d.3518/2, ll.95–96; *Journal of the Military Operations of the 3rd Western Army*, 224; Khrapovitskii, 117.

471. Khrapovitskii, 117.

472. Chichagov to Langeron, O'Rourke and Rudzevich, Nos. 1181, 1182, 1183, 26 November 1812, RGVIA, d.3517, 1.63–63b.

473. Chichagov to Grekov VIII and Czaplic, Nos. 1174–1175, 1179, 26 November 1812, RGVIA, d.3517, ll.61b–62b.

474. Khrapovitskii, 171; O'Rourke, 124; Bogdanovich, III, 267; Palageika to O'Rourke, No. 40, 27 November 1812, RGVIA, d.3518/2, l.112.

475. Czaplic to Langeron, [n.d. November 1812], RGVIA, d.3518/2, l.100.

476. Albrecht to Wittgenstein, 25 November 1812, in Kharkevich, 100; Buturlin, II, 247.

477. Clausewitz, 207–208.

478. Wittgenstein to Kutuzov, No. 181, 25 November 1812, RGVIA, d.3503, 1.45.

479. Vlastov to Wittgenstein, 27 November (2.30 a.m.) 1812, in Kharkevich, 118.

480. Volkonsky, 231–232.

481. Mikhailovsky-Danilevsky, IV, 167; Buturlin, II, 249.

482. Clausewitz, 208–210; Volkonsky, 231–232.

483. Fain, II, 378.

484. Junot to Berthier, 26 November (6 p.m.) 1812, in Chuquet (1911), 244.

485. Berthier to Ney, 25 November 1812; Berthier to Claparède, 26 November (9 a.m.) 1812, in Chuquet (1912), II, 214; III, 79; Mestre, *Géneral Claparède*, 332–333.

486. Napoleon to Berthier, 27 November 1812, *Correspondance de Napoleon*, No. 19,357, XIV, 319–320; Berthier to Ney, 26 November (7 and 11 p.m.) and 27 November (1 a.m.) 1812, in Chuquet (1912), II, 214–216; Bielecki, 132–133.

487. Fezensac, 129–130.

488. Krasinski, 100.

489. Berthier to Victor, 25 November (5 a.m. and 2 p.m.) and 26 November (4 a.m.) 1812 in Chuquet (1912), II, 227–230; Victor to Fournier, 25 November (9 p.m.), Victor to Berthier, 26 November (3 a.m.) 1812, in Fabry, 225, 226.

490. Davout to Berthier, 26 November 1812; Eugène to Berthier, 26 November (6.30 p.m.), SHAT 2C 133; Berthier to Eugène, 26 November 1812 (4 a.m.), *Mémoires et Correspondance du Prince Eugène*, VIII, 92; Partouneaux to Victor, [n.d. November 1812], in Partouneaux, 22.

491. Junot to Napoleon, 23 November 1812, in Chuquet (1912), III, 55; Lossberg, 274.

492. Viceroy Eugène to Davout, 26 November 1812, in Blocqueville, 191.

493. Caulaincourt, 245.

494. Raven, 144; Bégos, 191–192.

495. Legler, 202–203.

496. Muraldt, 105.

497. Raven, 143; Walter, 83.

498. Lejeune, II, 236.

499. Arnoldi, 104.

500. Oudinot to Berthier, 27 November (1 a.m.) 1812, in Chuquet (1912), III, 70–71.

501. Chapelle and Chapuis, 230.

502. Boulart, 275.

503. Chapelle and Chapuis, 230; SHAT, C2 286; Derrêcagaix, 516.

504. Pion des Loches, 325–326.

505. Brandt, 247–248.

506. Napoleon to Berthier, 27 November 1812, *Correspondance de Napoleon*, No. 19,357, XIV, 319.

507. Griois, II, 152.

508. Fusil, II, 525–526.

509. Fain, II, 385.

510. Kozlowski, 93.

511. Labaume, 263; Raven, 145; Brandt, 248; Muralt, 106.

512. Larrey, *Mémoires*, IV, 100–101; *Medical Record*, 4 September 1897, 344.

513. Brandt, 248; Fusil, II, 526.

514. Heckens, 160.

515. Dumonceau, 221–222.

516. Mikhailovsky-Danilevsky, IV, 169–170; Pils, 145.

517. Raven, 145.

518. Suckow, 250.

519. Dumonceau, 221–222.

520. Załuski, 274.

521. Fain, II, 388.

522. Suckow, 249.

523. Le Roy, 241.

524. Dumonceau, 221.

525. Gordeyev to Wittgenstein, 27 November 1812, in Kharkevich, 119–120.

526. Laugier, IV, 238; Capello, 265–266.

527. Napoleon to Berthier, 27 November 1812, *Correspondance de Napoleon*, No. 19,359, XXIV, 320; Eugène to Berthier, 27 November (4 a.m., 5 p.m.), Berthier to Eugène 28 November (7 p.m.), 1812, in *Mémoires et Correspondance du Prince Eugène*, VIII, 92–93.

528. Laugier, IV, 240.

529. Labaume, 262–263.

530. Napoleon to Berthier, 27 November 1812, *Correspondance de Napoleon*, No. 19,359, XXIV, 320; *Correspondance du Maréchal Davout*, III, 429–430; Gallaher, 268; Vigier, II, 110. Some authors note that General Zołtowski's brigade crossed together with the I Corps. Bielecki (1990), 143.

531. Coignet, 333.

532. Napoleon to Berthier, Napoleon to Maret, 27 November 1812, *Correspondance de Napoleon*, Nos. 19,358–19,359, XXIV, 320–321.

533. Suckow, 252–253.

534. Turno, 114.

535. Marbot, III, 199.

536. Castellane, I, 197.

537. Bertrand, 152.

538. Malinovski, 93.

539. Arnoldi, 104; Mikhailovsky-Danilevsky, IV, 170.

540. Chichagov, 'Pereprava cherez Berezinu …', 1166–1167.

541. Arnoldi, 104.

542. Czaplic, 515.

543. Chichagov, 'Pereprava cherez Berezinu …', 1165–1167.

544. Kharkevich, 165.

545. Vlastov to Wittgenstein, 27 November (2.30 a.m., 4 a.m.) 1812, in Kharkevich, 118.

546. Wittgenstein to Miloradovich, Yermolov to Wittgenstein, Yermolov to Miloradovich, 27 November 1812, Kharkevich, 120–123.

547. Vlastov to Wittgenstein, 9 December 1812, Kharkevich, 124; Mikhailovsky-Danilevsky, IV, 170. Vlastov commanded the 5th Bashkirskii, Platov IVs, Loshilin's, Rodionov's and Chernozubov's Cossack regiment, supported by the Combined Hussar, Finlandskii Dragoon, 25th Jägers, the Combined Grenadier, Azovskii Infantry Regiments and two *druzhinas* of the Novgorod *opolchenye*. Buturlin, II, 247f, 249. The Russian historian Bogdanovich claimed the troops Vlastov encountered at Stary Borisov were men from Gerard's division but all evidence suggests that it had reached Studyanka earlier that day.

548. Vlastov to Wittgenstein, 9 December 1812, Kharkevich, 124.

549. Buturlin, II, 250.

550. Vlastov to Wittgenstein, 27 November–9 December 1812, Kharkevich, 121, 125.

551. Victor to Berthier, 10 October 1812, in Fabry, 68.

552. Partouneaux to the editor of *Le Moniteur Universel*, 13 February 1821, in Partouneaux, *Addresse*, 11; Delaitre to Partouneaux, 15 December 1812, in Partouneaux, 16; Regis d'Oleon, 101.

553. Victor to Berthier, 10 October 1812; Victor to Berthier, Partouneaux to Berthier, 17 November 1812, in Fabry, 68, 185–186; Chuquet (1912), III, 53–54; Löwernstern, I, 354; *Historique du 51e Régiment*, 345; *Le 125e Régiment d'Infanterie*, 119.

554. Partouneaux to Victor (First and Fourth reports) in Partouneaux, 22–23, 30.

555. Partouneaux to the editor of *Le Moniteur Universel*, 13 February 1821, in Partouneaux, *Addresse*, 11.

556. Napoleon to Mortemart, 27 November (1 a.m.) 1812, *Correspondance du Napoleon*, No. 19,356, XIV, 318–319.

557. Partouneaux to Victor (First report), [n.d.] November 1812; Partouneaux to the editor of *Le Moniteur Universel*, 13 February 1821, in Partouneaux, 11, 23.

558. Victor's Order to the IX Corps, 27 November (5 a.m.) 1812; Victor to Berthier, 28 November 1812, in Fabry, 238, 244; Gourgaud, 254–255; Beulay, 79.

559. Victor to Berthier, 28 November 1812, in Fabry, 244.

560. Partouneaux to Victor (First report); Delaitre to Partouneaux, Camus to Partouneaux, 15 December 1812; Partouneaux to the editor of *Le Moniteur Universel*, 13 February 1821, in Partouneaux, 11–16, 23; Wagevier, 162.

561. Foord, 365.

562. Beulay, 75.

563. Khrapovitskii, 118.

564. Camus to Partouneaux, 15 December 1812, in Partouneaux, 10–11.

565. Wagevier, 46–47.

566. Delaitre to Partouneaux, 15 December 1812, in Partouneaux, 17.

567. Gourgaud, 255. That afternoon Victor ordered Partouneaux 'to re-occupy Borisov and remain there unless a superior enemy force appeared from the Lepel direction threatening to cut communications with the Grand Army'. His messenger could not reach Partouneaux (Victor to Berthier, 28 November 1812, in Fabry, 244).

Notes and Sources

568. Victor to Berthier, 28 November 1812, in Fabry, 244. The timing, however, varies between 3 and 6 p.m. depending on a source. Camus says he received Partouneaux order to advance at 4.30 p.m.

569. Partouneaux to Victor (First Report), [n.d.] November 1812; Delaitre to Partouneaux, 15 December 1812, in Partouneaux, 17, 23.

570. Beulay, 80; Sauzey, III, 189.

571. Partouneaux to Victor (First and Fourth reports), [n.d.] November 1812, in Partouneaux, 24, 32.

572. Ségur (1841), II, 257–258; Labaume, 265.

573. Rossetti, 171.

574. Partouneaux to the editor of *Constitutionnelle*, 4 March 1821, in Partouneaux, *Addresse*, 15.

575. Gourgaud, 255–256; Victor to Berthier, 28 November (12 a.m.) 1812, in Fabry, 244; Beaucour (2004), 36–37 (based on *Registre des Officiers du 55e Régiment*, SHAT, 2 Yb 313, 56, and 2 Yb 314, 34).

576. Rossetti, 174.

577. Partouneaux to Victor (First Report), [n.d.] November 1812; Camus to Partouneaux, 15 December 1812, in Partouneaux, 11, 24. Victor to Berthier, 28 November (12 a.m.) 1812, in Fabry, 244. Partouneaux referred to 'two *verstas*' [~2km] while Victor mentioned 'one *lieue*' or ~5km from Borisov.

578. Beulay, 81.

579. Camus to Partouneaux, 15 December 1812, in Partouneaux, 11.

580. Chambray, II, 313; Delaitre to Partouneaux, Sibille to Partouneaux, 15 December 1812, in Partouneaux, 17, 21.

581. Mahon, 211.

582. Sibille to Partouneaux, [n.d. December 1812] in Partouneaux, 21.

583. Camus to Partouneaux, 15 December 1812, in Partouneaux, 11.

584. Bogdanovich, III, 272; Buturlin, II, 251–252.

585. 'Spisok ofitserov Peterburgskogo i Novgorodskogo opolchenii, otlichivshikhsya 15 Noyabrya 1812 g. pod Starym Borisovom', 15 April 1813; 'Zapiska o sostave i deistviyakh Novgorodskogo opolchenya', 25 September 1836, in *Narodnoye opolchenye*, 311–312, 356. According to Steinheil's report, the Russians pursued the retreating enemy until 8 p.m., capturing twenty officers, some 400 soldiers and cannon (Steinheil to Wittgenstein, 28 November 1812, in Kharkevich, 132).

586. Camus to Partouneaux, Sibille to Partouneaux, 15 December 1812, in Partouneaux, 12, 21–22.

587. Mikhailovsky-Danilevsky, IV, 172–173; Buturlin, 252; Bogdanovich, III, 272.

588. Beulay, 82–87.

589. Camus to Partouneaux, 15 December 1812, in Partouneaux, 12.

590. Blanmont to the editor of *Constitutionnelle*, 18 February 1821, in Partouneaux, *Addresse*, 14.

591. Partouneaux to the editor of *Constitutionnelle*, 4 March 1821, in Partouneaux, *Addresse*, 15.

592. Partouneaux to Victor (First and Fourth reports), [n.d.] November 1812, in Partouneaux, 24–25, 33–34; Steinheil to Wittgenstein, 28 November 1812, in Kharkevich, 133.

593. Camus to Partouneaux, Delaitre to Partouneaux, 15 December 1812, in Partouneaux, 12–13, 17–19.

594. Wagevier, 49–50.

595. Beulay, 84.

596. Beulay, 84–85.

597. Camus to Partouneaux, Delaitre to Partouneaux, Partouneaux to Victor (Fourth report), December 1812, in Partouneaux, 14, 19, 34–35; Victor to Berthier, 28 November (12 a.m.) 1812, in Fabry, 245. The officers Camus selected were Charnaille and Blim from the 125th Line and an unknown from the 29th Légère.

598. Camus to Partouneaux, Delaitre to Partouneaux, 15 December 1812, in Partouneaux, 14, 19.

599. Beulay, 87.

600. Beulay, 85–87; Camus to Partouneaux, 15 December 1812, in Partouneaux, 14; Steinheil to Wittgenstein, 28 November 1812, in Kharkevich, 133; Mikhailovsky-Danilevsky, IV, 172; Buturlin, II, 252.

601. Holzhausen, 97; Ardenne, 110–112.

602. Mikhailovsky-Danilevsky, III, 172; Bogdanovich, III, 273; Berg, 266.

603. *Victoires, conquêtes*, XXI, 296.

604. Chandler, 843; Foord, 367; Nigel Nicholson, Napoleon 1812 (New York, 1985), 152; Nafziger, 319; Vasiliev, 242–243; Digby Smith, *The Greenhill Napoleonic Wars Data Book* (London, 1998), 407; *Otechestvennaia voina 1812 goda: Entsiklopedia*, s.v. 'Stary Borisov'. One recent study notes incorrectly that only one of Partouneaux's brigades was engaged in fighting and forced to surrender (Zamoyski, 470).

605. Partouneaux to Victor (Second report), Delaitre to Partouneaux, Camus to Partouneaux, Sibille to Partouneaux, 15 December 1812, in Partouneaux, 15, 20, 21, 26.

606. *Le 125e Régiment d'Infanterie*, 126; Martin, 215; Jongh, 22; *Résumé de l'historique du 36e regiment d'infanterie*, 80–81; *Historique du 51e regiment d'infanterie*, 346; Oleg Sokolov, 'Korpus Viktora pri Berezine', VIF, 1 (1998), 22; Andolenko, 185–186; Vlijmen, 224.

607. Castellane, I, 198.

608. Löwernstern, I, 354; Sauzey, III, 190; Holzhausen, 97.

609. Wagevier, 50–52.

610. Partouneaux to Victor (Third report), 2 February 1813, in Partouneaux, 28.

611. Partouneaux to the editor of *Journal Annales Politiques, Morales et Littéraires*, 24 August 1817, in Partouneaux, *Addresse*, 9–10.

612. Partouneaux to the editor of *Le Moniteur Universel*, 13 February 1821; Partouneaux to the editor of *Constitutionnelle*, 4 March 1821, in Partouneaux, *Addresse*, 11, 15; *Victoires, conquêtes*, XXI, 296.

613. Dumonceau, 224; Pils, 145; Wilson, 323.

614. Malinovski, 93; Bogdanovich, III.

615. Golitsyn, 145.

616. Mikhailovsky-Danilevsky, IV, 173.

617. Chichagov, 'Pereprava cherez Berezinu …' 1168–1169.

618. Martos, 500.

619. Yermolov, 205.

620. Yermolov, 206, 207f.

621. Chichagov to Czaplic, 27 November 1812, RGVIA, d.3517, l.63b; Czaplic, 510; Chichagov, 'Pereprava cherez Berezinu …' 1171.

622. Chichagov, 'Pereprava cherez Berezinu …' 1171.

623. Yermolov, 209–210; Davydov, 226.

624. Czaplic, 510–511; Arnoldi, 104–105; Bogdanovich, III, 276; Bielecki (1990), 167.

625. Chichagov, 'Pereprava cherez Berezinu …' 1171.

626. The III Corps consisted of the 10th Division of Ledru (~150 men), 11th Division of Razout (200 men) and the 25th Division (up to eighty men) led by Capt. Von Koseritz. The V Corps included Isidor Krasinki's 16th Division (~300), and Karol (Charles) Kniaziewicz's 18th Division (~300).

627. Sokolov, 409.

628. Tellegen, 66.

629. Pils, 146.

630. Langeron, 67, 73.

631. Arnoldi, 105.

Notes and Sources

632. Dąbrowski's report in *The Buturlin Papers*, RGVIA, d.3479, ll.52–52b; Chuquet, II, 200.
633. Czaplic, 511.
634. Pils, 146.
635. Legler, 204–205.
636. Legler, 204–205.
637. Legler, 206; Bégos, 193.
638. Buman, 191.
639. Bussy, 289–290.
640. Bégos, 193–194.
641. Fezensac, 131.
642. Jongh, 22.
643. D'Auzon de Boisminart, 276; Jongh, 19, 22.
644. Tellegen, 66–67; Lorencez, 76; Pils, 146.
645. Oudinot, 176.
646. Pils, 146–147; Tellegen, 67.
647. Fain, II, 396.
648. Pils, 148–150.
649. Oudinot, 176–177.
650. Fezensac, 131.
651. Bourgoing, 210–211.
652. Dembinski, 200.
653. Brandt, 250.
654. Gourgaud, 331; Fain, II, 401.
655. Dembinski, 200–201.
656. Dembinski, 203.
657. Marbot, III, 204.
658. Kirkor, 214–215.
659. Dąbrowski's report in RGVIA, d.3479, ll.52–52b; Davout to Vaudoncourt, 22 November 1814, in Blocqueville (1887), 112.
660. Larrey, IV, 102; Boulart, 276. Napoleon later rewarded Zajączek with 5,000 francs, which the General gave to his officers.
661. Szymanowski, 92.
662. Khrapovitskii, 118–119.
663. Arnoldi, 105–106.
664. Vasiliev mistakenly refers to the 18th Battery Company, but it was commanded by Staff Captain Nikolai Bulatsel. Pashenko was also in charge of the 18th Artillery Brigade which included the 18th Battery, 34th Light and 35th Light Companies. Vasiliev, 253.
665. Arnoldi, 106; Vasiliev, 253.
666. Czaplic says 2 p.m. but other sources suggest the attack took place before then.
667. Pils and Lorencez specifically note that Oudinot issued the first order for Doumerc to attack but it may not have reached the general. Doumerc, in his report, refers to Ney's order.
668. Bielecki (1990), 177. According to Doumerc's report, he had 1,200 men in the 3rd Cuirassier Division on 28 November. Doumerc to Berthier, 14 May 1813 in Sautai, *Héros de la Bérézina*, 5. The 29th Bulletin incorrectly refers to the 5th, instead of the 7th, Cuirassiers, a 'grave injustice' which General Dubois appealed to Louis Auguste Bourmont, King Charles X's minister of war, to correct in 1829. Dubois to Bourmont, 29 October 1829; Bourmont to Dubois, 5 November 1829, in *Historique du 7e Régiment de Cuirassiers*, 50–51.
669. Chichagov, 'Pereprava cherez Berezinu …' 1172.
670. Kharkevich, *1812 g. v dnevnikakh …*, IV, 58.
671. Buturlin, II, 254.

672. Czaplic, 512; Chichagov, 'Pereprava cherez Berezinu ...' 1171–1172.

673. Bogdanovich, III, 277.

674. Langeron, 74f.

675. Langeron, 74; Doumerc to Berthier, 14 May 1813 in Sautai, *Héros de la Bérézina*, 4; *Rapports du maréchal Berthier à l'Empereur pendant la campagne de 1813*, I, 494.

676. Legler, 207.

677. Czaplic, 513; Chichagov, 'Pereprava cherez Berezinu ...' 1172; Bogdanovich, III, 277.

678. Dubois to Doumerc, 21 January 1813, in Sautai, *Héros de la Bérézina*, 9–11; Napoleon's decree of 7 February 1813, *Historique du 7e Régiment de Cuirassiers*, 49–50.

679. Trip to Doumerc, 22 January 1813, in Sautai, *Héros de la Bérézina*, 11–13.

680. Dujon to Doumerc, 17 January 1813, in Sautai, *Héros de la Bérézina*, 7–9; Martinien, 525; *Historique du 4éme Régiment de Cuirassiers* (Bitche, 1994), 56.

681. Doumerc to Berthier, 14 May 1813 in Sautai, *Héros de la Bérézina*, 4.

682. Kamenskii, II, 205–206; Andolenko, 191–192.

683. Fain, II, 402; Joseph de Maistre's letter of 29 December refers to the body of Noailles and a female portrait found on it. *Correspondance diplomatique de Joseph de Maistre*, I, 298.

684. Berthezène, II, 169–170. Nafziger, without indicating a source, notes that Berthezène's men routed the Russian 12th and 22nd Jäger Regiments, 'reducing them from 4,000 men to 700 battered survivors in a matter of minutes'. Russian studies are silent on this account. Nafziger, 320.

685. Legler, 207.

686. Bégos, 195.

687. Bussy, 290–293.

688. Chichagov, 'Pereprava cherez Berezinu ...' 1174–1175.

689. For details see Martynov, 56; Kamenskii, II, 205–206; Bogdanov, 73–75; Boguslavskii, 326.

690. Czaplic, 513.

691. Langeron, 73.

692. Marbot, III, 204; Bourgoing, 211–212; Bégos, 196; Kharkevich, *1812 g. v dnevnikakh* ..., IV, 58.

693. Davout to Vaudoncourt, 22 November 1814, in Blocqueville (1887), 112; *Les Bulletins Français*, 101; Dumonceau, 225; Coignet, 333.

694. Chichagov, 'Pereprava cherez Berezinu ...' 1173; Langeron, 74; Rochechouart (1892), 193–194.

695. Dedem, 288.

696. For information on some Swiss officer losses see Tornere, 387–389; P. de Vallière, *Honneur et fidélité: Histoire des suisses au service etranger* (Lausanne 1940), 702.

697. Bégos, 192; Bussy, 291–292; Maillard, 205.

698. Bielecki, 181.

699. Dembinski, 202f.; cited in Bielecki, 182.

700. Tyrconnell to Cathcart, 20–30 November 1812 in Dubrovin, 347.

701. Mikhailovsky-Danilevsky, IV, 176; Buturlin, II, 255. For details on regimental losses see Vasiliev, 266.

702. Berthier to Victor, 27 November (5 p.m.) 1812 in Chuquet (1912), II, 232; Victor to Berthier, 28 November (12 a.m.) 1812, in Fabry, 245.

703. Chambray, II, 315; *Geschichte des 1 Badischen Feldartillerie-Regiments Nr. 14* (Karlsruhe, 1906), 89–90.

704. For a list of officers serving in the Baden brigade see *1812 Badische Truppen in Russland*, 34–36.

705. Sachs, 27.

706. Zech, 276–277.

707. Bielecki, 187.

708. Victor to Berthier, 28 November (12 a.m.) 1812, in Fabry, 245–246; Sauzey, III, 190–191; Vasiliev, 268–269; Holzhausen, 99–100; Hochberg, 64–66.

Notes and Sources

709. Mikhailovsky-Danilevsky, IV, 176–177; Berg, 267. On 14 December, the ten-day roster report showed 1,100 officers, 2,503 NCOs and 30,880 men in Wittgenstein's corps. Adjusting for losses and stragglers, the I Corps must have had some 36,000–38,000 on the 28th. *Destyatidnevnyi report*, 14 December 1812, in *General Staff Archives: Voina 1813 goda*, III, 3–7.

710. Sachs, 27.

711. Berg, 267.

712. Hochberg, 66.

713. Chapelle and Chapuis, 231; Laugier, IV, 246.

714. Dumonceau, 225.

715. Kergorre, 88–89; Kurz, 184.

716. Turno, 114–115; François, II, 830; Bourgogne, 213.

717. Hochberg, 66; Zech, 277.

718. Dumonceau, 226; Boulart, 276; Sachs, 29–30.

719. Sachs, 30–31.

720. Rapp, 204.

721. Vlastov to Wittgenstein, No. 378, 9 December 1812 in Kharkevich, 126–127.

722. Zech, 279.

723. Victor to Berthier, 28 November (12 a.m.) 1812, in Fabry, 245; Hochberg, 67; Zech, 279.

724. In 1842, Geither's son petitioned the French government to have his father's name engraved on the Arc of Triumph in Paris but was told there was no more space. Charles Schmidt, *Le Grand-duché de Berg (1806–1813)* (Paris, 1905), 165f.

725. Hochberg, 67; Zimmermann, 75; Zech, 279.

726. Berg to Wittgenstein, 1 December 1812, RGVIA, d.3514, ll.557b–558.

727. Wittgenstein to Alexander [n.d.] in Kharkevich, 161; Fetsov to Vlastov, No. 49, 29 November 1812, in *Narodnoye opolchenye*, 348; Bogdanovich, III, 279.

728. Wittgenstein to Alexander [n.d.] in Kharkevich, 161.

729. Victor to Berthier, 28 November (12 a.m.) 1812, in Fabry, 246.

730. Berg to Wittgenstein, 1 December 1812, RGVIA, d.3514, ll.557b–558; Wittgenstein to Alexander [n.d.] in Kharkevich, 162.

731. Bielecki (1990), 189; Vasiliev, 276.

732. Wittgenstein to Alexander [n.d.] in Kharkevich, 162.

733. Ségur to Blancard, Blancard to Ségur, 12 June 1825–28 July 1827 in Ségur, 2 (1898), 632–637.

734. Warchot's memoir in *Frantsuzy v Rossii*, III, 211–212.

735. Victor to Berthier, 28 November (12 a.m.) 1812, in Fabry, 246.

736. The 34th Jägers served in 4th Infantry Division of the II Corps and fought at Smolensk and Borodino in August–September. Its troops were then dispersed among the units as reinforcements in October. The regiment's newly-raised battalions rejoined the army only in the summer of 1813.

737. Ségur (1840), II, 287. Also see Zech, 280–281.

738. Bogdanovich, III, 279.

739. These were replacement squadrons of the Chevalier Guard and Horse Guard Regiments.

740. These battalions belonged to the Leib-Grenadier, Count Arakcheyev's Pavlovskii, Tavricheskii and Yekaterinoslavskii Grenadier Regiments.

741. Wittgenstein to Alexander [n.d.] in Kharkevich, 162.

742. Zech, 281–282.

743. Hochberg, 68–69; Zech, 281. Carl von Diersburg, *Geschichte des 1. Grossherzoglich hessischen Infanterie-(liebgarde-) Regiments NR. 115* (Berlin, 1899), 201.

744. Laugier, IV, 253.

745. Mikhailovsky-Danilevsky, IV, 179.

746. Zotov, 493.

747. Borcke, 223.

748. Victor to Berthier, 28 November (12 a.m.) 1812, in Fabry, *Campagne de 1812*, 246.

749. Victor to Berthier, 30 November 1812, in Fabry, 249–250.

750. Bielecki, 192; Sokolov, 22; Hochberg, 71.

751. *Narodnoye opolchenye*, 349. The Novgorod *opolchenye*, for example, presented a considerable force and counted over 9,000 men in its twelve *druzhinas* on 29 November. These included: twenty-five staff officers, 170 officers, 685 *uryadniks*, 105 musicians and 8,028 soldiers. In addition, there was a 400–men strong auxiliary personnel. The *opolchenye* was armed with 4,800 muskets which were given to the men in the first two ranks, while the rest carried pikes and halberds.

752. Fetsov to Vlastov, No. 49, 29 November 1812; Brovtsyn to Vlastov, No. 23, 30 November 1812, in *Narodnoye opolchenye*, 348, 350.

753. Wittgenstein to Chichagov, No. 520, 28 November 1812; Chichagov to Kutuzov, No. 1912, 29 November, in Kharkevich, 143–144.

754. Berthier to Victor, 28 November (7 p.m.) 1812, in Chuquet (1912), II, 233; Chapelle and Chapuis, 231.

755. Hochberg, 71.

756. Chapelle and Chapuis, 231.

757. Hochberg, 71.

758. Moritz, 78.

759. Chapelle and Chapuis, 232; Griois, II, 156; Séruzier, 255; *Historique du 1er Régiment de Pontonniers*, 111.

760. Foord, 372.

761. Bourgogne, 215.

762. Vossler, 81–82; Séruzier, 257.

763. Roos, 278; Chuquet (1912), I, 193–194.

764. Langeron, 71–72; Brett-James, 262.

765. Victor to Berthier, 30 November 1812, in Chuquet (1912), I, 197; Napoleon to Maret, 30 November 1812, *Correspondance de Napoléon*, No. 19363, XXIV, 323; Chambray, 341–342; Ney to Berthier, 2 December 1812, in Chuquet (1911), 258.

766. Kutuzov to Alexander, No. 569, 1 December 1812, RGVIA, d.3521, ll.90b–91; *Journal of Military Operation*, XIII, 70.

767. *Journals of Military Operation*, XIII, 70; Foerster's Memo, RGVIA, d.3701, l.2–3; François, II, 832.

768. De Maistre to King Victor Emmanuel, 30 April 1813, *Correspondance diplomatique de Joseph de Maistre*, I, 319. *The Gazette* also provided data on corpses found in Kaluga (1,027 humans and 4,349 horses), Moscow (49,754 and 27,849), Smolensk (71,735 and 51,430) and Vilna (72,203 and 9,405). Unfortunately, the data on the Berezina was not differentiated.

769. Brett-James, 262.

770. Generals of division (all wounded): Claparède, Girard, Legrand, Amey, Zajączek, Dąbrowski, Kniaziewicz; generals of brigade: Groisne, Simmer, Bartier St Hilaire, Albert, Blanmont, Castex, Delaistre, Fournier, Moreau, Devilliers, Mourier, Lingg, Dziewanowski, Geither, and Kamienski.

771. Napoleon to Maret, 29 November 1812; Napoleon to de Montesquiou, 2 December 1812, *Correspondance de Napoléon*, Nos. 19362, 19364, XXIV, 322, 324; *Kutuzov: Sbornik dokumentov*, IV, 421.

772. Caulaincourt (1933), II, 192; Bourgogne, 216.

773. Napoleon to Berthier, 28 November 1812, *Correspondance de Napoléon*, No. 19,360, XXIV, 321.

774. Chapelle and Chapuis, 233; Guillaume-Fréderic de Türckheim to Napoleon, 30 November 1812, in Chuquet (1911), 249.

Notes and Sources

775. 'Journal des Campagnes et Blessures de Charles-François Minod', Carnet de la Sabretache, 7 (1908), 522.
776. The detachment included the Belorusskii and Aleksandriiskii Hussars, Liflyandskii Dragoons and the 3rd Ural Cossacks.
777. Oudinot, 180–182.
778. Kutuzov to Alexander, No. 601, 5 December 1812, RGVIA, d.3521, ll.97b–98b; Tyrconnell to Lord Cathcart, 3 December 1812, in Dubrovin, 372–373.
779. Tyrconnell to Lord Cathcart, 3 December 1812, in Dubrovin, 373.
780. Khrapovitskii refers to the passage in Joel 3, which describes Jahveh destroying the coalition of Moab, Ammon, and Edom.
781. Cited in Tarle, 265; Wilson to his wife, 1 December 1812 in Dubrovin, 367.
782. William Napier, *History of the War in the Peninsula and in the South of France* (New York, 1862), IV, 167.
783. Hugh Seton-Watson, *The Russian Empire, 1801–1917* (Oxford, 1988), 140; Alan Schom, *Napoleon Bonaparte* (New York, 1997), 641; Vincent Cronin, *Napoleon* (London, 1994), 328; Michel Franceschi and Ben Weider, *The Wars Against Napoleon* (New York, 2008), 166.
784. *The English Historical Review*, 24 (1909), 413.
785. *1812 god v vospominaniyakh sovremennikov* (Moscow, 1995), 143; James Marshall-Cornwall, *Napoleon as Military Commander* (New York, 1998), 226.
786. Czaplic to Chichagov, No. 351, 3 December 1812, RGVIA, d. 3518/2, l.141–142.
787. Bogdanovich, III, 288. Also see Heinrich Leer, ed. *Obzor voin Rossii ot Petra Velikogo do nashikh dnei* (St Petersburg, 1893), I, 261f.
788. Oleg Sokolov, 'Berezinskaya pereprava', in *Otechestvennaia voina 1812 goda: Entsiklopedia*, 65.
789. Gunther Rothenberg, *The Napoleonic Wars* (London, 1999), 171.
790. David Gates, *The Napoleonic Wars*, 1803–1815 (London, 1997), 217.
791. David Markham, *Napoleon's Road to Glory: Triumphs, Defeats and Immortality* (London, 2003), 224.
792. Foord, 372–373.
793. Chandler, 846.
794. Chandler, 847.
795. George, 249.
796. Tarle, 265–266.
797. Bogdanovich, III, 294.
798. *The Cambridge Modern History*, ed. A. Ward, et al (Cambridge, 1906), IX, 503.
799. Zotov, 493–494.
800. Blond, *La Grande Armée*, 363. Also see Liubomir Beskrovnyi, *Otechestvennaia voina 1812 goda* (Moscow, 1962), 577–578; N. Garnich, *1812 god* (Moscow, 1956), 280; Pavel Zhilin, *Gibel Napoleonivskoi armii v Rossii* (Moscow, 1974), 304–305.
801. Tyrconnell to the Duke of York, Tyrconnell to Cathcart, 30 November 1812, Dubrovin, 355–357.
802. Bogdanovich, III, 289–290.
803. 'The King of Prussia's Military Instruction to his Generals', http://www.au.af.mil/au/awc/awcgate/readings/fred_instructions.htm (accessed on 6 October 2008).
804. Golitsyn, 145.
805. Mikhailovsky-Danilevsky, IV, 190.
806. Kharkevich, 140; Apukhtin, 249; Chambray, II, 302; Foerster's Memo, RGVIA, d. 3701, l.2.
807. Ségur (1877), V, 346–347; Jomini (1827), IV, 198–199; Dumas, III, 473.
808. Bogdanovich, III, 294.
809. Mikhailovsky-Danilevsky, IV, 196.

810. Buturlin, *Kutuzov v 1812 gody*, 145; de Maistre to King Victor Emmanuel, 14 June 1813, in *Arkhiv knyazya Vorontsova*, XV, 501; Golitsyn, 146.

811. Aleksey Shishov, *Kutuzov, Feldmarshal velikoi imperii* (Moscow, 2006), 278–280. Chandler, 846–847.

812. Bogdanovich, III, 293.

813. Kutuzov to his wife, 1 December 1812, in *M.I. Kutuzov: Sbornik dokumentov*, IV, part 2, 416.

814. Vasiliev, 316.

815. Golitsyn, 145.

816. Kutuzov to Wittgenstein, No. 562, 1 December 1812, RGVIA, d.3488, ll.280–281.

817. Kutuzov to Chichagov, No. 539, 29 November 1812, RGVIA, d.3518/2, ll.712–713.

818. Kutuzov to Alexander, [n.d., probably December 1812], in *M.I. Kutuzov: Sbornik dokumentov*, IV, part 2, 421–422.

819. Chichagov to Alexander, 29 November 1812, RGVIA, d.3700, ll.315b–316; Langeron, 87–88; Mikhailovsky-Danilevsky, *Imperator Aleksandr I i ego spodvizhniki*, vol. II, 'Sabaneyev,' 8; Edeling, 222.

820. Kudashev to Ekaterina Kutuzova, 1 December 1812, in *M.I. Kutuzov: Sbornik dokumentov*, IV, part 2, 417; *Literaturnoye nasledstvo* (Moscow, 1982), volume 91, 402.

821. F. Vigel, *Zapiski* (Moscow, 1928), II, 28; Zhukovsky to A. Turgenev, 9 April 1813, in V. Zhukovsky, *Sobranie sochinenii* (Moscow, 1960), 490; Gregory Derzhavin, *Sochineniya* ... (St Petersburg, 1866), III, 451.

822. Dokhturov to his wife, 3 December 1812, *Russkii arkhiv*, 1 (1874), 1107; Wilson to Lord Cathcart, 4 December 1812, in Dubrovin, 375.

823. Yermolov, 211.

824. Khrapovitskii, 120.

825. Golitsyn, 146.

826. Khrapovitskii, 120.

827. Yermolov, 213.

828. Wilson, Narrative, 356–357.

829. Rayevsky to his wife, 22 December 1812, in *1812–1814: Lichnye pisma generala N.N. Rayevskogo* (Moscow, 1992), 236; Yermolov, 215–216.

830. Davydov, 228–229; Chichagov, 'Zapiski ...' 51 (1886), 490–491; Yermolov, 211; Arnoldi, 110.

831. Edeling, 222.

832. Chichagov to Vorontsov, 15 September 1813, cited in Yulin, *Admiral P.V. Chichagov*, Part IV.

833. de Maistre to King Victor Emmanuel, 14 June 1813, in *Arkhiv knyazya Vorontsova*, XV, 500.

834. de Maistre to King Victor Emmanuel, 14 June 1813, in *Arkhiv knyazya Vorontsova*, XV, 502.

835. Cited in Yulin, *Admiral P.V. Chichagov*, Part IV.

836. Edward Wedlake Brayley, John Britton, Gideon Algernon Mantell, *A Topographical History of Surrey* (London, 1844), IV, Part 1, 61.

837. Jeremy Bentham to Samuel Bentham, 4 July 1814 in *The Correspondence of Jeremy Bentham* (Oxford, 1988), VIII, 385–386. Also see letters between Pavel Chichagov and Jeremy Bentham, ibid., 388–389, 411–416, 448–450, 488–490, 494–496, 497–502, 532–533.

Select Bibliography

A complete bibliography is available at www.napoleon-series.org

Archival Material

Rossiiskii Gosudarstvennii Voenno-Istoricheskii arkhiv (RGVIA) [Russian State Military Historical Archive]
Fond No. 846 (Voenno-Uchebnii Arkhiv; VUA), *opis* No. 16
  Delos 3385, 3471, 3472, 3479, 3484, 3490, 3491, 3503, 3515, 3517, 3518, 3521, 3522, 3524, 3546, 3558, 3572, 3573, 3655, 3700, 3701, 3836

Archives de la Guerre: Service historique de l'armée de terre (SHAT), Château de Vincennes
Cartons 1M 673, 1M 679, 1M 845, 1M 2138, 1M 2149, 2C 526, 2C 133, MR 109, C2 286

Bibliotheek Nederlandsch Legermuseum, The Dutch Army Museum
KHA-365 – D'Auzon de Boisminart, Willem Pieter. *Herinneringen uit den veldtogt van Rusland in den jare 1812.* Amsterdam, 1824.
KHA-364 – Wagevier, C J. *Aanteekeningen gehouden gedurende mijnen marsch naar, gevangenschap in, en terugreize uit Rusland, in den jaren 1812, 1813 en 1814.* Amsterdam, 1820.

Published Archival Material and Private Papers
Arkhiv admirala P.V. Chichagova. St Petersburg, 1885.
Arkhiv knyazya Vorontsova. Moscow, 1880, volume 15.
Beskrovnyi, Liubomir. *M.I. Kutuzov: Sbornik Dokumentov.* Moscow, 1954, volume 4.
——. *Narodnoye opolchenye v Otechestvennoi voine 1812 goda.* Moscow, 1962.
Fabry, Gabriel Joseph, *Campaign de 1812: Documents relatifs a l'aile gauche, 20 août – 4 décembre,* Paris, 1912.
General Staff Archives: Otechestvennaya Voina 1812 goda: Materialy Voenno-Uchenogo Arkhiva Generalnogo Shtaba. St Petersburg, 1910–1917, volumes 15, 16, 18, 19 and 20.

The Battle of the Berezina

General Staff Archives: Voina 1813 goda.: Voina 1812 Goda: Materialy Voenno-Uchenogo Arkhiva Generalnogo Shtaba. St Petersburg, 1914–1917, 3 volumes.

Journal of Military Operations of the 3rd Western Army, written by Lt. Col. Malinovskii, in Otechestvennaya Voina 1812 goda, XVII, 193–233.

Journal of the Advance Guard of the 3rd Western Army, written by Col. Ikskul., in Otechestvennaya Voina 1812 goda, XVII, 311–330.

Journals of Military Operations. 'Zhurnaly voyennykh deistvii' in Sbornik istoricheskikh materialov izvlechennykh iz arkhiva sobstvennoi Ego Imperatorskago Velichestva Kantselyarii. St Petersburg, 1906, volume 13.

State Council Archive. Arkhiv Gosudarstvennogo soveta. St Petersburg, 1888, volume 2.

RUSSIAN[1]

Primary sources

Anonymous. 'Bedstvennaya pereprava frantsuzskoi armii cherez r. Berezinu pri begstve Napoleona iz Moskvy v 1812 godu,' in 1812 god v vospominaniyakh sovremennikov (Moscow, 1995), 139–144.

Arnoldi, Ivan. 'Iz zapisok,' in Voyenskii (1912), 96–111.

——. 'Deistviya otryada Generala Kornilova pri Berezinskoi pereprave,' in Severnaya pchela, 56–57 (1840), 223–224, 226–228.

Bennigsen, Levin. 'Zapiski o kampanii 1812 goda.' RS, 1909, Nos. 11 and 12.

Bolgovsky, D. 'Iz vospominanii D.N. Bolgovskogo,' in Kharkevich, 1900, 226–243.

Bronevskii, Dmitri. 'Vospominaniya…,' RS, 6 (1908).

Chichagov, Pavel. 'Pisma admirala Chichagova k imperatory Aleksandru I.' Sbornik Rossiisskogo Istoricheskogo Obshestva, St Petersburg, volume 6.

——. 'Pereprava cherez Berezinu: Iz "Zapisok" admirala P.V. Chichagova.' RA, 7 (1869).

——. 'Zapiski…' ed. by L. Chichagov. RS, 50 (1886), 221–252, 463–486; 51 (1886), 247–270, 487–518.

Chicherin, Alexander. Dnevnik… Moscow, 1966.

Czaplic, Yefim. 'Otechestvennaya voina v rasskaze generala Chaplitsa.' RS, 6 (1886).

Davidov, Denis. Voennye zapiski. Moscow, 1982.

——. Sochineniya. Moscow, 1962.

Dubrovin, Nikolai. Otechestvennaya voina v pismakh sovremenikov, (1812–1815), St Petersburg, 1882.

Edeling, Countess. 'Iz zapisok…' RA, 2 (1887).

Eyler (Euler), A. 'Zapiski…' RA, 2 (1880).

Falenberg, P. 'Iz zapisok P.I. Falenberga,' RA, 10 (1877).

Golitsyn, Alexander. 'Zapiska o voine 1812 goda,' in Voyenskii (1912), 136–146; Voyennii sbornk, 10 (1910), 21–35.

Select Bibliography

Karpov, A. 'Iz zapisok…' in Kallash (1912), 219–225.

Khrapovitskii, Yason. 'Vospominaniya…' in Voyenskii (1912), 111–121; *Voyennii sbornk*, 10 (1910), 41–54.

Kolaczkowski, Klemens. 'Zapiski…' in Voyenskii (1912), 206–263.

Langeron, Alexander. 'Zapiski…' in *RS*, 7–9 (1907), 10–12 (1908).

Maistre, Joseph de. *Peterburgskie pisma*. St Petersburg, 1995.

Malinovskii, Silvestr. 'Zapiski…' in Voyenskii (1912), 88–96.

Martos, A. 'Zapiski inzhenernogo ofitsera Martosa.' *RS*, 77 (1893).

Muravyev-Apostol, M. *Vospominaniya i pisma*. Moscow, 1922.

Muravyev-Karsskii, N. 'Zapiski…' *RA*, 11 (1885).

O'Rourke, Joseph. 'Zamechaniya po povodu vzyatiya Borisova i srazheniya pri Berezine v 1812 godu,' in Voyenskii (1912), 121–124; *Voyennii sbornk*, 10 (1910), 55–58.

Otroshenko, Yakov. 'Zapiski…' *Russkii vestnik*, 10 (1877).

Radozhitsky, Ilya. *Pokhodnye zapiski artillerista s 1812 po 1816 god*. Moscow, 1835.

Shishkov, Alexander. *Zapiski…* Berlin, 1870.

Sukhetsky, Ivan. 'Diary…' in *Sbornik Imperatorskogo russkogo istoricheskogo obshestva*, 128 (1909), e-version at http://rpp.nm.ru/suhetsky/suhetsky.html

Tolstoy, Fedor. 'Zapiski…' *RS*, 7 (1873).

Vasyutinskii, A., A. Djivelegov and S. Melgunov, eds. *Frantsuzy v Rossii. 1812 g. po vospominaniyam sovremennikov-inostrantsev*. Moscow, 1912, 3 volumes.

Yelin, Christoph-Ludwig von. *Zapiski ofitsera armii Napoleona fon-Yelina*. Moscow, 1912 (on-line version at http://history.scps.ru/lib/ie00.htm).

'Zapiski generala Izyumova o deistviyakh Chuguevskogo ulanskogo polka v 1812 godu,' *Voyennii sbornk*, 11 (1910), 21–29.

Zhirkevich, Ivan. 'Zapiski…' *RS*, 10 (1874).

Zotov, Rafail. 'Rasskazy…' in *Rossii dvinulis syny* (Moscow, 1988), 461–497.

Secondary sources

Beskrovnyi, Liubomir. *Otechestvennaiya voina 1812 g.* Moscow, 1962.

Bogdanov, V. *Kratkaya istoriya 15-go pekhotnogo Kostromskogo polka*. Zhitomir, 1900.

Bogdanovich, Modest. *Istoria Otechestvennoi voiny 1812 g. po dostovernym istochnikam*. St Petersburg, 1859, volume 3.

Buturlin, Dmitri. *Istoriya nashestviya Imperatora Napoleona na Rossiyu v 1812 godu*, St Petersburg, 1838, volume 2.

Grutso, Igor. 'Istoriya sozdaniya pamyatnikov na meste perepravy voisk Napoleona cherez Berezinu v noyabre 1812 g.' in *Otechestvennaya voina 1812 goda* (Moscow, 2000), 52–55.

Kamenskii, E. *Istoriya 2-go dragunskogo S-Peterburgskogo general-feldmarshala kn. Menshikova polka*. Moscow, 1900.

Kharkevich, V. *1812 g. Berezina*. St Petersburg, 1893.

Martynov, A. *Kratkaya istoriya 46-go dragunskogo Pereyaslavskogo imperatora Aleksandra III polka.* St Petersburg, 1898.

Mikhailovsky-Danilevsky, Alexander. *Opisaniye Otechestvennoi voiny v 1812 godu*, volume 4, St Petersburg, 1839.

Otechestvennaya voina i Russkoye obshestvo, eds. A. Djivelegov, S. Melgunov and V. Pichet. Moscow, 1911, volume 4.

Sokolov, Oleg. *Armiya Napoleona.* St Petersburg, 1999.

Vasiliyev, I. *Neskolko gromkikh udarov po khvostu tigra.* Moscow, 2001.

Voyenskii, Konstantin. 'Napoleon i borisovskie evrei v 1812 g.' in *Istoricheskie ocherki i statii, otnosyashiesya k 1812 godu.* (St Petersburg, 1912), 191–199.

——. 'Admiral Pavel Vasil'evich Chichagov,' *Voprosy Istorii*, 2003 (2), 50–72.

Zhilin, Pavel. *Gibel Napoleonovskoi armii v Rossii.* Moscow, 1974.

——. *Otechestvennaya voina 1812 goda.* Moscow, Voenizdat, 1988.

BYELORUSSIAN

Frantsuzska-ruskaya vaina 1812 goda: eurap. dyskursy i bel. poglyad: materyaly Mizhnar. navuk. kanf., 29–30 November 2002, Minsk, 2003.

Joffe, E. *Stranitsy istorii evreev Belarusi.* Minsk, 1996.

Lukashevich, A. *Belarus' napiaredadni i u chas vainy 1812 h.* Minsk, 2004.

FRENCH

Primary sources

Ameil, Auguste, Baron. 'Notes et Documents provenant des Archives du Général Baron Ameil.' *Carnet de la Sabretache*, deuxième série, 5 (1906).

Beaulieu, Drujon de. 'Souvenirs d'un militaire pendant quelques années du règne de Napoléon Bonaparte,' in Georges Bertin, *La Campagne de 1812*, (Paris, 1895), 245–248.

Bégos, Louis. 'Souvenirs des campagnes…' in *Soldats Suisses au Service Etranger*, Geneve, 1909, 101–233.

Bellot de Kergorre, Alexander. *Un commissaire des guerres pendant le premier empire. Journal de Bellot de Kergorre*, Paris, 1899.

Bertin, Georges. *La Campagne de 1812 d'après des témoins oculaires*, Paris, 1895.

Beulay, Honoré. *Mémoires d'un Grenadier de la Grande Armée*, Paris, 1907.

Blocqueville, Louise Adélaïde d'Eckmühl. *Le maréchal Davout, prince d'Eckmühl: correspondance inédite, 1790–1815, Pologne – Russie – Hambourg.* Paris, 1887.

Boulart, Jean François. *Mémoires militaries…* Paris, 1892.

Bourgogne, Adrien Jean Baptiste François. *Mémoires du Sergent Bourgogne (1812–1813),* Paris, 1910.

Bourgoing, Paul. *Souvenirs d'histoire contemporaine,* Paris, 1864.

Brandt, Heinrich von. *Souvenirs d'un Officier Polonais. Scènes de la vie militaire en Espagne et en Russie (1808–1812),* Paris, 1877.

Select Bibliography

Buman, Louis de. 'Passage de la Beresina,' in Chuquet, II, 189–194.

Bussy, Jean-Marc. 'Notes d'un appointé de voltigeurs' in *Soldats Suisses au Service Etranger*, (Geneva, 1913), 218–312.

Castellane, Boniface de. *Journal...* Paris, 1896.

Caulaincourt, Armand. *Mémoires*, Paris, 1933.

Chapelle, Antoine, and Jean-Baptiste Chapuis. 'Relation du passage de la Bérésina, 26, 27, 28, 29 Novembre 1812,' in Fabry, *Campagne de 1812*, 227–236; a slightly revised version in Beaucour, 71–88.

Chichagov, Pavel. *Mémoires...* Leipzig, 1862.

Coignet, Captain. *Les Cahiers...* Paris, 1883.

Corbineau, Jean Baptiste. 'Passage de la Bérézina,' *Le Spectateur Militaire*, 1827.

Curély, Jean Nicolas. *Le Général Curély: Itinéraire d'un Cavalier Léger de la Grande Armée (1793–1815)*, Paris, 1887.

Davout, Louis N. *Correspondance du Maréchal Davout*. Paris, 1885.

Dedem van de Gelder, Antoine Baudouin Gisbert de. *Mémoires...* Paris, 1900.

Domergue, Armand. *La Russie pendant les Guerres de l'Empire (1805–1815)*, Paris, 1835.

Dumas, Mathieu. *Souvenirs...* Paris, 1839.

Dumonceau, François. *Mémoires...* Bruxelles, 1958–1963.

Fain, Agathon-Jean-François. *Manuscript de Mil Huit Cent Douze*, Paris, 1827.

Fezensac, Raymond-Aymery-Philippe-Joseph de Montesquiou, Duc de. *Journal de la Campagne de Russie en 1812*, Paris, 1850.

François, Capt. *Journal...* Paris, 1904, volume 2.

Fusil, Louise. *Souvenirs d'un actrice*, Paris, 1841.

Grouchy, Emmanuel. *Mémoires...* Paris, 1873, volume 3.

Heckens, E.F.C.A. *Mémoires...* The Hague, 1910.

Hogendorp, Dirk van. *Mémoires...* The Hague, 1887.

Langeron, Alexander. *Mémoires...* Paris, 1902.

Larrey, Dominique. *Mémoires de Chirurgie militaire, et Campagnes*, Paris, 1817.

Lassus-Marcilly, François-Anne-Nicolas. 'Notes sur ma Campagne de Russie,' *Carnet de la Sabretache*, troisième série, 2 (1914).

Le Roy, Claude François. *Souvenirs...* Dijon, 1914.

Lecointe de Laveau, G. *Moscou, avant et après l'incendie*, Paris, 1814.

Lorencez, Guillaume Latrille de. *Souvenirs militaires...* Paris, 1902.

——. 'Etat raisonné de mes services,' in *Le Carnet* IX (1902), 112–122.

Maillard, Jean-Pierre. 'Mémoires d'un lieutenant au service de France,' in *Soldats Suisses au Service Etranger*, (Geneva, 1913), 1–218.

Marbot, Jean-Baptiste Antoine Marcellin de. *Mémoires...* Paris, 1891.

Partouneaux, Louis. *Addresse...* Paris, 1815.

Pastoret, Amédée de. 'De Witebsk à la Bérésina,' *La Revue de Paris*, (1902 Mars–Avril), 465–498.

Peyrusse, Guillaume-Joseph. *Lettres inédites du baron Guillaume Peyrusse écrites à son frère André pendant les Campagnes de l'Empire de 1809 à 1814*, Paris, 1894.

——. *Mémorial et archives, 1809–1815*, Paris, 1869.

Pils, François. *Journal de Marche…* Paris, 1895.

Roguet, François. *Mémoires…* Paris, 1865.

Roos, Henri de. *Avec Napoléon en Russie: Souvenirs de la Campagne de 1812*, Paris, 1913.

Rosselet, Abraham. 'Souvenirs…' in Bertin, 265–270.

Rossetti, General. *Journal d'un compagnon de Murat*, Paris, 1998.

Schumacher, Gaspard. *Journal et souvenirs…* (Paris, [n.d.]).

Ségur, Philippe de. 'Note relative au passage de la Bérézina,' in *Le Carnet Historique et Littéraire*, 2 (1898), 632–637.

——. *Histoire et memoires*, Paris, 1877.

——. *Histoire de Napoléon et de la Grande-Armée pendant l'année 1812*, Paris, 1825.

Stuers, Lambert de. 'Mémoires…' in Ronald Pawly and Patrice Courcelle, eds., *Mémoires et Uniformes de Lambert de Stuers & Historique du 3e Régiment de Grenadiers à Pied de la Garde Impériale*, Brussels, 2004.

Suckow, Karl Friedrich. *D'Iéna a Moscou: Fragments de ma vie*, Paris, 1901.

Turno, Charles. 'Souvenirs d'un officier polonaise,' in *Revue des Etudes Napoléoniennes*, 1931, XXXIII, 99–116.

Vaudoncourt, Frédéric-François Guillaume de. *Relation impartiale du passage de la Berezina, par l'armée française, en 1812*, Paris, 1815(a).

——. *Mémoires pour server a l'histoire de la guerre entre la France et la Russie en 1812*, Paris, 1817 (from RGVIA, delo 3477).

——. *Quinze années d'un proscrit*, Paris, 1835.

Villeminot, Jean-Baptiste. 'Extraits des Papiers d'Un Cavalier de la Grande Armée,' in *Carnet de la Sabretache*, deuxième série, 7 (1908).

Secondary sources

Andolenko, Serge. *Aigles de Napoléon contre Drapeaux du Tsar*, Paris, 1969.

Beaucour, Fernand Emile et al. *La Bérézina: une victoire militaire*, Paris, 2006.

——. *Napoléon à la Bérézina, 26–29 Novembre 1812*, Levallois, 2004.

Bielecki, Robert. 'Les Ponts de la Bérésina: le rôle des Polonais,' in *Revue l'Institute Napoléon*, 143 (1984), 27–45.

Chuquet, Arthur. *Lettres de 1812*, Paris, 1911.

——. *1812. La Guerre de Russie: Notes et Documents*, Paris, 1912, three volumes.

Despiques, Paul. *Oudinot et Marbot*, Nancy, 1896.

Desplat, Jacques Joseph. *Fournier Sarlovèse, Général d'Empire, 1772–1827: un diable de hussard digne de leur légende,* Le Bugue, 2004.

Faivre d'Arciet, Captain, and Lieutenant Royé. *Historique du 37e regiment d'infanterie*, Paris, 1895.

Fillion, Alain. *La Bérézina: racontée par ceux qui l'ont vécue*, Paris, 2005.

Select Bibliography

Girod de l'Ain, Maurice. *Grands Artilleurs: Drouot – Senarmont – Eblé*, Paris, 1895.

Guillon, Edouard. *Napoléon et la Suisse*, Paris, 1910.

Jomini, Henri, Baron de. *Précis de l'Art de la Guerre ou Noveau Tableau Analytique*, Paris, 1894.

———. *Vie politique et militaire de Napoléon*, Paris, 1827.

Küpfer, Emile. *Nos dernières pages d'histoire héroique: La Suisse à Polotzk et à la Bérésina*, Lausanne, 1912.

'La Division de cuirassiers de général Doumerc à la bataille de la Bérézina,' in *Revue militaire*, 125 (May 1911), 347–350.

'La Division Dombrowski dans la Campagne de 1812,' in *Revue d'histoire, rédigée a l'état-major de l'armée*, 20 (1902), 389–401; *Revue militaire*, 18 (1902), 1299–1329.

Mahon, Patrice. 'Un pèlerinage au bord de la Bérésina,' in *Carnet de la Sabretache*, 5 (1897), 200–216.

Martinien, Aristide. *Tableaux par corps et par batailles des officiers tués et blessés pendant les guerres de l'Empire (1805–1815)*, Paris, 1899.

Martinien, M.A. 'Les Généraux du grand-duché de Varsovie de 1812 à 1814,' in *Carnet de la Sabretache*, deuxième série, 5 (1906).

Mestre, Lt. *Le Général Claparède: Sa vie militaire, ses campagnes*, Paris, 1899.

'Passage de la Bérézina,' in *Revue militaire*, 139 (July 1912), 137–165.

Regis d'Oleon, M. 'La Division Partouneaux a Borizow,' in *Sabretache*, 419 (December 1959), 92–114.

Sautai, Maurice Théodore. *Héros de la Bérézina*, Paris, 1912.

Sauzey, Commandant. *Les Allemands sous les aigles française: III – Les Saxons dans nos rangs*, Paris, 1907.

———. 'Les Allemands sous les aigles francais: Le contingent Badois,' in *Carnet de la Sabretache*, 2 (1903), 257–294.

———. *Les soldats de Hesse et de Nassau*, Paris, 1912.

Schaller, H. de. *Histoire des troupes suisses en service de France sous le règne de Napoléon I*, Lausanne, 1883.

Thiers, Adolphe. *Histoire du consulat et de l'empire*, Paris, 1856, volume 14.

Thiry, Jean. *La Campagne de Russie*, Paris, 1969.

Tornare, Alain-Jacques. *Les Vaudois de Napoléon. Des pyramides à Waterloo (1798–1815)*, Yens sur Morges, 2003.

Tranié, Jean and C. Carmigniani. *La campagne de Russie: Napoléon, 1812*, Paris, 1981.

Vigier, Henri. *Davout, maréchal d'Empire, duc d'Auerstaedt, prince d'Eckmühl (1770–1823)*, Paris, 1898, volume 2.

ENGLISH

Primary sources

Bourgogne, Adrien Jean Baptiste François. *Memoirs of Sergeant Bourgogne (1812–1813)*, London, 1899.

Caulaincourt, Armand de. *With Napoleon in Russia: The Memoirs of General de Caulaincourt, Duke of Vicenza*, New York, 1935.

Clausewitz, Karl von. *The Campaign of 1812 in Russia*, Hattiesburg MS, 1970.

Labaume, Eugène. *The Crime of 1812 and Its Retribution*, London, 1912.

Lejeune, Louis François. *Memoirs of Baron Lejeune, aide-de-camp to Marshals Berthier, Davout and Oudinot*, London, 1897.

Oudinot, Nicolas Charles. *Memoirs of Marshal Oudinot, Duc de Reggio, compiled from the hitherto unpublished Souvenirs of the Duchesse de Reggio*, ed. Gaston Stiegler, London, 1896.

Rochechouart, Louis-Victor-Léon. *Memoirs*... trans. by Frances Jackson, New York, 1920; French edition (1892).

Saint Denis, Louis Etienne. *Napoleon From the Tuileries to St Helena: Personal recollections of the Emperor's Second Mameluke and Valet*, New York, 1922.

Saint Elme, Ida. *Memoirs of a Contemporary*, New York, 1902.

Ségur, Philippe-Paul. *History of the Expedition to Russia Undertaken by the Emperor Napoleon in the year 1812*, London, 1840, volume 2.

Vaudoncourt, Frédéric-François Guillaume de. *Critical Situation of Bonaparte in His Retreat Out of Russia or a Faithful Narrative of the Repassing of the Beresina by the French Army in 1812*, London, 1815(b).

Vossler, Heinrich August. *With Napoleon in Russia, 1812*, London, 1969.

Walter, Jacob. *The Diary of a Napoleonic Foot Soldier*, New York, 1991.

Wilson, Sir Robert. *Narrative of the events during the invasion of Russia by Napoleon Bonaparte and the retreat of the French army*, London, 1860.

——. *Private Diary of Travels, Personal Services and Public Events During Mission and Employment in 1812, 1813 and 1814 Campaigns*, ed. by H. Randolph, London, 1861.

Secondary sources

Cate, Curtis. *The War of the Two Emperors. The Duel between Napoleon and Alexander: Russia 1812*, New York, 1985.

Chandler, David. *The Campaigns of Napoleon*, New York, 1966.

Foord, Edward. *Napoleon's Russian Campaign of 1812*, London, 1914.

Gallaher, John. *The Iron Marshal: A Biography of Louis N. Davout*, Carbondale, 1976.

Hattem, Mark van, Mariska Pool and Mathieu Willemsen, eds. *In the Wake of Napoleon: The Dutch in Time of War, 1792–1815*, Delft, 2005.

Nafziger, George. *Napoleon's Invasion of Russia*, Novato, CA, 1988.

Pawly, Ronald. *The Red Lancers*, Ramsbury, Wiltshire, 1998.

Yorck von Wartenburg, Maximilian. *Napoleon as a General*, London, 1902, volume 2.

Zamoyski, Adam. *Moscow 1812: Napoleon's Fatal March*, London, 2004.

Select Bibliography

Dissertations

Eidahl, Kyle. *The Military Career of Nicolas Charles Oudinot (1767–1847)*, Ph.D. dissertation, Florida State University, 1990.

Finley, Milton. *The Career of Count Jean Reynier, 1792–1814*, Ph.D. dissertation, Florida State University, 1972.

Hartford, Lee Shartle. *The Bavarian Army under Napoleon, 1805–1813*, Ph.D. dissertation, Florida State University, 1988.

Vovsi, Eman. *Service of Antoine-Henri Baron de Jomini in 1812–1813: A New Retrospective View*, MA thesis, Florida State University, 2006.

Weinzierl, John F. *The Military and Political Career of Claude-Victor Perrin*, Ph.D. dissertation, Florida State University, 1997.

GERMAN

Primary sources

Berg, Gregov von. *Leben von Gregor von Berg*, Dresden, 1871.

Bernhardi, Theodor von. *Denkwurdigkeiten aus dem Leben des Kaiserl russ. Generals von der Infanterie Carl Friedrich Grafen von Toll*, Leipzig, 1856–1858.

Bomsdorff, Otto Wilhelm Karl Röder von. *Mittheilungen aus dem russischen Feldzuge: an einen Offizier des Generalstabes*, Leipzig, 1816.

Borcke, Johann von. *Kriegerleben des Johann von Borcke, weiland kgl. Preuss. Oberstlieutenants, 1806–1815*, Berlin, 1888.

Boyen, Hermann von. *Erinnerungen aus dem Leben des General-Feldmarschalls Hermann von Boyen*, Leipzig, 1889.

Giesse, Johann Friedrich. *Kassel-Moskau-Küstrin, 1812–1813: Tagebuch während des russischen Feldzuges…* Leipzig, 1912.

Hochberg, Wilhelm. *Denkwürdigkeiten des Markgrafen Wilhelm von Baden*, Heilberg/Heidelberg, 1864, 1906.

Klinkhardt, Friedrich. *Feldzugs-Erinnerungen des Königlich Westfälischen Musikmeisters Friedrich Klinkhardt aus den Jahren 1812–1815*, Braunschweig, 1908.

Kurz, Hauptmann von. *Der Feldzug von 1812. Denkwürdigkeiten eines württembergischen Offiziers*, Leipzig, 1912.

Lehmann, Max. 'Clausewitz über die Schlacht an der Beresina' in *Historische Zeitschrift*, 61 (1889), 110–112.

Lossberg, Friedrich Wilhelm von. *Briefe in die Heimath: Geschrieben während des Feldzuges 1812 in Russland*, Cassel, 1844.

Minckwitz, August von. *Die Brigade Thielmann in dem Feldzuge von 1812 in Russland*, Dresden, 1879.

Moritz, Johann. 'Ein Mainzer in Napoleons Diensten Das Leben von Johann "Jean" Moritz: 1785–1837' in *Tagebuch – Briefe – Mainzer Skizzen*, eds. Eva and Helmit Lehr, Mainz, 2007.

The Battle of the Berezina

Muralt, Albrecht von, and Thomas Legler. *Beresina: Erinnerungen aus dem Feldzug Napoleons I in Russland 1812*, Bern, 1940.

Raven, Otto. *Tagebuch des Feldzuges in Russland im Jahre 1812*, Rostock, 1997.

Sachs, Carl. *Erinnerungs-Blätter eines badischen Soldaten an den Russischen Feldzug von 1812 bis 1813*, Ulm, 1987.

Steinmüller, Joseph. *Tagebuch Joseph Steinmüllers über seine Teilnahme am russischen Feldzuge 1812*, Heidelberg, 1903.

Wilhelm, Markgraf of Baden, *see* Hochberg.

Zech, Captain. *Beitrag zu der Geschichte des 9. Korps der französischen Armee im Feldzug gegen Rußland 1812*, Österr. mil. Zeitschr., 1821, Heft 3.

Zimmermann, P. *Erinnerungen aus den Feldzügen der Bergischen Truppen in Spanien und Russland*, Düsseldorf, 1842.

Secondary sources

1812 Badische Truppen in Russland, Karlsruhe: Armeemuseum Karlsruhe/Baden Deutsche Wehr Am Oberrhein, 1937.

Ardenne, Fr. von. *Bergische Lanziers – Westfälische Husaren Nr. 11,* Berlin, 1877.

Beitzke, Heinrich Ludwig. *Geschichte des russischen Krieges im Jahre 1812*, Leipzig, 1862.

Bleibtreu, Carl. *Die Grosse Armee (1812: Smolensk–Moskau–Beresina)*, Stuttgart, 1908.

Diersburg, Karl Christian Freiherrn Röder von. *Geschichte des 1. Grossherzoglich hessischen Infanterie (Leibgarde) Regiments Nr. 115, 1621–1899*, Berlin, 1899.

Ebstein, Wilhelm. *Die Krankheiten im Feldzuge gegen Russland (1812)*, Stuttgart, 1902.

Geschichte des 1. Badischen Feldartillerie-regiments Nr. 14, Karlsruhe, 1906.

Goethe, Theodor Daniel. *Ein Verwandter Goethes im russischen Feldzuge 1812*, Berlin, 1912.

Holzhausen, Paul. *Die Deutschen in Russland, 1812: Leben und Leiden auf der Moskauer Heerfahrt*, Berlin, 1912.

Keim, August Justus Alexander. *Geschichte des Infanterie-leibregiments Grossherzogin (3. Grossherzogl. Hessisches)*, Berlin, 1903.

Lindenau, Curt W.F. von. *Der Beresina-uebergang des Kaisers Napoleon*, Berlin, 1896.

Pfister, Albert. *Aus dem Lager des Rheinbundes 1812 und 1813*, Stuttgart, 1897.

Scholtz, Richard. 'Napoleons Rückzug über die Beresina Ende November 1812 ohne Schnee und Eis?!', in *Die Zinnfigur*, 1 (1989).

Welden, Franz Ludwig. *Der Feldzug der Oesterreicher gegen Russland im Jahre 1812*, Vienna, 1870.

ITALIAN

Cappello, Girolamo. *Gli Italiani in Russia nel 1812*, Città di Castello, 1912.

Laugier, Cesare. *Gl'italiani in Russia: Memorie di un ofiziale Italiano*, [s.n. 1827].

Select Bibliography

SWISS

Bleibtreu, Karl. 'Beresina und die Rückzugsverluste' in *Schweizerische Monatsschrift für Offiziere aller Waffen*, 1912, 459–ff.

Brunner, Emil. 'Ein Lied wurde zum Denkmal!: Der "Beresina-Legler" und "sein" Lied' in *Schweizer Soldat*, 15 (1962), 289.

———. 'Thomas Legler, der Sänger an der Beresina' in *Allgemeine schweizerische Militärzeitschrift*, 11 (1975), 410–414.

'Die roten Schweizer 1812' in *Allgemeine schweizerische Militärzeitung*, 1912, Literaturbl. Nr. 8.

'Die Schlacht an der Beresina' in *Allgemeine schweizerische Militärzeitung*, 1858, 45–46, 49–50.

Hellmüller, Carl Theodor. *Die Roten Schweizer 1812: zum hundertjährigen Gedächtnis an die Kämpfe der Roten Schweizer Napoleons I. an der Düna und Beresina*, Bern, 1912.

———. 'Die Schlacht an der Beresina und die Schweizer' in *Schweizerische Monatsschrift für Offiziere aller Waffen*, 1913, 58–ff.

———. *Die Schlacht an der Beresina und die Schweizer: Vortrag. Hiezu Uebersichtskarte und Situationsskizze*, Frauenfeld, 1913.

Kummer, Eduard. *Mühsale der Schweizer-Regimenter auf Napoleons Feldzug nach Russland im Jahre 1812*, Thun, 1972.

Legler, Thomas and Muralt, Albrecht von. *Beresina: Erinnerungen aus dem Feldzug Napoleons I in Russland 1812*, Bern, 1940.

Maag, Albert. *Die Schicksale der Schweizer-Regimenter in Napoleons I. Feldzug nach Russland, 1812*, Biel, 1890.

Streiter, Karl Heink. 'Kritik und Anregung: Beresina' in *Allgemeine schweizerische Militärzeitschrift*, 149/6 (1983), 352.

Walde, K. 'Vor 150 Jahren: Beresina: 28. November 1812' in *Allgemeine schweizerische Militärzeitschrift*, 11 (1962), 627–628.

DUTCH

Benthien, George Diederich (J. Eysten, ed.). 'Doorloopend verhaal van de dienstverrichtingen der Nederlandsche pontonniers onder den majoor G.D. Benthien 1797–1825' in *Bijdragen en Mededeelingen van het Historisch Genootschap*, XXXII (1911), 100–177.

Hoof, J.P.C.M. von. 'George Diedericj Benthien: een bruggenbouwer *pur sang*' in *Armamentaria: jaarboek legermuseum*, 33 (1998), 78–88.

Jongh, J.W. de. *Hollandse infanterie bij de bruggen over de Berezina, 1812*, Groningen, [n.d.].

Tellegen, Jacob Anthony. *Gedane Veldtochten, bekomene Wonden*, Oosterbeek, 2005.

POLISH

Bialkowski, Anton. *Pamiętniki starego zolnierza*, Warsaw, 1903.

Bielecki, Robert. *Berezyna 1812*, Warsaw, 1990.

Chlapowski, Dezydery. *Pamiętniki…* Poznan, 1899; French edition *Mémoires sur les Guerres de Napoléon, 1806–1813*, Paris, 1908.

Dembinski, Henryk. *Pamiętniki…* Poznan, 1860.

Dziewanowski, Dominik. 'Dziennik wyoraw wojennych z r. 1812' in Robert Bielecki and Andrzej Tyszka, *Dał nam przykład Bonaparte* (Krakow, 1984), 153–154.

Gawronski, Franciszek. *Pamiętniki…* Krakow, 1916.

Grabowski, Jozef. *Pamiętniki…* Warsaw, 1905.

Kirkor, Stanislaw. *Legia Nadwiślańsk, 1808–1814*, London, 1981.

Kolaczkowski, Klemens. *Wspomnienia*, Krakow, 1898.

——. *Henryk Dąbrowski twórca legionów polskich we Włoszech, 1755–1818*, Krakow, 1901.

Kozłowski, Józef. *Historya 1-go potem 9-go Pułku Wielkiego Księstwa Warszawskiego*, Krakow, 1887.

Krasinski, Jozef. *Ze wspomnien*, Warsaw, 1912.

Kukiel, Marian. *Wojna 1812 roku*, Krakow, 1936.

Mycielski, Franciszek. 'Relacja…' in Bielecki and Tyszka (1984), 152.

Nawrot, Dariusz. *Litwa i Napoleon w 1812 roku*, Katowice, 2008.

Pradzynski, Ignacy. *Berezyna*, Warsaw, 1920.

Rybinski, Maciej. *Moje przypomnienia od urodzenia*, Wroclaw, 1993.

Sanguszko, Eustachy. *Pamiętniki, 1786–1815*, Krakow, 1876.

Smarzewski, Marcin. *Pamiętniki…* Wroclaw, 1962.

Szymanowski, Jozef. *Pamiętniki jenerała…* Lwow, 1898.

Zaluski, Jozef. *Wspomnienia…* Krakow, 1865.

Note

1. Abbreviations: RS – Russkaya Starina; RA – Russkii Arkhiv; Voyenskii (1912) – Konstantin Voyenskii, *Istoricheskiye ocherki i statii otnosyashiesya k 1812 godu*, St Petersburg, 1912; Kallash (1912) – V. Kallash, *Dvenadtsatii god v vospominanyakh i perepiske sovremennikov*, Moscow, 1912.

Index

The Battle of the Berezina

Index